INDIAN NATIONAL ARMY
A Documentary Study

INDIAN NATIONAL ARMY

A Documentary Study

(In 5 Volumes)

Volume-V

(1944-1945)

T. R. SAREEN

GYAN PUBLISHING HOUSE
NEW DELHI - 110002

INDIAN NATIONAL ARMY—A DOCUMENTARY STUDY

Rs. 4,500/-

ISBN : 81-212-0833-5 (Set)
ISBN : 81-212-0848-3 (Vol-5)

Published in 2004 in India by
Gyan Publishing House
5, Ansari Road, Daryaganj
New Delhi-110 002
Phones-23282060, 23261060, Fax-23285914
Email : gyanbook@vsnl.com
Visit our Website at : http//www.gyanbooks.com

Lasertype Setting by: Tact Computer Graphics, Delhi
Printed at: Chawla Offset Press, Delhi

To
Anuradha

List of Documents

Introduction

Volume V of the document deal with the last phase of the Indian National Army after they were brought back to India from South East Asia. British officers of the Indian army were keen that the I.N.A. men should be treated as traitors and adequately punished for breaking their oath of allegiance to the King Emperor. In their view they were also.guilty of joining hands with the enemies of the Raj. Under pressure the government agreed to prosecute them now that the war was over. Surprisingly during the war the I.N.A. Soldiers who were captured during the Imphal campaign, were not punished or treated harshly. They were merely classified as 'White' 'Black' or 'Grey' according to the degree of their involvement with the Japanese. They were treated secretly and kept away from the public and even from their families. The idea was that no one should know about the existence of the I.N.A. After the war the situatiion had become different and had raised very difficult problems.The government was at a loss to decide as to how to deal with more than twenty thousands of them.

The problem had become more difficult on account of the facts, which had come to light after interrogating them. Earlier they were treated as deserters and traitors. But now it was known that they had collaborated with the enemies of the Raj for the liberation of their motherland and that they were not the puppet of the Japanese. It was further revealed that they had become nationalists in their outlook and were not now willing to serve under the British government as they were bound to the oath of loyalty, which they had taken in the I.N.A. after joining it. As regards the oath taken when they were in the British army earlier, their argument was that it was automatically annulled at the time of Singapore surrender and their being handed over the Japanese. [Document No. 4].

Even after knowing the above details, the British officers still considered them as traitors, though it was reluctantly conceded that the membership of the I.N.A. had made a deep impression on all those who joined it and they had still persevered their belief in the ideals of Subhas

Chandra Bose; that they were proud of Bose; of the I.N.A. and of their own efforts to free India. Keeping this in view, the higher authorities both in India and England decided to prosecute only those who were the worst offenders and those who were guilty of brutal behaviour towards some members of the Indian army who had refused to join the I.N.A. The British policy towards the I.N.A. had to be changed due to the political pressure and the mass upsurge in the favour of the I.N.A[Document No4, 6, 110.

All the political parties began to take deep interest in the fate of the I.N.A. soldiers, who became as Nehru puts it as 'a symbol of India's fighting for Independence'. The Indian National Congress, who had earlier denounced the creed of violence now came forward to defend the I.N.A. A Defence Committee was formed, who immediately urged the Viceroy that the trials be either postponed or abandoned until after the formation of the interim government at the centre and the functioning of the Provincial Governments' [Document No. 3]

The British government had no wish to postpone the trial. However keeping in view the mounting public demonstration in favour of these men, it was decided to put on trial only three officers of the I.N.A. in the first instance. It had become more or less a question of prestige for the British, as was reported by the American intelligence agency[Document No.9]. The trials began on 5 November1945. Soon after the authorities were faced with unprecedented, widespread popular demonstration in favour of the I.N.A. The reports came from the Director of the Criminal Intelligence that there had 'seldom been a matter which has attracted so much' attention of the public, and public sympathy as the I.N.A. isssue [Document No. 8]. Nehru warned the government that 'it would be very grave error leading to far reaching consequences if these men were treated as ordinary criminals' and the 'punishment given to them would be in effect be punishment to all India and Indians'. Other political parties also came forward to defend the I.N.A. men.

The Defense Committee of the Congress under the able guidance of Bhulabhai Desai fought the case. Desai spoke in their defense for nearly eight hours. He quoted precedent after precedent from international law in support of their actions. The main thrust of Desai's argument was that these men had the legitimate right to fight for the liberation of their motherland. He tried to prove that the Azad Hind Government was a recognized government and the I.N.A. was operating under the legitimate rules framed by this government. [Document No. 13]. The prosecution council, however did not accept the; pleadings of Desai [Document No. 14] As such all the three officers were convicted by the British and found guilty. They were sentenced to cashiering and transportation for life. During the trial the government had come to know that the punishment given to these officers by the court would be impossible to carry out in view of the strong public sympathy. As such the Viceroy issued an ordinance equipping the C-in-C with an authority of commuting the sentences of death or transportation for life just a week before the trial ended on 31 December 1945. Under this the C-in-C formerly decided to free the three I.N.A. officers only with cashiering and forfeiture of pay and allowances. [Document No 13].

In order to pacify the feelings of the British officers the C-in-C sent a memorandum saying that the 'confirmation of the sentences would have resulted in violent internal conflict, in India. As such he had taken a lenient view of their case and had commuted the sentences of all the three officers. [Document No. 18] With the above decision by the C-in-C, Shah Nawaz, P.K. Saghal, and G.S. Dhillon were released. Their release gave a fresh turn to the national movment in India, which made it difficult for the British to rely on the Indian Armed forces for the maintenance of their rule any longer.

Many are still alive, who joined the I.N.A. and there are others who were an eyewitness to the frenzied adulation of the Indian people for the I.N.A. soldiers. The author of these volumes belong to the second category who still remembers the heroic welcome given by the people to Shah Nwaz. Dhillion and Sahgal when they visited Lahore in 1946 after their release. This is evident from the report of the press included here. [Document no 16] It is interesting to note as to how the Congress afterwards under Nehru's leadership changed its policy towards the I.N.A. Some indication of this change in policy became apparent after the Congress came into power in 1946. This is evident from the record of the interview between Nehru and Lord Wavell, [Document no 19].

As mentioned earlier, the British Intelligence had closely kept an eye on the activities of the I.N.A. and detailed reports were prepared by the C.S.D.I.C., which was located at Red Fort. All their reports are not available at one place Some of these could be located in the I.N.A. papers, while others are available in the War Office papers at the Public Record Office, London. A few of these have been included in the earlier volumes, and a some are given in this volume. These reports are very informative especially the one on the Hikari Kikan, and the report containing the break up account of the soldiers of the British Indian Army who joined the I.N.A. after the fall of Singapore. Another report deal with the fighting capabilities of the I.N.A. on the Burma front.[Document No. 15,18,22]

This volume also contain a detailed report by a British agent who remained in Singapore. This report gives us a close view of many aspects of the I.N.A., not available anywhere else. The British Agent was in the special branch of the Police department at Singapore. [Document No. 10] However, it must be clarified that the reports of the Military Intelligence and the agents should not be taken at their face value. It is necessary to verify them with other evidence from the private and official records.

Death of Bose in the plane crash is still an unsolved mystery and an another commission of enquiry is looking into it at present. In this volume, only a few reports dealing with the last days of Bose are included which were prepared by the military intelligence. [Document No. 2,7.] Only one report deals with the death of Bose which was given by the Japanese doctor Tenneyashi Yoshimi, who attended him when Bose was brought to the hospital after the plane crash. Dr. Yoshimi has confirmed that Bose died of third degree burns. [Document No. 23]. Doubts have been voiced by many associates of Bose about these reports. They have never accepted the death of Bose in the plane crash. Initial doubts were circulated by Deb Nath Das who was very close to Bose. [Appendix III.] It was on account of these doubts that the Government had appointed various commissions to enquire into the mystery from time to time. It would be interesting to read the account given by John Figges, who submitted a report to the British Government on Bose more than fifty years back. In a recent book, he recalls his meeting with Habib-ur-Rehman, who was with Bose at the time of latter's death. He writes that Rehman whose left 'arm was heavily bandaged told me that after the Japanese army plane in which they were travelling crashed on take off at Taipei airport and burst into flames, he and the Japanese officers with them had great difficulty in getting Bose out of the wreckage because he was so corpulent. His clothes were on fire and he was badly burnt and died of his injuries in an hospital in Tapei a day or two later. The pilot of the aircraft also died. I could see no reason to doubt this story, which was later confirmed by G.H.Q. SCAP after detailed interrogation of the surviving Japanese officers concerned and signaled H.Q.S.A.CS.E.A. accordingly."[see Hugh Cortazzi, Post war Japan through British Eyes, Surry, 2001,p.9]

The appendices in this volume include mostly the memoirs of those who were very close to Bose, especially important is the account compiled by A.M. Sahey, who served as an interpreter to Bose when he was dealing with the Japanese. His recording of the Japanese policy towards the I.N.A. and other matters is very important in view of the absence of any Japanese records of what took place in these negotiations. Sahey's account can be further corroborated with the interrogation report included here. Another account of Bose included here is by Col. Yamamoto, who was with him in Germany and subsequently in Japan. Fujiwara's brief account is very important to understand the Japanese view of the I.N.A. and the personality of Bose. [Appendix I,II,IV]

Like the previous volumes, the documents included here were collected from different archival repositories in India and abroad and as far as possible these have been reproduced as they were found with hardly any change. I am thankful to these institutions for their help, but I am especially grateful to A.M. Sahey for giving me the copy of his memoris when I met him at Baghalpur. As I have pointed out earlier that the documents regarding the I.N.A. and other revolutionaries are lying scattered at different places. In order to understand the real contribution of those who fought for Indian's liberation from abroad, it will be essential to bring all these documents at one place. I am sure this task will be taken up by the National Archives of India for the benefit of research students.

T.R. Sareen

B-402, Kaveri Apartment,
Alaknanda,
New Delhi-110019

1

Circular Announcing the Termination of the War and Discontinuance of the Activities of the I.N.A[1]

6 September, 1945

To all Members of the Indian Independence League in Thailand, Comrades,

Jai Hind,

I have the melancholy privilege to inform you that your Azad Hind Fauj has been compelled to lay down its arms before the victorious army of occupation superior in number and superior in equipment. The Azad Hind Fauj has had to take this painful decision under the force of circumstances. This army of liberation has never thought of sparing its blood and as you all are aware, the Azad Hind Fauj has merited records of sacrifice, gallantry and chivalry second to none. Our fight was meant for liberation of India and on India frontiers and not abroad. Hence the decision to lay down arms and avoid unnecessary blood-shed and disturbance of public peace. At this fateful moment, I like to give you a few points of warning :

1. With the laying down of arms by the Azad Hind Fauj our armed struggle discontinues.
2. We must take our defeat in the coolest and most sporting manner.
3. Do not harbour any malice or hatred towards the Army of occupation, because we are vanquished today.
4. Be perfectly law-abiding, strictly disciplined and dignified in all your behaviour.
5. Avoid all possibilities of clashes with troops and one of the best means is to avoid trespassing the army camps and vicinity. Do not enter into unnecessary discussions or say or do anything likely to result in unpleasantness.

---

1. K.S. Giani, *op.cit.* pp 160-161.

6. Remember : (a) Your goal : "Independence of India."

(b) Your motto : "Unity, Faith and Sacrifice."

Remember always that with the discontinuance of armed struggle, the fight for India's freedom does not cease. We must and will continue our struggle till our goal of complete independence is achieved. Our countrymen inside India under the lead of the Indian National Congress are working with full determination to liberate India. We must be ready to do our mite in that struggle and for the sacrifices that will free India. when the call comes,

India is bound to be free and before long.

Jai Hind,

(Sd.) Parmanand,
Officer-in-Charge, Indian Independence League
Headquarters, East Asia.

2

Military Intellegence note on Last Movement of S.C. Bose[1]

10 September, 1945

S.C. Bose and his party left Rangoon on 24 April 1945 and reached Bangkok on 14 May. The party, at the time of leaving Rangoon, had in its possession gold, gold ornaments and diamonds contained in 4 boxes of varying sizes ranging between 9" × 9" × 4"and 6" × 4" × 2". An additional quantity of gold was purchased on the way at Moulmein to the extent of Rs. 700,000 drawn by S.C. Bose from Yokohama Special Bank, Moulmein Branch.

While at Bangkok several meetings of the Cabinet Ministers of the PGI were held between 18 May to 14 June, the object of which was to decide as to the future course of action so far as the existence of the PGI was concerned. No decision could be arrived at as S.C. Bose had to leave for Singapore in order to carry out his propaganda over the radio against the acceptance of "Wavell Proposal". In course of these meetings Lt. Col. (Maj-Gen) Chatterjee suggested that a nucleus of the PGI should be shifted to Yunnan Province in order to contact the communists who had more influence in that part of China, and through their help to contact the Soviet authorities in Siberia. At the same time it was thought desirable to leave behind certain Cabinet Ministers and high ranking I.N.A. officers to carry on the fight with HQ at Bangkok and Singapore. The following were the officers present in these meetings–

1. S.C. Bose.
2. Lt. Col (Maj-Gen) Bhonsle
3. Lt. Col (Maj-Gen) Chatterjee
4. Lt. Col (Maj-Gen) Kiani
5. Capt (Col) Gulzara Singh
6. Iyer[2]
7. A.M. Sahai

---

1. W.O.n 208/863, P.R.O.
2. S.A. Iyer.

7. A.M. Sahai
8. A.N. Sarkar
9. Isar Singh Gen. Secretary IIL Bangkok
10. Paramanand
11. D.M. Khan
12. Deb Nath Das
13. Karim Ghani (also attended the last meeting).

After the 2nd meeting (exact dates not remembered) Kiani left for Singapore to arrange accommodation for the Rani of Jhansi girls numbering about 120 who were at that time at Bangkok. At about the same time Chatterjee, Iyer and A.M. Sahai left for Saigon – Chatterjee to establish the site for the PGI, Iyer for broadcasting work and Sahai on a special mission at Hanoi not known to B1189.

On 16 Aug 1945 S.C. Bose came to Bangkok by a special Jap Bomber chartered for him, accompanied by Iyer and Capt (Col) Habib ur Rahman and Capt (Lt. Col) Pritam Singh. On 17 Aug 0700 hrs (Tokyo Time) Bose left Bangkok for Saigon accompanied by the following additional personnel of the PGI and I.N.A.:—

1. Gulzara Singh
2. "Maj" Hassan
3. Deb Nath Das

Lt. Gen. ISODA and two other H. Kikan personnel accompanied Bose and the party in a separate aircraft.

According to B1189's information received from H. Kikan and other sources, Bose and the parties reached Saigon on the same day (17 Aug). On the following day (18 Aug) S.C. Bose accompanied by Capt (Col) Habib ur Rahman left for Tokyo in a plane originally meant for the conveyance of some high ranking officials of Mori Butaui as placing of the special bomber at his disposal was no longer possible. The rest of Bose's party remained behind at Saigon where at that time Chatterjee and Sahai were also staying. ISODA who happened to be present at the Saigon aerodrome to see the party off, said that Bose took his seat in the passage of aircraft between the pilot and the tail and as such could not be seen to wave goodbye when the plane took off. According to the estimation of B1189, the remainder of the party at Saigon named above might have moved into any of the following places, as these were the names of the places suggested by various members in the Cabinet meetings mentioned before–

1. Yunnan Province
2. Hanoi
3. Shanghai
4. Harbin

In course of talk with ISODA on 21 Aug 1945 B1189 heard that the plane carrying Bose and the party landed at Taihoku (Formosa) at 1300 hrs (Tokyo Time) on 18th, and after about an hour's halt was taking off at 1400 hrs when the right engine failed resulting in the crash of the plane. The crew and the Chief of Staff Mori Butai were killed instantaneously, and Bose with Habib ur Rahman and 4 other Japanese officials were seriously injured. Bose and other injured persons were removed to an eye hospital at Taihoku where he died at 2400 hrs on the night of 18/19 Aug 1945 without regaining consciousness. No information about Habib ur Rahman could be obtained owing to restrictions put by the Allies on Jap communication. B1189 requested ISODA to keep photographs of Bose's funeral and other rites as well as his remains. No photographs or further information was received by B1189.

B1189 does not know whether Chatterjee ever met any of the nationalist Annamite leaders in course of his movements in French Indo-China. About Annamite leaders B1189 only knows that S.C. Bose on his way to Tokyo in Dec 1943 was prevented by the Japanese from meeting some of them who were eager to meet him (S.C. Bose) at Saigon.

B1189 has no direct information regarding the gold mentioned above. His own impression is, that a major portion of the gold was taken by S.C. Bose while the remainder was left with the rest of his party.

3

Representation from Defence Committee of the Indian National Congress to the Viceroy Requesting Him to Postpone the Court-Martial of the Officers of the INA[1]

15 October, 1 945

1. On behalf of the Committee appointed by the Working Committee of the Indian National Congress we make the following representation for your Government's consideration.

2. This Defence Committee consists of the following members:

   (a) The Rt. Hon'ble Sir Tej Bahadur Sapru, R.C. K.C.S.I.

   (b) Pandit Jawaharlal Nehru, Member, Congress Working Committee, Bar-at-Law.

   (c) Shri Bhulabhai Desai, Advocate.

   (d) Dr. K.N. Katju, M.A.L.D., Advocate.

   (e) Shri Raghunandan Saran.

   (f) Rai Bahadur Badri Das, Advocate.

   (g) M. Asaf Ali Esq., Member, Congress Working Committee Bar-at- law (Convenor).

   On the 22nd September 1945 the Working Committee of the Congress, having regard to the profound interest and anxiety felt throughout India in the fate and future of the officers and men of the Indian National Army now held as prisoners of the British Government, appointed this Committee to take necessary steps for their defence.

3. At present three officers namely, Shah Nawaz Khan, Sahgal and Dhillon have been formally charged with the offence of waging war against the King and other offences arising out of their activities as Officers of the INA. on active service. The 5th November 1945 has been fixed for their trial before a Court-Martial. These officers have

1. I.N.A. relief and enquiry committee file pertaining to I.N.A. trials.

formally entrusted their defence before the Court-Martial to the above mentioned Defence Committee.

4. According to press reports, trials of other officers and men for similar or cognate offences are likely to follow in the near future.

5. These trials raise questions of such grave public importance that the Committee considers it imperatively necessary to address your Government on the matter at once.

6. The circumstances which led to the formation of an Indian National Army are now common knowledge all over India. It is no exaggeration to say that while some may doubt the propriety of the policies which led to the establishment of such an Army as an independent military organisation under the command of its own officers, Indians of all communities, and persuasions and of all schools of political thought recognise and appreciate the selfless patriotism which actuated those who took part in this movement.

7. After the conquest by Japan of the French and Dutch possessions in South East Asia and the fall of Burma, Malaya and Singapore there arose a great desire in the minds of Indian inhabitants of these countries to organize not only for their own defence and protection, but also for active participation in the movement for the liberation of their home country from foreign rule. Rapid movement of events throughout the World led to the further intensification of this resolve and they appear to have determined to make a bold and resolute bid for the achievement of the Independence of India.Independence Leagues were established throughout the length and breadth of these countries and Provisional Government of Free India is reported to have been eventually set up, and a well-organized, well-trained and well-disciplined Indian National Army operated under its control. According to accounts available, this Government was not a mere puppet Government under Japanese control, but was an independent Government with a definite international status.

8. It is understood that in addition to a large number of Indian Civilians residing in the locality, numerous officers and men of the Indian Army, who had been surrendered by the British to the enemy, joined the Indian National Army.

9. We do not propose to enter here into any discussion about the legal status of the officers or men of the INA. and it would also be

inappropriate to discuss here the question whether they can be said to be guilty of any offence. The only question at this stage is whether it would not be contrary to public interest to bring them to trial and assuming that it is not so, when and by whom such a decision should be taken.

10. These men of the INA are virtually being charged with having endeavoured to enter India with armed force to liberate it from British domination. That alleged offence primarily concerns the Indian people, and the more so as the British Government have publicly announced that India will have the right to secede from the British Commonwealth if the Indian people so desire. So far back as 1924 the then Secretary of State for India, Mr. Wedgwood Benn, speaking on behalf of H.M.G. in the House of Commons said that whatever may be the deficiency in theory India already enjoyed "Dominion status in action". The first privilege of that status "in action" is that in a matter like this which vitally affects the lives and liberties of a large number of Indians drawn from all parts and principal communities of India, the wishes of the people of India should be ascertained and given effect to. Judging by the trend of public opinion in the country, this committee urges that this matter of the trial of the INA. should not be pursued any further.

11. At this juncture the Central Legislative Assembly and the provincial Legislative Assemblies have been dissolved. But by the middle of December, 1945, the Central Legislative Assembly will have been re-elected and by the month of March 1946 general elections in all the British Indian Provinces will have been held and the British Government expects that soon thereafter ministries in Provinces will be formed to undertake the task of Government in their respective spheres. H.E. The Governor General has also announced his intention to reconstitute his Executive Council soon after the general elections so that it may be representative of popular opinion in the country. All these constitutional events are due to take place in the next few months.

12. The Defence Committee believes that the Governor General with his reconstituted Executive Council will be in a much better position to gauge public opinion in this matter. Representatives of the people will also have opportunity to express their opinion upon it in the newly elected Central and Provincial Legislative assemblies, All the

Provinces are interested in the Indian National Army because men from every province have contributed to its personnel. The new Government will be able to arrive at a proper decision whether the intended trial of the INA should take place at all and if so when and how.

13. The Defence Committee therefore earnestly urges that the trial fixed for the 5th Nov. 1945 and all other contemplated trials should, if not abandoned, be at least postponed and the whole question relating to the INA. be examined afresh after the Governor General's Executive Council has been reconstituted and the ministries in the Provinces have begun to function.

14. The Defence Committee is convinced that it would be a tragedy if this matter were approached and disposed of in a narrow, technical and legalistic spirit. Unprecedented issues of this nature require to be decided in a broad and statesman-like spirit. There are various aspects of these issues of great public and political importance and hasty decisions not in consonance with popular will and sentiment, will have far reaching repercussions throughout the length and breadth of India, so deep and widespread is the appreciation of the motives and aims of the movement of which the Indian National Army was an expression.

The Defence Committee requests that the matter of the trials of the INA. by Courts-Martial be abandoned, or that in any event no proceedings before any Court-Martial be commenced until after the formation of the Interim Government at the centre and the functioning of Provincial Governments on the completion of the ensuing election, and all necessary directions may be given to the authorities concerned.

4

British Intelligence Assessment of the Feelings of the I.N.A. Soldiers in Malaya After their Surrender[1]

26 October, 1945

Japanese Indian Fifth Column[2]

Attiutde of the I.N.A. In Malaya

1. A report from Kuala Lumpur states that, of some 370 members of the I.N.A. who have been interrogated, 5% have categorically stated that they are unwilling, whatever is decided about their future, to continue to serve in the Indian Army. Two reasons are given for this attitude; firstly, that they feel strongly bound in their loyalty to the I.N.A. and are unwilling to break their I.N.A. oath and, secondly, that they have irrevocably spoilt their army records and also those of their families who have been connected with the Indian Army, with the result that it is not worth their while to carry on.

2. The emphases laid on the "I.N.A. oath" is interesting in view of the argument put forward by so many I.N.A. officers and men that their oath of allegiance to the British was automactically annulled at the time of the Singapore surrender and their being handed over to the Japanese.

Rani of Jhansi Regiment

1. It is estimated that the Rani of Jhansi Regt. reached, at its peak, a total strength of approximately 600 in Burma and Malaya. The leader of this unit, Dr. Lakshmi Swaminathan, is still in Rangoon (at liberty) and has set up a private medical practice. According to the Press, on 21 Oct 1945 she addressed a crowd of 3000 Indians gathered in Rangoon to celebrate Provisional Government Day. Her speech was

---

1. W.O. 208/804 Public Record Office London
2. This was the name used for the I.N.A. by the British.

an exhortation to remember their pledge to "Netaji" and to return home to fight the second round of the battle for freedom. This was greeted by cries of "blood, blood, blood" from the audience.

2. Of the other prominent members of the Regt. there is little of interest to report, except that Miss Gauri Bhattacharya, who is a medical student, has made her way by air to India in order to continue her studies. Her departure from Rangoon was unauthorised and irregular and her present whereabouts in India are not yet known.

3. Although most of the Amazons are not of Indian domicile there is an undoubted tendency amongst some of them to wish to go to India, about which they have been told so much by Bose's propaganda. Moreover, some of the more intellectual who find no facilities for studying in countries recently freed from enemy occupation may, like Miss Bhattacharya, turn for further education to India.

I.N.A. In India

1. Evidence of the dangerous state of mind of certain I.N.A. military personnel at present in India is found in a letter addressed to the Punjab Provincial Congress Committee by a "faithful soldier of the I.N.A." at present in Multan Holiday Camp. This soldier takes exception to Congress leaders' repeated assertions that Subhas Bose and his followers were "misguided" in seeding Japanese aid. He quotes from Bose's speeches and private conversations, and describes various episodes in Bose's career in the Far East to prove his point that his "Netaji", far from being a Japanese puppet, was merely using the Japanese as his tools, just as the British employ coloured troops to fight their battles for them.

2. Apart from these facts, he provides much authentic inside information about the I.N.A. for the Congress propaganda mill. Everything said by this man indicates the depth and determination of his devotion to "Netaji" and the goal he has given his followers. Particularly significant is his conviction that Subhas Bose is not dead but will return to lead his army at the opportune moment, and his belief that I.N.A. personnel who returned to India are biding their time until they rise against the British : "We are his time-bomb, and will burst when the right time comes.Our Leader will return to lead us."

Reactions to News of the I.N.A.

1. With reference to para 3 of F.S.I.S. No. 5 dated 12 Oct. 1945. public reactions to the I.N.A. and the proposed trials of I.N.A. officers have crystallized during the past fortnight. There has been an increasing volume of comment from the nationalist Press and spokesmen of all political parties. The almost universally expressed view has been that Bose and his I.N.A., although misguided in hoping to obtain freedom through Japanese help, acted with the highest motives of patriotism and the desire to free their country. From this follows on an equally widespread demand, supported by almost all shades of Indian opinion (though differing in the expression given to it), for extreme leniency on the part of Government in their treatment of the I.N.A.

2. Congress has been particularly vociferous in support of this campaign, which it started. The Congress I.N.A. Defence Committee has been very active in interviewing the three accused in the first court martial to take place early next month, and in providing and briefing counsel for the defence. There is evidence that an increasing number of relatives of Indian soldiers, if they know or suspect that the latter have joined the I.N.A., are approaching the Defence Committee for information as to their whereabouts and probable fate as well as for legal aid if they are put on trial. There is little doubt that this is drawing numbers of hitherto loyal families into the Congress net.

3. A noticeable feature of the whole of this Congree-sponsored campaign (aimed at increasing Congress' prestige and winning additional votes in the approaching elections, and emulated by the other political parties for the same reasons), is that very few references have been made in the Press or by political speakers to the fact that any member of the I.N.A. is accused of any crime other than treason. No mention has been made of the torture and oppression used to induce P.W. to join the I.N.A.' of the forcible collection of money from civilians for I.N.A. funds; or of the various other persecutions at which Bose and the Jif leaders connived when they did not themselves instigate them.

I.N.A.

1. In almost every Security Intelligence Report for Sep., views have been expressed on the treatment which should be given to members of the I.N.A. and these have varied according to the degree of

knowledge of units. These views may be summarized as follows :-

(a) By a few, who believe that men were tortured into joining no punishment.

(b) By some, who have heard of the ill treatment of loyal P.W. by Jifs, but who had not met the I.N.A. in the field : those guilty of ill treatment to be punished and the remainder treated generously.

(c) By many: that officers who joined are particularly guilty.

(d) The majority view, however, is that they are all traitors. There is also indignation at the championship of the I.N.A. by Indian politicians.

2. British troops are also indignant, but in their case more emphasis is laid on the sympathy, both real and feigned, expressed by Indian politicians and press on the death of Subhas Chandra Bose.

5

Auchinleck appreciation of the I.N.A. Trials; explains the attitude of the British officers of the Indian Army towards the I.N.A.[1]

31 October, 1945

1. Of the 20,000 military personnel who joined the I.N.A., a large proportion became traitors,

   (a) To avoid brutal treatment;

   (b) To secure better living conditions;

   (c) As result of persuasion by their seniors.

   Mass trials being clearly impossible because of the obvious desirability of disposing of cases as quickly as possible, it was decided to bring only the worst offenders to trial and these were grouped into the following categories:-

   (a) Officers of the I.A.

   (b) VCOs who became officers in INA.

   (c) VCOs who joined 950 Regiment.

   (d) Those who initially deserted from our lines as opposed to being taken prisoner.

   (e) IORs who became officers or under-officers in 950 Regiment.

   (f) Those instrumental in causing the death of any British or Allies subject, whether in or out of battle.

   (g) Those guilty of brutal conduct either to fellow JIFs/HIFs or to members of the Allied Forces.

   (h) Those who took part in the capture and handing over to the enemy of and British or Allied subject.

1. Military Department No. L/WS/1/1577. I.O.L. Record London.

(i) IORs who became officers in INA and took a leading part against us in battle, including front line intelligence duties.

(j) Fujiwara volunteers.

It was estimated that six permanent Courts Martial in continuous session could complete some 300-350 trials only in one year.

Subsequently, as a result of the tense political situation, it was decided to concentrate in the first instance on the trial of those guilty of murder or gross brutality. The first trial of this kind is due to open on Nov 5.

2. As soon as it became known to the public that trials were about to commence, all the main political parties, and especially Congress, made the I.N.A. a prominent political issue. The Indian Press is full of articles extolling the I.N.A. as heroes. This, together with the fact that popular ministries will be set up in the Provinces by April, make it highly desirable, if not essential, to dispose of the I.N.A. problem during the next six months.

It was therefore decided to bring to trial those included in the following categories only:-

(i) Any person actively instrumental in causing the death of any British or Allied subject, whether in or out of battle.

(ii) Any person responsible for the brutal treatment of any British or Allied subject.

(iii) Any person taking a responsible part in the capture and handing over to the enemy of any British or Allied subject.

(iv) Officers, VCOs and IORs who became officers in the I.N.A. and 950 Regiment and took a leading part against us.

(v) Fujiwara volunteers.

No person will be charged with "waging war against the King" unless he can also be charged with other crimes so that there will be no convictions solely on the charge of "waging war".

Men who deserted to the enemy, but do not also come into one of the above categories, will be tried solely for desertion.

All Blacks who are brought to trial by Court Martial will be dismissed by the end of April.

3. It is estimated that the number of offenders to be tried under the various heads will be:-

(a) 15 to 20

(b) 20 to 30

(c) 10 to 15

(d) 20 to 30

(d) 20 to 30

The intention is to complete the trials by the end of April but delaying tactics by defence counsel may retard this.

All sentences other than death will be confirmed.

It is probable that a proportion of the sentences of transportation will be commuted to shorter terms of imprisonment.

A rough estimate of the number in each category for which the death sentence is likely to be imposed, is :-

Offences in category

(i) 10 to 15.

(ii) 15 to 20.

Offences in categories (iii), (iv) and (v) 5 to 10.

On the assumption that approximately 120 persons are brought to trial, it is estimated that not more than twenty death sentences are likely to be confirmed, but it is not possible for obvious reasons to give a definite figure at this stage.

4. It has now been possible to assess the views held throughout the Indian Army regarding members of the INA and 950 Regiment. These vary according to the degree of knowledge available in different units but may be farily summarised thus:-

(a) a few, who believe that the men were tortured into joined consider no punishment should be inflicted;

(b) some, who have heard of the ill-treatment of loyal prisoners of war by members of the INA but who had not met that force in the field, think that those guilty of brutality should be punished and the remainder treated generously;

(c) many consider that officers who joined are particularly guilty;

(d) the majority view, however, is that they are all traitors and should be treated as such, though it is realised that it is not practicable to put all on trial.

5. I consider that, although the majority opinion is in favour of strong action, the Army as a whole will accept the policy of limited trials,

dismissals (Blacks) and discharges (Greys). I am strongly of the opinion that, although men may be tried for other crimes, the general feeling throughout the Army would be that they must be tried as traitors also. I feel even more strongly that the Army would strongly resent any measure which would allow any member of the INA or of 950 Regiment, who has not proved himself to be "White", to remain in the Army.

6

Home Department Memorandum on Policy towards I.N.A.

1 November, 1945

1. Since the conference with provincial representatives in the middle of August it has been necessary to give a great deal of further thought to this problem, and there have been various developments on which it is desirable to consult Provincial Governments. There are also points in the provincial replies to the Home Department letter of the 3rd September which could be settled more satisfactorily by personal discussion.

2. The governing factor, which accounts for the exceptional difficulty of the whole problem and the force of which must unfortunately be admitted, is that the Government in India, unlike the Government in any other country, cannot rely on public opinion to support – much less to press for- any action against "traitors" in the commonly accepted sense of that term. The most that political opinion will concede is that such persons are "mistaken patriots", but always with much more emphasis on the patriotism than on the mistake. It is now quite clear that Congress (followed willingly or otherwise by every other political party) is determined ot exploit the matter to the utmost and make a first class political issue of it.

3. The persons to be dealt with fall into two classes–

   (a) those subject to military law who, in addition to anything else they may have done, have broken their oath of allegiance; and

   (b) those not subject to military law who have broken no oath, but who have voluntarily helped the enemy either by joining the I.N.A. or in other ways.

   Certain general considerations are common to both classes. In the first place it is necessary to rule out any wide or sustained use of

1. Home Political Departments proceedings. The above memorandum by the Home Department was prepared after consulting the Provisional Government.

(a) the war time powers of restriction and detention without trial, or

(b) the powers of military custody pending enquiry which militry law provides but which cannot be used for more than a limited period. Secondly, it is necessary to discard the possibility of holding trials in camera (e.g. under the Enemy Agents Ordinance). It has been decided for good reasons to hold military trials by court martial in public.

It follows therefore that there is no half-way house between

(a) bringing the persons concerned to open trial and

(b) ignoring them or releasing those who are in custody.

4. The arguement in favour of trials are :-

(a) It is normal and right that the law should take its course; and not to set it in motion would betray weakness and a lack of courage which would react adversely on the ability of Government to govern successfully.

(b) There are some persons at least whom it would be repugnant to ignore or leave unpunished.

(c) To take no action against persons subject to military law who had committed one of the worst offences of which a soldier is capable might seriously impair the discipline of the whole Army.

The arguments against trials are–

(a) The numbers involved are in any case too great to make any complete solution on these lines practicable; and there is always a certain measure of amnesty by the victorious side on the termination of a successful war.

(b) Trials would be prolonged by every device known to the law; they could provide wide opportunities for anti-Government propaganda; and they would greatly increase the importance of the accused who might otherwise remain in obscurity.

(c) There would be little chance of obtaining convictions in civil trials unless the witnesses were thoroughly reliable or could be effectively protected against intimidation.

(d) There would be even less chance of enforcing capital sentences, if obtained, or even of maintaining sentences of imprisonment after a popular Government had come into power, unless the accused could be convicted of really heinous crimes abhorrent to popular sentiment, in addition to "treachery" or "waging war against the King."

On these premises the conclusion reaches is that it would do Government more harm than good to attempt prosecutions on any large scale and therefore that only a small number of the very worst cases should be selected for trial.

5. If the above conclusion is accepted, it will mean that a large number of disloyal persons must be ignored or released and the main problem will be the manner in which this should be done. The objects in view must be to face the resulting threat to law and order and reduce it to the smallest possible dimensions.

One possibility would be an immediate and complete amnesty for all except the few selected for prosecution. The opposite course would be the fullest possible examination of each case, either in India or abroad, with a view to assessing the risks that the freedom of each individual would entail and of delaying for as long as possible the release or return to India of those considered most dangerous.

However much there may be to be said for the first of these courses, it would mean throwing simultaneously on the countryside a large number of potentially dangerous and ill-disposed persons, quite a number of whom may have had previous terrorist associations or have received training in guerilla warfare and the methods of espionage (including the use of wireless). The strain on Provinces would probably be too great. The second course, or the other hand, would involve a very great deal of work it would take many months to complete the process; in the interval new Governments may come into existence, both at the Centre and in the Provinces which would take a different view of the whole matter; and the whole business would tend to become a running sore of which ever-increasing use would be made by the opponents of Government. In fact, under delay would merely intensify the dangers and aggravate the security problem.

6. The prevailing view therefore favours an intermediate course of action which would aim at the liquidation of the problem by stages within as short a time as possible in the hope that the persons concerned, if left alone abroad or widely disparsed to their villages in India and deprived of some of their most important leaders, would

be absorbed in the normal life of the country before they can be organised for dangerous political purposes. Such a course would have the additional advantages (a) of reducing the volume of agitation, much of which now comes from the relatives of I.N.A. men anxious to know their fate, and (b) of giving the Provinces early experience of the practical nature of the problem in the light of which the Future treatment of it may be guided.

So far as persons now in custody in India are concerned this would mean 'staggared' releases spread over a period of, say, six months. So far as persons outside India are concerned, it would involve arrangements (if the countries concerned can be induced to agree) to avoid the compulsory repatriation of ill-disposed Indians to this country, except for military parsonnel and the very few civilians who might be specifically wanted for trial, and to delay for a reasonable peroid the voluntary return of certain dangerous persons who might wish to come back and could not be indefinitaly prevented from doing so in view of their Indian nationality and domicile.

7. If these two conclusions are accepted, namely, (a) that the number of trials should be strictly limited and (b) that the process of releases etc. should be expedited, the resulting position as it affects the two classes mentioned in paragraph 3 may be presented as in the following paragraphs.

8. Persons subject to military law - that is to say, military members of the I.N.A. and 950 regiment.

(a) The Commander-in-Chief has decided to revise the order of the categories to be selected for prosecution, putting first those who may be charged not noly with waging war against, the King, but also with murder or other brutal conduct, etc., and leaving for trial later those who deserve prosecution on account of the rank and position that they held in the I.N.A.

(b) Three officers have been selected for trial by Court Martial in Delhi on charges that include the commission of certain atrocities as well as waging war against the King. Full publicity will be allowed to the trial and further action may depend upon its result; but it is provisionally proposed to bring about another 75 to 100 persons to trial and this numbers might be increased to 350.

(c) This will leave about 5,500 military 'Blacks' to be released after holding Courts of Enquiry and dismissing them from the Army. Of these about 3580 are already in India. The Courts of Enquiry can dispose of these cases expeditiously by releasing them in batches. As soon as an order of dismissal has been passed, there will be no legal authority for holding the person in military custody or escorting him in such custody to his home.

(d) The military authorities are anxious to release the 5500 'Blacks' at the rate of roughly 1000 a month, starting as soon as possible and maintaining a steady flow of releases throughout the month so as to avoid returning large batches at any one time to their Provinces. They propose to send the names and records of each batch to the Provincial Government concerned with the intimation that it had been decided to hold a Court of Enquiry on that batch by a given date thirty days in advance and that, if as was expected, the Court of Enquiry found that prosecution Ws not advisable, the men would then have to be released. The first lists are likely to be sent to Provinces in the near future.

(e) The whole process is likely to be delayed if Provinces make any extensive use of the right of consultation and interview as set forth in paragraph 3 of the Home Department letter of the 3rd September. The question therefore is what practical advantages are to be gained from this procedure and whether Provinces would agree to forgeing or restricting its use. It must be borne in mind that the action of the military authorities must be determined by what each individual had done as a member of the I.N.A. They cannot be expected to alter their decision in the light of the general character of an individual, which in any case had been "verified" by the provincial authorities before recuritmnet, or of how he is likely to behave in future. In fact, once the inevitability of large scale releases is recognised, it must be doubtful Whether detailed information about each man will be necessary or indeed readily obtainable and whether a rough and ready classification would not suffice, supplemented by such information as may be available regarding any particular man whose record and specialized training in the Army or the I.N.A. would suggest that he requires particular attention.

(f) The military authorities are prepared to release last those men who prove recalcitrant while in military custody and also to prosecute those whose breaches of discipline while in military custody justify such action.

(g) The number of military 'Grey' now in India is about 8000, to which must be added an indefinite number amounting perharps to over 5000, who may be sent back from occupied territories in future. The procedure in their case, as soon as they have been finally classified, is to send them to their regimental centres where they will come before Courts of Enquiry in bathces and they be discharged. Commanding Officers will send their names and a summary of each man's record to the Provinces concerned as far as possible in advance of actual release; but privinces cannot expect to be consulted further.. All these people will remain under military discipline until the expiry of their 42 days leave.

(h) All released military 'Blacks' and 'Greys' will be provided by the military authorities with railway tickets to their homes on dismissal or discharge. To send them in military custody would be difficult or impossible; but in view of the importance that some Provinces attach to this point, the military authorities would be prepared to discuss means of securing as far as possible that they travel straight to their destination- e.g. by limiting the time for which their tickets will be valid.

9. Persons not subject to military law, i.e.

(a) civilian members of the I.N.A. or 950 regiment and

(b) other civilian suspects or collaborators.

As regards (a) above the same general considerations apply as in the case of military members of the I.N.A. There are at present about 1150 civilian members of the I.N.A. in military custody in this country, whom about 230 are likely to be classified as 'Black' and the remainder as 'Grey'. There are known to be many more in Burma and Malaya but many of these may be presumed to belong to those countries and not to possess Indian domiciles. The following special points requirec notice:-

(a) The Military authorities regard all civilian members of the I.N.A. as a civil responsibility.

(b) The number likely to qualify for prosecution on the standards applied to military personnel all probably be very small.

(c) The Government of India have made it clear both to S.E.A.C. and the Government of Burma that, while they have no objection to the release in Burma or Malaya of civilian members of the I.N.A. whom it has been found unnecessary to prosecute on the spot for soecific offences, they are strongly opposed to the return of any of them in military custody to India. They would prefer them to remain where they are and this applies particularly to women who joined the Ranee of Jhansi Regiment. It has also been made clear that the Government of India realise that some of these people may have families and domiciles in India and cannot be prevented after release from eventually returning to this country, if they wish to do so. The request has therefore been made that the Government of India, or preferably Provincial Governments directs should be supplied with such information relating to 'Black' and 'Grey' civilian members of the I.N.A. as their interrogation and classification may have revealed.

(d) The immediate problem, is how to dispose of the 1550 persons now in India. The legal authority for holding these persons in the military camps where they now are is even more doubtful than in the case of military personnel who may be brought before military Courts of Enquiry. The desirability of dispersing them expeditiously to their Provinces is therefore even greater.

(e) As regards civilian 'Blacks' (apart from the few who may have to be prosecuted) the consideration mentioned in paragraph 8(e) apply with equal force. Before the problem attained its present dimensions, the cases of civilians members of the I.N.A. came to the Government of India after classification as 'Black' or 'Grey' by the combined DMI-DIB Section; the 'Black' were detained under Ordinance IV; and the Home Department passed temporary restriction orders on the 'Greys' and had them sent to their Provinces. A comparatively small number of such 'Grey' cases have been kept pending during the last few months; but these are now being disposed of by informing the Provinces concerned and asking them to take the men over without restriction orders. In future the cases of 'Greys' will not come to the Government of India at all and it is proposed to adopt the same procedure for 'Blacks'. This procedure would be for the various Commandants of the Camps concerned to inform Provinces direct of the names, classification and records of these take people and ask them to thank them over as quickly as possible. It will be for the Provinces to arrange for their reception in direct consultation with the Camp Commandants.

(f) The arrangements for securing that these people reach their destinations will be more difficult than in the case of military personnel, since the military authorities cannot undertake to provide them with tickets to their homes and have no other means of control over them. It might however, be possible for Provinces to send police parties to escort batches back to their Provinces.

10. As regards the other civilian suspects or collaborators mentioned at the beginning of paragraph 9, there are two classes to be considered.

(a) The first class consists of civilians hithereto detained by orders under Ordinances IV in the interest of "military safety". (Some of these may be members of the I.N.A.). The military authorities have recently informed the Home Department that they no longer consider it necessary to detain a number of these people. The number with which Provinces are concerned is about 115; and it is understood that provincial Criminal Investigation Department already posses full information with regards to them. Most of them were arrested while attempting to across the land frontier between Burma and India and were detained as suspected spies or as persons who knew too much about our military dispositions. Provinces have been addressed separately by the Home Department about these people.

(b) The second class referred to above consists of a number of persons, from Subhas Chander Bose downwards, who were known to have assisted the enemy abroad either in Europe or in Asia. Many months ago the Intelligence Bureau started making lists of these people and divided them into two categories:-

(i) persons whose surrender might be asked for on the terminations of hostilities with a view to prosecution and

(ii) Persons whose return to India might be required, even if it were found impossible to prosecute them.

On the termination of hostilities the western and eastern surrender lists contained the name of 13 and 12 Indian civilians, while the corresponding list of collaborators not actually earmarked for surrender contained 29 and 75 names respectively. The whole list of 129 names has been carefully examined and, for the general reasons set forth in the opening paragraph of this note, the conclusion has been reached that, with a few possible exception, it would be useless to have any of them compulsorily repatriated to India and that it would be better to leave them where they are, even at the long–term risk of their becoming centres of disaffection abroad. It is realised that some of them may eventually wish to return to India of their own accord and cannot be prevented from doing so indefinitely if they possess Indian nationality. Many of them, however, are comparatively old persons and some of them have married wives or established other connections in the countries concerned. Nearly all of them are comparatively unkown in Indian. Their importance would be greatly increased by bringing them back and attempting to prosecute them. Few, if any of them, have committed crimes, the punishment of which would command any degree of popular support. The possible exceptions referred to above are S.C. Bose himself; two persons (Nambiar and Habibur Rahman) who have broadcast for the Germans; and six persons (Hari Singh, M.G. Swami, Baba Amar Singh, N.K. Banerjee, C.B. Bhattachariya and S. Roy) who were prominent spy trainers under the aegis of the Japanese. It may be presumed that S.C. Bose is dead. The other eight parsons are hardly of sufficient importance to make their trial worth while.

The policy of leaving all these persons where they are and resisting their compulsory repatriation to India has been placed before the Secretary of State and awaited his orders. The implementation of the policy will, of course, require the cooperation of the military and other authorities now responsible for the government of the countries in which these people now are.

7

Note by the Military Intelligence on the Last Days of Subhas Chandra Bose[1]

6 November, 1945

Subject—Subhas Chandra Bose

The following information has been elicited from the conversations with the staff officers of the Japanese Army HQ. Saigon :-

1. In December 1944, Subhas Chandra Bose suggested that it would be expedient for the Japanese Government to come to terms with Chiang-Kai-Shek and further seek friendship with Russia. Bose's theory was that China would only too gladly accept a suggestion which would extract her from the convulsions of a long and weary war. In regard to Russia, he explained that he was convinced that the Russian alliance with Great Britain and America was brought about by force of circumstances and that with the completion of German defeat, Russian will repudiate her present mask of friendship and will openly revert to her well known hostile status towards Great Britain and U.S.A.

2. The Japs were in favour of such a move as they realized that their defeat was inevitable unless a paramount political event of this nature occurred. But they were doubtful if Bose was capable of procuring this new tripartite alliance. The Japanese therefore rejected this offer and conventionally reiterated their belief in their eventual victory as they intended to produce a large scale counter, attack which would turn the tide of war in their favour.

   There are indications that the Japanese Government evinced a keen interest when Bose put forth these suggestions and in fact plausible as these looked to them; it was in this connection that Bose visited Tokyo on Dec. 1944. But his preliminary effort to explore the possibilities and hence the Japanese rejections of the proposals.

1. W.O. 208/808. Public Record Office London

3. In June, 1945 while in Singapore, Subhas Chandra Bose, forseeing that the defeat of the Japanese was a matter of time only requested the Japs for permission to move his provisional Government and a part of the INA. to Japan proper or China, Southern Army, HQ passed this in turn to Tokyo. It is said that Lt. General Shidei, Vice Chief of Staff, Southern Army HQ opposed this permission on the ground that without Bose the INA in Malaya and Siam will not only disintegrate but become an administrative embarrassment at a juncture when it was least desired.

4. Again in July as the situation was fast deteriorating for the Japanese, Bose sought permission, this time to enter U.S.S.R. via Manchuria with a few selected members of his movement. No formal reply was made to this but Bose was advised to proceed to Tokyo in view of his request. Col. Yano Chief of the 2nd Sec. Southern Army HQ has been interrogated at some length on this point. He is emphatic that the Japanese decision to respect Bose's views does not denote that the Japanese Government had sought or received willingness from the Russians to accept Bose to go underground in their country.

   On the contrary, he believes that the Japanese Government was then approaching Russia to sue for peace and could not at this stage allow any complication which must have arisen from Bose's admission.

5. In the absence of any specific answer from Tokyo, Bose intended to give himself up to Chinese or American forces, if on his arrival in Tokyo, the Japanese Government did not permit him to enter Soviet Russia. But the fact remains that from Saigon Bose actually travelled in a plane which was taking Lt. Gen. Shidei to Manchuria via Japan where the latter had been posted after the surrender.

   Another source contends that there was no need for the Japanese to ask the Russians for Bose's entry because Bose wanted to go to Manchuria from where he thought he would be able to get in touch with the Russian forces and obtain necessary admission independently.

6. It was in view of this that S.C. Bose had left Singapore on 16 Aug. On his way, he stopped at Bangkok where he took a formal farewell of everybody. He arrived in Saigon at 1200 hrs on 17 August, 1945. Lt. Gen. ISODA had come from Bangkok to bid Bose farewell and the former returned after two or three days.

7. After the accident at Taihoku on 18 Aug. Bose and Habib- In-Rehman were admitted into military hospital where Bose died the same night.

   Habib-ur-Rehman after his recovery left for Tokyo on 5 Sep. 1945 with ashes of Bose. Formosan Army informs that Habib-ur-Rehman took with him a package containing photographs taken at the time of Bose's death and also the jewellery that Bose was carrying with him.

8. It is generally recognized here that Subhas Chandra Bose had actually died. Also it is beyond doubt that he had plans to go underground together with a number of selected friends of his movement. There is nothing further by way of details or documentary evidence that can be obtained from Southern Army HQ. In the absence of substantial proof, it is still difficult to state conclusively the fate of Bose but the belief that he is dead is growing stronger and widespread.

   Further investigntions are being conducted on the following lines :

   (a) Allied HQ Tokyo has been requested to fly Staff Officer TADA to Saigon for examination.

   (b) Interrogation Report on "Col" Habib-ur-Rehman is on the way to this H.Q. and the details of it will be checked at this end.

   (c) The photographs will probably furnish best proof of his death.

8

Note by the Intelligence Bureau on the Public Reaction to the British Policy Towards INA.[1]

24 November, 1945

Reactions in India to the INA

1. There has seldom been a matter which has attracted so much Indian public interest and, it is safe to say, sympathy as the fate of the I.N.A. Public feeling is based on political, racial and sentimental considerations, and has been very greatly influenced by the Press and platform propaganda of political leaders and organisations. Generally, the nationalist Press and the politicians have spoken with one voice, and this Press campaign has had an undoubted effect, for many of the papers in question are most popular and widely read. The general theme of the nationalist case is that the men of the I.N.A. were actuated by patriotic motives. The demand is therefore made that none shall be punished, coupled with the statement that punishment would result in racial bitterness which would continue down the ages. The emphasis of current nationalist propaganda is on the treason aspect of the I.N.A. trials, and other crimes are ignored. There is no doubt that this campaign has largely captured the ear of the Indian public, to the exclusion of the other side of the case.

2. Congress has led this outcry since its commencement and continues to do so. Whatever its motives, it is certain that it attaches great importance to this matter, and there is so far nothing to suggest that its efforts will be reduced or that Congress will allow itself to be diverted from its present course without complete acceptance by Government of the demands put forward. On the contrary, there is every indication that Congress will use all available means to create still greater countrywide interest and to inflame public opinion in

1. W.O. 208/761. Public Record Office, London.

support of its demands, pursuing this line with determination throughout the election period and beyond, as long as events serve its purpose. The election campaign now in progress provides convenient platforms and growing audiences. Demands for no action against the I.N.A. have been constant at the many Congress political meetings all over the country during October and November.

3. Other political parties have followed the Congress lead, some of them with marked determination, as in the case of the Sikhs and the Hindu Mahasabha. The influence of the Sikhs in the Central Punjab rural recruiting areas needs no emphasis. The Hindu Mahasabha lacks the rural influence of the Sikhs, but their strongly worded appeals have had effect. The Muslim League also has sided with the I.N.A., but there is some reason to believe that in this, as a party, it is less earnest than others. Nevertheless, the trials of Muslims may make their effect increasingly felt on the Muslim public and the League alike, particularly now that the Muslim League I.N.A. Defence Committee has been approached to undertake his defence by a Muslim officer who is to appear before the next Court Martial.

4. The effect of all this propaganda for the I.N.A. is seen in reports which state that growing enthusiasm was obvious at meetings held in connection with I.N.A. Weeks and I.N.A. Days and that this is not only true of the towns but also of the villages. Indeed, it was recently stated that politicians engaged in their election campaign had to speak of the I.N.A. in appreciative terms to interest their audiences. This was attributed partly to a wave of anti-British feeling which is now being deliberately fostered, and partly to a genuine sympathy for the I.N.A. This report also stated that the licence apparently permitted to speakers about the I.N.A. had given rise to the feeling that anything could be said with impunity, and had its effect on those who might otherwise have supported the Government view openly, but now feel that silence is their best policy.

5. It is clear that sympathy for the I.N.A. is not confined to those who are ordinarily against Government. It is equally clear that this sympathy cuts across communal barriers. This is partly explained by the fact that the thousands in the I.N.A. have many thousands of relations who are anxious about their fate. A considerable measure of support is therefore found for the political bodies who are helping the I.N.A. and is accompanied by a growing general bitterness. There

is already evidence of some rather surprising approaches to Congress for assistance and the effect of the open association of ex-judges of the High Courts and gentlemen with titles in the defence of such cases is not negligible. Indication of any public appreciation of Government's position or responsibility for taking action are rare.

6. So far, the campaign in favour of the INA has not resulted in any overt action against Indian Armymen or Europeans. There has been no hint of social boycott of the former, for instance, and apparently nothings of this kind is intended.In respect of Europeans, however, threatening posters have appeared in towns. Although the experience of earlier terrorist movements in India justfies respect for anonymous warnings of this character, it is unnecessary to take the matter too seriously at this stage.

7. There have been numberous reports that military personnel and particularly returned prisoners-of-war, feel very bitterly about the attitude the country and its politicians have adopted, and that their animosity towards the INA is deep-seated. On the other hand, a recent informal sounding of military opinion shows a rather different picture. While animosity does exist among Armymen who have fought against the INA or have suffered at their hands as prisoners of war, the wartime Indian soldier in India usually takes a more lenient view, depending on the extent of his knowledge. He feels that members of the INA should be removed from the Indian Army, but that in general stern action is neither necessary nor desirable, for he finds extenuation in the circumstances which prevailed under Japanese occupation. The offence of the INA, in his opinion, was not so much treason as foolishness and weakness. It seems that this leniency does not extend, however, to INA personnel who were guilty of atrocities against Allied personnel. Some support for this reading of Indian Army sentiment is found in donations to INA Defence Funds by men of several Army and Royal Indian Air Force units.

8. On the whole, nationalist leaders have prudently avoided making public any plans they may have for the future use of INA personnel. There is, however, ample evidence of the interest of Congress, at least, in the men of the INA as well as in its propaganda value. It is interesting to note that in some of his speeches in Bombay earlier this month, Vallabhbhai Patel declared that Government ought to make the INA the nucleus of a new Indian Army. Similarly, Nehru,who

has publicly referred to the INA as the soldiers of independence, has been credited with ideas of using INA men as instructors in volunteer bodies: indeed, an INA officer has already been to train the Congress volunteers in Allahabad. Another report states that a Sabha is being formed in the north of India, with the object of contacting released INA officers and men in order to enrol them as members and train them, in the expectation that they will be of use to Congress in its day-to-day activities and in time of emergency. It appears that the Congress offices in the Punjab have an arrangement of advance warning of the arrival of discharged INA personnel going home and several cases have been reported of sepoys being immediately contacted by Congress officials while passing through Lahore. From these men enquiries are made, in accordance with the terms of a circular from the Congress High Command, about the locations, members and strength of INA holding camps in India, particulars of their class composition and of the officers in charge, and the names, addresses and INA histories of individual soldiers. In both the Punjab and other provinces, reports also state that in some instances the discharged soldiery contact Congress on their own initiative, offering their services and full information about the INA. A batch who visited a Congress office in Lahore were described as being "as zealous as soldier meeting their officers after having done a deed of exceptional valour in the course for their duty". INA men such as these give credit to the Congress for their release. The dangerous possibilities inherent in the mutual attraction and interest for each other of Congress and the INA merit very careful attention.

9. Briefly, the conclusions to which the information set out in this note leads are, *firstly*, that public feeling is generally sympathetic towards the INA while genuine disapproval of its conduct is lacking, *secondly*, that this sympathy is substantial and widespread, being confined neihter to the towns nor to any particular community and that it is being intensified by the day-to-day campaign of nationalist speakers and the nationalist Press; *thirdly*, that there is here a threat to the security of the Indian Army itself; and *fourthly*, that there exists the real possibility that this agitation, with its accompanying personal interest in INA members, may develop in dangerous directions.

9

OSS Report on the Feelings of Different Indian Groups Regarding the Trial of I.N.A.[1]

25 November, 1945

1. The current Indian uprising among students are sympathetic demonstration in protest against the trials of members of the Indian National Army. These outbreaks cannot be regarded as symptomatic of any revolutionary trend.

2. Many Indians feel that the members of the Indian Nationa Army who are now on trial will be convicted and then freed and on the whole programme of trials and publicity is an effort to restore British prestige, and that the anticipated releases will be intended to win the favour of the people.

3. The Muslim community and Army personnel look on the trial with tolerance, and do not wish those on trial to suffer any with punishment although they are not in sympathy with the INA program.

4. Hindu Army officers are strongly critical of the Government of these trials. According to one informant the feeling among thepeople is that they will stage uprising if the men on trial are executed.

5. The bulk of the Hindu population in general; and particularly in the Punjab are fully aware of these trials, and are strong opposed to any punishment of members of the INA. Defense have been set up, and in the Punjab more than a lakh of rupees has been given to aid the work of these groups. Signs have been erected and badges are being worn which claim that the men on trial are patriots and not traitors.

6. The Hindu Mahasabha is strongest in defense of the INA, but Communitst Party has taken a neutral position in the matter. It is claimed that the Congress is active in defense merely reasons of

1. Office of the Strategic Services, Record Group No.226 U.S. National Archives, Maryland, U.S.A.

publicity, and the Muslim organizations have maintaind a discreet silence on the subject.

7. At date of report there were no signs of an imminent uprising in Delhi.

10

Report by a British Agent on the Indian Independence Movement in East Asia (Extract)[1]

25 November, 1945

The Indian Independence Movement was planned by the Japanese, before the European War, with a view to creating disturbances amongst the Indians in India as well as outside and thus hampering the war efforts of the British in the event of war against Japan.

After hostilities broke out between Germany and the Allies, Japan encouraged the movement through her agencies employing Indians in the Far East for propaganda amongst Indians in countries under the government of the Allies.

Amongst others, one Hari Singh Osman, who, I am told was a member of the *Kamagata Maru* and was implicated in the Budge Budge incident and who was living in Batavia, Java, under the name of Osman Khan and had married a Malay, was taken to Shanghai where he was secretly working for the Japanese under the Japanese Navy.

Similarly Pritam Singh was another employee of theirs who was deputed for propaganda in Siam.

After the landing of the Japanese in Siam and when they were advancing towards Malaya they came across the British Indian Troops who had advanced into Siam.

The Japanese forces captured the Commanding Officer, Capt. Mohan Singh and Lieut. Mohamed Akram Khan of 1/14 Punjab Regiment at the outset.

Major Fujiwara, Officer in charge of the (Fujiwara Kikan) the Japanese political propaganda party who was following the advanced parties contacted Capt. Mohan Singh and Lieut.Mohamed Akram Khan and started negotiating with them through his agent Pritam Singh.

1. I.N.A. papers F.No. 164/I.N.A. This report was prepared by N.A.K. Mufti, Special Branch, Police, Singapore.

Capt. Mohan Singh, who in the past had anti-British inclinations, asked for the release of the Indian soldiers taken prisoners by the Japanese forces.The discussions were held in Alor Star and it was decided that the Indian Soldiers who had been taken prisoners and were kept in Alor Star Jail be released and Capt. Mohan Singh would make use of them for Fifth Column and propaganda work by sending them into the lines of the retreating army. Batches of the Indian Soldiers were sent to join the retreating Indian Soldiers, and propaganda which was of assistance to the Japanese commenced. The Nationalistic feelings of the Indian soldiers were roused and communications were cut, thus causing disturbances in the Indian Army.

Pritam Singh was responsible for propaganda and the Civilians of the occupied areas and the formation of the Indian Independence League.

After the occupation of Penang by the Japanese Military, Pritam Singh arrived in Penang and came into contact with Dr. Jagat Singh and then with N. Raghavan and Dr. Menon.

N. Raghavan in concert with Dr. Jagat Singh arranged for a general meeting of the Indians.

I personally did not attend the meeting but I was told that N. Raghavan and his party and the Sikh Community with few exceptions took a prominent part. Pritam Singh, in his address to the gathering, praised the Japanese power and sincerity in the cause of delivering the Asiatics from the clutches of the European and American powers and exhorted the Indians to cooperate wholeheartedly with the Japanese.

Muslims of Penang in general neither attended the meeting nor came forward in support of the movement *firstly* because they were anti-Indian National Congress party and *secondly* because there was no Indian Muslim propagandist with the Japanese to influence the Indian Muslims.

On the suggestion of Pritam Singh, N. Raghavan and Dr. Menon decided to change the name of the Indian Association of Penang to the Independence League of India (as the movement was called Indian Independence Movement) with the same office bearers to carry out the programme. Later the name was changed to Indian Independence League.

Sikhs and Hindus in general supported the movement wholeheartedly. The following were the leading figures at the commencement :

N. Raghavan, Dr. Menon amongst the South Indian Hindus, Dr. Jagat Singh, a Sikh who was the Secretary of the Sikh Temple whose name I have forgotten amongst the Sikh Community and another Gujarati or Marwari Hindu Makan Lal amongst the Northern Hindus.

Lawyer Gurcharan Singh was very anxious to take a prominent part but had no open support against Dr. Jagat Singh.

Gurcharan Singh got in touch with the Japanese Gestapo and worked as their informer. He endeavoured to cause Dr. Raghavan and his party and Dr. Jagat Singh to lose favour with the Japanese. He was instrumental in the arrest of H.H. Abdul Kader and Saravana Muthu of Penang.

The Indian Independence League, Penang Branch, started functioning under the presidentship of Dr. N.K. Menon.

The League succeeded in taking over the essential foodstuff, etc. from the Japanese authorities for sale to the Indian Community and appointed Abdul Kader of R.E. Mohamed Kasaim to take charge.

The League refused to sell the foodstuff etc. to those Indians who did join as Dollar members of the League.This policy helped the League to collect money and swell its membership. Many poor Indians who had little money and were not in a position to spare a dollar or who had no hope of any income in the near future underwent hardships from hunger.

The Muslim Community who were against joining the League faced the same situation. In addition they could not obtain passes to leave Penang in search of work or business, etc. as these passes were in the beginning issued by the Indian Independence League.

Hafiz Ghulam Sarwar M.C.S. retired District Judge attempted to take up the matter with the officials of the Indian Independence League but he did not receive satisfaction from Dr. Menon who refused to consider any amendments or change of their policy in this connection.

Some of the Pathans approached me for advice and I advised them to try to join the Malay Association which would solve their problem. I myself used to get rice, sugar or anythings I needed from my Chinese friends.

Seeing all these difficulties confronting the Indians especially the Indian Muslim Community of Penang and the high handedness of the Indian Independence League Officials, Hafiz Ghulam Sarwar and several other Indian Muslims decided to approach the Japanese authorities to express the difficulties of the Indian Muslims who were not willing to join the League and to request for separate arrangements to be made for the supply of foodstuffs to them. As no one was allowed to approach (personally or through the Japanese authorities in any other way than through the Japanese Association or his own Communal Association,they decided to forward an application to the Japanese Governor of Penang requesting him for an interview, through the Chairman of the Indian

Independence League. But the application was turned down by the president (Dr. Menon) of the League.

Hafiz Ghulam Sarwar then went personally to see Dr. Menon requesting him to forward the application for an interview Dr. Menon demanded the objects of the interview and when a position was explained to him, he nevertheless turned the request down.

Then a few Muslims held a private meeting and decided that, as the Japanese did not permit the formation of any other society of Indians but the Indians Independence they should approach the authorities for permission to form an Indian Commercial Association through which they would be able to solve the problems of all Muslims.

They proposed that I be on the Committee but I refused as I was not a businessman but I was persuaded to be one of the delegates to approach the authorities which they decided to arrange through the president of the Japanese Association.

Learning of the Muslim party's opposition to the Indian Independence League with whose officials he was at loggerheads, and being anxious to become a leader of Indians, Gurcharan Singh expressed his sympathies to a couple of Muslim Members, but later withdraw on finding that president of the Japanese Association by saying that the Muslim wished to create a split in the Indian Community. The President of the Japanese Association had at first intimated to some of the Indian Muslims that he would lead the Indian delegates to the Japanese Governor for the purpose of forming the Commercial Association.

Gurcharan Singh wanted me to support him and indirectly wanted me to recommend him for the leadership of the Muslim Commercial Party but I wanted the Muslim members against him. During my stay in Penang, knowing Gurcharan Singh's connection with the Japanese Gestapo I kept him under the impression that I was his supporter.

As the Japanese troops advanced to Malaya Fujiwara Kikan (the Japanese Political Department) alongwith its Indian propagandists followed them and contacted the political minded Indians on the way and formed Indian Independence Leagues in the important cities. Many Indians offered their services to help the Japanese forces, to do sabotage work or propaganda.

One Hari Chandaran of Ipoh followed the Japanese troops. On reaching Singapore he offered his further services in the Andamans and Nicobars and he was taken there.

Similarly a members of the military personal Alla Dutta who was a V.C.O. in the British Indian Army helped the Japanese and it is from his own lips that I heard that he was the first Indian to offer his services alongwith his party, to cross the straits of Johore. He was an important figure in the beginning and was considered second to Capt. Mohan Singh and was given the rank of Captain.

Prince Rawthore was another important figure in those days. He met the Japanese somewhere in Malaya, and expressing his anti-British views and professing himself a Prince followed them. He used to carry revolver and was a prominent figure in Singapore carrying out Japanese propaganda. He tried to pose as a leader and got Japanese support. The Japanese realizing that he was a quarrelsome person and had no standing here took away the privileges they had given him. Later on he was involved in a connected case of being in possession of parts of arms and taken into custody for a few days. He was then released. He then adopted the role of a Sanyasi—a holy man––a fakir—and took his shelter in the Sikh Temple off the Singapore Railway Station. He went upcountry and was last heard of in K.L. or Malacca.

After the surrender of Singapore on 15 February 1942, the British Indian troops were separated from the British and Australian Troops and they were ordered to collect in Farrer park. On the Second Day of the surrender they were addressed by Major Fujiwara, Capt. Mohan Singh and Pritam Singh. Their speeches emphasised the sincerity of Japanese and their offer to help Indians to gain Independence of their country. Taking advantage of the emotional nature of Indians and the suffering they had endured during their retreat and emphasising the fact of the Japanese over-whelming military power in success in Malaya within such a short period, they asked the Indian prisoners of war whether they were ready to fight for their country, all the gathering unanimously raised their hands and shouted yes. But soon after the majority of them, especially the officers, realised their hasty action and regretted it. Major Fujiwara also told them that they will not be considered as prisoners of war and they will be separated under Capt. Mohan Singh.

Similarly the Japanese of the Fujiwara Kikan contacted the civilians. On the second day of surrender they interviewed Dr.K.P.K. Menon and discussed with him the same subject of Indian Independence and Japanese assistance and continued interviewing him now and then. They requested Mr. K.P.K.Menon to broadcast a speech to the Indians explaining the sincerity of the Japanese for the cause of Independence of India but he kept putting them off and refused to commit himself.

Mr. S.C. Goho was also approached by the Hikari Kikan and he and Raja Ram were taken to Saigon by aeroplane.

Pritam Singh and the party also addressed the civilian population of Indians and the Indian Independence League (Singapore Branch) was formed with Mr. S.C. Goho was the president. On the premises of the old Anzac Club in Waterloo Street as established the office of the Indian Independence League (Singapore).

About a month after the fall of Singapore an Indian Independence Conference was arranged by the Hikari Kikan to take place in Tokyo (Japan) and the following representatives of the Indians of Malaya attended it:

1. Mr. N. Raghavan, 2. Mr. K.P.K. Menon, 3. Mr. S.C. Gobo, 4. Capt. Mohan Singh, (5) Lt. Col. N.S. Gill—members of the goodwill mission from Malaya. Messrs Pritam Singh, Satyanand Puri of Thailand, Lt. M. Akram and Nilakanta Ayer of Malaya who were to attend this conference met with a fatal accident on their way to Tokyo.

The conference was also held under the chairmanship of the late Rash Behari Bose and lasted for three days from 28th to 30th March 1942 at Nanno Hotel,Tokyo.

The conference was also attended by Col. Iwagaro, Chief Officer in charge of Hikari Kikan, representing the Government of Japan.After welcoming the members of the Conference, he, on behalf of the Imperial Government of Japan expressed whole hearted support to the conference in its noble effort to achieve Independence of India.

The main idea of Rash Behari Bose and the Japanese was that the conference should elect Rash Behari Bose as a dictator with full power to deal with the situation. Mr. K.P.K. Menon opposed it and he was supported by other members of the Malayan Party.

Mr. K.P.K. Menon, who was against a dictatorial organisation and wanted the movement to run on democratic lines, opposed some of the items of the constitution which were put up by the Japanese through Deshpande. He was against the movement being under the control of one person and stated that as the representation at the conference was very poor,decision could not be binding on the Indians of Malaya and that a more representative conference of Indians of various parts of East Asia should be held at Rangoon or some other place at the earliest opportunity.

The conference appointed Mr. Rash Behari Bose as Interim President of the Council of Action.

The conference was of the opinion that the movement for the complete Independence of India be started immediately.It adopted as its motto Unity/Faith/Sacrifice.

After the return of the Goodwill Mission Delegates from Tokyo, Messrs S.C. Goho and K.P.K. Menon started reforming the Indian Independence League, Syonan and appointed a Representative Council consisting of 75 members.

On 31st May 1942, a meeting of the Representatives was called. Some of the nominees did not attend. An objection was raised that the number of Muslims on the Representative Committee was too small upon which some of the Hindu members present objected on the ground that the communal question should not be brought in. Mr. K.P.K. Menon suggested that as they had directly appointed members and had decided not to increase the number of members to more than 75, it would be difficult to deal with any adjustment then but agreed that the Muslims should be given 1/3 seats as soon as vacancies occured.

This agreement was verbal. On the same basis election of office bearers and the numbers of the working committee would be made.Before the election of office bearers and the members of the working committee. Muslim members present asked that the President or Vice-President and one of the other 3 office bearers and 5 out of the 15 of the committee members be Muslims but Mr. S.C. Goho pointed out that the Japanese required him and Mr. K.P.K. Menon to be President and Vice-President in the Committee. It was then decided to elect a Muslim as a second Vice-President. It was decided that the Committee of the Indian Independence League (Singapore) should side by side with political work carry out social and welfare work under the name of Indian Community. This committee assisted by purchasing foodstuff from the Japanese and selling it to the members at fixed prices. It also repatriated displaced and homeless persons from Singapore.

At this time another body composed of Indian Muslims was formed under the name of "All India Muslim Club" under the presidentship of K.S. Anwari which was sponsored by Japanese.

After the formation of the Representative Council and the Working Committee of the Indian Independence League, Syonan Branch, Messrs S.C. Goho, K.P.K. Menon, Amir Mohammad Khan, B.A. Mallal, Hardit Singh as nominees of the Indian Independence League, Syonan Branch Left for the Bangkok Conference on or about 6th of June 1942.

There were about 30 nominees from the officers of the Indian National Army some of whom were Capt.Mohan Singh, Lt. Col. Gill, Lt. Col.Gillani, Capt. Jahangir, Capt. Malik of Bhawalpur, Capt. Burhanuddin, Lt. Col.Aziz, Capt. Inayat Kiani, Capt. Parkash, Capt. Arshad, Capt. Patnack, Capt. Hussain and Major Brar.

H.H. Abdool Cadar of Penang was also representative for the Bangkok Conference for his own safety as he thought that he was suspected by the Japanese, and had just come out of prison.

An open session of the Bangkok Conference took place at the Silapakaram Theatre Hall under the chairmanship of Rash Behari Bose on the 15th June 1942. Representatives of Thailand, Japan, Italy and Germany also attended.

After the singing of Bande Mataram (National Anthem) and silent prayer for the martyrs in the cause of India's freedom the Conference commenced with a message from H.E. the Premier of Thailand read by a Thai girl in which he praying for the success of the Conference said that it was auspicious occasion in which all the Asiatic people may collaborate as one in doing away with the hardship imposed on them by the oppressive rule of alien races and as Japan had taken the lead to liberate Asia it was an opportunity for all Asiatics to unite and join with Japan for the accomplishment of the task.

Mr. Debnath Dass of Bangkok, Chairman of the Reception Committee welcoming the delegates said "India is passing through a most crucial period in her history of the struggle for freedom which has now become the world struggle. Indians who meet today under the able guidance of Rash Behari Bose the pioneer of our movement for Freedom in East Asia should now make their decision that they will accelerate the creation of a free happy united India."

Mr. Rash Behari Bose in his presidential address thanked the delegates for his election as the President of the Conference. After narrating the incidents leading to Bangkok Conference he said "Let us all fully realise our responsibility towards our land of birth and let us realise well that our down trodden country cannot afford to lose this golden opportunity that comes only once in centuries. Our brothers and sisters have suffered and sacrificed for more than a century so that our country may be once more free. Let us rise to the occasion in order to please the soul of the Martyrs and act so that the great preparations that Mahatma Gandhi has made may bear fruit." He also impressed on the Indians that they should not doubt their friends otherwise the world will go on and they will be left behind and they will regret it.

Then Mr. N. Raghavan addressing the Conference said, "For a hundred years, we fought the British in India inch by inch and it took them till 1857 a full hundred years before they could say that India was theirs. We have since been fighting in various other ways. Today we are fighting for our independence again. But with a little difference. For well over a century we have been trying to convince the world that the agonies of India will one day be the agonies of the world. We condemned the British at the bar of public opinion of the world. That is the change that has come in the independence movement of our nation. Until now we have been struggling all alone. Today we are getting international cooperation not in a diplomatic sense but in practical language. Never before India has been able to achieve this purpose and that is the reorientation of the movement that has come about today."

Referring to assistance from foreign powers he said, "It is said that we may be asking assistance from others, but what objection can there be if that assistance is forthcoming from other nations who have condemned Britain? What objection can there be if the hand extended to us from across the Seas is in the full conviction that the problem of India is the problem of the World". Making an appeal to Indians he continued "After all the greatest Dharma we believe in is the Dharma to our own Mother. Our Mother is calling with her dishevelled, hair, dress torn, tears streaming down her eyes. She is calling her sons abroad. She is saying 'how long more is my agony to continue'? Have I not forth nearly 400,000,000 sons and daughters, and can they not raise their little fingers in answer to my call?" Are we going to ignore the call? Are we not going to say we are coming. Yes mother we are coming, we are coming. We will act now and shall always be by your side. We are going to free you from your shackles. That will be our answer. Yes we are coming and that answer will reverberate through our hearts and throughout the world. Let us go forward at this opportunity not because our enemy is in difficulty but because our enemy stands condemned before the world opinion and because we after 39 years of development of soul force by our great leader, Mahatma Gandhi, are ready to strike for our liberty and to raise our flag of freedom."

Mr. Sahay, Capt. Mohan Singh and Col. Gill also delivered speeches on the occasion. The Japanese Ambassador of Thailand read his congratulatory message.

Messages from Subhas Chandra Bose, General Tojo and the Foreign Minister of Japan, and from the Friends of India Society, Italy were read.

The Japanese Ambassador to the Court of Thailand the Italian and German Ministers in their congratulatory speeches said that it is their intention to make it clear to the Indians that they will be backed up by joint strong support of Japan, Germany and Italy. It was also said that the war which the Tripartite powers were victoriously waging against India's oppressor was destined to create a new order in contrast with the old one ruled by Anglo Saxon selfishness and abuse and that they have no territorial interest whatsoever in India but have one desire that India and her people are set free.

After two days of general discussion and the deliberation of the subject committee, the full conference *in camera* adopted various resolutions.

It was decided to take immediate steps for achieving the object of the movement for which a Council of Action consisting of Rash Behari Bose as President and Messrs N. Raghavan, K.P.K. Menon, Capt. Mohan Singh and Col. G.Q. Gilani as members were elected.

Unity/Faith and Sacrifice was adopted as the motto of the Indian Independence Movement and that all its activity would always be on a national and not a sectional or communal basis. It was also resolved that India should be considered as one and indivisible and the programme and plan of action of the movement should, in general be to supplement from outside the valiant efforts that India's National Leaders have been making within India to achieve complete and immediate independence free from foreign domination, control or interference of whatever nature.

They also adopted the resolution requesting the Imperial Government of Japan to make a formal declaration that Japan shall respect the territorial integrity and the full sovereignty of India free of any foreign influence control or interference of a Political, Military or Economic nature on the severance of India from the British Empire and that it will also exercise its influence with other friendly powers in inducing them to recognise National Independence and absolute sovereignty of India.

It was also decided that the copy of the resolutions adopted be sent to the Imperial Government of Japan for its acceptance and the resolutions were forwarded to Col. Iwakuro for favour of transmission to the Imperial Government of Japan.In order to take the public into confidence regarding the Conference the President of the Council of Action permitted delegates to show some of the resolutions.

After the Conference the delegates waited at Bangkok for a few days—in the hope of receiving reply from the Government of Japan to their request for acceptance of the Bangkok Conference Resolutions but later on they were given to understand verbally by the Iwakuro Kikan that the Bangkok Resolutions had been sent to Tokyo and that on receiving the reply it would be transmitted to the Council of Action.

The delegates then decided to disperse but agreed that the movement should go on in the meantime with the proviso that vital and important steps should be taken only after the receipt of a reply from Tokyo.

Rash Behari Bose stayed at Bangkok where the Headquarters of the Indian Independence League was formed.

The delegates of Malaya returned. Mr. K.P.K. Menon was placed in charge of propaganda, Mr. N. Raghavan of Education and Welfare and Capt.Mohan Singh of the Military.

The delegates of Malaya also received a complaint against Dr. D.M. Khan, a delegate from Hongkong.This man became a prominent figure in the movement.

The Indian Community, Committee of the Indian Independence League (Singapore) felt the urgent need for relief. To meet these needs a Distress Relief Committee was formed under the Chairmanship of B.A. Mullal. The instructions to this Sub-Committee were to pay their full attention towards relief work only, the object of which were

1. To feed and clothe the Indian destitutes from up-country who had come to Singapore prior to its fall, and the local Indian destitutes who were homeless as a result of bombing and the destruction caused in Singapore.
2. To assist the clerical classes who were badly off and without jobs, with money to feed themselves and their families.
3. To provide medical attention to the sick and ailing destitutes.

This sub-committee opened a Distress Relief Camp at Waterloo Street to accommodate the homeless Indians to feed them and to give them medical attention.

Funds were raised by Voluntary public subscriptions and by contributions made by the Singapore Branch of the League. Some merchants gave food-stuff. Old clothing was collected and distributed to the destitute. Non-Indians such as Malayans were also received in the Camp.

Shortly after the Bangkok Conference N. Raghavan took over the portfolio of Education and Welfare and organised amongst others a school known as "Swaraj Institute" in Penang where pupils were trained for fifth column work in India.

Mr. K.P.K. Menon who was appointed as head of the department of propaganda resigned from the Vice-Presidency of the Indian Independence

League. Syonan Branch and M.V. Pillai was elected in his place. He was working as a District Judge then.

Mr. K.P.K. Menon started a Broadcast section for Indian Propaganda from the Syonan Station under the Directorship of Capt. Jahangir, Civil and Military personnel were employed for different jobs. Hikari Kikan had appointed one Ishikawa as a censor and the verbal understanding between Hikari Kikan and Menon was that the Indian Broadcasting Propaganda and its personnel will be under his direct control and that the Japanese could have nothing to do except the censoring.

He also intended to take over the Indian papers, one in Hindustani and the other in Tamil and third in Malayan which were then run by the *Syonan Times* edited by Raja Ram and V.P. Abdulllah respectively, after completing the broadcasting arrangements.

A leaflet committee was also formed for preparing propaganda leaflets in different languages and cartoons were prepared for despatch into India by aeroplanes, Mr. K.P.K. Menon was its Chairman. Some members of this committee were civilians and the others the majority officers of the Indian National Army. A Japanese officer attached to Hikari Kikan used to attend the meetings. The Japanese were not satisfied with the wording of the leaflets and wanted stronger words (abusive language) to be used. But Mr. K.P.K. Menon opposed their wishes.

Indian Independence League Headquarters in Bangkok also started Indian Broadcasting. Indian propaganda was also broad cast from Saigon by the Indian Miliatary officers amongst whom were Lt. Col. Nagar and Capt. Irshad I.M.S.

N. Raghavan implementing the Constitution passed at Bangkok converted the Central Indian Association of Malaya into Indian Independence League Malaya Branch, with himself as the President and the same office bearers as before. Although his highhanded action in thus appointing this body was criticised, Raghavan paid no heed. Mr. B.K. Das who was the Secretary of Indian Independence League of Malaya, later became the Secretary of Indian Independence League, South East Asia.

Capt. Mohan Singh,who was given full power over the Indian Military irrespective of whether or not they had joined the movement, had given 400 A.A. unit personnel to the Japanese Authorities before he left for Tokyo. One hundred persons of this unit were sent to Cebu by the Japanese without consulting Mohan Singh.

Captain Mohan Singh then started organising the Indian National Army, with the assistance of Major M.Z. Kiyani. He also started propaganda for which Major Barar was appointed and Capt. Patnaik was deputed officer in charge of the Welfare Department. Propaganda was started amongst the Indian National Army through different agents and a great amount of money as well as persuasion and force was used.

One Capt. Shingara Singh together with Lt. Fateh Khan and some others of the Indian National Army were appointed as Military police. Shingara Singh was known as a terror of the Indian National Army. These people did not hesitate to shoot non-volunteers. In Kranji Indian soldiers were fired upon by members of the Indian National Army and similarly up-country at Kuala Lumpur.

Shingara Singh was later on transferred and Major (Capt.) Rashid Khan was appointed as Chief of the Military Police.

He was equal to Shingara Singh in all respects when torturing and threatening the non-volunteers.

On one occasion some members of Non-Volunteer officers were rounded up. Their belongings were looted and they were put in a separate concentration camp. They were later taken to another area and were put under the charge of Col. Aziz of Kapurthala Regiment.

These officers were ordered to salute the Indian National Army sentries and to be their scavangers. They were given uncooked rice mixed with sand for their consumption and had to cook themselves in garbage tins etc. as they had not been provided with cooking utensils. My nephew Lt. Ismail Khan of 2/10 Baluch Regiment and many of my friends were in this group of non-volunteers.

A few of them who could not bear the hardships agreed to join the movement but most of them stuck on. Later on when some objections were raised in the Council of Action these officers were released.

In 1941 I had made a report against Capt. Mohan Singh's cousin who was also a Captain in the same Regiment as Mohan Singh then stationed at Alor Star for his anti-British views and his efforts to incite the soldiers of his regiment against the British. He was later sent back to India after a long corresponence between (I.G.P.) the then security officers and the Military Department. The said Captain whose name I have forgotten and with whom I had no acquaintance visited me in Penang on his way to India and from his talk I gather that he had some knowledge of the report against him and that he suspected the informer who was my friend and was an officer in his platoon.

I feared that Capt. Mohan Singh might suspect me of being involved in this matter and I consequently kept friendly with him. For the same reason my friend who had given me the information agreed to join the Indian National Army when he was taken to Alor Star from Taiping (where he was in hiding) by the Late Lt. Mohamed Akram Khan in the beginning.

A.S.P. Mr. Finch then in charge of Special Branch Penang knew of this fact and we had discussions on the matter with the Commanding Officer of the said regiment then. Capt. Mohan Singh who was given the rank of G.O.C. by the Japanese was negotiating directly with the Japanese authorities in the formation of the Indian National Army and drew up a scheme for the Indian National Army organisation without submitting the Scheme to the Council of Action for its approval. He was also taking unconditional pledges from the volunteers to support him as the general officer commanding and started giving promotions. He used to receive $225,000 per month from the Japanese directly for the upkeep of the Army in addition to rations.

The Japanese policy was to keep the Indian National Army separate and away from the influence of the Indian Independence League or its Council of Action. They supported Capt. Mohan Singh in his resolve to deal with the Army personally, as they had great faith in him after his conduct in the Malayan Campaign.

At the end of November the surplus volunteers and the non-volunteers who were under the control of Capt. Mohan Singh and the supervision of Hikari Kikan were taken by Beppon Department (P.O.W. Department).

Capt. Mohan Singh played into the hands of the Japanese. He later sent Rahman to Burma without informing or obtaining permission from the Council of Action. It had been decided that the Army was to be under the directions of the Council of Action and that no move was to be made before acceptance of the Bangkok Conference resolutions by the Japanese Government.

After the Bangkok Conference, the Indian National Army was formed with 12,000 men and officers and although Hikari Kikan had agreed to the further enlistment of 3,000 civil volunteers this did not materialise. Mohan Singh became the G.O.C., Col. Gilani holding no portfolio. A scheme was drafted by Lt. Col. Kagawa. Later on Mohan Singh wanted to raise the forces by enlisting 10,000 more soldiers but the surplus volunteers were not allowed to be taken into the Indian National Army.

On one occasion the Indian Independence League requested the Indians of Singapore to hoist the Indian National Congress Flag (Tricolour flag) and Hinomaru (the Japanese flag—the Rising Sun) but the majority of the Muslims hoisted the Muslim Flag (Crescent and Star) and Hinomaru. Some of the Tamil Hindus objected to the hoisting of the Muslim flag instead of the Congress flag and broke into a Muslim shop in Serangoon Road and also started trouble in Arab Street by pulling down one of the Muslim Flags and treading upon it. A fight ensued but police and Japanese intervened. In the meanwhile K.P.K. Menon went to a shop in Arab Street in order to negotiate with T.A.M. Abdul Aziz and to request the Muslim but on his coming out of the shop he was slapped by the Japanese and then taken to the M.P. Station at Y.M.C.A. Later he was set free.

Mr. Rash Behari Bose came to Syonan (Singapore) via Penang from Bangkok in the end of August 1942 and brought with him a letter sent by Col.H. Iwakuro, Head of the Hikari Kikan of the Japanese Imperial Army expressing wholehearted support of the Japanese Government as evident from General Tojo's statement, etc.

The letter was produced by the President (Rash Behari Bose) in the meeting of Council of Action in or about September 1942 and N. Raghavan was of the opinion that the reply was unsatisfactory and the Council decided to write again. This reply, copy of which is attached was sent but subsequently withdrawn on the ground that the letter was more or less a declaration of the no confidence as was indicated by Col. Iwakuro in his conversation with the President.It was pointed out to Rash Behari Bose by Col. Iwakuro that the receipt of that letter would be deemed to be a declaration of non-confidence in the Japanese Imperial Government. Rash Behari Bose explained the attitude the Japanese would take to the Council of Action and suggested that it be withdrawn. The Council of Action withdrew it, Raghavan not being present.

Meanwhile as stated above Syonan Broadcasting Station was in charge of K.P.K. Menon who made appointments and set out programme.

Without consulting or informing K.P.K. Menon,Capt. Arshad was appointed Director by Capt. Mohan Singh in consultation with Hikari Kikan. Capt. Arshad I.M.S. who was formerly in Saigon Broadcasting Station had great influence with the Japanese Authorities and refused to obey K.P.K. Menon's directions. The Japanese started appointing new hands and revised the scale of salary and in some cases refused to employ Menon's appointees.

Ishikawa who was appointed as a Censor (Officer) by the Hikari Kikan started altering the message, etc. to suit Japanese propaganda.

Col. Iwakuru and Major Ogawa were approached but with no result.

In connection with the Press Hikari Kikan was insisting in July and August 1942 that Menon should take up the Indian Press but Menon held to the view that he would take it over after he had set up the Broadcasting Station. In October Kikan intimated that the press would not be handed over to K.P.K. Menon.

Japanese Authorities employed various channels for infiltration into India. This infiltration campaign was known to members of the Council of Action but the details were not known. The following methods were employed

(a) Infiltration work by Indian National Army.

(b) Infiltration work by Ram Swarup's Party in Burma.

(c) Swarajia Institute Penang from where some students were taken away for infiltration.

(d) Osman (Hari Singh) infiltration group which was recruited by Amir Mohammed Khan,carpet dealer of Singapore. Osman was doing it for the Japanese Navy and he had no connection with the Indian Independence League although he was using the League name.

The Indians in general experiencing and hearing of the atrocities of the Japanese and being humiliated again and again by slaps and beatings for no apparent reason, lost all enthusiasm.

The anxiety amongst the educated Indians increased at receiving no satisfactory reply from the leaders of the movement who in turn had received no reply from the Japanese Imperial Government.

In addition, relations between Captain Mohan Singh, G.O.C. and Mr. Raghavan took an unpleasant turn due to Mr. Raghavan challenging Mohan Singh's power and criticising his actions in connection with the Indian National Army.

The anxiety turned into suspicion when no satisfactory reply to the letter and resolutions of the Bangkok Conference came.

In the meantime Capt. Mohan Singh who was playing in the hands of the Hikari Kikan had agreed to send the personnel of the Indian National Army to Burma and had requested the Kikan to arrange passage for them without referring this matter to the Council of Action became suspicious. Lt. Col. Gill who had come from Burma gave many stories connected with Burmese Kikan and their opinion about the movement and the Council of Action. He reported the full text of conversations that had taken place between Lt. Col. Kitabe, Captain Tsuchi and Yutani's of Iwakuro Kikan and Desh Pande and Mr. Parshad, in which the Political Officers were of the opinion that, as the Bangkok. Resolutions were not accepted and there had been no announcement by the Japanese Government, the Japanese Government has not recognised the Council of Action and any its orders or decisions were worthless and that Indian Independence League not being an independent body had to obey the orders of the Commander in Chief of the territory concerned.

Captain Mohan Singh who was very much impressed by the frankness of K.P.K. Menon was on close terms with him.

Mr. K.P.K. Menon's influence and knowledge of political matters and Col. Gill's information in connection with his suspicions against the Japanese opened the eyes of Capt. Mohan Singh and he in turn began to suspect the Japanese.

During the sittings of the Council of Action from 26th November to 5th of December 1942 members of Council put forward their complaints in connection with mistakes made by individual members and resolved to follow decisions made in the sittings and also disclosed to failure of Japanese Authorities to fulfil promises in connection with the Indian Military and Civil Volunteers.

Council also decided to and did send a further letter to Col. Iwakuro asking for a formal reply to the Bangkok Resolutions, Col. Iwakuro on receiving the letter called a joint Conference of the Members of the Council of Action and the Japanese on 1st December 1942 and expressed his inability for the reasons given to forward the letter mentioned above to Tokyo Government.

Mohan Singh, on receiving instructions from Major Ogawa to send 900 Indian National Army to Burma on the 5th of December, in spite of his previous request for transport, refused to send the Indian National Army to Burma and brought the matter to the notice of the Council of Action on 2nd December, 1942. Capt. Mohan Singh (G.O.C.) was interrogated on the night of 1/2 December 1942 by Lt. Kunizuka who had been sent by Col. Iwakuro to find out the reasons for Mohan Singh's sudden loss of confidence in the Japanese.

On the evening of 2nd December 1942 Major Ogawa discussed with Captain Mohan Singh his refusal to send personnel to Burma.

Soon after Col. Iwakuro tried to bring round Mohan Singh as the thought that Mohan Singh had been influenced against Japanese.

Next day Major Fujiwara had a discussion with Mohan Singh, and explained his sincerity, trying to persuade Mohan Singh to send the 900 men of Indian National Army but with no success. Major Fujiwara also met Raghavan and Rash Behari Bose in the same connection and said that if the transport were refused it would jeopardise Indo-Nippon friendship. Rash Behari Bose and Raghavan were inclined to send the soldiers but Mohan Singh and Col. Gilani strongly opposed.

Next day in the Council Rash Behari Bose stated that Col. Iwakuro had promised that he would try his best to get a satisfactory reply from Tokyo on the point raised by Council of Action and said that his impression was that Col. Iwakuro was genuine. K.P.K. Menon and Mohan Singh requested that Col. Iwakuro should promise in writing to send the letter dated 29th November to Tokyo failing which they would have no alternative but to resign. The President said that this could not be done.

Raghavan tried to persuade them to give time and suggested that the President should take up the matter with Tokyo Government if necessary but K.P.K. Menon, Mohan Singh and Col. Gilani said that the position was just as unsatisfactory and after some discussion stated that unless Col. Iwakuro gave an assurance that he would forward the letter to Tokyo and that the reply would be given on or before 1st January, and no major action would be taken regarding Indian National Army etc. the three of them would resign. The President said that he would place these matters before Col. Iwakuro and would obtain his views.

The President of Council of Action induced them, not to do so until he had further discussed the matter with Col. Iwakuro.

On the morning of 8th December, Col. Gill was taken away by the Japanese Military Police without the knowledge of the members of the Council of Action. This enraged Mohan Singh, K.P.K. Menon and Col. Gilani who on receiving the message of President's failure in his talks with Col. Iwakuro, sent in their resignations from membership of the Council of Action. The president accepted their resignations.

On 7 Dec. 1942, the eve of 1st anniversary of Japan's entering into this war, N. Raghavan, Goho and others gave statements to Domai agencies.

Raghavan also submitted his resignation but separately.

The President informed Iwakuro Kikan about the resignation of the members of Council of Action and his acceptance of it. He also informed K.P.K. Menon and others about the acceptance of the resignation on 9th December.

On the 8th morning Major Fujiwara and Senda met Mohan Singh in Senda's house where Fujiwara brought in the subject of Col. Gill's arrest and explained the charges against him, he was a British espionage agent and that he was responsible for sending 6 officers 2 of whom succeeded in crossing to India to convey to the British Government of India information about events in the Far East. He also said that the Japanese authorities had come to know about Gill's being a British agent from 6 Parachutists who landed in Pegu in November 1942 and by deciphering a British Code letter.

Captain Mohan Singh asked Major Fujiwara for an interview with the parachutists and Col. Gill but was refused.

Capt. Mohan Singh (G.O.C.) not believing Fujiwara's story about Gill said that "In 1939 after the outbreak of the European War certain officers (Sikhs) planned to capture Punjab. It was then we decided to put up the claim of Maharaja of Patiala and one senior officer amongst us took the scheme to Col. Gill at Army Headquarters, Simla. Col. Gill kept that secret to this date. He advised us to wait as it was not the proper time."

I cannot say whether or Mohan Singh was telling the truth and Col. Gill was consulted/connected with the above mentioned conspiracy but judging from Mohan Singh's activities and his cousin's views already mentioned there may be something in it. I have no proof or witness to the effect.

N. Raghavan who did not resign from the post of the President of Malaya Branch and seeing the crisis facing the Council of Action called a meeting of the Presidents of the State Branches at Syonan to (Singapore) which was held at the Headquarters of the Malaya Branch on the 8th and 9th December. The idea behind it was to get the support of the Presidents of the Branches for Rash Behari Bose and the carrying on of the movement.

It is interesting to note that N. Raghavan gave as his reason for resigning from the Council of Action the arrest of Col. Gill whereas the rest of the members did so on the ground that the Japanese Government would not clarify the position of Indepenence Movement and further it was not possible or desirable to go on with it.

On 10th October 1942 the President of Council of Action Rash Behari Bose gave out a written statement. In this statement he expressed his regret at the resignation of the members of the Council of Action and his acceptance of it and expressed that they should not have resigned at all and thus precipitated a crisis and a deadlock which would result in hardship misunderstandings and unhappiness and damage to the cause. He further declared that he had taken control of the movement on 9th December 1942 in order to save the movement from collapsing and appealed to the Indians to continue to render him and the movement their support and cooperation.

In general the Indian public had no faith in Rash Behari Bose and considered him a Japanese Puppet and a mouthpiece. The resignation of the members of the Council and his persistence confirmed the opinion of the general public as mentioned above, but some who were paid by him especially his lieutenants like Linghan and D.M. Khan and similarly men from Indian National Army and the Bengali Hindus either from civil life or Indian National Army started propaganda for him and worked as informers for him.

On the 11th December Rash Behari Bose asked Mohan Singh (G.O.C.) Indian National Army to arrange for an interview with some high ranking officers of the Indian National Army upon which Mohan Singh challenged his authority and refused to obey him which enraged Rash Behari Bose. He purported to remove Mohan Singh from the post of G.O.C. of Indian National Army and to dismiss him from the membership of the Indian National Army.

Mohan Singh sensing trouble called a private meeting of the High ranking officers of the Indian National Army. Mohan Singh G.O.C. Indian National Army issued a special order stating that the Indian National Army would be dissolved shortly as it was impossible for the Indian National Army to achieve its goal, and that a confirmatory order would be issued as soon as arrangemens with the Japanese were completed. He added that in the events of his being taken before such confirmation the dissolution would take place automatically and immediately and that the members of the Indian National Army would be released from all their obligations and undertakings to him and the Indian National Army. On the same date he issued the order of immediate Dissolution of Indian National Army. Later on Mohan Singh was taken to some neighbouring island alongwith Lt. Ratan Singh, his A.D.C. and Lt. Iqual. They were provided with boarding and lodging. Mohan Singh was not allowed to communicate with any civilian or military personnel.

Mr. Rash Behari Bose issued another statement addressed to the Civilian and Military in which he criticised Capt. Mohan Singh for his activities in connection with the Indian National Army and the Indian Prisoners of War and blamed him for the crisis.

It was followed by a statement issued by the Chief of Iwakuro Kikan explaining the circumstances leading upto his dismissal.

There was no doubt that Mohan Singh was responsible for the organisation of the Indian National Army and helped in making the movement a success and was ultimately responsible for the atrocities committed against the Indian prisoners of War with a view to forcing them to join the movement. He lost his head somewhat in trying to be the sole master of Indian National Army, a belief encouraged by the Japanese as well as members of the Council of Action who did not object or check him at the beginning. Similarly the Iwakuro Kikan did not question his authority or the power of Council of Action until they found that he, having became suspicious, started opposing their plan.

This crisis created a deadlock amongst the supporters of the Indian Independence Movement, and was a blow to the Sikh Community, as they considered themselves very important in view of the presence of Capt. Mohan Singh as G.O.C. of the Indian National Army and the helpful activities of the late Pritam Singh in support of the Japanese. The Sikh community in general wholeheartedly supported the Japanese and the movement and even went out of their way to please the Japanese by adopting a harsh and severe attitude towards the internes and prisoners of War. The removal of Mohan Singh shattered their hopes.

Shortly after the arrest of Mohan Singh, opinion was divided amongst the members of Indian National Army. Some claimed that it was dissolved,others that it was not. A questionnaire was issued to the officers of the Indian National Army.

On 13.12.1943 Rash Behari Bose issued a circular touching upon the replies to the questionnaire.

Col. Bhonsle was now appointed Director of Indian National Army Bureau, which meant that he was in virtual Command of Indian National Army which was reorganised by him.

Some of the Indian officers who had joined the Indian National Army as a result of persuasion and some who had joined under pressure, did not rejoin the Indian National Army on its reorganisation. Some also refused to rejoin as they were strong supporters of Mohan Singh. All these were sent to Prisoner of War Camps.

After a short time about 7 officers were separated on the charge of propagating views unfavourable to the reformation of the Indian National Army. They were kept in Hill Street Police Station lock up for about 6 months. They were released some time after the arrival of Subhas Chandra Bose and were sent to the Prisoner of War Camp.

Rash Behari Bose asked Raghavan the President of the Malaya Branch of the Indian Independence League to take over the Department of Publicity and Information and Civil Volunteering. N. Raghavan delegated his power to two members of the executive Council of the Malaya Branch. S.C. Goho was entrusted with the Department of Publicity and Information and Dr. Lukhshimayah with Department of Civil Volunteering. Mr. Dalal was appointed as a Chief Executive Officer under S.C. Goho.

Criticism was now levelled against Rash Behari Bose for not withdrawing from the Presidentship and against Raghavan for not sending in his resignation jointly with K.P.K. Menon, Capt. Mohan Singh and Col. Gilani.

The Japanese appreciating the unpopularity of Rash Behari Bose wanted to set up another organisation under the name of the Youth Movement being of the opinion that if the Indian Independence League movement ceased they would be able to pull strings through that organisation.

Raja Ram who was employed as a publisher of the Indian Press and was in League with the Japanese was taken into confidence of the promoter of the Indian Youth Organisation. One Mr. Mizumo got in touch with Raja Ram, K.R. Menon and Narayanasamy who were members of the former Indian Youth League and Indian Passive Defence and started encouraging them to start the Indian Youth Movements. I believe a large sum of money was given to them for expenses.

On the other hand Rash Behari Bose was trying to become a dictator and his Lieutenants V.C. Linghan, Desh Pandey and Dewan Das were busy doing propaganda for him.

Mr. Goho learning about the Japanese intentions to start the Youth Movement tried to stop it on the ground that was an understanding with the Japanese that no other political organisation would be allowed to function other than the Indian Independence League, but without success. He suggested that the organisation be run under the Indian Independence League and wanted to consult N.Raghavan and promulgate a scheme for it.

N. Raghavan seeing that he had become unpopular with the public and fearful of losing the support of the Japanese,who were instrumental in the formation of Youth Movement, called a meeting of the Territorial Committee at Penang. The Territorial Committee met from 18th to 21st February 1943 and discussed the Japanese policy, cooperation between the civilian and military side of the movement, reorganisation of the Indian National Army and liaison between them, direct dealing between the Japanese and the workers and members of the League and Indian Youth Movement, help to be extended to the League in matters of communal questions and collections and few other subjects, and passed some resolutions, and also decided to send a memorandum to Rash Behari Bose, President of the Council of Action with a request to solve the difficulties which confronted them.

In this meeting resolutions were passed in which Dictatorial Powers were given to the President of Malaya Branch and the Presidents of other Branches with the President of the Malaya Branch for removing and appointing President of any Branch or sub-Branch and its members.

The said memorandum was brought by S.C. Goho on 22/2/1943 as Raghavan was not well and sent to Mr. Rash Behari Bose through Mr. Watan be of Iwakuro Kikan.

Two days after his return Goho met Rash Behari Bose.

At the instigation of Raja Ram, K.R. Menon, and Narayanasamy the organisers of the Youth Movement, Japanese M.P. sent for S.C. Goho and warned him against hindering the formation of the Youth Movement.

Next day, S.C. Goho was asked to resign from the Presidentship of the Indian Independence League, Syonan (Singapore) Branch and Rash Behari Bose also told him to tell N. Raghavan to resign from the Presidentship of the Malaya Branch of the Indian Independence League.

On 7/3/43 S.C. Goho sent in his resignation from the Presidentship of the Singapore Branch of the Indian Independence League.

The Representative Council of the Singapore Branch after accepting Goho's resignation elected Mr. Yellappa as the President. Mr. S.C. Goho after handing in his resignation requested Raghavan to tender his resignation by telegram through him,where upon Raghavan also sent his resignation from the Presidentship of the Malaya Branch of Indian Independence League.

On 8th March 1943 a body of Indians mostly composed of the coolies from Seleter were taken round the town in lorries carrying Indian Congress Flag and shouting slogan, and then collected at Victoria Memorial Hall, Singapore. Kumarasamy of Singapore Traction Company presided, the meeting organised an Indian Youth Movement. The people who went to attend the meeting were asked to sign forms before entering.

In the meeting they condemned and impeached the office bearers and the members of the Indian Independence League and passed a resolution to the effect that they have organised the movement in order to get rid of the pro-British elements and those who are hindrance to the Independence Movement.

They again held a meeting in the Capital. Theatre where officers of the Indian National Army were also present and in that meeting Raja Ram blamed the leaders of the Indian Independence League movement and their committee and called them British fifth columnists without mentioning names. They expressed their full faith in A. Yellappa the then President of the Indian Independence League, Singapore Branch. They also exhorted the people to support the movement and have full faith in the Japanese and Mr. Rash Behari Bose their leader.

A. Yellappa was also responsible for this impeachment as he was against Mr. S.C. Goho and wanted him discredited. The reasons for sponsoring this Youth Movement by the Japanese were firstly to revive enthusiasm which had lagged as a result of the crisis that arose and secondly to stop the pressure that the leaders of the Independence League were bringing for a declaration of Japanese policy towards India by the Japanese Government which the Japanese found inconvenient to comply with. Sometime later, this Youth Movement was absorbed by the Indian Independence League. Later on Youth Sections were opened in all the places under the name of Independence League Youth Section.

The Territorial Committee held meetings from 16/3/1943 to 18/3/1943 in Singapore under the Chairmanship of Dr. M.M. Lukshmeyan. In these meetings resignation of Mr. N. Raghavan from the Presidentship of the Malaya Branch and S.C. Goho from the membership of the Territorial Committee were accepted.

Dr. M.K. Lukshimeyeh was elected President of the Malaya Branch.

Mr. Thivy stated that objectionable speeches were made by the Youth Movement members impeaching the leaders of the Indian Independence League movement and calling them fifth columnists and suggested to the President of the Malaya Branch to approach the President of the Council of Action and requested him to take action to have such statements withdrawn and apologies tendered.

Mr. A. Yellappa was of the opinion that they should ignore the incident as the Youths had been silent and inactive and he thought that the speeches must have been scrutinised by Rash Behari Bose before they were delivered as he had directed the Indian National Army officers to be present at the meeting. But it was decided that the President of the League Malaya Branch should take up the matter with Rash Behari Bose President of the Council of Action.

The President met Rash Behari Bose who was of the opinion that the incidents should be ignored in view of the fact that the Youth Movement would cause under the Singapore Branch League (as a Section) and it should be left to the President of the said Branch to deal with this matter.

The weekly journal in English *New Light* edited by Raja Ram stopped publication and it was replaced by another weekly journal in English called *Young India* after the organisation of the Youth Movement.

A. Yellappa suggested that a band of young men be sent on tour in Malaya to rouse up the public as in Syonan (Singapore) the public spirit was lagging behind and it was necessary to whip up their enthusiasm and set the movement on progressive lines.

Dr. Lukshimeyah the president moved a resolution in Territorial Committee reaffirming its confidence in the sincerity of Japan which was unanimously carried. K.A. Narayanasamy moved many resolutions.

During these days a women's section was created in the Indian Independence League, Singapore Branch. On the refusal of Mrs. Davies and Dr. Lakshmi to become the Chairman Mrs.Chidambaram was elected. Dr.Lakshmi agreed to be Vice-Chairman and Miss S.N. Saraswathi Secretary.

Similar sections were opened in the other places of Malaya. Beside these sections a school for the training of fifty young Indians was also opened in Singapore on 20th April 1943 under the name of "Azad School." The students were given revolutionary training and Raja Ram was incharge.

I am attaching a rough translation* of Hindustani speech of one Jai Ram Bali of the Indian Army delivered to the personnel of the Indian National Army, in the Headquarters of Hind Field Force, Biddadari on 9th April, 1943. The speaker was captured by the Japanese troops in Burma. He also delivered the same speech on 13th April 1943 at a Mass Meeting on the occasion of Jallianwala Bagh Day.

At the meeting of the Representative Council of the Indian Independence League Singapore Branch held on 16/4/43 at which Yellappa presided, it was decided to appoint a sub-committee to arrange for the celebration of Tantryo Batau (Tenno Heika's Birthday) on 29th April 1943. The sub-committee decided to release $20,000 out of which $10,000 were to be given to Nippon Red Cross Society for the benefit of the Japanese soldiers and at the second meeting held on 23rd April under the Chairmanship of Mr. M.V. Pillai it was reported that $10,000 had been collected upon which the Chairman said that the amount will not meet with the expenses of the celebration and at least $15,000 had to be collected.

It was decided to spend not more than $2,000 on decoration feeding and other incidental expenses and $3,000 to be set aside for donation to the Indian sick soldiers.

A Committee was nominated for handing over $10,000 to Mr. Shinozaki for the Nippon Red Cross Society.

The president authorised Udharam Manager of Chotirmall and Co., to fix up an appointment with Mr. Shinozaki.

During this period an Officers Training School was also opened at Neesoon with Lt. Col. Habib and Major Dara of the Indian National Army as supervisors.

After acquiring control of the Civil and Military (Indian National Army) organisations Rash Behari Bose, the president of the Council of Action, tried to change the constitution framed in Bangkok Conference, and in order to assume dictatorial powers (which he was already in fact practising) invited Indian Representatives from the different places in East Asia to hold the Indian Independence League Conference of Delegates at Singapore on 27 April 1943.

A Reception Committee was formed from the members of the Representative Council of the Indian Independence League Singapore on the instructions of Rash Behari Bose. Programme of the Conference and arrangements in connection therewith were prepared in consultation with Col. Chatterjee by the various sub-committee appointed.

Representatives from Java, Sumatra, Hong kong, Manila, Burma, Thailand and Malaya including persons from the Indian National Army attended Conference which was held in Singapore Branch of Indian Independence League for 5 days from 27th April under the presidentship of Rash Behari Bose.

Besides the representatives in the list of the subject committee Dwarka Dass from Java and Amar Singh and Moulvi from Bangkok, one Banerjee from Burma and many others from Indian National Army, and other delegates appeared for the Conference.

The following persons were nominated by the President as the Members of Council of Action who according to the rules formed could function only in an advisory capacity and then only when their advice was asked for by the President.

1. Rash Behari Bose, President
2. A. Yellappa.
3. J.A. Thivy.
4. Lt. Col. Bhonsle of the Indian National Army.
5. Lt. Col. Zaman Kiani of the Indian National Army.

The word President was only used for the President of the Indian Independence League and the other Presidents of the Branches were designated as Chairman.

Many changes in the way of organisation in the League Headquarters as well as branches took place.

The following departments were formed and were run by the secretaries deputed.

1.	Secretary General		Lt. Col.Chatterjee
2.	"	Finance	"
3.	"	Supply	Hardial Singh
4.	"	Recuriting	Lt. Col. Gilani
5.	"	Training	Lt.Col.Ihsan Kadir
6.	"	Health and Social Welfare	D.M. Khan of Hong Kong
7.	"	Housing Deptt.	-do-
8.	"	Transport	-do-
9.	"	Education and Culture	Mr. Thivy
10.	"	Reconstruction	Mr. Sarkar
11.	"	Propaganda	Iyer of Bangkok
12.	Members Overseas Deptt.		A.M. Sahai
13.	Director of Military Bureau		Lt.Col. J.K. Bhonsle.

The President appointed Mr. Yellappa the Chairman of the Singapore Branch of Indian Independence League and the following amongst others were chosen to look after the various affairs, beside their names:

1. Maganlal of Maganlan Nagindas, Treasurer or Finance Officer.
2. G. Sarangapany in charge of Propaganda and Publicity.
3. Dr. P.T. Nathan in charge of Social Welfare.

During the open session of Bangkok Conference one person went to the stage and protested that they have been played with by the leaders who had given the impression that Subhas Chandra Bose will be coming and he will lead the movement but to his surprise he was not there. He started blaming the leaders present there. He was removed from the stage by force on the ground that he was mentally affected.

One of the resolutions of the Bangkok Conference was to request S.C. Bose to come to East Asia and an appeal was made to the Japanese Government to obtain permission from the German Government to enable Subhas Chandra Bose to come to East Asia.

The Japanese who had fully realised the unpopularity of Rash Behari Bose, whom the Indian public in India as well as outside in general thought to be a tool in the hands of the Japanese, and realising the need for Indian propaganda to support them in causing disturbances in India had no alternative but to bring Subhas Chandra Bose from Germany to East Asia. As he was then of no practical value to Germany who had failed in her advance towards Persia and was then in retreat. They were able to persuade the German Government to send him out to the Far East.

Subhas Chandra Bose was taken to Japan from Germany where he stayed for sometime on account of his health. Rash Behari Bose was taken to Japan to meet Subhas Chandra Bose.Thereafter Subhas Chandra Bose was brought to Malaya by aeroplane accompanied by Rash Behari Bose and reached Singapore on 2nd July, 1943.

They were received at Singapore Airport by Indian National Army and Indian Independence League representatives. The prominent figure were Lt. Col. J.K. Bhonsle, Lt. Col. Zaman Kiani, Lt. Col. Raju of Indian National Army, A. Yellappa, Amir Mohamad Khan and others.

Subhas Chandra Bose was provided with a guard of honour from the Indian National Army after which he was taken to a residence near Katong Park which was fully guarded by the Indian National Army slodiers. Japanese in plain clothes were also on duty there.

On 4th July, 1943 a Conference of the Indian Independence League Delegates from East Asia was held at Dai Toa Gekijo (Cathey Cinema) where admission was by tickets issued by the Chairman of the Indian Independence League Syonan Branch (Singapore). Besides the Military and Malayan representatives the following represented the places mentioned against their names:-

1. Daswani	2. Daljit Singh	—Manila
3. Dewarka Dass	4. Tejunal	—Java
5. Matani	6. Ibrahim	—Sumatra
7. Mr. Karkata	8. Matani	—Bangkok
9. D.M. Khan		—Hang Kong

Rash Behari Bose in his Presidential address after explaining the then war situation and the sincerity of Japan towards India and Indians gave up his presidentship and appointed Subhas Chandra Bose as the Leader of the Independence Movement, Mr. J.A. Thivy, Chairman of the Malai Branch in his address welcoming Subhas Chandra Bose said that the Indians in Malaya will show their faith and trust in him as their leader.

Lt. Col. J.K. Bhonsle D.M.B. (Director of Military Bureau) welcoming Subhas Chandra Bose on behalf of the Indian National Army said they had placed their lives and the destiny of India in his hands. He added that he was certain that they will meet the enemy in the field and destroy him there and rid India from the evil influence of Anglo-American Imperialism forever.

Subhas Chandra Bose before starting his address praised Rash Behari Bose for his services to his country. He also expressed his desire that Rash Behari Bose should continue his activities as his Supreme Adviser.

Subhas Chandra Bose in his address asked the Indian gathering to line up in one solid flank under one Leadership and prepare themselves for action and the fight that lay ahead of them. He expressed that the final victory will be won by the Tripartite Powers and their allies. He added that if anyone had still any doubt about Japanese intentions to help in the liberation of the Asiatic Nations, he should place his trust in him. He also indicated that he intended organizsing a Provisional Government of Free India to lead the Indian Revolution to a successful conclusion and to prepare the Indian people for an armed struggle.

A Resolution was passed thanking General Tojo for his congratulatory message.

On 5th July, 1943 a Military (Indian National Army) review was arranged on the field opposite the Municipal Office. Subhas Chandra Bose after inspection gave a speech to the Officers and men of the Indian National Army expressing full faith in their victory and said that battle cry would be "To Delhi" "To Delhi" and the ceremony ended after the March Past.

On 6th July a review of the Indian National Army was again held in the same place in honour of General Tojo who had come to Singapore on 5th instant.

Mass Rally of Indians in Singapore was held on July 9th on the Padang opposite Municipal Offices in honour of Subhas Chandra Bose. Men, women and Indian youths participated in great numbers.

Subhas Chandra Bose addressed the audience in a speech in which he gave reasons for running away from India and his experience and faith in the victory of the Axis Powers. He asked for total mobilisation and money and manpower. He expected to enrol at least three hundred thousand soldiers and collect thirty million dollars. Addressing the women he said that he wanted a death defying regiment of women.

The title Netaji was conferred upon Subhas Chandra Bose by public acclamation. Netaji means the leader.

A mass meeting of Indian women of Singapore was organised under the auspices of the women section of the Indian Independence League, and the Supreme Commander of the Indian National Army on 19th July, 1943.

Subhas Chandra Bose after inspection of the guard of honour composed of 40 women with fixed bayonet addressed the gathering and exhorted them to sacrifice for the freedom of their country and called for volunteers for the "Rani of Jhansi Regiment".

Indian Independence League East Asia appointed recruiting officers for Singapore and applications were invited on the understanding that they would have to parade in the evening at the different centres and they would be sent for when required.

Subhas Chandra Bose contacted some of the Senior Indian Officers of the prisoners of war to find out their reasons for not joining the Indian National Army and also to hear their complaints regarding the atrocities committeed on those who did not want to join during Capt. Mohan Singh regime.

I understand that amongst them was Lt. Col. Choudhari I.M.S. a Bengali who told Subhas Chandra Bose that as he had pledged to serve the King Emperor he could not break that pledge but would have no objection to join if he was absolved by the British Government from oath.

Subhas Chandra Bose also visited the Macpherson Road Camp where the Indian Prisoners of War were present. There, after delivering the lecture which was not well received he asked those who wanted to join the movement to collect under the Indian National Flag (Congress Flag) which was then hoisted up. Only one soldier who has gone there from the Changi guard stood under the flag. Subhas Chandra Bose called the Indian Prisoners of War British dogs. The Prisoners of War were highly insulted by this remark of his.

Subhas Chandra Bose took the command of the Indian National Army in his own hands on 8th August, 1943 and designated himself the Supreme Commander of the Indian National Army and the Director of Military Bureau (Lt. Col. Bhonsle) became Chief of Staff of the Indian National Army.

Sometime later Rash Behari went back to Japan accompanied by his A.D.C. V.C. Lingan, sometime in August 1944. Rash Behari Bose died in January, 1945.

Desh Pande the other Lieutenant of Rash Behari Bose who had a Japanese wife in Japan was in the independence Movement. He, in the beginning had great faith in the Japanese but some time after the crisis started suspecting the Japanese. He was frank in his talks and views and aired them daringly. The Japanese began to suspect him after his conversation, with the officer in charge of the Hikari Kikan Burma. He was sent back to Singapore from Burma and was just passing his days in silence.

He was allowed to go to Japan to see his family but met with sudden death on board the Ship Awa Maru on 1st April 1945.

I am told that Subhas Chandra Bose met Mohan Singh and had talk with him about the movement but Mohan Singh did not agree with Subhas Chandra Bose's views and expressed in strong terms his complete lack of faith in the Japanese.

After sometime Mohan Singh was sent by air to Sumatra as he was run down in health and Lt. Ratan Singh followed him by boat.

Lt.Iqbal who remained behind was sent to a Prisoner of War Camp in Singapore.

On the representation of the Ceylonese a Ceylonese Department was also started in the Indian Independence League Headquarters. Hotchawala became the Secretary. Similar sub-branch of the Ceylonese was also started in the Indian Independence League Syonan Branch under the Chairmanship of M.V. Pillay.

At its inception the Indian Independence League then known as Indian League of Independence Syonan Branch had S.C. Goho as its President and Kanan Pillay as the Secretary of the Syonan Branch League.

After Goho's return from the Tokyo Conference, Kanan Pillay who was suspected of selling League Newspaper and pocketing the money and misappropriating other things, e.g., foodstuffs, papers, etc., to the Malaya Branch as Secretary by arrangements between Raghavan and S.C. Goho who did not wish to take drastic steps as he was one of their staunch supporters.

On the transfer of Kanan Pillay, Muthiah and Kadar were elected Assistant Secretaries of the Singapore Branch of the League.

The Education Department was under the Municipality and Muthiah who was by profession a teacher found it difficult to discharge his job as a teacher. The Municipality raised objections and requested the League to release both Bhag Singh and Muthiah from their posts in the League so that they may attend regularly to their duties as teachers. Bhag Singh resigned from the League and Muthiah from the school becoming a full time paid General Secretary of the Singapore Branch of the League.

In February 1942 Mr. S.C. Goho was not available to attend to some Japanese celebration and the address which he had to read was passed on to Muthiah to give to Mr. M.V. Pillay to deliver. M.V. Pillay found himself in an awkward position when the leaders of the other communities brought properly drafted and decorated addresses whereas the one he had to read was not.

Mr. Pillay got very annoyed about this and Mr. Muthiah on learning that the Mayor had felt that there was neglect on the part of the Indians went to see Shinozaki and apologise for such neglect.

Mr. Pillay who was not on good terms with Mr. S.C. Goho the President thought that the Secretary Mr. Muthiah who was henchman must have played with him and let him down in the eyes of Japanese, strongly protested against the Secretary's slackness in the meeting of Representative Council and demanded Muthiah's resignation or alternatively offered his resignation from the Committee. Mr. Muthiah realising the seriousness of the situation and also feeling that Mr. Yellappa who was against Mr. Goho and his elique had been elected as President of the League, resigned from the post of secretaryship of the Indian Independence League.

K.R. Menon took over the Secretaryship temporarily and during this time the post was advertised and applicants called for. I was served with a notice from K.R. Menon the Hon. Secretary on the instruction of the President A. Yellappa informing me that I had ceased to be a member of the working committee as well as a member of the Representative Council for not attending meetings. After sometime one K.R. Ramanathan was taken in as the paid secretary of the Indian Independence League in the middle of April 1943. Later on there were misappropriations from the monies donated and loss of jewellery received from the public for the League and Rani of Jhansi Regiment. Ramanathan, A. yellappa President and Chidambaram were suspected of having a hand in the losses.

On enquiry Ramanathan was held responsible as the person whose duty it was to issue receipts for money and jewellery received. Yellappa and Chidambaram were trying to hush up the matter but public criticism was loud against them and at last the matter was referred to the Police and Ramanathan was charged and convicted. He was recently released on 11/45 when the convicts were released from Jail.

After the Sohan Singh who was very friendly with the high officers of the Indian National Army and Indian Independence League and helping them by supplying various articles was given the post of Secretary as one who could be relied upon.

When Subhas Chandra Bose came to Singapore he was not in favour of wasting time and energy in looking after the sick or poor Indians and expressed that as they were in the midst of a war they could not pay any attention to the sickly and the dying.

Those who were very sick were removed from the Camp established by the Distress Relief Committee to Pungol with no proper arrangement and the others were sent away from the camp. Distress Relief Committee ceased to function furthermore its funds were exhausted.

This camp became the headquarters of the Rani of Jhansi Regiment, with Captain Lakshmi as its Commanding Officer.

In 1944 when the question of providing rice for the Indian sick and destitutes who were housed at Pungol arose Municipal Authorities were approached. They refused to give rice but Shinozaki of the Municipal Department suggested that it will be helpful to Indians if they were to start Indian Welfare Association under the (Tokubetu Si) Municipality similar to the Associations formed by Eurasians, Malaya and Arabs.

The members of the social welfare branch of the Indian Independence League Singapore agreed to it. The Indian Welfare Association started to function under the Chairmanship of Mr. M. V. Pillay and used to meet at Indian Independence League, Singapore Branch premises. Amongst others were Balbir Singh, Dr. Nathan, Maganlal, Paul, Sammy, Rev. Handy, Davies, Anwari.

The Indian Welfare Association, which had no connection with the Indian Independence League, utilised the premises of the Indian Independence League, Singapore Branch, for its purposes, and began to collect donations from the public independently for the support of the Indian destitutes and bulit huts behind the Indian Independence League, Singapore Branch, Waterloo Street.

Mr. N. Raghawan who had rejoined the Indian Independence League Movement and was Minister of Finance in the Azad Hind Government did not approve of this formation of the Welfare Association probably for personal reasons. Nor did Subhas Chandra Bose approve of the Association, as the Indian Independence League had no control over it.

A meeting was called by the Indian Welfare Association at Jalan Bazar for collection of money, and during the opening address by M.V. Pillay, objections were raised for omitting to Sing at the outset "Bande Mataram". Heckling and disorder prevailed. I am informed that soldiers of the Indian National Army and the members of Azad School Singapore were sent in plain clothes to create confusion at the meeting.

Subhas Chandra Bose on the advice of N. Raghavan made strong protests to the Japanese against this organisation on the ground that no other body outside the Indian Independence League should be formed in connection with Indian affairs and it was later dissolved.

In order to carry on the work of Indian Independence League and to support the Indian Independence Army, Subhas Chandra Bose made an appeal to Indians for funds which appeal met with a good response especially from the Hindus of the United Provinces. Contributions from the rich class were not so satisfactory and questionnaires were issued by the League Headquarters to individuals known to be well off calling for information regarding their income and wealth. This scheme did not succeed as many did not return the questionnaire forms at all.

On the instructions of the Indian Independence League Headquarters the local League Branch issued a circular to members of the Representative Council to help the persons nominated to collect statistics of Indians residing in Singapore in every way possible.

Most of the Muslims either did not join the League or did not cooperate whole-heartedly on the ground that they did not approve of the Indian National Congress and the singing of "Bande Mataram". Nor did the leaders who were mostly Hindus care for the feelings of Muslims. This attitude of the Muslims offended the Leaders of the Indian Independence League.

Non-Muslims especially Hindus started a propaganda to the effect that Muslims were pro-British and anti-Japanese. They did not trust the Muslims who were in the movement whether they were members of the Indian Independence Army or the Indian Independence League.

During the time of Rash Behari Bose, A. Yellappa the President of the Indian Independence League, Singapore Branch sent for T.A.M. Abdul Aziz who was a representative of the South Indian Muslims along with Haji A. Mohammed Hussain, B. Mohammed Ibrahim, and few others and hold a meeting in which Rash Behari, A. Yellappa, Lt. Col. Bhonsle, Lt. Col. Z. Kiyani, Lt. Col. Chatterjee, Lt. Col. Ihsan Kadir, M.V. Pillay were present. Col. Chatterjee accused the Muslims of lack of cooperation and non-participation in the movement calling them enemies of India, and warned them that unless they changed they will be the sufferers. On the objection raised by Muslims regarding the singing of "Bande Mataram"and the Congress Flag Col. Chatterjee replied that the League will not stop the singing of "Bande Mataram" and will continue the use of the Indian National Flag. Lt. Col. Ihsan Kadir and Lt. Col. Bhonsle supported Col. Chatterjee and also used harsh and threatening words. Lt. Col. Zaman Kiani dealt leniently with them and suggested that the League should give some privilege to the Muslims and consider their objections.

Sometime after his arrival Subhas Chandra Bose called at his house, Abdul Aziz and a few others Muslims. Lt. Col. Chatterjee and M. K. Chidambaram were present. Subhas Chandra Bose asked the Muslims the reasons for not coming forward for the Independence of their country upon which the representatives said that they objected to the song "Bande

Mataram", the Congress Flag and that as they were followers of the Muslims League of India which is also fighting for the Independence of India and as they were unaware of its policy and attitude towards the Indian Independence League they could not participate in the Movement. Subhas Chandra Bose told then that he will consider their objections but that they should participate in the movement.

Under the persistant threats of A. Yellappa who had asked for $ 250000 from Indian Muslims only $ 130000 was collected and given to Subhas Chandra Bose.

The Muslim objection against *Bande Mataram* was that it formed part of a song written by a Hindu Bengalee, to excite the Hindu population in Bengal against the Muslim rulers of Bengal. It contains many objectionable references to Muslims and although these references do not appear in the stanzas which form the supposed national song, yet the implication is there. Subhas Chandra Bose ordered the substitution of another song for *Bande Mataram* but in practice *Bande Mataram* used to be sung at meetings.

After sometime A. Yellappa took T. A. M. Abdul Aziz to Penang with him in order to persuade the Penang Muslims to participate in the movement and make contributions. T. A. M. Abdul Aziz at a meeting in Penang asked the Muslims to join and contribute. Thereafter a Committee of Muslims under the Chairmanship of Abdul Wahab of Penang was formed to collect money. Although Muslims were not willing but not desiring to bring trouble on themselves collected about $ 5,000.

After a speech made by Subhas Chandra Bose (soon after his arrival) circulars for total mobilisation were issued to the members of the Representative Committees by the League Branches asking them to exert and try their best to raise volunteers for the Indian National Army.

On 21st October 1943 the fifth Conferences of the Indian Independence League in which delegates from all the centres of the East Asia including Malaya participated was held at Dai Toa Gekijyo (Cathay Cinema) Singapore.

M. K. Ramachandran read an address welcoming the delegates which was followed by a report on the working of the League, by the General Secretary Lt. Col. A.C. Chatterjee.

After that Subhas Chandra Bose delivered an address in which he dealt with all aspects of the current world situation with particular reference to India. He also declared that the formation of the Provisional Government had become a necessity for the final fight for freedom.

The Conference reassembled in the afternoon. Subhas Chandra Bose appeared at the Conference accompanied by Col. Yamamoto the then chief of the Hikari Kikan. Before proclaiming the inauguration of the Provisional Government of Free India Subhas Chandra Bose read two messages of congratulations he had sent to Burma and Philippines and another to the Japanese Government expressing the thanks and gratitude of the Indians for their kind help in the movement. The message were adopted by the Conference.

Subhas Chandra Bose announced the composition of the Provisional Government comprising a cabinet of ministers consisting of the representatives of the Indian National Army and a body of advisers.

Subhas Chandra Bose then made a statement in Hindustani explaining the significance of the extablishment of the Provisional Government which was translated into Tamil by Mr. M. K. Chidambaram.

Then Subhas Chandra Bose the Head of the State and Prime Minister took the following oath:

"In the name of God I take this sacred oath that to liberate India and the 38 crores of my countrymen I Subhas Chandra Bose, will continue the sacred war of freedom till the last breath of my life. I shall remain always a servant of India and to look after the welfare of 38 crores of my Indian brothers and sisters shall be for my highest duty. Even after winning freedom, I shall always be prepared to shed even the last drop of my blood for the preservation of India's Freedom".

This was followed by the oath taking ceremony of the members of the Government. The oath ran as follows

"In the name of God I take this holy oath that to liberate India and the 38 crores of my countrymen I will be absolutely faithful to my Leader Subhas Chandra Bose and shall be always prepared to sacrifice my life and all I have for fulfilling this pledge."

Subhas Chandra Bose shook hands with each member and this was followed by the Proclamation of the Provisional Government of Free India which was read in Hindustani by Mr. A.M. Sahay, in Tamil by Mr. M.K. Chidambaram and in English by Subhas Chandra Bose.

A luncheon party was given by the Indian Independence League in honour of the delegates at the Indian Independence League organisation of East Asia at Cricket Club, Singapore. Lt. Col. Mitabe of the Hikari Kikan Burma was also present. Subhas Chandra Bose spoke on that occasion and said that all arrangements necessary for a revolution were completed and that they should be ready for the last phase of struggle. He appealed to the rich Indians to sacrifice whatever they possess.

On 22nd October 1943 Birthday of Rani Lakshmi Bai of Jhansi and the opening ceremony of the "Rani of Jhansi Regiment Training Camp" was celebrated at the Indian Independence League, Singapore Branch, Waterloo Street. Subhas Chandra Bose was received by Mrs. M.K. Chidambaram the President of the Women Section Syonan. Mr. Bose then inspected the guard of honour presented by an armed unit of the Rani of Jhansi Regiment in company of Capt. Dr. Lakshmi.

Subhas Chandra Bose in his speech said "It was not merely political movement but on the other hand it was engaged in the great task of regenerating the nation. He added that India has a glorious tradition of producing brave women like Rani of Jhansi and others and it did produce a Lakshmi Bai today for the war of Independence of India. He further said that the women of India have not only taken part in the Passive Resistance Movement but in the history of the Revolutionary party also there are many examples of the Indian women. He gave a short history of Rani of Jhansi and her fight against the British for freedom of Jhansi. He added that 156 Indian women are going to start their training in the Central camp but hoped that the numbers in Syonan (Singapore) will reach to 1000 and added that Training Camps for women had also started in Thailand and Burma and declared the Rani of Jhansi Camp Syonan opened. The first meeting of the Council of Ministers of the Azad Hind (Free India) met at the residence of Subhas Chandra Bose at 9.00 p.m. on 22/10/43.

On the night of 23rd and 24th October the Provisional Government of *Azad Hind* declared a war on Britain and the United States of America.

On 24 Oct. 1943 a military parade of the members of the *Azad Hind Fauz* (Indian Independence Army) was held in the playing ground in front of the Municipal Building, Singapore and Subhas Chandra Bose after inspecting the Indian National Army gave a speech to the members of the Army.

On 24 Oct. 1943 Provisional Government of Free India was host to a Banquet to high ranking Japanese Army and Navy officers as well as prominent Japanese civilians at Japanese Army Officers' Club. Subhas Chandra Bose gave a short speech in which he said that since the war broke out in Europe in 1939 Britain and her Allies professed that they are fighting for democracy in the world and similarly the United States of America has repeated it after joining in the War but the truth can be judged by the refusal to apply the Atlantic Charter wherever any suppressed nation asked for it. The domination of India by the British is by itself a proof of this false declaration. Praising the Axis Powers he said that they are fighting on the Principle of Justice and Right. Japanese Air Commander and High Ranking Officers of the Burmese Army also spoke.

A general meeting of Businessmen and Chettiars for collection of funds was held at Jalan Bazar Stadium on 25/10/1943 in which Subhas Chandra Bose demanded money for carrying on of the movement. Nearly 7 million dollars were promised. On 26th at another meeting held at the Indian Independence League, Singapore Branch Office, about six million dollars in promise were added to the above contribution.

A gold plated silver Charkha (Spinning wheel) was bought by the Chettiar (Nagarathers) of Negri Awmbilan for a sum of $ 500000 at the auction.

The general procedure in these collections was that some important figure such as A. Yellappa the President of the Singapore Indian Independence League, Branch Singapore, Mr. M.K. Chidambaram or Udha Ram of Chotirmall & Co. used to tax the people in whatever amount they thought best and a garland was sold for so many dollars to such a person who had no option but to accept it and pay the sum specified.

Furthermore people were summoned to the League Headquarters and the Singapore Indian Independence League Branch where they were compelled to agree and pay the amount at which they were assessed. The collection was made by threat of confiscation of all one's money and property or handing one over to Japanese Military Police and calling one Pro-British. Men responsible for these extortions were A. Yellappa, M. K. Chidambaram, Udha Ram and Magan Lal and in the case of wealthy persons, Subhas Chandra Bose, Raghawan, Thivy and Dr. Lakshmeyah used to interview and force contribution out of them.

Many cases have occurred wherein persons who could not afford to pay the amount demanded or were not willing to pay were taken by the Japanese M.P.'s.

Besides the above mentioned extortions the Manager of the Indian Overseas Bank Mr. Jagathesan was giving them full information about the account of deposits of individuals in his bank or their other businesses. After the formation of the Provisional Government of Free India a fresh oath of allegiance and pledge were asked to be taken by the Indians and the old membership card of the Indian Independence League was cancelled and a new card issued.

The Provisional Government of Free India was officially recognised by the following countries.

Japanese Government recognised the Provisional Government of Free India on 23rd October 1943.

German Foreign Minister Her Von Ribbentrop officially notifying Subhas Chandra Bose, by telegram that the Reich Government extended the recognition to the newly formed Provisional Government of Azad Hind Fauj (Free India).

On 25th October, 1943 information was received in Syonan that the Independence State of Burma had recognised the Provisional Government of Azad Hind.

The Philippine Republic's recognition of the Provisional Government of Azad Hind was conveyed to Subhas Chandra Bose, Head of the Provisional Government of the Free India by Jose P. Laurel, President of the Republic of the Philippines.

Croates extended its formal recognition to the Provisional Government of Free India on October 27, 1943.

On November 1st, 1943 Nanking Government of China officially announced its recognition of the Provisional Government of Free India.

Manchouko Government as announced on 1st November 1943 in Hainking that Manchouko formerly recognises the Provisional Government of Free India.

Fascist Republic of Italy recognised the Provisional Government of Free India on November 9th, 1943.

On November 18th 1943 Bangkok Radio announced the recognition of the Provisional Government of Free India by the Government of Thailand.

Central Bureau of Free India Berlin issued a declaration.

A few days after the formation of the Provisional Government of Free India Subhas Chandra Bose alongwith Lt. Col. Bhonsle, Lt. Col. Raju, I.M.S., A.M. Sahai and Mr. Hassan who was his Private Secretary and hand followed him from Germany flew to Japan and on arrival at Tokyo on November 1st, 1943 was officially received by the Government of Japan as the Head of the Provisional Government of Free India to attend the East Asia Conference as an observer.

General Hideki Tojo Premier of Japan in response to a speech made by Subhas Chandra Bose at the Assembly of Greater East Asiatic Nations on 6th November 1943 made a declaration transferring the Andaman and Nicobar Islands to the Provisional Government of Free India headed by Subhas Chandra Bose.

Nippon Territorial Committee of the Indian Independence League entertained Subhas Chandra Bose at a Tea Party at the Imperial Hotel on

11th November 1943 and also a Rally was held jointly sponsored by the Taisei Yokusankai and the Japan Indian Society at the Hibiya Public Hall on November 14th, 1943 where Subhas Chandra Bose gave speeches.

Subhas Chandra Bose also made Radio speeches from Tokyo to his compatriots in Germany and other places in Europe on 16th November, 1943 and on 17th to the people of India.

On his way back to Malaya Subhas Chandra Bose visited Philippines and Nanking in China where a welcome Rally was held in his honour on November 19, 1943. There in his speech he called upon Chiang Kai Shek and other leaders to shake off Anglo-American influence and do the utmost for the unification of China and stress that India and China should both fight for freedom and liberation of Greater East Asia. The intention of the Provisional Government of Free India was to establish its Government at Andamans so that they may have their own territory but it was not agreed to by the Japanese *firstly* because in handing over the Islands to the Provisional Government the interests of Japanese who were defernding the place and were in full control would have clashed with that of the Provisional Indian Government. *Secondly* in Japan there was public criticism of the action of the Prime Minister. *Thirdly* the Japanese wanted to strengthen the Burma front and furthermore Subhas Chandra Bose wished to be on the borderline of India for opportune moment to enter India.

A suicide squad of selected volunteers from the Azad Hind Forces (Indian National Army) was formed under the Command of Lt. Col. Shah Nawaz (formerly Captain of 1/14 Punjab Regiment) who had offered himself and the personnel of this squad signed an agreement with their blood and they were moved to Burma. At the same time the 1st Division of the Indian National Army under the Command of Col. M.Z. Kiyani also left for the Burma front. Subhas Chandra Bose on his return from Japan addressed a gathering in front of the Municipality on 2nd December 1943 to celebrate the Andamans and Nicobar Day.

Subhas Chandra Bose visited Sumatra, Borneo and Java on a four days tour where he delivered lectures and collected money. I was told by Lt. Col. Giani who was there that the Japanese did not allow the Indian National Congress Flag to be put on Subhas Chandra Bose's car and also the lecture in Batavia was arranged in a hall where only Indians and some Japanese were present. He further told me that the President of Java was the only Javanese who was invited but was not allowed to enter. The reason for this restriction was, he said, that Japanese did not want the Indian Independence movement to come openly as the Indonesian may start demanding their freedom too.

After that Subhas Chandra Bose visited Andamans and Nicobar Islands which were renamed as Shaheed (Island of Martyr) and Swaraj (Independence) Islands respectively on 30th December 1913 and hoisted the Indian Tricolour Congress Flag.

During this time arrangement were made for transferring Headquarters of the Provisional Government of Free India and the Supreme Command of the Indian National Army to Burma. Subhas Chandra Bose reached Burma on 7th January, 1944, Rear Headquarteres were left in Singapore under the control of Col. Chatterjee.

Colonel (later on Major General) Loganathan who was the Minister of State was appointed the first Chief Commissioner of the Shaheed and Swaraj (Andaman and Nicobar) Islands where he went with one Capt. Alwi his private secretary. Col. Loganathan was just a nominal figure and his work consisted at looking after the Indian Independence Movement there.

Long before Subhas Chandra Bose departed to Burma arrangements were made to send some of the Indian boys for higher military training to Japan and for that purpose Dr. N. K. Menon brought his son from Penang for an interview and later on Mr. Gurcharan Singh of Penang also came down with his son, Menon's son and two sons of Gurcharan Singh were selected for training and were sent to Japan and are still there with some others.

Two months after the transfer of Headquarters of Azad Hind Provisional Government and the Azad Hind Army to Burma Lt. Col. Chatterjee the Secretary-in-General of the Rear Headquarters was also called there and Lt. Col. Alagapan was appointed in his place.

Lt. Co. Bhonsle Chief of the Staff of the Indian National Army who had also gone was replaced by Lt. Col. Nagar in the Rear Headquarters as acting Chief of Staff. By this time the 2nd Division of the Indian National Army also left Singapore on its way to Burma under the Command of Lt. Col. Bhagat Lt. Col. Nagar was also appointed the commander of 3rd Division formed with the Malayan recruits in the main.

A. Yellappa, Chairman of the Indian Independence League, Singapore Branch and the adviser of the Azad Hind Government also went to Burma and M.V. Pillay was appointed to act as Chairman in his place.

Azad Hind Government in the official announcement declared 21st March to be observed as Azad Hind Day, and that the 21st Day of every month shall be observed as Azad Hind Day.

A public meeting of the Indians was held in the playing field of Waterloo Street on 21st March for the celebration of Azad Hind Day and the victories on the Arakan Front and Indo-Burma Front.

Indians of Johors also held a meeting on the 21st under the Chairmanship of Major Dara.

Lt. Col. A.C. Chatterjee the Finance Minister of the Provisional Government of Azad Hind was appointed as Governor of Liberated Areas of India Azad Hind 22/3/44.

A public procession and Mass Rally was organised by the Indian Independence League. Singapore Branch to celebrate the entry of Indian National Army into India and the Bhagat Singh Day in which Lt. Col. Alagappan and Lt. Col. G.R. Nagar were speakers and resolutions were passed.

At a meeting for the celebration of Azad Hind Government Day in Burma Major I.S. Misra of the Indian National Army was personally garlanded by Subhas Chandra Bose and was awarded the Sardar-E-Jung for his meritorious services in the Akyab Sector, Subhas Chandra Bose the Head of the Government of Azad Hind issued citations and awards to 15 members of the Indian National Army including Major I.S. Misra for the act of gallantry during the Arakan operation in February 1944.

A ceremony was held on 30th March 1944 at Waterloo Street playing ground on the occasion of Passing out Parade of the first batch of volunteers of the Rani of Jhansi Regiment in which Lt. Col. Bhonsle, Chief of Staff of the Indian National Army and Capt. Lakshmi, Minister and Commandant of Rani of Jhansi Regiment, Syonan (Singapore) spoke. Most of the members who were willing to go to Burma were sent there.

The following Lt. Colonels were promoted to the rank of Colonels:—

1. A.C. Chatterjee, Administrative General of Free India from 28th March 1944.
2. J.K. Bhonsle, Chief of Staff, Indian National Army from 28th March, 1944.
3. A.D. Loganathan, High Commissioner of Andaman & Nicobar from 31st March 1944.
4. M.Z. Kiyani, 1st Division Indian National Army Commander from 1st April 1944.

In Indian National Army the Muslims units refused to sing the *Bande Mataram* and were singing Iqbal's Poem *"Sare Jahan se Achcha Hindustan Hamara"* (Our India is far better than the rest of the world) which was generally not taken up by the Hindus as it was a composition of a Muslim poet, although Iqbal's song was the only one sung by the Indian National Army during Mohan Singh's regime.

The translation of Tagore's poem and also the songs of Jai Hind and "On to Delhi" were composed by Syed Mumtaz Hussain on the instructions of Col. Chatterjee. The songs are in Hindustani and besides these many songs in Tamil and Hindustani languages were composed by different people which I have lost.

On April 1944 Provisional Azad Hind Government opened the Azad Hind Government Bank in Burma.

Although the arrival of Subhas Chandra Bose put fresh enthusiasm in the hearts of the members of Indian Independence League yet most of the educated classes still had doubts about the Japanese intentions and deplored the Japanese behaviour towards the Indian labourers and employers.

The news of the Indian National Army's entry into Indian territory shook the determination of most of them and fearful at losing the chance of becoming great men they joined the movement. Enlistment in the Indian National Army and other Schools and organisations of the Indian Independence League started again. On the other hand the poorer class of people were dying of hunger and the wages paid were not sufficient to support them owing to high prices prevailing of food stuffs and the difficulty of procuring food and also the ill-treatment of their Japanese employers had forced them into the arms of the Indian National Army.

Mr. N. Raghavan had expressed his willingness to Subhas Chandra Bose in his first interview to rejoin the movement. Subhas Chandra Bose wanted him to go to Burma but he was not willing to do on the pretext that he was ill.

After learning of the favourable turn in the fighting in Burma was taking and of the successes of the Indian National Army and the Japanese entry into India he expressed his willingness to go to Burma and work there. Subhas Chandra Bose sent for him and N. Raghavan took along with him, some of his followers to Burma.

N. Raghavan was then made Minister in the Azad Hind Government and was later given the Portfolio of Finance.

In compliance with the appeal made by Subhas Chandra Bose on 29th March 1944, National Liberation Week was celebrated in remembrance of Jallianwalla Bagh, Amritsar incident of 1919 in Singapore from the 7th to 13th April 1944. The programme for the celebration is attached.

Special prayers for the success of the Indian National Army and Liberation of India were offered in Temples and Rama Krishna Mission on 7th April.

On 8th a public meeting of Indian women was held in the Indian Independence League, Singapore Branch and Mrs. M.K. Chidambaram. Members in charge of the women section of the Indian Independence League made the presentation of $ 6500 collected by the women section of the Indian Independence League, Singapore Branch for the Rani of Jhansi Regiment.

On 9th April Indian National School Children held a Mass Rally which was attended by Lt. Col. S.C. Alagappan, Minister of State and Secretary General, Rear Headquarters, Brahmachari Kailasam, Principal of the Indian National School and Mr. S. Raja Ram representing the Indian Independence League Rear Headquarters and several others. Lt. Col. Alagappan gave a short speech.

A mass meeting was held under the chairmanship of J.A. Thivy the General Secretary of the Rear Headquarters in place of Lt. Col. Alagappan (who had left for Burma) at the Waterloo Street Playing Ground on 13 April 1944. The Chariman addressed the meeting and Major A.S. Dara of Indian National Army also spoke. It was also announced by Mr. M.V. Pillay acting Chairman of the Indian National League, Singapore Branch that seven hundred and fifty dollars were donated by the Indians during the week.

Sikhs of Singapore also had a prayer meeting at Queen Street Sikh Temple, Singapore in observance of "Jallianwallah Day" on the13 April 1944 in which Sohan Singh sports dealer the General Secretary of the Indian Independence League, Singapore Branch exhorted them to follow the example set by Udham Singh who assassinated Michael O' Dwyer who was responsible for the incident and slaughter of Indian people at Amritsar.

Penang Indians under the auspices of the Indian Independence League, Penang Branch held a route march headed by Dr. R.K. Menon the Chairman of the Indian Independence League, Penang in commemoration of the Indian Liberation Week on 9th April 1944. At the close of the march Dr. N.K. Menon urged the gathering to exert greater efforts for their fight for freedom.

On an appeal made by Subhas Chandra Bose a Youth Corps of Indians was formed in order to be instructed in political matters and to imbibe the love of their country. A children's group under the name of "Balak Sena"(Youth Corps) was formed in Singapore and their Headquarters were in the Indian National School No. 9 Morris Road, Singapore. Similar parties of children, girls and boys, were formed in Johore and other parties. A weekly organ was also started under the name of "Balak-E-Hind".

On 21st April 1944 Azad Hind Day was celebrated in Singapore by a free Cinema show at Dai Tea Gekijo (Cathey Cinema) and lectures by M. Siva Ram, Director of Indo Shimbum Sha (Newspaper) and the spokesman of the Provisional Government of Azad Hind and Lt. Col. Kaslival of the Indian National Army.

On 22 April 19444 the Provisional Government of Azad Hind announced the appointment of 5 new Ministers:-

1	A. Yellappa	formerly the advisers to the Provisional
2.	Ishar Singh	Government of Azad Hind and S.B. Basir of Rangoon was appointed advisor.
3.	N. Raghavan	
4.	Lt. Col. G.R. Nagar	
5.	Lt. Col. Habibur Rahaman	

Lt. Col. Alagappan who was Minister without portfolio was appointed as Minister I/C of Supplies in addition to his other duties.

As usual Indians, with other communities took part in the Tenchu Satau (Tenno Heika Birthday) celebrations on 29th April 1944 and the leaders of the communities of Singapore renewed their pledge of loyalty to the Japanese Government. T.A.M. Abdul Aziz representing the Indians.

On 10th May, 1944 "First War of Independence Day" was celeberated by the Indians under the auspices of Indian Independence League in Singapore. By this was meant the Indian Mutiny of 1857 on which occasion Mr. J. Thivy and Lt. Col. Nagar spoke.

On 21st May "Azad Hind Day" and the victories on the Indo-Burma Front were celebrated by holding mass meetings and small group meetings at Indian Independence League, Singapore Branch Waterloo Street, Ramakrishna Mission, Indian Chamber of Commerce and 976 Geylang Road in which (1) Mr. M.V. Pillai, J.Thivy, (2) Brahma Chari Kailasam, (3) G. Maganlal, (4) M.K. Chidambaram spoke respectively and resolutions were passed.

The Civilian Police Training Centre was opened on 3rd June 1944 in Singapore by the Indian Independence League Rear Headquarters under its Reconstruction Department known as "Azad Hind Dal" and this centre formed are of sub-branches of Reconstruction Department. The object was to train policemen for the liberated areas of India.

On 13 June 1944 "Udham Singh Day" in commemoration of the fourth anniversary of the execution by the British of Udham Singh for assassinating Sir Michael O'Dwyer at a meeting of the East India Association in Caxtion Hall, London was celebrated as by the Indians under the auspices of the Indian independence League, Singapore Branch. A meeting was arranged at "Dai Toa Gekijyo" (Cathay Cinema Hall) in which J. Thivy, Lt. Malik of Indian National Army, M.M. Pavalliar and A.M. Nair spoke.

As usual Azad Hind Day was celebrated on 21st June 1944 in which Lt. Col. Gilani of the Indian National Army and Dr. R.T. Nathan spoke at a meeting held in the Indian Independence League, Singapore Branch, Waterloo Street.

Under the instructions of the Provisional Government of Azad Hind issued on 27th June 1944 Netaji Week was celebrated from July 4th to 10th by the Indians in East Asia by displaying Indian Tricolour Flags on houses and holding flag hoisting ceremonies and processions and public meetings under the auspices of the Indian Independence League branches in order to commemorate the taking over of the Leadership by Subhas Chandra Bose in June 1943 as the President of the Indian Independence League of East Asia and Supreme Commander of the Azad Hind Fauz (Indian National Army).

On July 4th a mass rally of Indians after a march in procession from Bidadari was held in the Padang opposite Municipal Building under the Chairmanship of J.A. Thivy. Messers. J.A. Thivy, M.K. Chindambaram and Lt. Malik of Indian National Army spoke.

On 9th July Open Air Cinema shows depicting the events connected with the Independence Movement since the arrival of Subhas Chandra Bose and the formation of the Indian National Army into India were shown in front of the Indian Independence League office, Singapore Branch. A meeting of women was also held in the preeincts of the Indian Independence League, Singapore Branch, on 8th July in which Mrs. Davies, Mrs. Subramaniam Ayer, and Lakshmi Devi Raida of the Rani of Jhansi Regiment expressed their gratitude to Subhas Chandra Bose for having allowed them to form the Jhansi Regiment for the emancipation of their motherland.

A training camp for civil administrations and labour agencies was inaugurated at Bidadari Camp by the Reconstruction Section of the Azad Hind Government by Mr. Thivy., Lt. Col. Gilani, Secretary of Reconstruction Department spoke briefly of the work to be done by the organisation. The trainees were to be sent to the liberated areas to run the affairs of the Provisional Government.

On 21st July "Azad Hind Day" was celebrated as usual by hoisting flags on the Indian Houses and holding a meeting at the Indian

Independence League, Singapore Branch. The meeting was addressed by J.A. Thivy, Daljit Singh of Manila and G. Sarangapani.

Towards the end of July 1944 the Provisional Government of Azad Hind created a new department known as "Man Power" with A.N. Sircar the former legal adviser as its head (Minister of Man Power).

Karim Ghani of Burma was appointed Minister of State. N. Raghavan who was Minister of State took over the portfolio of finance from Col. A.C. Chatterjee and in addition to his duties as Minister of Finance he was placed on special duty to undertake the task of National Planning for a Free India. Col. Chatterjee continued holding the rank of Minister without portfolio.

Mrs. M.K. Chidambaram was appointed as Deputy Minister of the women's organisation.

Besides helping the Jhansi Regiment and the Training of Nurses the women section of the Indian Independence League, Singapore Branch used to treat now and then sick soldiers of the Indian National Army Camp Bidadari, Singapore to parties. Later in August 1944 it organised charity concerts to collect funds for the comfort of the front line soldiers and for the Health and Social Welfare section of the Local League Branch. A Committee of the following women was formed and authorised to collect money. Dr. Narula (Convenor), Mrs. Davies, Mrs. Jamnadas, Mrs. P.C. Nair, Mrs. Doshi, Mrs. Chatterjee, Mrs. Issac, Mrs. Subramanian Iyer, Miss. S.N. Saraswathi.

Indian Independence League, Singapore Branch, also arranged Boxing matches in aid of charity the proceeds being given to Health and Social Welfare work among Indians.

On 21/8/44 Azad Hind Day was celebrated as usual, Mr. Thivy and 2 others spoke at the meeting.

In or about 8th September 1944 Mr. M.K. Chidambaram was appointed acting Chairman of the Singapore Indian Independence League Branch in place of M.V. Pillay who resigned. Mr. M.V. Pillay continued to serve as a Chairman of the (Singapore) Syonan Indo-Jin Kosei Kyokai Singapore Welfare Association.

On 21st September " Martyrs Day" was observed by the Indians on the instructions of the Indian Independence League. The Indian Tricolour Flag draped in black was flown at half mast side by side with Himomaru (Japanese Flag).

A public meeting was held at Dai Toa Gekijyo (Cathay Cinema) the same evening. Lt. Col. G.Q. Gilani, the acting General Secretary of the Rear

Headquarters, Indian Independence League, presided at the meeting. Lt. Col. Gilani, M.K. Chidambaram, acting Chairman of the Independence League, Singapore Branch and Lt. Col. Hassan of Indian National Army spoke. This celeberation was observed in memory of 5 Indians who were employed for fifth column work and had gone to India where they were executed.

On 2nd October 1944 "Gandhi's Birthday" was celebrated by hoisting Indian Tricolour Flags and Himomaru on most of the shops and houses of the Indians and free food was distributed at some places. A meeting was held under the auspices of the Indian Independence League, Singapore Branch the same evening at Waterloo Street playing ground under the Chairmanship of M.K. Chidambaram.

Mr. Chidambaram and Lt. Col. Alagappan spoke on the life of Mahatma Gandhi.

Azad Hind Government anniversary week was celebrated from the 18th to 24th October 1944 throughout East Asia by the Indian Independence League Branches.

In Singapore on 18th October the Army Day in memory of those who sacrificed their lives for the cause of India's Freedom was celebrated.

Flags were hoisted at the Indian Independence League Rear Headquarters and Singapore Branch. In the afternoon a meeting was called at the Indian Independence League, Singapore Branch premises, Waterloo Street where the pictures of Messrs. Agail Singh and T.P. Kumaran Nair, which were available out of the five who had gone to India as advance agents and were executed in India, were unveiled by Col. J.K. Bhonsle.

Col. Bhonsle, J.A. Thivy, Lt. Col. S.C. Alagappan and Mrs. Sinha spoke on that occasion.

Indian National Army Hospital and Training Camp were visited, speeches to the Indian National Army and lectures were given exhorting them to place their services at the disposal of their country. 21st October was celebrated as Anniversary of formation of the Provisional Government of Azad Hind by holding a military parade at Bidadari Camp and Mass meeting at Cathay Cinema under the Chairmanship of Lt. Col. G.Q. Gilani who spoke and was followed by Mr. Chidambaram.

Lectures were given to the students of the "Azad Hind Dal" (Free India Reconstruction School) by Lt. Col. Gilani and J.A. Thivy on 22/10/44.

On 24th October a State Luncheon Party was given by J.A. Thivy Vice-President of the Indian Independence League Rear Headquarters as a round off to the anniversary celebrations of the Azad Hind Government in which representatives of the Nippon Army and Navy, prominent officials of the Indian Independence League and Indian National Army and other well known Indians were invited.

On 26th October 1944 passing out ceremony of Second Batch of Jhansi Volonteers which was scheduled for 23rd was held at Waterloo Street playing field. A batch of about 180 graduated, Mrs. Thavar and Col. Bhonsle spoke on the occasion.

The creation of a War Council Cabinet proposed by Subhas Chandra Bose to consider all problems concerning the war, its future development and speeding up of war efforts was approved by the Minister and advisers of the Azad Hind Government on 19th October 1944. The following Military and Civil personnel were appointed:

Col. J.K. Bhonsle, Chief of staff, Col. M.Z. Kiani, Col. Aziz Ahmed, Divisional Commander, Lt. Col. Ihsan Kadir, the Minister of Man Power, N. Raghavan Finance Minster, S.A. Ayer, Propaganda Minister, Parmanand, Deputy Minister of Supplies, Col. A.C. Chatterjee, Governor of liberated area, Lt. Col. Galzara Singh, Regimental Commander, A. Yellappa. Transport Officer and Lt. Col. Habib Rahman.

At the end of October 1944 a new Ministry known as Revenue Ministry was formed in order to exercise general supervision over the Income and to exploit all possibilities of increasing the income of the Azad Hind Government in close cooperation with the Finance Ministry. A.N. Sircar took over the Revenue portfolio.

Early in November 1944 Subhas Chandra Bose alongwith Lt. Col. Chatterjee, Col M.Z. Kiani, Lt. Col. Habibur Rahman went to Japan to attend the first anniversary of the Joint Declaration adopted at the Greater East Asia Assembly at Tokyo which had taken place on November 6th 1943.

In order to celebrate Joint Declaration Day a meeting of the Indians was arranged at the premises of the Indian Independence League, Singapore Branch on 6th November under the Chairmanship of J.A. Thivy., M.K. Chidambaram, Dr. H.H. Moonshi and Brahma Chari Kailasam were the speakers.

Mrs. Krishna Gouri Jamnadas who had been taking an active interest in the women section of the Indian Independence League, Singapore Branch was elected by the committee as its member in charge in place of Mrs. M.K. Chidambaram who went to Burma for special duty.

Indian Independence League, Local Branch had appointed Committee for Local Affairs in the Seven Police Divisions of the island under seven divisional chiefs with ward representatives on line similar to the Japanese

Auxilary Police Organisation. These appointments of committees were made in the middle of August 1944 with S.G. Sarangapani (Chief of publicity) as the head for the purpose of giving publicity to news among the Indians in their respective areas and to help obtain recruits for Indian National Army and to assist the league in any other matter concerning Indians.

This committee held its first meeting on the 5th of November 1944 at the local League premises under the Chairmanship of J.A. Thivy and unanimously decided that it was essential in the battle for Liberation of India that propaganda relating to the work and activities of the Indian Independence movement must be carried out.

The usual monthly meeting for celebrations of Azad Hind Day was held under the auspices of the local Indian Independence League at its premises on 21st November under the Chairmanship of Lt. Col. Gilani, R.S. Naidu, and G. Maganlal were the speakers.

J.A. Thivy General Secretary of the Rear Headquarters of Independence League was transferred to Burma and Dr. Lakshimayah who had gone to and returned from Burma advance headquarters in the middle of May 1944 took over the General Secretaryship of the Rear Headquarters from him.

Indian National School, Singapore entertained Mr. & Mrs. Thivy at a farewell Tea Party at Ramakrishna Mission Hall on 27th November, Brahmachari Kailasam, Principal of the Indian National School praised Thivy for his untiring service in the Movement and help and interest in the working of the Indian National School and the "Balak Sena Corps".

Indian Independence League, Singapore Branch also gave a farewell party to Thivy and welcomed Lakshimayah at the Nanno Hotel on 1st December 1944. Dr. Chidambaram who presided at the functions lauded the services of Mr. Thivy and extended a cordial welcome to Dr. Lakshimayah.

On 5/12/44 the Christening ceremony of the 14 aeroplanes ten of which were given by Subhas Chandra Bose and 4 by the Chinese, Malays and Eurasian Committees to the Japanese Air Force, was held at Kallang Airport.

Mr. M.K. Lakshimayah, Secretary-General of Indian Independence League Rear Headquarters represented the Indian Independence League, Azad Hind Fauj (Indian National Army) being represented by Lt. Col. J.K. Bhonsle, Chief of Staff Col. Loganathan, Lt. Col Alagappan.

The third anniversary of the Dai Toa Senso (Greater East Asia War) was celebrated by Indians of Singapore at a meeting at Theatre Royal Hall on 10th

December under the Chairmanship of M. V. Pillai. After M. V. Pillai's Presidential address M.M. Pavallar, Bashista Raj and M.K. Chidambaram spoke.

Subhas Chandra Bose visited Singapore on his return from Japan where he had gone to attend the first anniversary of the Joint Declaration adopted at the Greater East Asia Assembly. A meeting was arranged by the Indian Independence League, Local Branch at the Waterloo Street, playing ground on 17th December, Subhas Chandra Bose gave a speech in which he expresed the firm determination of the Indian National Army to fight to the end and said that people should not lose heart and slacken their enthusiasm for the failure to capture Imphal, which he said was due mainly to the setting in of Rainy Season. He threatened those who were carrying on anti-League propaganda by spreading false rumours. Large contributions were made to him.

Another mass meeting was organised on 24th December in which he, amongst other things expressed the certainlty of the Axis victory in the War.

Subhas Chandra Bose on his way to Burma toured Malaya and at different places delivered lectures and collected money for the League.

On 27th March 1945 Martyr's Day was observed and a meeting was arranged by the Indian Independence League, Singapore Branch on the same evening in which M.Raghavan the Finance Minister of the Provisional Government of Azad Hind delivered a speech.

"National Liberation Week" was observed by Indians in Singapore by hoisting Tricolour Flags and Hinomaru, by a drive for recruiting and collection of funds by the Local Branch League, by a meeting of the Indian women on 8th March, by a rally of children at which Raja Ram and Sarangapany spoke and comfort visits to the Japanese wounded soldiers hospital and by special treats to the inmates of the Indian Distress Relief Camp and Rama Krishna Orphanage, and by a meeting on 13th April at the Branch premises, Waterloo Street. Dr. M.K. Lakshimayah, Secretary General of the Rear Headquarters of the Indian Independence League addressed the gathering. As usual Azad Hind Day was celebrated on 21st April, 1945 by holding a meeting in the premises of the Indian independence League, Singapore Branch. Col. S.C. Alagappan addressed the gathering on the significance of the day.

On 10th May, 1945 "First War of Indian Independence" was Commemorated by the Indian Independence League, Singapore in which speeches were made in remembrance of the mutiny of 1857.

By this time the British offensive in Burma was progressing favourable and the Japanese Army was retreating from their advance positions. Subhas Chandra Bose left Rangoon for Bangkok and formed his headquarters there. He then came down to Singapore on 18th June 1945 and kept himself busy broadcasting to Indians in India and to the Congress Leaders to reject Lord Wavell's offer.

Furthermore, collections were made and meetings and lectures were delivered and sports and show were held in order to keep up the morale of the populace who had also heard of the fall of Germany and of defeat and retreats of Japan in other places.

On 30th July 1945 a united mass meeting of communities sponsored by the Indian Welfare Association at Dai Toa Gekijyo (Cathey Cinema) under the Chairmanship of M.V. Pillai was held to pledge wholehearted cooperation of the various sections of the local populace to the Japanese Military administration and the Japanese Forces in the defence measures against any attack.

"Netaji Week" was celebrated. During this week mass meetings were held, sports and parties and dramatic shows were given. Collections were made. On 8th of July 1945 Subhas Chandra Bose laid the foundation stone for a Memorial to Heroes who had lost their lives in the Battle of Freedom at the water front at Connaught Drive; Subhas Chandra Bose addressed the gathering comprising Azad Hind Fauj (Indian National Army) Volunteers of the Jhansi Regiment, the Balak Sena Unit, high ranking Japanese Officers, high officials of the Azad Hind Government, Community Leaders and leading members of the Indian public. Wreaths were placed.

The opening ceremony of this memorial took place in the end of August 1945. Major General M. Z. Kiani who was the highest officer of the Indian National Army present in Singapore organised a rally for the opening ceremony. Indian public and officers and personnel of the Indian National Army attended the parade.

This memorial was blown up on September 1945 on the re-occupation of Singapore[2].

Many changes in the Ministry and ranks of the Indian National Army had taken place by this time. Col. A.C. Chatterjee later Foreign Minister along with S.A. Ayer the Propaganda Minister had gone to Saigon to raise funds and also to obtain the cooperation of Indians there.

The Japanese seeing the imminent danger of war coming to Malaya specially Singapore pressed the evacuation of the necessary part of the population to camps up country.

The Japanese and Indian National Army retreated from Burma and by the end of July 1945 Subhas Chandra Bose went to Bangkok. He, soon after peace was declared and the cease fire given left by plane with Col. Habibur Rehman for Tokyo after issuing an order of the day praising the Indian National Army for its brave fight against great odds and said that their fight was not over yet.

It is reported that the plane in which Subhas Chandra Bose was flying met with an accident and Subhas Chandra Bose succumbed to the injuries suffered and Habibur Rehman, although injured, survived.

There are two different views held by the Indian Public in Singapore regarding the death of Subhas Chandra Bose. One view is that the news of his death is genuine and that he was deliberately killed by the Japanese. The other view is that Subhas Chandra Bose is still alive and is probably hiding in Russia and awaiting for an opportune movement to start the Independence Movement again.

The desertion of Subhas Chandra Bose is criticised by some Indians who are of the opinion that he should have faced the situation and shared with his troops the trials consequent upon the re-occupation of Malaya by the British.

I attach printed copies of the Indian Independence Movement in East Asia and also speeches and writings of Subhas Chandra Bose from the time of appearance composed and edited by Narayan Menon in Bangkok named "On to Delhi" and also a copy of discourses on cultural and national subjects published by Indian Independence League Headquarters, Singapore.[2]

These documents which I have attached are mostly taken from Mr. B. A. Mallal whom I had asked to collect as I was afraid to do myself being under suspicion of the Japanese.

I was arrested by the Japanese on 22nd April 1944 and released on the 20th August, 1945. I was during this period not in a position to follow the political situation but I have endeavoured to collect the information from my friends and others.

This report has taken some time to prepare as I have been recovering gradually from the effects of my incarceration in prison and I have found it painful to exert my mind continuously. Nor I had any facilities or assistance in its preparation with the result that it has taken longer than I expected.

---

2. Not included

11

Viceroy to the Secretary of State for India Regarding the Revised Policy towards I.N.A.[1]

1 December, 1945

No.13860. Our telegram No.13814, November 30th. Follwing is the tesxt of press communique put out last night and published this mornings:—

Begins. Since there is clearly much misconception regarding the policy that has been adopted towards the officers and men of the Indian Army who joined the so-called I.N.A., It will be useful to summarise the intntions of Governemnt and the various communiques which have appeared. It will be appreciated that fresh evidence come to light almost daily, and it is therefore now possible to give more information than when the communique of 27th August was issued.

Of the 60,000 men of the Indian Army who were taken prisoner, some 40,000 stood firm to their oath of allegiance, resisting throughout the period of their captivity the propaganda to which they were subjected and in some their captivity the propaganda to which they were subjected and in some cases also facing starvation and torture, thus setting and example of soldierly qualitites and steadfastness in endurance worthy of the highest praise. There were, however, 20,000 who joined the I.N.A. who joined the I.N.A. Of these rather more than 5,000 have yet to reach Indian while less than 1,000 are still untraced. Of the 14,000 in India, some 2,500 have been exonerated of having intended at any time to aid the enemy and will rejoin their units in the same way as other prisoners of war.

Of the remaining 11,500 some 6,000 are men who are believed to have joined the I.N.A. because they were persuaded eirhter by enemy propaganda or by threats or torture that it was in their best interest to do so. In dealing with these men, the Government of India took into account the conditions in which the founded themeselves, at a time when it appeared that the enemy's arms were successful on all fronts, and when

1. L/8/0/10/25, India Office Library and Records, London.

they had no access to any news, except enemy propagands. In spite of the serious nature of their offence, which in ordinary circumstances is punishable by death under the laws of all countries, the Government of India decided from the beginning to treat these men with clemency and generosity, and this was announced on August 27th. Throughout the time that they were in arms against the forces of the Allies, their families continued to be in recipt of their family allotmetns as though no change had taken place in their status as ordinary prisoners of war of the Japanese; and thesee allotments are not to be forfeited. They will also be given pay from the date of their recovery from enemy hands and 42 day's leave with pay in order to enable them to settle down in their villages or to find employment. They are being realsed as fast as Court of Enquirey can settle their case.

There remain some 5,500 of these, the examination of some 1,700 is still in an early stage, while 3,800 are believed to have gone over to the enemy with the clear intention of helping the Japanese in an invasion of India, which would, if successful, have led to her subjegation by the Japanese. Many of them were captured with armsin their hands against their fellow contrymen, whose lives they were endeavouring to take. Nevertheless it is believed that although they were fuly aware of wath they were doing, a large number(though by no means all) were genuinely misled and had no realisation of the bloodshed and misery that would have resxulted to theri fellow countrymen from a Japanese conquest of India. The Government of Inda therefore decided from the begining to extend clemency to the grat majority of theis category also. Such men will be dismissed from the army and will forefeit their pay, but their families will keep the allotments paid in full while they where supposed to be prisoners of war and no further caction will be taken against them.

There is evidence, however, that of these men a small number have committed acts of gross brutality, resulting in some cases in death, upon their fellow countrymen who wre prosoners of war or members of the I.N.A. Crimes of this nature are abhorrent to all civilised peoples, and it would be worng for the government to refrain from bringing to trial men against whom therre is prima facie evidence that they have committed such offences. Trial by court-material of such persons, and of no others, will therefore take place, and Government are confident theat public opinion will support them in this decision.

In reviewing any sentences which may be passed by Courts-Martial, whether in the present or any future trial, the competent authorities will have regards to the extent to which the acts proved offend against the canons of civilised behaviour.

In order to relieve the anxiety of the men and their relatives and friends, decisions not to bring to trial will be intimated as soon as they are reached and the men concerned will be given facilities to communicate with their relations.

The name of persons whom it is intended to bring to trial will be published as soon as the decisions are reached.

The Government of India wish to take this opportunity of pointing out that they have refrained from publishing in advance the allegations made against the accused because such allegations migh have prejudiced the accused in their defence. All possible steps have neen and will continued to be taken to afford every facility to the defence and to ensure a fair trial. They would also point out.that in no case is the finding of a court of justice a foregone conclusion. They would therefore urge persons of all shades of 0opinion to refrain from forming concllusion until the facts of each case have been brouught in evidence in the course of the trial, and until the court has reached its findings.

Until all investigations are complete, it is not possible to state the number who will be brought to trial but the total is unlikely to be as many as fifty and may be as few as twenty: and, as explained above, trials will be limted to those against whom brutality is alleged.

12

Commander-in-Chief Remission of Life Sentences Awarded to I.N.A. officers at Red Fort Trial[1]

1 January, 1946

Captain Shah Nawaz Khan, Captain Sahgal and Lieut. Dhillon have stood their trial by Court-Martial on charges against all three of waging war against the King Emperor; Lt. Dhillon being also charged with murder and the other two with abetment of murder. The findings of the court are that all three are guilty of the charge of waging war, while Captain Shah Nawaz Khan is also convicted of the charge of abetment of murder. Lt. Dhillon is acquitted of the charge of murder and Captain Sahgal of the charge of abetment of murder.

Having found the accused guilty of the charge of waging war, the court was bound to sentence the accused either to death or to transportation for life. No lesser sentence was permissible under the law. The sentence of the court on all three accused is transportation for life, cashiering and forfeiture of arrears of pay and allowances.

No finding or sentence by Court-Martial is complete until confirmed. The confirming officer in this case, the Commander-in-Chief, is satisfied that the findings of the court are in each instance in conformity with the evidence and he has, therefore, confirmed them.

The confirming officer is, however, competent to mitigate, commute or remit the sentences. As already stated in the press, it is the policy of the Government of India to bring to trial in future only such persons as are alleged, in addition to waging war against the state, to have committed acts of gross brutality, and it has been announced that in reviewing sentences in any trials, the competent authority will have regard to the extent to which the acts proved offend against the canons of civilised behaviour.

Lieut. Dhillon and Captain Sahgal have been acquitted of the charges of murder and abetment of murder and it has not been alleged that they

1. *Tribune*, 3 January, 1946.

were guilty of other acts of brutality. Although Captain Shah Nawaz Khan has neen found guilty of abetment of murder and the acts proved against him were harsh, the prevailing circumstances have been taken into account by the confirming officer.

The Commander-in-Chief has decided, therefore, to treat all three accused in the same way in the matter of sentence and to remit the sentences of transportation for life against all three accused. He has, however, confirmed the sentences of cashiering and forfeiture of arrears of pay and allowances since it is in all circumstances a most serious crime for an officer or solider to throw off his allegiance and wage war against the state. This is a principle which it is essential to uphold in the interests of the stability of any Government by law established, present or future.

12

I.N.A. Defence By Bhulabhai Desai[1]

1 December, 1946

During the last many days, you have heard evidence on the two charges with which my clients, the accused before you, have been arraigned. Shortly stated, the two charges are waging war against the King and, without detailing anything, murder and abetment of murder, in that certain deserters were tried and ordered to be shot. My submission to the Court is that substantially there is really one charge before the Court, because in so far as the charge of murder is concerned it is a part of the first charge; and I say so for this reason that it would be quite possible in the case of a charge of waging war against the King, to be able to charge every single act of firing a shot, which would be, I think, *reducio ad absurdem;* and therefore it will be my duty later on to point out to the Court that really and truly there is only one charge before the Court and that is waging war against the King. Evidence has been admitted on other matters to which I do not wish at this stage to refer, so that for the moment, I will occupy the time of the Court for the purpose of considering what facts have been established in support of the first charge, namely, waging war against the King; and in due course it will also be my duty to point out to the Court that in so far as the second charge is concerned, there is no foundation fact for it except to this extent that in reference to the four persons who are alleged to have been shot there is on record evidence that they were tried and sentence passed. In reference to Mohammed Hussian, there is nothing on record to show that any sentence was passed. In all these cases it will be my duty to submit that on the evidnece the Court is bound to come to the conclusion that though sentence was passed in one case and not at all passed in

1. I. N. A. Trial Papers. See also Bhulabhai J. Desai, *I. N. A. Defence* (Delhi 1946) This booklet containing the address by Desai was published separately also.

the other, none of these sentences was actually carried out. That is the nature of the examination on facts which will be necessary for me to place before this Honourable Court.

There are one or two matters which I am bound to mention to the Court before I come to the actual facts of the case. This case raises issues which are not of the normal type which a Court Martial is called upon to decide, because most, if not all, of such cases are generally cases of individual dereliction of duty or individual offences. Here is a case in which, I venture to say—and the evidence supports it—that it is not at all a case of what you might call three individuals waging war against the King. The evidence amply bears out the fact that these men charged before you were a part of an organised army which waged war against the King even according to the prosecution. Therefore the case before the Court is not a personal case of any kind or sort. The honour and the law of the Indian National Army are on trial before this Court. What is now on trial before the Court is the right to wage war with immunity on the part of a subject race for their liberation. I shall be able to cite authorities on International Law that a nation or part of a nation does reach a stage where it is entitled to wage war for tits liberation, and I shall be able to prove that point to your Honours' satisfaction.

There is another thing I wish to say, and I say it with a certain degree of earnestness. This case has naturally aroused a considerable amount of public interest. It is not for me to say whether it is right or not but the fact remains that it is so, and opinions have been expressed from the point of view of the public and from the point of view of what I might call 'official sources' beginning with the Viceroy of India. You, Sir, having sworn to do justice to these men on the evidence before you will, I have not the smallest doubt, come to your own decision guided by your conscience and entirely unaffected by oipinions for or against them. For in all trials of this kind—and in a few of them I have had the honour to be engaged—it is very difficult for the human mind to maintain that detachment which justice requires. In the case of Juries I have had to caution them against the use or abuse of the effect of public expressions of opinions on matters which it is for them to decide. In this case what I wish to say is this. Having studied the rules which guide the proceedings before this Court I find that you, Sirs, are the judges both of law and of fact. I am aware that the Judge-Advocate who is your adviser, will take care to do justice to everything that myself or my learned friend on the other side will place before you on questions of law and fact, and while you will very seriously regard his advice in the end, the final decision is your privilege and your responsibility. Therefore what I might have done in another place I do not do before you and that is, I cannot say that I will address the Judge on law and the Jury on the facts. There it is an easier process because I must confess that before a trained Judge it is easier to deal with the question of law than before a tribunal of this character. At the same time I have this consolation that sometimes of the law is plain—as I submit it is in this case, it will probably be much easier, appealing to commonsense, to establish the law on which I rely, and I desire to ask your indulgence and your attention in the somewhat difficult task which I am undertaking.

My next submission to the Court is that I desire, as far as possible, to state categorically the conclusions of fact which are established in this case. Having done that I will proceed to deal with the law applicable to them. In dealing with any single item, should any doubt arise in the Court's mind, I trust that you will be pleased to tell me, so that, if it is necessary, I will go into the details of evidence, because as at present advised, I do not desire, unless there is a real doubt about it, to weary you with reading over 250 pages of evidence and about 150 pages of exhibits, which are before the Court. A few important ones I will certainly read where necessary. Having regard to the attention which the Court has paid to the evidence as it was recorded, I will avoid reading them in extenso.

With these remarks I now proceed to place before the Court what I submit are the conclusions of fact justified by evidence. Before I do that, I will give you a few important events. In the month of December 1941, war was declared by Japan against Britain and America. Then followed certain events which are the subject-matter of controversy to a certain extent before this Court. The next event of importance is the surrender of the British Indian forces at Singapore, which took place on the 15th February, and then the most important material event took place on the 17th February at Farrar Park.

The next event of importance, after that which the Court will have to bear in mind, is the formation of what I shall shortly describe as the first Indian National Army in the month of September 1942. The next event of importance is the dissolution of that Army in the month of December 1942 and the arrest of Capt. Mohan Singh. The next important events thereafter are the efforts which were being made for the formation of the second Indian National Army. On 2nd July 1943, Sri Subhas Chandra Bose arrived in Singapore. He later took command of the Indian National Army and there was a conference of what is called Greater East Asia, attended by Indians, with delegates belonging to the Indian Independence League from different parts of the Far Eastern countries. One of the resolutions at that Conference was that a Provisional Government of Free India should be established. The next event of importance is that on the 21st October 1943 there was proclaimed a provisional Government of Free India which for brevity I will call "Provisional Government". That Proclamation is one to which I shall refer later, but now I will try to give the Court events of importance which the Court will have to bear in mind. On the Proclamation of that Government the different Ministers concerned with the functions of the State took Oath of Allegiance, of course headed by Nataji Subhas Chandra Bose as the Head of the State. The next event of importance is the Declaration of War by that Government on Britain and America. The next event of importance thereafter is that so far as the I.N.A. was concerned, it began to carry out its functions under the orders of the new State. Thereafter the events of importance so far as the actual facts are concerned, are only three : the movement of this Government from Singapore to Rangoon; the movement of the Indian National Army from Burma into, beyond and within the territories of India right up to Kohima; and the rest, dealing with the retreat of that Army back again until the event which took place at Rangoon slightly before, at the time, and slightly after the occupation of Burma by the British Forces. These, Sirs, are the main undisputed events with which the Court is concerned. Bearing in mind these events, I shall now place before the Court the conclusions of facts which we submit have been established either in cross-examination of the evidence of the prosecution or in the affirmative evidence which we have called in defence.

The first conclusion of fact which we ask this Court to accept is that the Provisional Government of Free India was formally established and proclaimed. I submit, Sirs, there can be no doubt about this event and no cross-examination of withesses who have been called to prove that event, as far as I can see, has been seriously attempted. You have to remember, Sirs, the picture of the Proclamation of that Governemnt and Exhibits put in on that point. Before I proceed any further, I wish to call attention to that proclamation. It is Exhibit FFFF[2] before this Court. I do not wish to read the whole of that document; the only passages

2. These exhibits were placed before the court. Some of the relevant ones have been produced in these volumes. For the rest, see the Trial Papers at National Archives of India, New Delhi.

which I wish to rèad are passages which bear on the issue before this Court.

Reads the following from the document:

"Forcibly disarmed by the British after 1857 and subjected to terror and brutality, the Indian people lay prostrate for a while—but with the birth of the Indian National Congress in 1885 till the end of the last World War, the Indian people, in their endeavour to recover their lost liberty tried all possible methods—namely, agitation and propaganda, boycott of British goods, terrorism and sabotage—and finally, armed revolution. But all these efforts failed for a time. Ultimately in 1920, when the Indian people haunted by a sense of failure, were groping for new methods, Mahatma Gandhi came forward with the new weapon of non-cooperation and civil-disobedience.

"Thus, on the eve of the present World War, the stage was set for the final struggle for India's liberation. During the course of this war, Germany, with the help of her allies, has dealt shattering blows to our enemy in Europe—while Nippon, with the help of her allies has inflicted a knockout blow to our enemy in East Asia. Favoured by a most happy combination of circumstances, the Indian people today have a wonderful opportunity for achieving their national emancipation.

"For the first time in recent history, Indians abroad have also been politically roused and united in one organization. They are not only thinking and feeling in tune with their countrymen at home, but are also marching in step with them along the path to freedom, In East Asia in particular, over two million Indians are now organized as one solid phalanx, inspired by the slogan of "Total Mobilisation",

I stop here to submit to the Court that evidence have been adduced as to the numbers of Indians in East Asia and the figure mentioned here is more or less what is borne out before this Court.

"Having goaded Indians to desperation by its hypocrisy, and having driven them to starvation and death by plunder and loot, British rule in India has forfeited the good-will of the Indian people altogether, and is now living a precarious existence.

"It will be the task of the Provisional Government to launch and to conduct the struggle that will bring about the expulsion of the British and of her allies from the soil of India. It will then be the task of the Provisional Government to bring about the establishment of a permanent National Government of Azad Hind constituted in accordance with the will of the Indian people and enjoying their confidence. After the British and their allies are overthrown, and until a permanent National

Government of Azad Hind is set up in Indian soil, the Provisional Government will administer the affairs of the country in trust for the Indian people.

"The Provisional Government is entitled to and hereby claims, the allegiance of every Indian. It guarantees religious liberty, as well as equal rights and equal opportunities to all its citizens. It declares its firm resolve to pursue the happiness and prosperity of the whole nation and of all its parts, cherishing all the children of the nation equally and transcending all the differences cunningly fostered by an alien government in the past.

"In the name of God, in the name of bygone generations who have welded the Indian people into one nation, and in the name of the dead heroes who have bequeted a tradition of heroism; and self-sacrifice, we call upon the Indian people to rally a round our banner, and to strike for India's freedom."

Then follows the signature of the members of the Government. The reason why I called attention to this document is the purpose for which the Provisional Government was formed, and the means by which that Provisional Government intended to carry out its purpose. The fact that it failed to achieve its purpose is entirely irrelevant to the issue before this Court.That is the first fact which we say has been established. The second fact which we say has been established is that is was an organised Government. It does not require many words to establish that proposition. Witnesses have spoken before the Court as to the allocation of duties which appear at the end of the document which I have just read to the Court, and it is also in evidence before the Court that the Indian Independence League became the executive of the Provisional Government which organized, so far as it was possible to do in those warlike conditions, the care of the people who owed allegiance to it. In the month of June 1944, as the evidence is quite clear—it is also in the Exhibit—in Malaya alone, 2,30,000 persons actually took written Oaths of Allegiance to the Government. That was in June 1944, and it is in evidence that thereafter the process continued. The object of stating the figures is that is was not a case of a Government of what you may call, or what somebody being my opponent may facetiously call, a set of rebels, a desultory sort of crowd of no consequence. I wish to give a lie to that kind of suggestion, and that is the reason why I suggest that the provisional Government was an organized Government to whom the whole of the two million odd people owed allegiance, and out of whom 2,30,000 persons actually took the Oath of Allegiance in Malaya.

Then, Sir the next fact which I submit is established before the Court is that this Government was recognized by the Axis powers. I use that expression briefly because it is quite unnecessary either in law or in fact to prove that the recognition must be by a particular number of Government or by a particular class of Government. The recognition is proof and more than proof that it had the right to declare war for the purpose for which it intended to fight, and having the right to declare war in so far as its armies were concerned they became subject to the international laws of war.

On the question of recognition, I wish to call attention to certain cross-examination by my learned friend. Of course in so far as recognition by Germany or Italy was concerned there could be no cross-examination and none was attempted. But with reference to certain East Asia matters in those days, a suggestion was made that those Government were under the control of Japan. I for my part, with very great respect, fail to understand the significance of the suggestion. Supposing Japan had an empire, that is to say succeeded in keeping the territories it conquered without giving them liberty, the recognition would be nonetheless effective because it makes no difference whether and which Government recognised this particular Government of Free India. The point still remains, and I assert that the recognition is but a proof of what I may call a statehood which gives it the capacity of declaring and making war for the liberation of its own countryment. The material point therefore is whether it had attained that degree of statehood which gave it that power. Once you have a State which can and is entitled to declare war, the war itself is its own justification. There is no question that any two independent States have a right to declare war. Any, act done in the prosecution of that war is justified by the mere fact of the war itself. Barring this, it may be asked why trials are going on in parts of Asia and elsewhere, and in Germany. In fact they themselves emphasize the truth of the correctness of the proposition that any act done in due prosecution of war cannot be the subject of any municipal court by way of examination. What has happended is that in addition to the due prosecution of war according to civilised laws, individuals have been guilty of acts outside the pale of civilized warfare, which we popularly call now war crimes. But the very fact that you can only deal with and do deal with war crimes, emphatically and clearly proves that in so far as the normal civilised conduct of war is concerned including the use of an atomic bomb, is outside the pale of examination by way of right or wrong by any municipal tribunal.

Then, Sirs, the next fact which I submit is established is that this State had an army which was properly organised, having its own distinctive badges and emblems, functioning under regularly appointed officers. I am obliged to the prosecution in this matter for I was spared the necessity of having to prove this proposition. They put in document after document to show that the Indian National Army was properly organised. First, that it was regulated by an Indian National Army Act. The only point as far as I could see from the cross-examination which was made was with reference to certain items of corporal punishment. On that it is necessary to point out to the Court that for the moment those who pursue that course forget the course of legislation in British India itself. It is true that Liet. Nag told the Court that apart from the Indian Army Act certain provisions relating to corporal punishment were incorporated in the Indian National Army Act. It was probably forgotten that a little while before, in the Indian Army Act were incorporated provisions in Section 45 of the that Act, headed "Corporal Punishment". I am reading from Section 45 of the Indian Army Act of 1911:

"Where any person subject to this Act, and under the rank of warrant officer—

(a) on active service, is guilty of any offence; or (b) at any time is guilty of the offence specified in clause (c) of Section 31 or (d) at any time is guilty of a civil offence which would be punishable with whipping under the law of British India, and is triable by court-martial under this Act,

it shall be lawful for a court-martial to award for that offence corporal punishment not exceeding thirty lashes."

It is true that about the time of this war this particular provision was omitted. But it is a mistake to think that a similar provision in the Indian Statute Law did not exist. As a matter of fact, in so far as the Defence of India Act and certain Ordinances are concerned, the provision was definitely made, making corporal punishment as part of the punishment applicable to the personnel of the Indian Army. Ordinance 37 of 1943 practically replaced the provisions of the Indian Army Act which were not found in it; a certian amount of effort was made as if under an Act governing a civilised army corporal punishment was not permissible as against the provisions which were to be found in the Indian National Army Act. I am quite certain that it was done under misapprehension.

The Military Operation Areas Special Powers Ordinance, Part II, Sections 22 and 23 read :

"Sec. 22 : Whoever commits an offence punishable under Section 121-A, 122, 125 or 131 of the Indian Penal Code (XLV of 1860) may, in lieu of any punishment to which he is liable under the said code be punished with death.

"Sec. 23: Whoever contravenes any of the provisions of Rule 36 of the Defence of India Rules or is deemed under the provisions of the said Rules to have contravened such provision, may, in lieu of any punishment to which he is liable under the said Ruled, be punished with death, or with whipping, in addition to any punishment to which he is liable under the said Rules. I will be able if necessary to read out all the Rules which clearly show that under the Indian Law, taken as a whole, the punishment with reference to whipping exists, such as the provision which was made in the Indian Army Act. I have got, Sirs, a *summary* made out of the provision with reference to *whipping which I shall afterwards hand over to the Court.* Shorlty stated, my submission to the Court is this that the only attack made by the Advocate-General on the making and framing of the Indian National Army Act, was the provision with reference to whipping, and I submit to the Court that that was done under a misapprehension, got it is as much a part, though not technically quite, in the Indian Army Act but in the defence of India Rules and the Ordinance. It makes no difference. But taking in the aggregate, Indian legislation does sanction corporal punishment throughout the period with which we are concerned and therefore it is that I say and submit to the Court that this was a properly organised army, having a code of its own, which for all practical purposes is the Indian Army Act and any condemnation of the rules under which that army functioned is a condemnation of the Indian Army Act itself, which I submit is not the purpose of the prosecution in this case. Therefore, we come back, Sirs, to this point that this was an organized army functioning under a civilised code. As regards the appointment of officers and the regular method by which it was done, as regards the different branches and the functions, you, Sirs, are more competent than myself to judge from the documents which have been placed before you. They are in the shape of army orders or orders of the day and so on, which have been placed before the Court. On a question of fact we have arrived so far that there was a state which declared war for the purpose of fighting for the liberation of the country and it had an organised army organised under a code which for all practical, substantial purposes, accorded with the aggregate law on the same subject prevailing in British India. I use the word aggregate, because I must bring in the other laws also which provided for and permitted the infliction of corposal punishment in all these cases. The next fact whch is established beyond all dispute was that the object of the declaration of war by the Provisional Government of Free India was the liberation of India.

The next important fact which I think must be mentioned is that the Indian National Army was formed with two purposes. The main purpose was the securing the liberation of India and no doubt, Sirs, from the most important witness that the prosecution called, it has never been difficult to establish that that was the object with which that Army was formed and that was the object with which the individuals who joined it. The other object also was which was somewhat subordinate, but useful purpose, the protection such as could be afforded to the Indian inhabitants of Burma and Malaya, particularly during the days when law and order in those parts of the country was poorly looked after, the lives and the honour and the property of the people was not quite so easily protected. The first object is the one which the army was called upon to fulfil as a part of its duties. Again taking the evidence as a whole, I submit it has been amply proved before this Court that the I.N.A. was formed with the object of fighting for the liberation of India and also with the object of protecting the lives, honour and property of people residing in East Asia at that time.

The next point which is established, I submit, is this—though I speak with less confidence because I do not see it admitted—but the fact has been proved and it is my duty to examine the evidence on it, is that the Japanese Government or the Nippon Government as it is called, ceded to the new Indian State the islands of Nicobar and Andamans, that the Indian State acquired territory in the form of Ziawadi, which was about fifty square miles in area, and that it administered for a period of four to six months the Manipur and Vishnupur areas.

As regards the first, in so far as Lieut. Nag was concerned, he has given definite evidence that the two islands were ceded. The evidence falls under three parts : the first is a declaration to that effect by the Japanese Government, announced by a document which has been proved before this Court. That document is a statement by General Tojo that they were about to concede the islands of Andamans and Nicobar to the Free Indian Government. That document is UUUU. (Counsel reads relevant portions of the document). This was on the 5th November 1943.

Statement by Prime Minsiter General Hideki Tojo regarding the Independence of India

(Delivered before the Assembly of Greater East Asiatic Nations, November 6, 1943)

"Not only India but all Greater East Asia was, without doubt, highly invigorated by the speech just given by His Excellency the Head of the Provisional Government of Azad Hind, in which His Excellency made it clear that the Indian people under the Provisional Government, with the future destiny of India and of Asia at heart, have risen resolutely to realise their long cherished aspiration to regain Indian's freedom, independence and prosperity.

As has been reiterated in the various statements already issued, the Empire of Japan means to give India every possible aid so that she may free herself from the American and British yoke and attain her long-cherished ambition. Now that the foundation of the Provisional Government of Azad Hind has been solidified still further and the Indian patriots under the same Government, bound in close units as never before, are firmly determined to accomplish their steadfast aim, I take this occasion to declare that the Imperial Government of Japan is ready shortly to place the Andaman and Nicobar Islands, Indian territory now under the occupation of the Imperial Japanese Forces, under the jurisdiction of the Provisional Government of Azad Hind, as the initial evidence of her readiness to help in India's struggle for independence.

The lofty ideal that guided Japan's national founding of enabling all peoples to have each its proper status and to enjoy well-being has been and is being steadily carried out. The Japanese Empire today has been strengthened further in its determination to extend all-out co-operation to India in her fight for freedom. Japan is anxious that the Indians on their part shall extend redoubled efforts in that direction.

From the spirited utterances by Their Excellencies the representatives of various countries of East Asia at yesterday's and today's sessions of this Assembly, I note with assurence and satisfaction that these countries, in concert with Japan, are extending every support to the cause of India's independence. I trust and hope that they will give even greater support to- that cause in the future."

Then followed events which clearly, showed that that purpose was carried out. You have in evidence that the declaration was made and that the new Indian state was called upon to administer it by means of a Commissioner, that a commissioner was in fact appointed, that the Commissioner in fact went, and you have evidence of a definite ceremony at which the naval and military authorities then in charge handed over the islands to the Commissioner on behalf of the Indian State at Port Blair. These are points on which, as far as I am able to see the evidence, very little criticism has been made by way of croos-examination.

The point on which there has been a difference between the prosecution and ourselves is the actual form and extent of the administaration of the islands. But it is clearly a misconception to confuse the ceding of a territory and taking over every item of administration of that territory, particularly under the conditions then prevailing. The fact and it is commonsense I submit-that a house might well be sold and completely sold, sold outright and yet possession for time may not be wholly given. It is a familiar illustration I am giving, so that it is easy to appreciate. In the somewhat elaborate cross-examination for this purpose of Col. Loganadan, it was intended merely to point out that the whole of the administration was not taken over-which is not dnied-he said it over and over again; and I think It is established and I ask the Court to hold it is estalbished that he went for the purpose of taking over the administration. It is true that he did not take over more than two items-one, education and the fact that the area was small and the people ignorant is hardly an argument that he had not taken ove the administeration daresax in other countries where the standard of Literacy is something like 99 per cent, ther eare may more shcools than in this unfortunate country whre the standard of literacy is probably 15 per cent. Therefore the argument that schools were few and the expenditure was so little I think there is very little point in the cross examination on this matter. I did enter a protest but it was overruled and it is not for me to say anything more about it. but you do not detract form the cession of a territory in quantity or tie by pointing out that hte whole of the administaration was not and vcould no be taken over. Colonel Logandan told the Court again and again—almost painfully over again—of the fact that until he got complete control of the police in the matter of spies (which seemed to be a sore point with the local inhabitants), he was not prepared to take over any other part of the administration. But there is one significant thing that my learned friend got out of Colonel Loganadan, and that is that one of the officers who went with him, administered what you may call very elementary justice which it was possible to do in the conditions then revailing in the islands. So much so that having asked it and got it, he tried to shake it off but he could not, and it was proved to the hilt that Justice and Education were taken over. True, police was not taken over because the Japanese from the point of view of defence wre keen on retaining control over what you may call the spy population of these islands. But one thing remains and that is the most significant fact, and that is the renaming, of the islands. So that any amount of examination as to why or how month by month or day by day further acts of administration were not made, cannot possibly get rid of three important facts : first, the clear solemn declaration that the islands would be handed shortly. A suggestion was made—it remained at a suggestion only—that they would be handed over after the war. Where my friend got the words "after the war" I do not know. I hope he will point it out and that is why I read out this document. The document clearly shows that they were to be very shortly handed over.

The second fact was that it was to be administered through a Commissioner, which was a definite proposition made at that time. A Commissioner was in fact nominated by the Provisional Government and the Commissioner in fact reached there and began to function. No doubt, as in every case of this kind, I presume this Court will take almost judicial notice of the fact as to how Germany and other countries are being administered today. No doubt the man will be qualified, and he may be the best educated man from amongst his staff, and he may hope that hte local machinery would soon adapt itself for the purpose of continuing the administration, because it is unthinkable that you can transfer quickly and at one stroke the whole administrative machinery from one country to another. Anybody who is familiar with the administration fo this very country, is aware that Britain administers this country through practically the entire machinery of the Indian people themselves. So that the number of men and all the rest of it, I submit, is so much, without any disrespect, hot air. The real point is, were or were not the islands ceded? And I say there is so much evidence that they were.

The last point is the renaming of the islands : Shahid and Swaraj.

I submit that it is clearly established on the evidence before this Court that though by reason of the exigencies of the situation, it may not have been possible to take over the complete administration, in law and in fact the islands were given over to the Indian State, or to what I would call the Provisional Government.

Next I deal with the question of Ziawadi. The position is this, accordance to the evidence on the record : that this was property, about 50 sq. miles in area, with 15,000 inhabitants who were Indians. It had on it a sugar factory and various other means of production, agricultural or otherwise and every branch of administration of that territory was carried out by men appointed by the Indian National Army and belonging to the *Azad Hind Dal.*

My learned friend did not even venture, in the course of cross-examination, to challenge the truth of the statements made before this Court by witness Shiv Singh and Arshad on this head. Shiv Singh said that every branch of administration was taken over. He gave the name of the person who was the officer in charge of every branch of administration, Revenue, Police, P.W.D., Justice, both civil and criminal. Under these circumstances, the legal position is simple. I shall come to it in greater detail afterwards. Japan conquered Burma. By right of conquest it was in a position to dispose as it liked of the whole or any portion of any territory and as the witness told you clearly, by reasons of the agreement between the Provisional Government and the Nippon Government this territory was handed over as a part of the liberated territory to the I.N.A. and the Azad Hind Dal. At this stage let me point out to the Court that the Azad Hind Dal, it has been proved, was an organisation of men trained for the purpose of administering areas as soon as they came under the control or occupation of the I.N.A. or as soon as they were handed over to them. I must also remind the Court that it has been proved beyond question—because as far as I see there was no cross-examination or effective cross-examination any way, that as soon as the I.N.A. crossed the borders of Burma into India a proclamation was issued in two parts, one signed by the Head of the Indian State and the other signed by General Kawabe under the orders of the South Eastern Command. In that it was distinctly stated that any part of the Indian territory which would be acquired by conquest or otherwise by the Japanese Army whould be handed ober to the I.N.A. for the purpose of forming part of the liberated territory and to be administered by them. That is the history of the ceding.

Then we come to Manipur and Vishnupur areas. Evidence has been given before the Court without any reasonable demur to the effect that during the time, the Japanese and the I.N.A. were operating, those portions of India were in fact adminsitered by the I.N.A. through its organisation, the Azad Hind Dal, and the area was 150,000 square miles. The duration, of administration has no bearing on this issue, for indeed it can happen, as it did happen in this war, that territories were as easily acquired as lost. This Court is not concerned with the question of duration. I would ask the Court to hold that the two islands, Andamans and Nicobar, were in fact ceded, that Ziawadi became a part of liberated Indian territory, and that, though for a short period of time, Manipur and Vishnupur areas were exactly in the same position.

The next point to which I wish to refer is the resources of the State. I order to judge the existence of the State the resources of the State is also one of the matters to be considered. It has been proved before the Court that some 30 crores of rupees were in fact donated to the State, out of which was maintained the civil government and the army. Dina Nath, who impressed this Court, gave extremely clear evidence on this head. He was one of the Directors of the Azad Hind Bank and he told the Court that between Burma and Malaya, during that short period of time, the State had resources to the tune of 20 crores of rupees, in addition to the produce of Ziawadi. It is a remarkable thing to notice that on the reoccupation of Burma and Malaya every single document which was in the possession of this Indian State was found intact. It was amazing. See the monthly reports which the Prosecution was able to produce with reference tot he administration of the Andamans and Nicobars! It only emphasizes—and I wish to make a point of this—that there was a complete organization, and that organisation was as good as could reasonably be expected. That alone accounts for half the documents which my learned friend was able to produce.

The point is that we were a little handicapped owing to the lack of certain documents. As the evidence before the Court shows, this Bank was closed after the occupation of Rangon, and in fact it is in evidence that some 35 lakhs worth of property was sequestered. I am not complaining of the sequestration. That I think was the right of the conquerors. What I am saying is that in so far as the resources of the State were concerned, they were full and adequate for the purposes which the new State had then in view.

Here I wish to refer to a bulletin. It is not what I might call technical evidence before the Court by it may be my duty to submit that it is a document of which the Court should take judicial notice. The document is dated the 10th November 1945 and called Stamp Collecting.

Mr. N.P. Engineer : My learned friend is reading from a document which as not been accepted.

Mr. Desai : I am only making a submission to the Court. Is it my friend's contention that if I read a book on law, it should be put in as an exhibit?

Judge-Advocate : The document itself cannot be admitted at this stage.

Mr. Desai : All I am doing now is to make a submission to the Court Section 57 says :

"The Court shall take judicial notice of the following facts:

"In all these cases and also in all matters of published history, literature, science or art the Court may resort for help to appropriate books or documents of reference"

And if the learned Advocate General solemnly suggests that every single book of history, literature, science, and art is to be an exhibit before it can be refered to, I am very sorry that it is a statement which defeats itself.

Judge-Advocate : Mr. Desai, will you read out what you want the Court to take judicial notice of ?

Mr. Desai: May I not apply that the Court may consider it ? And I am asking is that this application be considered. Of course the Court may reject it; I am not suggesting that the Court is bound to accept it. My submission is that under Section 57 it may be taken as judicial notice.

I was referring to an issue of November 10, 1945, of a weekly publication called "Stamp Collecting" Published in London and edited by Douglas Armstrong, a well-known philatelist. In that issue at page 136, column 1, the following appears :

"Imphal Stamp that failed.

"So confident were the Japs that they would occupy Imphal, when they invaded Southern Assam that they actually prepared a special issue of stamps for use there . Needless to say these stamps failed to materialise, but our correspondent, Flying Officer T.A. Broomhead, informs us that he has seen proof impressions in the hands of the man who was responsible for the printing (in Rangoon). Two denominations appear to have been prepared, viz., 3 pice plum and 1 anna red, both in the same design and roughly perforated 11½ x9½ (approx.). The subject of the vignette (illustrated is the old Moghul Fortress at Old Delhi accompanied by the slogan "On to Delhi". Bi-lingual inscription reads "PROVISIONAL GOVERNMENT OF FREE INDIA". When it becameevident that the Imphal stamps would not be required, the dies were destroyed and the bulk supply of sheets printed in readiness was burnt with the exception of a small quantity salvaged by the printer."

At the top corner on the left-hand side is a facsimile of the stamp referred to in the above quotation.

It is submitted that this document should be taken judicial notice of in support *inter alia* of proof that the Provisional Government of Free India had got prepared, issued or were about to issue postal stamps of that character. As appears from the above quotation, the dies were prepared under the direction of the Japanese.

Counsel for the Prosecution: I submit.................

Judge-Advocate : Would it not be more convenient to deal with this point in your arguments, and so shall I. There is no point, when the document is read whether the Court accepts it or not.

Mr. Desai : I frankly submit to the Court that it is not a matter of such importance, but as the document was brought to my notice I thought it was my duty to put it before the Court. Nobody should question books of history, science, literature and art. It is a very accepted magazine in England 'ealing with this subject, edited by a very well-known man indeed.

Then, Sir, it appears from the evidence that this Indian State had a

Civil, and what I may call, an Army Gazette of its own. That is also established before this Court.

On these facts, Sir, the first question of law which I wish to raise is this: Having regard to the condition in which this Free Government of India had been formed and was functioning, it was entitled to make war and it did make war for the purpose of liberating this country. That is the first and the main issue before the Court. This Court is trying civil offences under the Indian Penal Code, and there are two ways of looking at this question. One is that when two States declare a war—and I may assume for the purpose of this argument, because I cannot do more than place evidence before this Court for its acceptance, that the condition in which the new Indian State found itself, it was in a position to declare war—and having declared war, in so far as any acts in the prosecution of that war are concerned, they are outside the pale of municipal law. I will tell you, Sir, what I mean because I will elaborate this sufficiently to make myself understood by the Court. Supposing a German during the prosecution of the war had shot two or three or ten Britishers in England and was found in England, the question is, could he be charged with having committed murder. I submit never, for the simple reason that those acts were done during the due prosecution of the war which, unfortunately, in the present world of infirmities the International Law accepts. That is to say, what International Law accepts is that two independent countries or two States, as they are called, may make war on each other, and those who carry out any action in due prosecution of the war (apart from war criminals) is outside the pale of municipal law. Alternatively, if that is not sufficient for this Court (though I submit it should be in view of what I am going to read to you from accepted authorities on International Law) under Section 79 of the Indian Penal Code the acts done in due prosecution of the war were not offences. Section 79 of the Indian Penal Code reads thus:

"Nothing is an offence which is done by any person who is justified by law.........." And my submission to the Court is that under the term 'law' is covered 'International Law', and for that reason in so far that German—continuing the example which I was giving—who was arrested in England was concerned, his defence would be :

"My country, my State, was at war with your States. Under the orders of my State, and in due prosecution of the war, I did the acts which under ordinary normal circumstances might be offences, but which having regard to the circumstances are no offences at all."

Sir, it is unthinkable that any member of any organized army could be charged with an offence merely because he fought one or ten or a million men belonging to an army of the State with which he is at war. It is perfectly obvious to anybody that during the prosecution of the war, the municipal law relating to that country does not apply, except, I quite agree, when one soldier steals the pocket-book of another soldier. That I appreciate. But the question which we have got to bear in mind is the very important distinction. Was that act done in due prosecution of the war which one State declared upon another.

Once you get to that state, it is perfectly obvious that that municipal law must and is bound to remain in abeyance. It is impossible to arraign any individual for carrying out as a matter of duty acts which might otherwise be offences—killing a man every day, destroying property every day. In fact it is a very part of the war itself. Therefore the agreement is twofold. The alternatives are either that any act done in due prosecution of war is outside the pale of municipal law—that is why I pointed out to you in the commencement that the charge against these young men before you is not as if they had committed an act of private murder by reason of some private quarrel. The documents accepted by the prosecution clearly bear out that whatever they did, they did as part of the prosecution of war. Remember that always, because without that the law cannot be appreciated with reference to the facts in issue.

But there is another way of looking at it, if you must. That is whether the exception provided by Section 79 is not equally applicable to the case. My submission to the Court is that whether you accept the one or the other makes no difference to the decision that I am asking for as to the immunity from those acts being offences at all ; because the very language of Section 79 is : "Nothing is an offence which is justified by law." The Section assumes that in private life it might otherwise have been an offence. If you, gentlemen, in the due prosecution of war committed murders, could be civil laws as propounded by the other side be put into action against you, when in all honour you acted in prosecution of your duties as members of an organised army of a State that had declared war ? It stands to reason—and it must—that any act done by a member of an organised army fighting under the order of one State against another State between which war exists, is an act entirely outside municipal law. But assuming for the purpose of argument the Court requires some nearer justification. In the eye of the Court in so far as the administration by this Court is concerned, it is fortunate that I am able to find the exception in the Indian Penal Code itself, because the young men are being charged either under Section 121 or Section 302 of the Indian Penal Code and I am relying on

Section 79 of the same Code which says in terms that it is not an offence. Supposing war was declared between two States and when peace time returned every individual soldier is called upon to say whether he killed so and so. I am quite sure that as I am addressing men of commonsense, you would laugh at the idea. But then quite agree that I would have to satisfy you that the new Indian State that declared war was entitled to do it in the sense of international law.

And now I will proceed to quote from books of international law on the question of right to make war. I am reading to you Vol. II of Dick Corbett's Cases of International Law under the heading of "War", 1937 Edition.

"International war is a contest carried on by an armed force either between States or between a State and some community or body which is treated as a State for the purpose of the conduct of hostilities. International war differs from other kinds of war in that it has the effect of setting up a new relation in law both as between the belligerents themselves and as between each of them and the other States. As between the belligerents, the State of war although it departs from normal relations, is nevertheless a State of regulated violence in which the conduct of hostilities is governed by certain principles and rules which rest part on custom and part on convention, and which are sanctioned in the last resort by the action of international society however uncertain may be their operation."

I next call attention to Wheaton's International Law. I am reading Wheaton's "International Law", 1945 edition, Vol. II, page 98:

"War in the absence of any international authority competent to suppress effectively international wrongs has always been held legal by international law."

Remember that as a definite proposition that so long as there are two states, if they declare war against each other, there is no justification required for it. And once you have a war, any person being a member of an organised army or one of the warring States, cannot be called upon individually to account for the acts, which in civil matters or normal times if done individually in a private capacity for private motive, be considered to be an offence.

"War, in the absence of any international authority competent to suppress effectively international wrongs, has always been held legal by international law.... Even the creation of the League of Nations leaves war in certain cases legal, there is now on record the unanimous. Assembly condemnation of aggressive war. War is essentially a struggle between States, involving the application of force. Mere armed occupation, as in the seizure of Strassburg by Louis XIV in 1680-81 or as in that of Corfu by Italy in 1913, is not war unless the State affected declares it so, and similarly, as regards pacific blockade. The States need not necessarily be fully sovereign: in 1876, Serbia and Montenegro warred on Turkey through vassal States: in 1877... Rumania followed suit. In 1855, Bulgaria warred on Serbia, then fully sovereign, and in the treaty of peace of March 8, 1886, though Turkey as suzerain took part, Bulgaria appeared independently as a party. So the South African Republic warred on the United Kingdom in 1899.

So, the first step in the argument is that the State which declares war is and must be in a position to do it. But once it declares war against any other State, then there can be no question of its propriety, or right. In the particular case before the Court, and not with standing their territories which were occupied, I do say that this war at all events was completely a justified war. International law in the question of war is not static. It is law that has grown from time to time with the progress of civilization.

Therefore, the question really is, once it comes to war, there is no question of justification. But hitherto at all events now in the global war a great many events have occurred of which international conscience takes note. I will read out to you two passages, one from Mr. Winston Churchill from the Hansard and another from Mr. Eden. The position now is that international law has reached this stage that if liberty and democracy are to have any meaning all over the world, and not merely just for a part of it, and this is not politics, it is law—any war made for the purpose of liberating oneself from foreign yoke is completely justified by modern international law. And it will be travesty of justice if we were to be told as the result of any decision arrived at here or otherwise, that the Indian may go as soldier and fight for the freedom of England against Germany, for England against Italy, for England against Japan, and yet a stage may not be reached when a free Indian State may not wish to free itself from any country, including England itself. We maintain that this particular war, according to the decisions, requires no justification. If one State can declare war, then the other State can also declare war and fight, and anything done in its due prosecution has no civil consequences of any kind. In other words, not one of these men now charged before you can be called upon to account for his actions. We can show that they have done nothing outside the scope of the due prosecution of war on a civilized basis. That is an emphasis which I always wish to put. It is not alleged against these men that there was any question about the acts with which they are charged. They were acts carried out in due prosecution of the war, under what you may call civilised rules. Therefore the question before the Court is a very narrow one.

To continue what I was reading :

"A civil war between different members of the same society is, what Grotius calls, a mixed war. It is according to him public on the side of the established Government and private on the part of people resisting its authority. The general usage of nations is as regards such a war as entitling both the contending parties to all the rights of war as against each other and even as respects neutral nations. It seems to be now settled that it is unnecessary in order to constitute war that both parties should be acknowledged as independent nations or sovereign States."

There was at one time the old idea that you had to be an independent State or a sovereign State in order to be able to declare war. Of course that created a vicious circle, that a subject race will remain in perpetuity a subject race. It can never make a legitimate war for the purpose of liberating itself. Hence modern international law has now recognised the right of subject races which are not for the time being or at the moment independent, to be so organized, and if they are organised and fight an organized war through an organised army, the individual members of that army are unanswerable before any municipal court for what was done in due prosecution of that war.

It seems to be now settled that it is unnecessary in order to constitute a war that both parties should be acknowledged as independent nations or sovereign States. A war may certainly exist between a State and its suzerain as in the Boer War. May I appeal to this Court and all of you are familiar with British history—what about Charles I and his death? What about the Magna Charta? What about James II? It is all recorded in history. In other words, you do reach a stage where the organisation, call it rebel if you like, call it insurgent;—insurgents or rebels may reach a stage of organisation for the purpose of liberating themselves when what they do after declaring war is subject to the laws of war.

"A war may certainly exist between a State and a suzerain as in the Boer War. Moreover, a war may exist where one of the billigerents claims sovereign rights as against the other, whether in a federal or a unitary States......."

But it is quite an unnecessary requisite. If ever a subject race finds itself in a position where its organisation is able to declare war, then acts done by the armies on either side come under this. I put a very simple question: What about the acts of those who fought on the side of the British in this War? They killed lots of people. Would they be put up before this Court under Section 302? Most amazing! It was a properly fought war, no doubt as in order wars one or the other side lost, and the fact that a war is lost has no effect on the immunity from the consequences in acts done in due prosecution of the war. He says further :

"Whether the struggle is a war or not is to be determined, not from the relation of the combatants to each other, but from the mode in which it is carried on. The Government of the State may recognize its subjects as belligerents, in which case other States will normally but need not follow the same course. Or other States may recognize belligerency, in which case the parent State will all but certainly follow suit."

That is the crux of the matter. I quite agree that if ten persons in a village declare war. British, they are rebels, and I am not here to justify it. What I am saying is this that struggle between two organizations a stage must be reached where the organisation of the State and the organisation of the army are such that it is a war recognised by civilised nations; and if it is once recognised, then the immunity follows. As the books point out, we had the instance of the war between the South and North of America and you have a declaration from Abraham Lincoln downwards that it was a proper war and there was nothing more to be said about it as soon as the hostilities ceased. It goes on to say :

"Among the tests are the existence of a de facto political organization of the insurgents sufficient in character, population and resources to constitute it, if left to itself, a State among nations capable of discharging the duties of a State; the actual employment of military forces on each side acting in accordance with the rules and customs of war..... If all these elements exist, the condition of things is undoubtedly war; and it may be war before they are all ripened into activity."

Therefore what I wish to say is this : that the test by which you will judge this case is, have we or have we not proved the existence of a *de facto* political organization of insurgents? I do not deny that they wree insurgents. Apart from the other question to which I shall come presently, I will assume against myself that the people who declared war and who declared the Provisional Government of Free India were a set of insurgents, a set of rebels—I will assume that against myself.

"As President Grant said in his message of June 13, 1870 : 'The question of belligerency is one of fact not to be decided by sympathies for or prejudices against either party. The relations between the parent State and insurgents must amount, in fact, to war in the sense of international law".

I call upon you to do the same. It is not a question of prejudice; it is not a question of prestige or what happens to the Army, to this or the other person. Please remember that you are here as judges; you are not politicians, I agree, and I do not want you to be such. If you find that there is a *de facto* political organization sufficient in numbers, sufficient in character and sufficient in resources to constitute itself capable of declaring and making war with an organised army, your verdict must be in favour of these men—no more and no less than the verdict on your own men for killing others, of which act you are justly proud.

That is the position in law.

Then I wish to call attention to another book on International Law—an accepted book and what is more it is borne out by all the earlier cases in which war was waged by what you may call insurgents against their own sovereign, if you must use that expression. This book is by Lawrence—page 309. The whole question before the Court under this particular head is whether or not there was a properly declared war in presecution of which the accused before you did the acts which they did. And if they did that in due prosecution of that war, then there can be no question of any civil offence, as I think all of you in your own person will easily realise. I am not obliged in my civil life to kill anybody except on pain of conviction, but you are.

Lawrence says :

"War may be defined as a contest carried on by public force between States, or between States and communities having with regard to the contest the rights of States, the parties to it having the intention of ending peaceful relations, and substituting for them those of hostility with all the legal incidents thereof".

These were no private acts done with a private motive or done for private individual benefit. They came to be done by them as members of an organised army, having declared war and the law says to them that no such consequences as the government demands can arise. Lawrence goes on:

"It is true that two States are said to be at war as soon as one of them has received a declaration of war from the other."

Here there was in fact a formal declaration of war. Then I call attention to a well-known work of Oppenheim on International Law. Oppenheim was Professor of International Law at Cambridge University. He says this—(Vol. II, page 166):

"War is a contention between two or more armed States through their armed forces for the purpose of overpowering each other.... War is a fact recognised, and with regard to many points, regulated but not established by International Law."

Once you get to the stage of war, naturally it is the primary purpose of each party to overpower the other. Therefore in due prosecution of it, acts which might be called offences under civil law are not offences : the very purpose is to destroy men and property : the very thing which would otherwise be unlawful becomes right, becomes patriotic, becomes a duty.

"In any case it is universally recognised that war is a contention, i.e., a violent struggle through the application of armed force......

To be war, the contention must be between States...... On the other hand, to an armed contention between a suzerain and its vassal State the character of war ought not to be denied, for both parties are States, although the action of the vassal may, from the standpoint of constitutional law, be rebellion." (Para 56)

I have already said that States are those which have the right to make war *like States.*

The first proposition for which I stand before this Court is this, that the two States sufficient in number, in organisation and in resources may make war against each other. That is the proposition to which I stand, and if they made war against each other, then there is complete immunity for what might otherwise be a private offence. That must necessarily follow from the acceptance of war as a necessary evil in this infirm world, and no individual member can be called upon to answer for the consequences of his acts so long as it is a properly declared war. I shall call the Court's attention to Mr. Hyde's book on 'International Law', Vol. III, page 1792, para 648.

"So soon as a man is armed by a sovereign government and takes the soldier's oath of fidelity, he is a belligerent; his killing, wounding or other war-like acts are not individual crimes or offences. No belligerent has a right to declare that enemies of a certain class, colour or condition, when properly organised as soldiers, will not be treated by him as public enemies."

In other words the position is simple. Any act done by members of an armed force against any opponent, which in ordinary times in a personal case would be a civil offence, ceases to be an offence altogether. Otherwise, war and recognition is not a possibility.

There is a very important decision of the Federal Court of the United States expressing the same thing. I may be pardoned for multiplying authorities, but I do so because I feel that instead of paraphrasing the idea myself, if I do it through the medium of an accepted authority, I might be able to carry better conviction. It is Vol. 168 United States Reports, page 250. It is the case of *Underhill* v. *Hernandez*. I am reading the judgement of Chief Justice Fuller. The opinion of the Court is as follows :

"Nor can the principle be confined to lawful or recognised Governments or to cases where redress can manifestly be had through public channels. The immunity of individuals from suits brought in foreign tribunals for acts done within their own States in the exercise of Governmental authority, whether as civil officers or as military commanders must necessarily extend to the agents of governments ruling by paramount force as a matter of fact. Where a civil war prevails, that is, where the people of a country are divided into two hostile parties, who take up arms and oppose one another by military force, generally speaking, foreign nations do not assume to judge of the merits of the quarrel. If the party seeking to dislodge the existing government succeeds, and the independence of the government it has set up is recognised, then the acts of such government from the commencement of its existence are regarded as those of an independent nation. If the political revolt fails of success, still if actual war has been waged, acts of legitimate warfare cannot be made the basis of individual liability."

Chief Justice Fuller was deciding the case arising out of the war between the North and the South. A war might exist between what you might call an existing State and insurgents, and yet the insurgents, as they were called by the Federal Government, may have such organisation, force and strength that the relation between the two parties is one of the existence of war. Once the war exists, what is the legal position? If the party seeking to dislodge the existing Government succeeds, it is now accepted law that a successful rebellion is a Government established by law. The question is—what is the position in case of an unsuccessful rebellion. The law is, I submit, that if the stage is reached where the rebels or insurgents are sufficiently organised and are sufficiently resourceful to make war, then it is entitled to be regarded as war, and there will be no individual consequences to persons who take part in it. If actual war has been waged, and my learned friend himself was at pains to prove that a regular war was being waged, and he put forward document after document to prove it, then the question is: What is the distinction between a private individual waging war on his own and his waging war as a member of a force or organized State. That is the real distinction which makes one immune from the consequences. If actual war has been waged, then acts of legitimate warfare cannot be made the basis of individual liability.

There is another case belonging to the same period. It is *Ford* v. *Surget,* 97 United States Reports, page 594, (equal to 24 Law F.D.).

"The Confederate Government can be regarded by the Courts in no other light than as simply the military representative of the insurrection against the military authority of the United States.

"To the Confederate Army was however conceded, in the interest of humanity and to prevent the cruelties of reprisals and retaliation, such belligerent rights as belonged, under the laws of nations, to the armies of independent Governments engaged in war against each other; that concession placing the soldiers and officers of the rebel army, as to all matters directly connected with the mode of prosecuting the war on the footing of those engaged in lawful war and exempting them from liability for acts of legitimate warfare."

The first proposition is this that in view of the fact that a state of war existed between the Provisional Government of Azad Hind and the British, any act done in prosecution of that war has not the consequences which the Crown claims or might have claimed in the case of a private individual.

In International Law it is permissible for those who are subject to a foreign authority to organize themselves, and having reached that stage of organisation and having an organized army to fight for liberation, whether it is successful or not, during the process while the war is being carried on, there is immunity, so far as individual members of the organized army are concerned for all acts done in due prosecution of war on a civilized basis (other than war crimes like those which are the subject of trial now in different parts of the world). That being so, my submission is that the accused men before you are entitled to be declared innocent in that there is no civil or criminal responsibility for those acts. In terms of the language of the books on law, the liability is on the State under whose direction they fought, and such liability in international law on the cessation of hostilities does not exist. Of course if a rebellion is successful, then it becomes a new Government, and there is the end of it and there will be no tribunals, but it is only in a case in which it is not successful that the question arises and the answer is given in my clients' favour by International Law.

The next point to which I wish to advert is the alternative point which I made under Section 79 of the Indian Penal Code. The issue which arises, apart from the Indian Penal Code, is an issue of great international importance. It has arisen, if I may say so, in its actual form for the first time though the authorities directly or indirectly support the principles on which my contention is based. At the same time, appearing before this Tribunal, it becomes my duty to justify it on what I may call a narrower ground to the extent to which it is necesary, for I do feel that before a Tribunal constituted as this is, it is equally important that I should put myself within the narrow sphere of the Indian Statute itself. Then I submit, assuming my submissions are correct and accepted, the hands of the Tribunal are fairly strengthened. The words which I referred to in Section 79 of the Indian Penal Code are 'justified by law'. The question is what is the meaning of the word 'law' appearing in Section 79 of the Indian Penal Code. If I can satisfy this Court that the law there comprehends and includes international law, I submit my Honourable Friend on the other side would have hardly any case to present to the Court at all. If the word 'law' in Section 79 includes International Law so far as the immunity which I have described before is concerned, then I submit the three men at your bar are entitled to plead that they were so justified in the actions which in ordinary private personal life might have been offences under the Indian Penal Code. I wish to call your attention to a certain number of authorities on the question. The first authority to which I call your attention is Blackstone's Commentaries in Book IV, but it is volume II in this binding. It is accepted at all events by British lawyers that Blackstone's Commentaries are the fountain-source of Common Law of England and it is a matter which I wish to particularly assert before this Court. The page that I am reading is 2237 (Vol. II, edited by W.C. Jones). Most of us who are not lawyers are familiar with Blackstone's Commentaries and know that he is father, to a very large extent, of Common Law. Blackston's Commentaries are relied upon in British Courts as a very authoritative exposition of the law on the particular question which he has dealt with.

"In arbitrary States this law, wherever it contradicts or is not provided for by the municipal law of the country, is enforced by royal power; but since in England no royal power can introduce a new law, or suspend the execution of the old, therefore the law of nations (wherever any question arises which is properly the object of its jurisdiction) is here adopted in its full extent by the common law, and is held to be a part of the law of the land."

So that, as soon as the Court has ascertained what is the International law on a particular point before the Court, it is the bounden duty of the Court to administer that part of International Law as a part of the law of the land, and hence it is that I am submitting to the Court that the word 'law' in Section 79 should be given that extensive meaning which the law has by the Common Law of England.

The next work on which I rely for the purpose of the meaning of the word 'law', meaning thereby that 'nothing is an offence which is justified by law', is Oppenheim's International Law. The question is what is law, and it is in support of that I am submitting next Oppenheim's International Law Vol. I, Fifth Edition, page 36, article 21a :

"In view of this wide divergence of doctrine it is necessary to inquire into the actual legal position in the principal countries in the matter of International Law and Municipal Law.

(I) As regards Great Britain, the following points must be noted :

(a) all such rules of customary International Law as are either universally recognised or have at any rate received the assent of this country are *per se* part of the law of the land. To that extent there is still valid in England the Common Law doctrine to which Blackstone gave expression in a striking passage, that the Law of Nations is part of the law of the land. It has repeatedly been acted upon by Courts. Apart from isolated *obiter dicta* it has never been denied by judges. The unshaken continuity of its observance suffered a reverse as the result of the *dicta* of some judges in The Franconia Case in 1876, but *West Rand Central Gold Mining* Co. v. *The King* decided in 1905, must be regarded as a reaffirmation of the classical doctrine."

So that ever since the time of Blackstone, untile the last edition of Oppenheim, which belongs to the year 1937, there has never been any question that on any issue in which the doctrine of international law is accepted to be the international law it becomes a part of the law of the land, law of the land in England, and law of the land here.

Next, I call attention to the work of an American Jurist Hershey on International Public Law and Organisation, page 14, 1927 Edition.

"International Law is a part of our law, and must be ascertained and admitted by the Court of Justice of appropriate jurisdiction as often as questions of right depending upon it are duly presented for their determination. For this purpose, where there is no treaty and no controlling executive or legislative act or judicial decision, resort must be had to the custom and usages of civilized nations, and, as evidence of these, to the works of jurists and commentators who, by years of labour, research, and experience, have made themselves peculiarly well-acquainted with the subjects of which they treat. Such works are resorted to by judicial tribunals, not for the speculations of their authors concerning what the law ought to be, but for trustworthy evidence of what the law really is."

So, you will see from this quotation which has come from Justice Gray in the case which is cited—195 United States Reports, page 113 at page

163, that it has been accepted that while administering justice it is your bounden duty to find out, recognise and apply the principles of international law where a person at your bar seeks justice on the ground that the act with which he is charged is an act justified by law and that for the purpose of ascertaining it you may have resort as it is stated by the learned Judge himself to "the usages and customs of civilized nations, and as evidence to this to the work of jurists, commentators, who by years of labours, research and experience have made themselves peculiarly well-acquainted with the subject of which they treat."

Therefore, I plead that when the time comes for your deliberation you will carefully, of which I have no doubt, and diligently, of which I am perfectly conscious, study and apply your mind to the citations which I have already given and which I am about to give. Because, according to the well-accepted canons, the commentators who by years of labour, research and experience have made themselves peculiarly well-acquainted with the subjects of which they treat, and such works are resorted to and have to be resorted to by judicial tribunals. I have got, Sirs, the original judgment from which this quotation is given. The judgment is reported in 175 United States Report in the judgment at page 700. The case is Paquet Habana, Appeals from the District Courts of the United States for Southern Districts of Florida. The judgment of Mr. Justice Gray on this question is to be found at page 700. I do not wish to read it again, because I have already read it from the textbook in which it is now accepted. At the same time I may be pardoned for pressing this point upon the Court because then the issue before this Court becomes exceedingly narrow. If I am able to presuade this Court, as I submit I hope to do, that in administering the law you are bound to have regard to international law, there will be no difficulty whatever in the way of the defence which I am presenting. Then the Statute law has made it incumbent upon you, and in fact has declared that nothing is an offence which is justified by law. If therefore the acts which are said to be offences are declared not to be offences, and if I am able to show that the law so declares them, then it will be your duty to declare that, notwithstanding apparent confusion of thought, words like treason and so on, will have no value.

The law of treason in India is codified. It is to be found in Chapter VI of the I .P.C. (Offences against the State) in Sec. 121 and following Sections. Therefore let me caution the Court against the general use of words like "treason". The question is whether my clients who have been charged under Sections 121 and 302 have or have not, in doing those acts, been justified by law, i.e., the law of nations, and if they are so justified the law of this country declares that it is not an offence. In other words the law of this country recognises that there may be acts which if done in private life for private motive might be an offence but which in public life or public duty are not an offence. A judge is not liable as an abettor of murder because he orders a man to be hung, because he is justified by law. Similarly and equally, if not more emphatically, the member of an armed force having declared war, if during the state of that war he has committed acts which in private life might be offences, the law says nothing shall be an offence. Therefore, I do wish in so far as in me lies, to press this point upon your attention, because the first line of argument which I submitted to the Court stands, and I submit to the Court that is the law. In other words the law is that in the prosecution of war the acts which take place are beyond municipal law. But assuming for the purpose of argument, I have to take my stand on a narrower ground. Then the law of this country, the Indian Statute Law itself enjoins upon you that if I can show justification by means of international law for those acts, then my clients are entitled to a verdict in their favour. I say this to you in the language of one of your greatest poets that if in so far as God grants me the tongue of persuastion and you the ears of hearing, I have not the least doubt that when you have considered the cases before you, you will have no difficulty or hesitation to decide in my favour on that narrow ground.

The next point to which I wish to call attention is Moore's International Law and Digest page 2, Vol. I, and this is how it is stated :

"It is thus apparent than from the beginning the scene in question denoted something more that the positive legislation of independent States and the term international law which has in recent times so generally superseded the earlier titles served to emphasize his fact. It denotes a body of obligations which is in a sense independent of and superior to such legislation. The Government of the United States has on various occasions announced the principle that international law as a system is binding upon nations, not merely as something which they may be tacitly assumed to agree but also as a fundamental condition for their admission to the full and equal participation in the intercourse of civilised nations."

I therefore cannot more emphatically assert than the ground on which I appear before the Court and I have no doubt that it will rise superior (in the language of one of the cases that I read) to all question of prejudice and come to the right conclusion in considering Section 79 and the immunity granted by it.

Just one more passage to which I wish to call attention. It is the judgment of the Privy Council on this question. The last under these heads is a judgment of Their Lordships of the Privy Council, reported in a recent number, 1939 appeal cases, page 168. There a question of international law arose. The name of the case is Chang Chi Chu. It was a case of murder committed on a Chinese ship and that is how the question arose of the liability of the prisoner to be tried. And the question arose to what extent in international law it was necessary to consider whether the prisoner was liable. The contention shortly stated was that the Chinese ship was so much floating Chinese territory. That was the claim made under the international law. Their Lordships of the Privy Council held that under international law it is probably not correct to say that a floating ship of foreign power is so much, what you may call, island foreign territory. But they have ruled by reason of the respect accorded to comity of nations, that anything that occurs on a foreign ship is not within the authority or jurisdiction of municipal law. In this particular case what they held was that in as much as the ship itself accepted the authority of the power which was exercising authority in those waters, they held it became an exception. But in considering the applicability of international law to the question whether or not the Court had jurisdiction to try this particular Chinaman, the question arose to what extent international law has to be considered and the judgment of Their Lordships delivered by Lord Aitkins is very important from this point of view. I would not enter into the question of details which arose in that case though by themselves they are interesting enough. But I may say this that the observations which I propose to read are necessary and essential because the whole defence to the charge of murder, and the want of jurisdiction of the Court, were based on the ground that under international law the Court had no jurisdiction and for that purpose the Court went into the question of what was the appropriate international law on the question. Their Lordships said with reference to the necessity of the application, or rather with reference to the obligation to ascertain and apply international law ourselves was a part of the law. That is how that part of the case is stated.

Page 167 : "Their Lordships entertain no doubt that the law is the correct conclusion, namely, that a ship is not so much floating part of a foreign territory, but that immunity is granted for whatever happens in that ship in so far as jurisdiction is concerned. It more accurately and logically represents the agreement of nations which constitute international law, and alone is consistent with the paramount necessity expressed in general terms for each nation to protect itself from internal disorder by trying and punishing offenders within its boundaries."

It must always be remembered that in so far as, at any rate, the courts of this country are concerned, international law has validity in so far its principles are accepted and adopted by domestic law. There is no external power that imposes its rules upon our code of substantive law or procedure The Court acknowledge the existence of a body of rules which nations accept among themselves. On any judicial issue they seek to ascertain what the relevant rule is, and having found it, they will treat it as incorporated into the domestic law so far as it is not inconsistent with the rules enacted by any Statute or finally declared by their tribunals. What then are the immunities of public ships of other nations accepted by our courts and on what principle? I say that in this particular case not only there is no Statute to the contrary, but in fact the Statute imposes that obligation, coming back to the action of Section 79, *viz.*, nothing is an offence which is justified by law. Therefore what you have got to do, Sirs, is to ascertain the relevant body of international law, and having done so, apply it to what is described as domestic law. Therefore there can be no reasonable doubt that in the construction and application and application of Section 79 the submission which I have already made on the immunity of individual members of an armed force fighting i· a war properly declared, that immunity is a part of international law and therefore is a part of national law. And I submit that your own experience whenever emergencies of war have arisen should bear ample testimony to that position. Each time a soldier fights under the orders of a state in a war properly declared, if he were to consider what would be his liabilities, I am afraid the efficiency of war would be a very difficult process indeed. It is an assumed part of the law of nations that once you become a member of a fighting force of a properly qualified State entitled to make a war, there is an end of all individual liability for the acts which if they were private acts for a private purpose might be an offence within the law. Though according to may submission the first is an essentially correct ground, in any case the justification by law is a sure ground on which I stand before this Court. Hence I submit that nothing is an offence which is justified by law, and I therefore say that the acts with which the accused are charged before the Court are justified by law, that is to say by the international law, and therefore, there can be no question of a personal or individual liability.

This questions has been considered in a different from or perhaps in different language because I wish to point out to you, as you have seen in the earlier works to which I referred, the law of war is often described as the law of belligerency. I wish to point out to the Court, as I shall presently do, what is the law of belligerency ; in other words, who are entitled to be treated as billigerents in the light of international, and what I may call, municipal or domestic law.

For that purpose I wish to call attention to the authorities which clearly show where and how the law of belligerency rests. I again refer you to Oppenheim on International Law, 1944 edition, Vol. II : he was professor of international law at Cambridge and falls within the description which I gave of men who have by their labour and research and experience and knowledge, contributed to the formulation of international law on many questions. The present question is dealt with on page 200—Article 76 A :

"Recognition of belligerents by other States is not as a rule binding upon the State. Notwithstanding such recognition, it is entitled to treat the insurgents as traitors ; but the position is controversial with regard to recognition as a belligerent power granted to separate armies which comprise subjects of the enemy who are fighting to free their nation from this rule and which are responsible to an authority recognised as representing the nation in question."

That really epitomises the whole of the issue—"but the position is controversial with regard to the recognition as a belligerent power granted to separate armies which comprise subjects of the enemy who are fighting to free their nation from this rule and which are responsible to an authority recognised as representing the nation in question."

To translate it according to law, the accused before you were members of an army responsible to the Provisional Government of Free India, fighting to liberate themselves from the rule of the army of those who were fighting against them, and I submit that is precisely the case before us. The author goes on and gives instances of cases of that kind, and I want to draw your particular attention to those historical instances which fortunately have occurred before, so that I stand before you on much more solid ground than if this were perhaps actually the first instance:

"Thus, in the year 1918, during the world war, Great Britain, France Italy and the United States of America recognised Czecho-Slovaks as co-belligerents. Similar recognition was granted in the year 1917 to the Polish National Army, composed to a substantial degree of the subjects of the enemy powers. It has been maintained that as in the case of insurgents in a civil war—(quotations of which I have already given)—the enemy is entitled to disregard such recognition and treat the members of the insurgent army when they fall into his hands, in accordance with the provisions of the criminal law. The better opinion is probably that when such recognition is granted by and adversely to large bodies of men effectively organised on foreign soil in anticipation of independent nationahood, a point is reached at which the belligerents, confronted with disaffection and desertion of a considerable number of his subjects engaged in hostilities against him, can no longer, without exposing himself to justifiable retaliation, assert the provisions of his own criminal law as the only legally element in the situation."

I want to draw your attention pointedly to the conditions which are here laid down and which, I submit, we have more than amply fulfilled. I ask this Court to declare that is the better opinion, and I do say that we have reached a stage far in advance of the illustration given by Oppenheim. In this case not merely men were effectively organised, but there was a regularly organised army. This has been amply proved by the Prosecution—thanks to them for that. They have amply proved that there was a regular army, a properly organised army—on foreign soil it is true—but with this added qualification in my favour, that Indians residing in places where the army was organised, numbering not a few hundreds, even a few thousands, but two million men and women and children, through 230,000 adult men and women swearing allegiance to that Provisional Government, for the purpose of liberating their country—which unfortunately failed, but nonetheless the condition required that you may at your peril call to aid the criminal law of the country against such an organisation—effectively organised on soil in anticipation of an independent nationhood. It is true—and that is why I read the Proclamation to this court—I read it with a view to show to you that the object with which on foreign soil an independent government was formed was the liberation of their country : It was undoubtedly in anticipation of independent statehood ; and of course if the independent state had been established by the successful prosecution of force, as I said, this tribunal would not have been there to try them. It was because it was done in anticipation, which failed, and which does not detract from the point, that a stage is reached in which a belligerent confronted with the disaffection and desertion of a considerable number of his subjects engaged in hostilities against him, can no longer assert the provisions of his own criminal law as the only legally relevant element in this situation. In other words, the legally relevant element in this situation is that we, meaning the two armies, had reached a stage where, having reached a stage of war—there can be no question at all that under Section 79 we are entitled to the justification which the laws of war give to belligerent armies. And that no acts done during the course of the prosecution of the war are matters of what you may call domestic law, pure and simple ; which would be as if any one of these three accused went and did any of these acts out of private motive. Therefore, it is essential to remember that in all these cases the substance of the law is this : two independent States can always make war and the members of their combatant forces are unanswerable for their acts. Only the question, or the intermediate stage arises, whether without having reached the stage of independent statehood (to take the words of Oppenheim) you have attained a stage, and whether having founded a state for the purpose of liberating your own country, you are so organised, both the state and the army, that it assumes the proportions of a state and as a result of the war-as much a war between two independent states. I am pleading before you that we have proved before this court, and the documents which otherwise we would not have had the benefit of and have generously been produced by the prosecution all of them distinctly and clearly showed that we had reached that stage and this court would not only be justified, but, I submit, bound in law and in consciences to regard the accused as belonging to that organisation, and as member of such a belligerent army they are entitled to all the privileges of the laws of war. In other words, immunity for personal acts carried out in due prosecution of the war, as you yourself in your own person would claim.

The next book to which I call attention is the British Year Book of International Law, 1937, page 18. It says:

"What we call belligerent recognition is not so much recognition, even temporary and provisional, of a new government, so the recognition of the existence of awar."

I may explain what is meant here, because the recognition comes as a stage when it has not yet succeeded in establishing its own government. Of course, if for instance perchance this very army had succeeded in its aim, as the maxim of international law is, the successful revolution is the government established by law. But earlier than that there is the stage at which it is in a state of war and that is all that is necessary for the purposes of my case. If I can establish that they were making war, which is regarded as a stage of belligerency by international law, they are entitled to the same privileges and immunities as would be accorded to the armies of two independent nations. It continues :

"The existence of war is purely a question of fact; but if we recognise the fact that a war is being carried on, then the recognition of the insurgent government follows as a necessary consequence. Wars can only be carried on by governments, and there must be at least two parties to every war. Much of the confusion which obscures the current discussion of the Spanish problem arises form the failure to observe this correct logical consequence. The true doctrine is that recognition of the insurgent government is the necessary and logical consequence of recognising the fact of war."

Therefore I submit that once you recognise, as I submit this court is bound to do on the evidence before it, that there was a regular properly declared and properly prosecuted war, then I submit there can be no question that the acts of these men, done in due prosecution of that war, are completely justified by international law and therefore by law.

The instances are given in the Year Book of International Law. This is what it says :

"Lets this should seem to be merely doctrinaires, that is the kind of criticism with which we people are sometimes apt to run away-and theoretical opinion, I shall try to fortify my doctrine by authority. In 1828 Don Miguel, the Pretender to the throne of Portugal, was carrying on war by sea and land against his niece and nominal fiancee the child-Queen Donna Maria, who was recognised by Great Britain and other powers as the legitimate Sovereign of Portugal. At no time during the struggle was Don Miguel recognised by Great Britain under any form *de jure or de facto.* In 1828 he proclaimed naval blockades of Opor to and of the Azores. These blockades were notified to the British Government which published the notices in the London Gazette and communicated them to the committee of loyd's. The king's advocate Sir herbert Jenner advised the British Government that the blockades, if effectively maintained, might be recognised as valid, although no form of recognition had at any time been conceded to Don Miguel."

In other words the distinction that is sought to be made is that you may recognise the state of belligerency without necessarilly recognising the state.

Refusal to recognise the blockade, so Jenner advised, would be a departure from the neutrality which this country had professed in the civil war. Twenty years later the Palmerston Government, following the advice of Sir John Dodson- and I hope that Judge Advocate will advise you accordingly-then the Queen's Advocate decided to recognise the blockade of Trieste by the Italian insurgents during the Revolution of 1843, although there had been no other act of recognition of the insurgent government.

The point I am trying to emphasize is this that you need not necessarily recognise you opponent as a government, and yet during the course of the war, once you recognise that it was a proper state of belligerency, then the immunities and privileges which I described before follow, because the men, and in modern times the women, who are fighting for the insurgent government, are recognised for the purpose of these immunities. It goes on :

"Upon the point which we are now discussing Dodson's opinion is very clear. 'It is sufficient he says to justify a blockade if duly maintained that a *de facto* war is carried on by Sardinia and Venice on one side and Austria on the other'."

Even more clear is the opinion of a later Queen's Advocate Sir John Harding when advising the Government in 1860 upon the question raised by Garibaldi's rebellion. This is perhaps nearer in its application. This is he quotation from the opinion of Harding:

"If Her Majesty's Government considers that a civil war actually exists between the dictatorial Government of southern Italy ad that of is Majesty the King of the two Silicious in which Great Britain is to be strictly natural and that the dictatorial government has in fact attained (howsoever) an independent and sovereign existence and governs de facto a portio of the Neapolitan dominions, then Her Majesty's Government may without violating or disregarding the law of Nations and without encouraging piracy, so far recognise the acts of this de facto government as to admit the validity of an effective blockade, maintained by a competent naval force acting under its orders, for to acquiesce in the capture and condemnation buy it of articles of contraband of war designed for use of the King of the two Sicilies."

The belligerency which existed was between what you might call the King of Italy and the insurgents, and the advice of Sir John Harding was that if there was a de facto war between the two, then the rights of the belligerencts should be accepted and acknowledged. In other words, supposing they took as prize of war ships belonging to what you might call the constituted King of Italy, it would still be a perfectly good prize.

In the course of the same opinion, Harding pointed out that Garibaldi and his officers could not possibly be regarded as pirates, since they were carrying on war in a regular manner and had been dealt with on equal terms by British naval officers. The three opinions which I have just cited are those of British law officers ranging over the period from 1828 to 1860.

Without further multiplying citations, I will therefore summarise their effect by saying that what we recognise in these cases is the existence of war. The recognition of the insurgent government is merely incidental or consequential since a war implies the existence of some independent authority which carries on the war.

The next thing to which I wish to call your attention is the recognition this matter has received from the British Government through the then Foreign Secretary, Mr. Eden. I am reading from the Hansard which is the recognised report of the Debates of the House of Commons. I am reading from the debates of the 14th April 1937, page 113. This is what I have here :

"The leader of the opposition spoke earlier today as though the Government had given something up in this case. Of Course, we have not given anything up, because you can never grant belligerent rights to one side only; they must be granted to both sides, if they are granted at all."

This issue arose on the question of the Spanish war.

"The Honourable Gentleman remarked that he thought that never in history had there been any question of granting belligerent rights early in a dispute. As a matter of fact, in the American Civil War we did grant belligerent rights within six weeks of the outbreak of the Civil War."

"Mr. Noel Baker said : The Government themselves declared a blockade, which, as all international lawyers will agree, comples them to grant belligerent rights to both sides."

"Mr. Eden: We ourselves made, in point of fact, a declaration of neutrality out to which arose the granting of belligerent rights to both sides. That is what we did in the American Civil War. Of course, that does not stand alone. It is not the only example. The Honourable Gentleman is probably familiar, I think, as I know something of his associations in this respect, with the Greek rebellion against Turkey in 1821-25. At that time also—remember that in each case these were insurgents against their parent State fighting for their liberation, and it was during the course of that struggle that the rights of belligerents were granted by Britain. At that time also, belligerent rights were granted and His Majesty's Government voiced this opinion to which I would draw the attention of the House; the character of belligerency was not so much a principle as a fact that a certain degree of force and consistency acquired by any mass of population engaged in war entitled that population to be treated as a belligerent and even if this title were questionable, rendered in the interest well-understood of all civilised nations so to treat them."

The position of British politicians and British law on the question of the recognition of belligerency even as between what I might call the parent State and the rebel States has always been recognition of belligerency.

At that time Canning was the Foreign Secretary of this country and Professor Philips in his History of Europe deals with this very interesting chapter of modern Greek independence. He says :

"Curiously enough as in the affairs of Spain, so now his (Canning's) attitude was frankly based upon the interests of England. The interests of England in his opinion demanded peace ...... The recognition of the belligerent character of the Greeks was necessitated by the impossibility of treating as pirates a population of a million souls and of bringing within the bounds of civilised war a contest which had been marked at the outset on both sides, by disgusting barbarities.

"Those were both cases in which belligerent rights were granted. A third and perhaps, in a way, even more remarkable case, was the revolt of the Spanish Americans Colonies against the Spanish Government, from which resulted the establishment of the South Ameracan independent Republics as we know them today."

So that you have instances on both sides of the line. You have instances where those who rebelled against a State for their own independence ultimately succeeded, but while they were in a state of war both were recognized as belligerents. Those others in which they did not succeed but nonetheless during the interval of the struggle, they were both recognized as belligerents.

"A third, and perhaps, in a way, even more remarkable case was the revolt of the Spanish American Colonies against the Spanish Government, from which resulted the establishment of the South American independent Republics as we know them today. In that dispute we recognized the rights of the belligerent colonies..."

People were actually revolting against their own Government for their own freedom, and one need not be apologetic in this period of world history to say that the subject race may free itself.

"In that dispute we recognized the rights of the belligerent colonies long before we recognised them in any other way, and, when I heard the Right Hon. Gentleman below the Gangway speaking earlier this afternoon, I bethought me that he might well have remembered the enthusiasm shown by the Liberal Party of that day for those new State across the Atlantic to whom we accorded belligerent rights, though they were rebels against their own mother country."

Sir, I say that I could not quote a stronger authority for your adoption than the action of the British Government as stated authoritatively by the Foreign Secretary of Britain and I would like to read it again in order that I may not miss the point:

"I bethought me that the might well have remembered the enthusiasm shown by the Liberal Party of that day for those new States across the Atlantic to whom we accorded belligerent rights, though they were rebels against their own mother country."

And I say that the same point arises for you. It is true that those who fought were rebels from the point of view of constitutional law as against their own King—and later on I will come to the question of zallegiance it will be my duty to analyse before you what that means, though it is irrelevant to the issue as I shall point out. The very fact that those colonies were fighting against their mother country as it is called, shows that at that time there was what you may call 'legal allegiance', but legal allegiance cannot be a matter of perpetuity because if it becomes a matter of perpetuity no subject race will ever attain freedom. For the moment, the point with which we are concerned is merely this : that while in a state of belligerencey Britain recognized the rebels as proper belligerents, those who were fighting against their mother country, and if that belligerency is recognized, I venture to submit it will be far too much to ask this court to refuse it to this Provisional Government of Free Inda and the Armies fighting under them. Mr. Eden goes on—because he wanted to make the point that the State will be recognized not only when it comes into existence, but while still the struggle goes on. New I read :

"What I wish to deduce from these three examples is that the natural thing, ..." mark the words—

'........ when a struggle has reached the large dimensions of the present war in Spain, would have been to recognise its belligerent character, and for States whose maritime interests are involved, as ours are, to grant belligerent rights to both sides."

In other words, as he put it before, it is essentially a matter of fact. If we find that the struggle, - call it rebellion, call it what you like—has reached such proportions that you connot control it by normal means, then you must recognize that it is a state of war, and once you recognize that it is a state of war, those who fight in pursuance of the declaration of war and in prosecution of it are entitled to all the rights of belligerency. Then he goes on :

"That would have been the natural thing to do. Recognition of belligerencey is, of course, quite distinct from recognising anyone to whom you give belligerent rights as being the legitimate Government of the country."

And that is what I want to impress upon you, that if it is asserted on the other side that it is required for the purpose of immunity from all acts done in due prosecution of the war that the Provisional Government should have been recognized by Britain, it is a completely futile argument. In fact, the very hypothesis cannot exist. The hypothesis is this: The rebels as I have called them—I do not mind it—are fighting for their freedom against another country. If they succeed, the Government will be recognized, but, in the meantime, during the course of fighting, the Government won't be recognized, but what is recognised is belligerency. I shall presently point out what it involves,—immunity from all acts done in due prosecution of the war.

"Recognition of belligerency is, of course, quite distinct from recognising anyone to whom you give belligerent rights as being the legitimate Government of the country.'

It is a fact that the Provisional Government was not then and did not become the actual Gvoernment of India, but that does not matter at all. What are the rights and privileges during the course of the struggle, and if I am right in my submission to the Court, there can be no doubt that during the course of struggle there was only one duty owed by men like the accused before you, and that is to prosecute that war under the orders of the Provisional Government,—and anything that they did by way of prosecuting that war gives them complete immunity.

"It has nothing to do with it. It is a conception simply concerned with granting belligerent rights which are of convenience to the donor as much as they are to the recipients. I will not go into the reasons, but for a variety of reasons in the present dispute we are not granting belligerent rights."

So that you have here recognition of an adoption of the principle supported by precedents as stated by the Foreign Secretary of that day.

Then there is a quotation from Mr. Churchill's speech during the course of the same discussion to which I wish to call your attention. That is on the 14th of April 1937, page 1068:

"When I hear my Right Hon. friend opposite speak of rebels, I must remind him that, sitting there as he does in the seat of the Whigs, he is departing from Whig principles. The saered rights of rebellion was one of their first doctrines. In regard to liberal statesmen, there the Right Hon. Gentleman sits, the successor to Mr. Gladstone, striving to uphold the great principles for which his party stands. But what was Mr. Gladstone's record? He was a stong supporter of rebles. He was a strong supporter of the rebels in the war of American secession. There, we had a civil war in which the rebels were not only rebels but slave owners. Mr. Gladstone went about the country, and in a famous speech either at New Castle or Hull proclaimed that the Confederate States (i.e., the Southern States had not only founded an army, but that they had founded a navy, they had founded a Government, and more than that, they had founded a nation. (An Hon. Member :"He was a Tory then.") He was not a Tory then. Therefore before one takes the view that rebels are like mad dogs to be put down and shot at sight, we should remember these things."

In other words, in that debate the Government of the day in England recognized that while a rebellion may or may not be successful, while it had attained a stage of war, you must recognize and give immunity to those people who fight on either side, for what justification is there on the part of one set of them to fight and claim immunity as against the other side? If the I.N.A. shot, I daresay the British Indian Army equally shot from the other side. The justification is equal in both cases in so far as this particular struggle is concerned. Mr. Churchill goes on :

"If we search the history of the 19th century we shall find many cases where the British Government have actually espoused the cause of rebels. The Hon. Member (Mr. Maxton), the leader of the Glydeside party, with this customary candour and frankness, made no bones about supporting rebels. He declared that the question was whether or not they were rebelling for the thing you wanted."

I am quite certain that we have proved to the hilt that they were rebelling for a thing they wanted which is fully approved of by any civilised human being. There cannot be two different laws for two different sets of people. "Everyone will support rebels who are fighting for the things of which they approve and they will criticise the Government which is for the things which they dislike. Therefore do not let us have too much of an attempt to make out that the Government in Spain have all the right on their side and the rebels none."

The Court will appreciate that I am pleading for a very limited right. I am not here before this Court on the question of the recognition or non-recognition of the unfortunate failure of the Provisional Government to obtain the independence of India. That is not the issue. There is a very narrow issue. It is this. While they were fighting and struggling, were they or were they not entitled to the rights of belligerents.

Mr Churchill goes on : "Therefore do not let us have too much of an attempt to make out that the Government in Spain have all the right on their side and the rebels none. It is one of the most evenly balanced struggles and one of the most unpleasant and certainly it is the least cause for us to espouse. If we were to take the course which is recommended by the Right Honourable gentleman and to break the blockade, if we throw the might of the British Navy into the scale, could he guarantee or could he be sure that we might not provoke that very alignment and crystallisation in Europe along those unnatural and idiotic—perhaps I had better say ideological—lines which it is our whole message and mission to rupture, or least to avoid. "So that Sir, even up to the very last war, up to the year 1937, just on the eve of the last war, it is perfectly obvious that a distinction has been maintained, a distinction which I cannot too often insist upon between a state of belligerency which may be recognised and the rights accorded without the ultimate success of those who fought for the cause for which they could fight. They may fail but nonetheless in the interval they are entitled to the rights of belligerency."

Then, Sirs, there is a further point and I tell the Court that it is a question of fact. This Court should find that this Provisional Government had ceded to it the territories which I have described. But while insisting on that finding of fact, because we submit that it was a fact, I wish to point out to you that from the point of view of belligerency it is quite unnecessary that the particular government for the time being need have any territory in its possession at all, and for that purpose, I wish to give you illustrations in history. Take Belgium in the last war and all the emgre Governments residing in London during the last but one war and the last war, what were those emigre Governments? Not an inch of territory which they could call their won at that time and yet who ventures to say before this Court that a member of the Dutch Army or for that matter the Polish or the French or the Yugoslavian Army may not fight to liberate its own country and not have the right to claim, even if they failed, all the rights and immunities as far as their soldiers are concerned of belligerencey. I think, Sirs, the last war has illustrated more than any other that some of these old principles may be overdone and that it is quite unneccessary in order that you may have a state of war, that country that is fighting a war on one side need not necessarily at that time have, what I may call in the common English parlance, a local habitation though it may have a name. Many of these emigre Governments were deprived of their territory and the fact that they were deprived of their territory temporarily, or the fact that the Indians were deprived of their territories for 150 years, makes, not the slightest difference to the point that we are submitting to the Court. What we submit to the Court is this. They were all liberating armies, trying to liberate their country and therefore were entitled to the immunities of those who were fighting. The next question before you, Sirs, is this. There is no such thing as the law of limitations in dealing with nations so that if either the Dutch or the French or anybody else was trying to fight for the liberation of their country while having lost their territory to the enemy, can it ever be argued in a British Court that those who were fighting to liberate their country were not fighting a struggle where they there entitled to the rights of belligerents. Supposing any one of them failed, is it to be said in a British Court that they were not fighting a struggle to which all the laws of immunities and privileges of a fighting army exist? I therefore urge upon you not to take the instance that you have before you as any different because we happen to be Indians. Remember that. They were trying to liberate their country. I am not here to espouse the cause of the Provisional Government. I am pleading for men who fought under the orders of their Government for the liberation of their own country. If therefore they were entitled to fight for their own county. Country for the purpose of liberating their country, I am centitled to tell this Court that they are entitled to hte privileges of belligerency. One more instance on which there was a certain amount of struggle in proving the facts is the case of the Maquis in France. Remember the facts. At the time when the Maquis were fighting, the *de facto* and the *de jure* Government in France was Marshal Petain's Goverrnment and the latter were allied witht Germany. The Maquis were fighting in order to release France from their own French Government which was allied with Germany, and what did Eisenhower say? I am going to read that to you because it is a very short document and it is very important. At that time it was apprehended that the Maquis might be dealt with unjustly by the then French Government, because it was the *de jure* Government of the time and would shoot as rebels, very much the same as the Advocate-General will later on argue to say about the persons who took part in the Indain National Army. But you have the Pronouncement of no less a person as Field Marshal Eisenhower that that shall not be. In other words, if persons with a view to liberate their Government fight against their own Govrnment, they are entitled to the rights of belligerents. That was the reason why I was very anxious that I should be able to prove that statement. Sirs, this is the statement which has been proved and I army incidentally agree to what my learned friend insisted upon That I should put in also the German view of the matter. If he prefers that it is his look-out. I do not. I prefer the American and the British view.

"There is conclusive evidence that the German forces in France are—(I am obliged to my honourable friend for saying that he does not doubt the authenticity of the source, meaning that it came from General Eisenhower. Of course, he insisted that I should put in the second passage and I leave it to you to judge which of the two you should prefer, with the submission that you should prefer Eisenhower to General Keitell.

"Now recruiting members of the French resistance group as France Tireurs and today an announcement from SHEAF in the name of General

Eisenhower makes these four points :

1. That the French forces of the interior constitute a combatant force commanded by General Koeniggaud forming an integral part of the Allied Expeditionary Force.
2. That the French Forces of the interior in the Maquis bear arms openly against the enemy and are instructed to observe the rules of war they are provided with a distinctive emblem and regarded by General Eisenhower as an Army under his command.
3. Reprisals against resistance groups violate the rules of war by which Germany is bound."

This is what I ask you to do : that anything done against the members of the Indian National Army fighting for their freedom according to the rules of war—I submit that any action taken against them is a breach of international law.

4. "Every effort will be made to trace the authors of any atrocities against members of the forces under General Eisenhower's command. Steps to this end are already being taken."

Then the rest reads :

"General Eisenhower in a declaration broadcast to the B.B.C. tried to legalise the French partisans as a fighting force ...."

The question that arose was somewhat delicate from a constitutional point of view, because for the time being the then French Government was still under the thumb of Germany. The people of France for the time being fighting against their Government which was pro-Germany were undoubtedly guilty of fighting against their won Government, but the ground of immunity accorded was that they were fighting alongside the allies for the purpose of freeing France. What is the distinction, I ask, between those who fought on the side of, even if we say Japan, for the purpose of freeing their own country? With very great respect it is difficult to understand any distinction. In other words, if the Maquis were entitled to all the privileges and immunities of a good fighting force for liberating their own country, I cannot see how you can fail to accord a similar treatment to those standing in the position of the Indian National Army.

Then, I read on:-

"General Eisenhower in a declaration broadcast by the B.B.C. tried to legalise the French partisans as a fighting force. From responsible circles in the Wilhelmstrasse the following statement has been given out :

"This attempt by the Allied High Command is unjustified. French partisans revolt against the legal French Government and violate the French laws, which enforce capital punishment for such violations."

Now you are asked solemnly to adopt what the Germans said in a similar situation. With what face could ever such an argument be presented to a British Court?

"The activities of the French partisans do not constitute regular war conduct ...."

(Precisely the kind of argument that is likely to be advanced).

"The activities of the partisans do not constitute regular war conduct but a malicious system of ambush fighting against the occupation power. Thus the partisans have forfeited the right to be treated as regular troops."

I submit that the view put forward by General Eisenhower is the more correct of the two. But the other view clearly shows what I have to establish before you in order to claim immunity, namely, that it is a regular organised army, fighting according to the laws of war, and not guilty of any personal atrocity beyond and outside merely fighting a regular war, and it is fortunate in this case, the first test of its kind, because the issue is neat. There is not even a charge of any personal atrocity. My submission to the Court is that the British, and I mean no empty compliment, civilised instinct has recognised that if a struggle for freedom is waged, then if it reaches a stage at which there is an organised Government and an organised army, it must be accorded all the rights, privileges and immunities of fighting army, and that is what I plead for.

The question which arises under Section 79 of the Indian Penal Code is that by all rules of civilised warfare what you claim for yourself you must accord to your opponents, even though you may have succeeded in defeating them. You are entitled to come to your own conclusion on the merits of the controversy at issue before you. But the Government says this:

"The policy of the Government of India is, however, that only these cases will be brought to trial where there are serious charges, apart from that of waging war against the King."

As I said it is not law and in no manner binds you. I must frankly confess that much, because it must not be said that I was trying to take refuge behind any executive statements. But the fact remains that behind that statement is almost a reluctant admission that waging war is in this case not an offence, or at least seriously treated as an offence. That is perfectly obvious, not because waging war per se not an offence, but because in the circumstances of the case, where, with an organised government and an organised army, a war was carried on, then waging that kind of war is not an offence. I am not denying that if ten individuals in India collected arms and began to fight the Government of India, waging war is not or would not be an offence. But what is meant is that waging war, meaning the prosecution of war in the circumstances of the case, namely, of the Indian National Army under the Provisional Government that is not an offence. But it is a matter which I want to be judged entirely on the merits of the legal and factual submissions which I have made.

The next issue which really, I submit, does not arise, but inasmuch as I have only one address before this Court I must try and anticipate things and answer them,—sometimes it is unjust to one's self, because one may raise more things than the opponent is likely to think of and I may make a present of an argument to him—but having regard to the rules of this Court, I am obliged to resort to that course—it cannot be helped; otherwise I should have preferred to have a short reply to any new point which may be raised by my learned friend on the other side. The short way to deal with the issue is this: the cases which I have cited and the authoritative works which I have quoted to the Court, clearly show that in judging this case, no question of allegiance arises. All insurgents, while they are fighting, are still held by allegiance, and all the books which I have read will be worth nothing if the question of allegiance had been raised,—because until you successfully throw it off, the *prima facie* allegiance, if I may so call it, exists; and nonetheless while it is not successfully thrown off, while it is in that ambulatory stage, the rights of fighting and the rights of war, if it is a properly declared war and a properly conducted war (I will not repeat that qualification again, you will assume it from me that when I talk of the rights of war, I am talking of a properly declared war and a properly prosecuted war as to which I have made my submission)—in such a case *ex hypothec* the allegiance exists. They want to throw off the foreign yoke, and the rest is that undoubtedly if the question of allegiance arose or had everyone's , no grant of immunity to insurgents fighting for liberty against the parent State would have ever arisen; but the fact remains that notwithstanding the fact of allegiance remaining , the right and freedom to liberate their own country being recognised at the same time, it is given effect to by recognising belligerency; that is to say, when an organised force is fighting under an organised government for its own freedom, while they have not completely succeeded and taken allegiance remains, they are still entitled to fight. That is recognised by the law of nations. But should such a question ever be raised by my learned friend—which I submit is irrelevant—I have important submissions to make. First, that on the events which took place at Farrar Park on 17th February, there was no allegiance left and hence it is very important that I try to concentrate my attention on what occurred at that meeting.

The fact, which probably may remain unnoticed, but which was most important, was that the British officers and British other ranks were separated from Indian officers and Indian ranks. It is an extremely important fact to remember, in order to be able to appreciate the events and the occurrences of that day. They having been separated, the Indian officers and ranks, numbering anything between 30,000 to 45,000, were all asked to assemble at Farrar Park —Colonel Hunt made a short statement or speech, saying that he was handing them over on behalf of the British Government to the representative of the Japanese Government, Colonel Fujiwara. Colonel Fujiwara then made a speech in Japanese which, as the evidence now show, was translated both in English and in Hindustani; and the statement of Col. Fujiwara amounted to this—using my own language—that those of the Indian prisoners of war who wanted to join an army for the purpose of liberation of their own country were free to do so, and handed them over to Captain Mohan Singh. Captain Mohan Singh then addressed them saying that he was prepared to organise the Indian National Army for the purpose of fighting for the liberation of India; and we had the evidence—uncontradicted—that he was acclaimed by the whole of the Indian prisoners of war present. I wish even at the risk of repetition to submit that when an insurgent fights against the then constituted government to free his own people and his own country from the alien, the question of allegiance does not arise. I want in that connection to take the statement of Captain Arshad —it is a most emphatic statement he made.

"We believed that the only allegiance we owe is allegiance to our country." I cannot describe better than in his words the result of that day's proceedings.

That brings me up to a somewhat difficult subject like the case of any subject people, in particular India. All of you are aware that every charge of treason in England is a charge of working against the King and the country. The last one is the reported case of John Amery. In the situation in which an Indian finds himself, the question is under what circumstances and to what extent this question of allegiance can be raised at all, because once you divide the King from the country, it becomes a very difficult issue altogether for any human being to decide, and hence I would prefer to rest my argument on the occurrences of 17th February. The position of an Indian in a case of this kind is difficult and I am going to submit to the Court on first principles what its true solution is. Where the King and the country coincide there is no question of an alternative. If you fight against the King and also fight against the interest of your own country, the question does not arise, but the question does arise where there is a fight for freedom, and I propose to read passages to show to what extent the world has progressed in the matter of the recognition of human rights. When you are nominally fighting against the King but really fighting to liberate the country, then the point is whether the question of allegiance can arise at all. Unless you sell your own soul, how can you ever say that when you are fighting to liberate your own country there is some other allegiance which prevents you from so doing. That means that if that happens there is nothing but permanent slavery.

Therefore, it is that I submit that in the circumstances of this case a choice was presented by the force of circumstances to those prisoners of war who were surrendered by Britain—I do not say wrongly—because there are reverses in the fortunes of war. Who am I to say whether it is rightly or wrongly done? At the same time you cannot disregard this most important fact that for the time being by reason of the exigencies of the war Britain found itself unable to give any protection to her soldiers to fight for the country and that being so, they found themselves in a very unenviable position. My learned friend may say : "you ought to have remained prisoners of war, and he may argue that they may do anything under the circumstances short of making war. I concede that proposition where allegiance to the King and country coincide, but where the two do not coincide, a different situation arises altogether. My learned friend may say that they were fighting on behalf of a puppet Government or they allowed themselves to be used as stooges of the Japanese. Even accepting this somewhat unenviable expression of stooges or otherwise, the question is one of fact, namely, whether or not it was a regular army honestly believing that it is fighting for the freedom of its country. The question of a bad name that may be given has really no relevancy to the legal issue by inasmuch as a great deal of dirt has been thrown by expressions of this character—puppet Government and puppet army and words to that effect—and the question of the strength of—that army may be raised, it is my duty to tell the Court how the evidence stands on record. The evidence that stands on record is that the No. 1. I.N.A. was formed and was dissolved in December. I shall forget that for the purposes of this case, because waging war which is the subject of the argument applies to what you might call I.N.A. No. 2. I have attempted to prove that I have established that the I.N.A., though small in numbers, was fighting as allies of the Japanese Army and there is no ignominy in admitting that or in doing that, because the objective at that time of both the armies was undoubtedly to free India from Britain. The objective was no more and no less than that of the allies in fighting to free France or Belgium or any other country, and if in that process there was a unified command or a single strategy, you, Sirs, will not say with your knowledge of military affairs that makes one army the stooge of the other. It is a phrase with which my learned friend will not be able to walk away if he uses it, and that is why I want to tie his legs, if I can. If the British and the American armies fought under the command of General Eisenhower, Britain may not be called the stooge of the Americans, and I hope my learned friend will not descend to the level of calling the I.N.A stooges of the Japanese. The evidence given by Lt. Nag is very important from this point of view. He was extremely prolific in the results and he came to prove at the instance of the prosecution that there was a very organised regular army, and that a big war was fought. My submission is that he was hoisted with his own petard. If he proved that a regular war was fought that is precisely my defence. He was qualified to speak about it. He was legal adviser of the I.N.A. and he told this court in effect—I am quoting his words —that the two armies fought as Allies. Whether the alliance was right or wrong is not before this Court. The only thing that is before this Court is whether or not this army fought as an organised army. My learned friend will not be able to support any allegation that they fought for any other objective except the liberation of India. If an allegation of that kind is made, it is a false allegation, and we have given a complete lie to it. The prosecution witnesses from beginning to end admitted that the object of the I.N.A. was to fight for the liberation of India, and everyone, whether volunteer or non-volunteer, willing or unwilling, has admitted that they had no other objective except the liberation of their own country. That being so, my submission to the Court is that in so far as any allegation is made to the contrary it is only put forward as a point of prejudice, and I had to meet it with a view to remove the prejudice, because as I said it is not in human hands to choose your allies under the circumstances which may be forced upon you. And whether you fight with the aid of X, Y or Z for the purpose of liberation of your own country, the fact that Y was otherwise a bad person has got nothing to do with the case. But in all human discussions there is always an argument at a tangent; many human minds confuse the issue, and hence it is that I have attempted to cross-examine, at all events in the briefest possible way, to make this point clear. The point that I tried to bring out was that the I.N.A. was, though small, a very organised army, inspired by the best of motives, and fought for that purpose, though unsuccessful for the time being.

There is one other thing which I ought to have mentioned and I regret I omitted it while I was talking on the first issue. That was with reference to the Minister sent by Japan to the Government of Azad Hind. I ought to have stated earlier, because the points which I have mentioned were proclamation, recognition, declaration of war, followed by possession of territory, and also the Minister of the Nippon Government accredited to this Government. The last is not essential, but still in point of fact it was alleged, and I will state how the facts stand under that head. The fact is that a Minister was sent in fact. No less a person than Mr. Sawada of the Foreign Office told the Court that it was decided to send a Minister to the Provisional Government of Azad Hind, while he was the Vice-Foreign Minister and he was competent to speak about their decision that a Minister in fact was sent. As it happened he came without letters of credit or his credentials, and as if it mattered the whole argument was to show that a Minister ceases to exist because he did not bring the papers. Supposing one of you, Sirs, sent me your agent, and I choose not to demand from him his letter of authority and I accept him, it is a most extraordinary argument that the agent ceases to exist. That is a sort of logic which my learned friend wishes to apply to this case. But a good reason was given founded on diplomatic practice which you should accept. The evidence says that being a Provisional Government, in accordance with the dignity of nations, or comity of nations, no credentials are required. In other words, the important point is whether the man came and was recognized by the person for whom he was intended. During the evidence, my learned friend got an answer from one of the witnesses to the effect that the head of the State, Netaji Subhas Chandra Bose, did not receive him. But there is further evidence which really destroys any other points on this question : Thereafter credentials were asked for, the head of the State according to his conception required it, and you have the evidence that credentials were prepared and that they were signed by the Japanese Emperor and were despatched but the then conditions of war they did not reach. But because the Japanese Minister was duly accredited I submit it is a reinforcing argument in my favour. When he came, the two Governments—meaning the Provisional Government of Azad Hind and the Japanese Government-took a different view of what you may call diplomatic practice, but that does not affect the issue. The sending Government in the end, when so required, actually sent letters of credit, and the fact that it reached or did not reach does not affect the issue: at all events it completely cured such defect or deficiency as there was in the procedure. And in point of fact I ask the Court to hold that there was a duly appointed Minister, which is all that arises here. The reason why we brought in the evidence was among other things that the Provisional Government of Azad Hind was a properly organized Government, and accepted, and the acceptance does not require necessarily the sending of an envoy, or an ambassador, or a Minister, or whatever the position or the relation between the Governments may be.

What is it that the I.N.A. embarked upon in collaboration with the Japanese? According to their agreement which I submit I have proved, any part of Indian territory which may be liberated would be immediately. handed over to the I.N.A. If you, as men of affairs, understand things rightly, it is the only thing to do. Where is the question of being an instrument. If, however, there was any instrument, it was the Japanese, because it is they who wee assisting in liberating India, with a view that the liberated parts of India would be handed back to the I.N.A. The facts of the case are that two proclamations were issued by the representatives of both the Governments—Gen. Kewabe on behalf of the Japanese Government and Mr. Subhas Chandra Bose on behalf of his Government. You may say nobody fights a philanthropic war. But whether or not it was philanthropic remains to be seen. I can well understand, and I submit it for your consideration, that Japan, as indeed one of the witnesses said, that the East would be better protected by a free India or that they might have better prospects of trade which is their only means of maintaining their standard of life, which incidentally is also the means of Britain. It was not a philanthropic war at all. So far as the freedom of India was concerned, it was, I submit, the object of that war, and you have it in evidence on oath before the Court. It may well be, I presume it was, that a free India might better be able to assist by means of trade and otherwise to enable the Japanese to maintain their high standard of life. Therefore, it is idle, unless people appreciate the true issue for them, to say that unless you conquered territory there can be no other object in assisting in getting its freedom. It is that idle argument which I wish to meet before this Court. But we are not left to speculation. My learned friend cross-examined one of the witnesses. He said, Oh yes, you are assisting the Indian National Army with a view to attain your Japanese war aims, and he thought he had got away with it. But when we asked what were the war aims, then I am afraid all this cross-examination fell to the ground. He said it was with a view to assist war aims which was to free India. There may be many who doubt promises in this country but I am not one of them. I am one who looks on the brighter side of life and believes that if India could be freed in that way, why honest men should not believe it, it is difficult to understand. The question before the Court shortly is this. What were the relations between the I.N.A. and the Japanese Army. That is the short point. It is a point of prejudice and yet it is my duty in defence of the honour of those whom I am defending and the group to which they belong that they were not the stooges of the Japanese, as cheaply might be said by the opponents. That is the short history of the position of the I.N.A. vis-a-vis the Japanese Army. I was speaking about the quality of allegiance, and I submitted to the Court that in a case of this kind where you have got to administer the law as a matter of justice, equity and good conscience, you may have a case where the country and the King do not coincide and where there is an imposed allegiance on a subject people; and I am not talking merely as a matter of theory. I am going to give you an instance of a case of this kind which has occurred in the days when the British Commonwealth was called the British Empire; and the statement that I wish to read is the Declaration of Independence by the United States of America on the Declaration of war and before they had attained any statehood, as it is called in the cases which I have given. I am reading from a book called "Speeches and Documents on Colonial Policy", edited by Keith and published by the Oxford University Press in London. It is at page 70. It says :

"When in the course of human events, it becomes necessary for one people to dissolve the political bonds which have connected them with another, and to assume, among the powers of the earth the separate and equal station to which the laws of nature and of nature's God entitled them, a decent respect to the opinions of mankind requires that they should declare the causes which impel them to the separation.

We hold these truths to be self-evident, that all men are created equal, that they are endowed by their Creator with certain inalienable rights; that among these are life, liberty, and the pursuit of happiness"—(and here I would like to point out that the recent pronouncement of Mr. Truman and of Mr. Churchill are to the same effect)—

"that, to secure these rights, governments are instituted among men, deriving their just powers from the consent of the governed, that, whenever any form of government becomes destructive of these ends, it is the rights of the people to alter or to abolish it, and to institute new government, laying its foundation on such principles, and organizing its powers in such form, as to them shall seem most likely to effect their safety and happiness. Prudence, indeed, will dictate that governments long established should not be changed for light and transient causes; and accordingly all experience hath shown, that mankind are more disposed to suffer while evils are sufferable, than to right themselves by abolishing the forms to which they are accustomed. But, when a long train of abuses and usurpations, pursuing invariably the same object, evinces a sign to reduce them under absolute despotism, it is their right, it is their duty, to throw off such government and to provide new guards for their future security. Such has been the patient sufferance of these colonies, and such is now the necessity which constrains them to alter their former systems of government. The history of the present King of Great Britain is a history of repeated injuries and usurpations, all having, in direct object, the establishment of an absolute tyranny over these estates. To prove this, let facts be submitted to a candid world:"

(Then they cite the grievances—I will not read them at all). Then the statement says :

"Nor have we been wanting in attention to our British brethren. We have warned them, from time to time, of attempts made by their legislature to extend an unwarrantable jurisdiction over us. We have reminded them of the circumstances of our emigration and settlement here. We have appealed to their native justice and magnanimity, and we have conjured them, by the ties of our common kindred, to disavow these usurpations, which would inevitably interrupt our connections and correspondence. They too have been deaf to the voice of justice and of consanguinity. We must, therefore, acquiesce in the necessity which denounces our separation, and hold them, as we hold the rest of mankind, enemies in war,—in peace, friends. We, therefore, the representatives of the United States of America, in General Congress assembled, appealing to the Supreme Judge of the World for the rectitude of our intentions, do, in the name and by the authority of the good people of these colonies, solemnly, publish and declare"—(and this is the point)—"That these United Colonies are, and of right ought to be, Free and Independent States;"—(and then comes the important sentence)—"That they are absolved from all allegiance to the British Crown, and that all political connection between them and the State of Great Britain is, and ought to be, totally dissolved; and that, as Free and Independent States they have full power to levy war, include peace, contract alliances. Establish commerce, and to do all other acts and things which Independent States may of right do. And for the support of this declaration, with a firm reliance on the protection of Divine Providence, we mutually pledge to each other, our lives, our fortunes and our sacred honour."

Here you have a case in which this quality of allegiance came to a test. They owed allegiance in the familiar sense to the King of England. They owed allegiance to their own country, and they realised that the time had arrived when the question became one of conflict between the allegiance to the King and the allegiance to the country. So that in accepted history, we have got a classical instance of a case where the choice between allegiance to the King and the allegiance to the country was presented to the world, and men of honour chose allegiance to their own country to the imposed allegiance to a foreign king. Therefore I venture to stand before this Court today with the most classical illustration, the illustration of a race, of a country, that has saved the world today, and in the last war and did marvels in the cause of civilization; and if that illustration is not going to be respected, I submit justice would be denied completely. I submit that what happened at Farrar Park, by reason of the actual state of events in this country, was perfectly legitimate, and indeed legitimised by what I may call the course of history. Indeed it is amazing how from the year 1776 to today the words are as true as they were then :

"We hold these truths to be self-evident that all men are created equal, that they are endowed by their Creator with certain unalienable rights; that among these are life, liberty, and the pursuit of happiness."

And I commend this to you, Sirs, in order that you in your wisdom will consider it just, if ever any question arises. This declaration took place on the 4th July, 1776; and ultimately a war was fought, which resulted in 1781 in establishing what is today the United States of America as an independent republic of the world. I venture to submit this a historical instance, important in its character, valuable as showing the way in which the world has functioned. I want to call attention to the oath of allegiance to the Provisional Government of Azad Hind and its context, for it is important that you should know it.

"Indians in East Asia today are not more the subjects of an alien power; they are the proud citizens of the Provisional Government of Azad Hind. To bring this home to the mind of every Indian in Malaya and to rouse our community to a full realisation of the responsibilities of the new status, it has been decided to ask each member of the Indian Independence League to take an oath of allegiance to the Provisional Government of Azad Hind. Detailed directions regarding this have already been sent to all the State branches along with the form of the oath. Each member, on taking the oath, will be given 'oath of allegiance card', and the "Indian Independence League membership card " he or she now holds will be taken back by the officer administering the oath and destroyed. The privilege of owing allegiance to our government will be extended only to members of the Indian Independence League as any Indian who is not a member of the League cannot be considered as a true Indian. As Netaji said in his speech in Syonan on 25th October 'we will not treat them as Indians or friends. There is no place for them in India."

What I wish to point out is that in so far as these documents are concerned they evince the same interest as was evinced by those who issued the Proclamation of Independence of the United States of America.

The next point to which I wish to call attention in this context is the law of treason with reference to India. So far as India is concerned, it is a loose expresssion. The whole of the law on this subject has been codified in the Indian Panal Code and I call attention to Chapter VI of the Indian Penal Code—Offences against the State. There you find codified what is the law of treason in other countries. Section 121 is waging or attempting to wage war against the Queen, 121A is conspiracy to commit offences punishable by 121,122 is collecting arms; 123 is concealing with intent to facilitate design to wage war; 124 is assaulting Governor-General, etc., 124A is sedition; 125 is waging war against any Asiatic power in alliance with the Queen, 126 is committing depredation on territories of a power at peace with the Queen; and 127 is receiving property taken by war or depredation mentioned in Sections 125 and 126; 128 is public servant voluntarily allowing prisoner of State or war to escape; 129 refers to a public servant negligently suffering such prisoner to escape. These are the offences against the State.

My submission to the Court is this. In so far as the question of the law of treason is concerned in this country, my learned friend cannot talk of treason. For what would be called treason in the common law of England, my learned friend would have to look to the language of Chapter VI of the Indian Penal Code. In other words my submission to the Court is this—that generally speaking, apart from Section 121, my learned friend will not and has no right to resort to what he calls the principles of treason.

The next point to which I shall call attention is a classic book on the Law of England written in the old English. I have got a transcript of it here. It is on page 95:-

When a nation has placed itself under the protection of another that is more powerful, or has even entered into subjection to it with a view to receiving its protection—if the latter does not effectually protect the other in case of need, it is manifest that, by failing in its engagements, it loses all the rights it had acquired by the convention, and that the other being disengaged from the obligation it had contracted, re-enters into the possession of all its rights, and recovers its independence or its liberty. It is to be observed that this takes place even in cases where the protector does not fail in his engagements through a want of good faith but merely through inability. For the weaker nation having submitted only for the sake of obtaining protection—if the other proves unable to fulfil that essential condition, the compact is dissolved—the weaker resumes its right, and may, if it thinks proper, have recourse to a more effectual protection. Thus the Dukes of Austria, who had acquired a right of protection and in some sort a sovereignty over the City of Lucerne being unwilling or unable to protect it effectually, that city concluded an alliance with the three first cantons; and the Dukes having carried their complaint to the Emperor, the inhabitants of Lucerne replied "that they had used the natural right common to all men by which everyone is permitted to endeavour to procure his own safety when he is abandoned by those who are obliged to grant him assistance."

This is the law which has been enunciated and accepted in England ever since. This was in 1797.

My submission is that the insurgents are in the position of rebles up to a stage, but a stage is reached where if the State has an organised army it becomes possessed of the right of belligerency, even though they may ultimately fail. The question of allegiance does not arise then, but I would not be surprised if with a view to divert the discussion into a wrong channel any such statement is made.

Before I go further, I wish to make quite clear a point about the prisoners of war. The prisoners of war may submit even to the extent of assisting the enemy—that is passive assistance up to the point of labour. You will find in the same books that they may not actually join the enemy and in this connection I wish to submit to the Court what was the relation of the I.N.A. to the Japanese. You belong to the profession of arms and will appreciate what I am submitting to you. I have stated the position as much against myself as possible. I am now assuming the events which took place at Farrar Park did not take place. I am assuming against myself that they were just prisoners of war. The question still remains what it is that they did. The question arises whether they ever allowed themselves to be used as what I might call tools of the enemy or any other instruments, whatever the phrase used. Having been surrendered as prisoners of war, if the Japanese chose to leave the Indians to secure their liberty—I am willing to agree that it suited them—that by itself does not bring the I.N.A. and the accused before us within the prohibition imposed upon the prisoners of war. It is a point that I wish to elaborate up to a stage. I wish to state that there is no obligation whatever which prevents a person who is a prisoner of war from fighting on his own for the liberty of his own country. I submit that my learned friend will not be able to controvert that, and therefore I wish to make it quite plain that the question of the relation between the Japanese Army and the I.N.A., the question of the Objective of the Japanese Army and the I.N.A., the question of the objective of the

Japanese as regards India—these points have got to be re-emphasized before this Court. Unless they are borne in mind, the Court may easily go into a wrong track.

The point is this. I quite agree that the Court or any member of it may say: "They were fools in believing the Japanese". That has nothing to do with the case. Other men may have been wiser. The question is whether those who formed the I.N.A. did believe in a *bona fide* manner that they would be able to secure the freedom of the country. If they *bona fide* believed it, the fact that there are wiser men on earth does not alter the issue so far as the renouncement of the guilt of that army fighting for the liberation of India is concerned. Hence it is that I wish to submit that the evidence which I submitted yesterday and a few more passages to which I wish to call attention today is relevant for that purpose. You have it in evidence and it is a matter again in which the question is of one's own belief. The question is not whether that belief was something which probably the Court or any member of it may think was of very credulous people. That has nothing to do with the point. You have it definitely in evidence before this Court, in the evidence of prosecution witnesses, that if any nation or any race or any class came into being to oppose the independence of India, they were prepared to fight that, including the Japanese. That is why I was very anxious to point out that it is only when a story is completely pieced up and comes before the Court that its significance can be appreciated. The whole point of it is that the question is not so much as to whether you or I or anybody else would have relied upon it as a promise. From that point of view probably we are a credulous race. We have relied on many promises of others and of Japanese also. But that has nothing to do with the point. The point is that if these people honestly believed, as I say they did, that they were securing the independence of India, then the question of what a prisoner of war cannot do, does not actually arise and will not arise.

In this connection I would like to read the evidence of Nag. The question that I put to him was: Do you remember ever attending a meeting in Singapore at which Capt. Mohan Singh told the prisoners of war that if need be they would fight the Japanese in addition to the British? He said he would fight anybody who stood in his way even if it were the Japanese or anybody else. The next is P.W. 9 Havildar Sucha Singh, and this is the passage to which I wish to refer: "He said that the I.N.A. has already been started in Singapore and a good many people had joined it; and the I.N.A. will only fight for the freedom of India and for no other cause. If we go to India the Japanese go with us, we are equipped with arms, and we will fight the Japanese if they turn round against us. This is a golden chance for us and we may not get such a chance again." The next witness is P.W. 18. He said: "After I was posted to Bose Brigade, Captain Shah Nawaz Khan delivered a lecture which I heard. He said that the Bose Brigade which was formed was to go first of all to the front, and this Brigade is composed of picked officers and men." And then the passage goes on: "He also said that if and when we fight with our allies the Japanese nations, it should not happen that we remain as second rate in the fight and thus disgrace our nation. When we reach India we shall meet Indian men and women, and those who are elders to us we should consider them as mothers and those who are younger we should consider them as our daughters and sisters, and if anybody will not obey these instructions he will be shot dead; and if and when India is freed and the Japanese who are now helping us tried to subdue us, we shall even fight them. He also said that even now if a Japanese gives you one slap, you should give him three in return, because our Government is parallel to their Japanese Government, and we are in no way subservient to them, and that when we reach India, if we notice any Japanese maltreating an Indian lady he should be first warned by word of mouth not to do so, but if he continued to do so, we were at liberty to use force and even shoot him in order to prevent it, because the fight which we are making now is for the freedom and well-being of India and not for the benefit of the Japanese. This lecture was delivered in Taiping." Then, I come to P.W. 19. He said : "I was aware of the declaration of the Provisional Government of Free India. Prior to my joining the I.N.A. I was in a prisoner of war camp." Then I came to the other passage which is relevant for the purpose. "I knew after joining the army that the sole ambition of the I.N.A. was to fight for the freedom of India against any army in the world, but my own idea was not to fight but escape. By 'any army in the world' is meant also the Japanese." Then I come to P.W. 24. He said : "In August 1943 I was in Neesoon Camp. Captain Shah Nawaz came to address the Heavy Gun Battalion there. He said that the I.N.A. had been formed for the liberation of India and it would fight not only British Imperialism but also those would put obstacles in the way of India's freedom or any other party which wished to subjugate India."

I had hitherto avoided reading any evidence because there was no substantial contest as to the facts which have been proved. The record of evidence clearly shows that in so far as the I.N.A. was concerned, they acted on their own. No doubt, they accepted the alliance with Japan on promises which they, at all events, honestly and sincerely believed, and if they believed them, I submit there can be no question of any obligation.

There are so many matters which have been gone into and which in patience we suffered in the belief that there was no relevancy to the charges before the Court. But now that they are before the Court, I must separate them as best as I can and, while separating them, give answer to every single suggestion that was made or is likely to be made. Hence it is that I am here before the Court to point out that in doing what the I.N.A. did, there was no question of any breach of any obligation or the prisoner of war obligations or duties, remembering the extreme obligation, which, I submit, I have stated as strongly against myself as it is possible to do.

The next point to which I wish to call attention is this. In addition, there is the evidence of the last witness, P.W.12, and that sets out more or less fully the point of view of those who honestly believed in doing what they did. I am not saying that the Court is not called upon to examine the matter in its own light. At the same time, the Court has got to see not so much what any individual member might have done as that whether you believe what they said before this Court and that was their object.

This witness said: "My reasons for joining I.N.A. were many. I admit that it was a difficult question to decide whether I should join the I.N.A. or not, because there were many factors which I had to consider. It was a momentous decision. Uptil that time I was not greatly interested in politics or the political welfare of India because I was educated that way, and moreover when I joined the Indian Army in 1936, I felt that politics was not encouraged in the Indian Army and hence I stayed away, but when the question of I.N.A. arose and we had to decide whether we should join it or not, I had to think deep, but it was such a big question that I could not make a decision myself."

The reason why I am reading this to the Court is this. He was a witness of truth and the very fact that they had a conflict in their minds is illustrative of the extreme *bonafides* of the men who chose to take the course which they did. Hence it is that I shall read a few more lines of that evidence: "I remember sometime in the beginning of July 1942, when we were being asked whether we were going to volunteer for the I.N.A. or not, I was staying at Mount Pleasant, Singapore, where Capt. Mohan Singh had his Headquarters. I know Capt. Sahgal for the last 12 or 13 years; we were in College together and we were friends there. I felt that if I had a discussion with him along with a few other officers, we may come to some decision regarding volunteering for the I.N.A. So in the beginning of July, he and two or three other officers came to my bungalow at Mount Pleasant and we went through this question of joining the I.N.A. We discussed all the pros and cons. We unanimously decided that under the circumstances we all owed our allegiance to our country.

"We also felt and agreed upon that so far concerning our career in the Indian Army, there had been distinctions between the British Officers and the Indian Commissioned Officers. The Indian Commissioned Officers had not been treated as well as our English comrades or brother officers. We also felt that if the senior officers present in Singapore or in Malaya did not join the I.N.A., it was quite possible that the Japanese would exploit the Indian prisoners of war, because then the Indian prisoners of war would be split up into small groups. Some people would join and some would not, and the Japanese would take advantage of that and enrole people from amongst the prisoners of war who would be willing to do any service for them. We felt that that would be a disgrace to Indians. We agreed that if the senior officers joined the I.N.A. and formed a strong party and organised the I.N.A. as a regular army and fought the Japanese on every point regarding the army, we would have a far stronger position with the Japanese than otherwise. We also felt that if we created an army of our own, we may be able to establish a certain amount of standing with the Japanese, and by doing that we may be able to stop the Japanese from committing any atrocities on the Indians in Malaya. We had seen what the Japanese were doing to the Chinese and Anglo-Indians and the Malayans. They were not treating them very well. Certain atrocities had been committed on the Chinese and also on the Eurasian community, and we thought that if the Indians refused to join the I.N.A., it was quite possible that the whole of the Indian community in Singapore or in Malaya might suffer. So we had a discussion on all these points. But then arose the question that if we did join the Indian National Army, what would be the reaction of our people in India?"

My suggestion to the Court is this that, apart from the process, the thought which the last witness brought to bear upon it and the discussions which he had with other people, clearly show that they did not take the steps either dishonestly or hastily. They took this step after taking into account the whole of the situation in existence at that time, and the future as they saw it.

And if that is the condition in which they did it, I ask the Court to hold that they honestly believed in the propriety of the step they took and the justice of the cause for which they took it. And hence it is that I wish to point out to the Court that it was not a case, as the text-books say, of a prisoner of war joining the enemy in order to fight his battle. That, I quite agree, according to the text-books, he may not do. But where a prisoner of war already of war released, as I have told you earlier, finds himself in the situation in which he did and then fights for himself and for his own country, being prepared to fight against the Japanese themselves if they ever became untrue to them, in such circumstances, I submit, there was no question and there could be no question of the Indian National Army being guilty and of those who joined that army being guilty of any act which may be regarded as contrary even to what you may call the code of duties imposed upon a prisoner of war. I have already submitted and at the risk of repetition I will say, that it is entirely irrelevant and there is no such thing as a charge against these men before you of a breach of duty as prisoners of war. In fact there is no such charge in the Indian Penal Code, so far as I can see. There may be a charge under the Indian Army Act but no such charge is at present before you. There is not even a charge of desertion and indeed there cannot be, for when the prisoners of war were surrendered there was no occasion for desertion. So let us not be carried away by what you may call the popular language of desertion, breach of duty and all the rest of it. Let us concentrate, and I ask the Court so to do, on the charge on which the accused are on trial before the Court, and on that only. The rest is a matter of prejudice; and if one has a complete answer even on a matter of prejudice, it is a matter of satisfaction. It is a matter which I understand—and I appreciate— that tribunals of this kind are likely to take account of, namely, that general *bonafide,* honestly and integrity all goes to the credit of individuals who are on trial as so much in their favour.

Then, Sir, there is one piece of evidence in so far as this particular matter is concerned, a piece of evidence of extreme importance, and that is how the first I.N.A. broke up. As to how it broke up you have evidence before the Court and it is unanimous as to the reasons for which that event occurred. Rash Behari Bose was for many years in Japan and he was too easily inclined—to put it most mildly—to believe in the Japanese. Mohan Singh on the other hand was very cautious. Mohan Singh in fact has himself evinced by his conduct that should anything happen to him, that is to say, if he is arrested or removed, the army should be dissolved. And the real reason is this, that while on the one hand Mohan Singh was anxious that there should be an army formed for the liberation of India, at the same time he was equally anxious that the army should not serve as a mere instrument of Japan. And it is because he had his suspicions, is because—of the Resolutions in the Bangkok Conference with regard to making clear the aims of the Japanese for the purpose of fighting the war so far as India was concerned—that Mohan Singh began to lose faith in the promises of the Japanese. And as soon as the Japanese realised that through the agency of Rash Behari Bose—and you have picturesque evidence here—Rash Behari Bose came along, collected all the senior officers and declared that Mohan Singh had been removed. I could not quite appreciate, with all the throught that I devoted to it, the point that my learned friend made or attempted to make as to whether he was actually removed by Rash Behari Bose or by the Japanese. For my own part I do not mind the suggestion that my learned friend made that the Japanese arrested him. That is precisely the point, that the first I.N.A. was at a stage at which there was a trial of strength between those Indian National Army and those who were likely or wanting to join it were not prepared to become tools in their hands, that there was a break, and hence when you come to the second I.N.A., when Subhas Chandre Bose took command of the Indian National Army, the second time you find an association between the two armies—may be very unwilling on the part of the Japanese. Very often one has to make a choice when one finds strong man on the otherside; and hence it is that I wish to insist before this Court that throughout the dealings between the I.N.A. and the Head of the Provisional Government of Free India at the time, the position taken up by them was not an instrument of the Japanese, but a body formed with the object of liberating themselves, no doubt getting all the assistance that they could from the Japanese as an allied army. And that, I submit, is the key to the *bonafide* of the belief of every individual man who at all events thinkingly—if I may use that expression—joined the I.N.A. I dare say it often happens in the world that once you find a thinking and leading man taking a course, other people *bonafide* believe it to be the true course and join it. Therefore I submit there is ample evidence on record, evidence emanating from witnesses which in ordinary courts and tribunals is the best to be relied upon by the defence, evidence from prosecution witnesses, not all willingly given, that they fought their own ground, they fought their own cause, and therefore there was no question whatsoever of their breaking any duties which they owed as prisoners of war. But you have to remember to all the time and again and again that there is no such charge in the trial before you. There are only two charges before you which I need not repeat. But I want to be quite careful because it will be my duty to deal with the material, lest it might be suggested that I did not deal with it, and I wish to point out its relevancy and its significance to the extent to which these points bear on the conduct of the men on trial before you. I have no desire to shirk an inquiry; in fact I am here as far as I can—apart from any question of private opinions on political issues—to impress upon you the truth, integrity and sincerity of men, which after all is a bigger asset sometimes than the legal technical issue. There is also the evidence of Lt.-Col. Loganadan, D.W.7 with reference to the question; and I am obliged to refer to it particularly because of the pamphlet called " Our Struggle" which was placed before you. There is just one point which I must make before I read the evidence, that all that is proved is that the pamphlet was issued. But I hope and trust that my learned friend will not suggest that the mere fact that a pamphlet is issued, that by itself proves the truth of the statements made therein. Let me therefore begin by saying that I am not obliged to explain why Rash Behari Bose said what he did. It will be an error on the part of the Court to say that because Rash Behari Bose said something about Mohan Singh, therefore it is true. At the same time I wish to call attention to this evidence with a view of pointing out the terms on which Mohan Singh and Rash Behari Bose stood, with a view to point out that any allegations emanating from the disappointed Rash Behari Bose at that time are not to be taken as words of truth. Secondly, in any case an allegation made by A against B, neither of whom has appeared in Court as a witness, is no proof of the allegation made by him.

With this observation I now call attention to the evidence of D.W.7 (Lt.-Col. Loganadan).

"I know Captain Mohan Singh. When I joined the Indian National Army, he was G.O.C. The relations between Captain Mohan Singh and Rash Behari Bose were not very happy. Of my own personal knowledge I knew that Rash Behari Bose, having lived so long with the Japanese, was inclined to be guided and controlled by them. Whereas Mohan Singh said he felt that the Japanese should be dealt with a firmer hand than what Rash Behari would be able to do."

I then come to P. W.12 (Captain Arshad). The passage to which I call attention is this:-

" I was in the first Indian National Army Headquarters, they as General Staff Office in 'G' Branch. The first I.N.A. was dissolved in December 1942. The I.N.A. had been raised after the Bangkok resolutions were forwarded for ratification to the Japanese Government. The Bangkok resolutions were the result of a Conference held in Bangkok in June. There were many resolutions in that and they were passed by the Conference and then sent to the Japanese Government for ratification, and we hoped that the ratification would come quickly; but as the days went by, Captain Mohan Singh, who was then G. O. C. of the Indian National Army, felt that the Japanese were delaying the ratification of the Bangkok resolutions and he asked the Japanese liaison body which was attached to us, called the Iwakuru Kikan to expedite the ratification of the resolutions. They were not very clear in their replies. They tried to delay them as much as possible. I was present. Captain Mohan Singh kept his Headquarters informed of all the correspondence and the arguments which he was having with the Japanese. Captain Mohan Singh told us his doubts of the intentions of the Japanese. He said that he noticed that the Japanese were not playing the game, and he said that if the Japanese continued with that attitude of theirs he would dissolve the Indians National Army, and we all agreed with him because we felt that unless and until there was a clear understanding between the I.N.A. and the Japanese we would not continue the Indian National Army. Besides that, there was another main point of dissension between the Japanese and Captain Mohan Singh. At the Farrar Park meeting the Japanese had handed over all the Indian prisoners of war to Captain Mohan Singh. Until that time the members of the I.N.A. as well as those prisoners of war who had not joined the I.N.A. were under the command of Captain Mohan Singh. But in December the Japanese wanted to take those people away from Captain Mohan Singh who had not joined the I.N.A. Captain Mohan Singh felt that the Japanese were not keeping to their word and he refused to part with the prisoners of war. These main reasons as well as the other minor reasons forced us to dissolve the I.N.A.

And, Sir, the Bangkok Resolution No.13 which is referred to, reads thus :

"(13) Resolved that the Indian National Army shall be made use of only.

(a) For operations against the British or other foreign powers in India.

(b) For the purpose of securing and safeguarding Indian National Independence, and

(c) For such other purpose as may assist the achievement of the object, viz., Indian Independence."

Lt. Nag (P.W.1) refers to the same subject in these terms :

"Capt. Mohan Singh left written instructions that if he was arrested, the I.N.A. should be dissolved. 'In the event of my arrest the I.N.A. will be dissolved and all the I.N.A. badges of rank and records will be destroyed.' There was a general feeling from the beginning that the I.N.A. should not be subordinated to the Japanese and that we would not allow it to be subordinated to the Japanese. There was no question of dissolving it at any time during those days. The predominant motive was to free India for the sake of Indians.

"After the 2nd I.N.A. was formed the same feeling was there, untill Subhas Chandra Bose arrived in July 1943. After that everybody thought that they had got a leader who could guide them on proper lines without being subordinated to the Japanese. Thereafter the two armies fought as Allies, i.e., the Indian National Army and, the Japanese."

This, Sir, is the evidence which has been placed before this Court. As I said, my submission before the Court is that it was when the I.N.A., which was formed on the second occasion, felt confident that they would not be subordinated to the Japanese that they really fought as Allies. And hence it is that I submit to the Court that in so far as relations between the I.N.A. and the Japanese Army were concerned, it has been established by evidence that they were of the character which I claim for them, namely as allies. So far as the I.N.A. was concerned, it was actuated by only motive and one business, and that was to secure the freedom of India. That is the issue, which as I have said, does not actually arise, but was bearing on the integrity of purpose of those who are on trial as members of the Indian National Army.

Then the next point of which I wish to call attention is the evidence before the Court that the Indian National Army was completely officered by Indian officers. True, an attempt was made by my learned friend in cross-examination as to the question of the High Command. I do not deny for a moment, though I do not understand or profess to understand very much the organisation of armies when they fight together for apparently the same purpose in any case, but knowing what you do about the last but one war and the last war, when any question arises of unified command it serves very little purpose to suggest that in so far as the higher strategy is concerned, it was no doubt in the hands of the Japanese. No doubt probably they claimed at all events that they understood the art of war better, and that after all the Indian National Army consisted of men of not that standing. But apart from accepting better judgment on what should be the proper strategy, when it came to a question of internal administration of the I.N.A., it has been amply proved before the Court that the I.N.A. was entirely independent in its composition, including every officer. The evidence of Lt. Nag is in these terms:

"The whole of the Indian National Army was trained by Indian Officers and not by the Japanese. It was entirely and throughout officered by Indian officers and not by Japanese officers.

The colours of the Indian National Army were the Indian National Congress colours, i.e., saffron, white and green. Their badges were distinct from the Japanese badges."

And then he answered other questions which are immaterial, namely, that among the colours in the middle of one of the badges there was a brown star and it was resented by the personnel of the I.N.A. as it might be mistaken for the Rising Sun.

P. W. 19 gave the following evidence:

"So far as I am concerned, I took instructions from our own Indian officer a only and not from the Japanese. As far as I am aware, there were no Japanese in command in our area or otherwise in the I.N.A. I was Assistant to Lt. Abdur Rehman who was left in charge of the rations at Falam. There was a long carry of 48 miles for rations. The rations consisted of rice, salt, oil and sugar. Sugar was very scarce. The rations were very short consisting of rice, salt and a little oil. The Indian National Army was fighting under great hardship on that front. Whilst I was in the I.N.A., I carried out my duties faithfully."

The next point which I wish to make is that apart from what you may call the general higher strategy, the Indian National Army was completely independent. And through I am not anticipating a point which it will be my duty to argue, namely, whether or not the question arose that people joined the I.N.A. because they might be worse off as prisoner of war, the less said about it the better. The evidence clearly shows that the only ration that the I.N.A. had, apart from sugar and oil which was nominal, was rice, and that was the luxury which attracted men to the I.N.A. My learned friend will consider twice over before trying any such argument. The question really is that one set of men believed in a cause and the other set of men either from supineness or otherwise did not, and nobody ever gave thought to the question as to whether one would be better off or not. One thing is quite certain: that apart from what actually happened by the Japanese, those who joined the I.N.A. were certainly facing the possibilities which every soldier has to face, unless he wishes to avoid it, which prisoners of war could, namely, fighting with the opponent army. And, therefore, my submission to the Court is that this idea of contrasting the comforts of the I.N.A. and the comforts of the prisoners of war under the Japanese, is entirely overdone. It is entirely a question as to what points of view appealed to one or the other sets of men, and therefore, Sir, my submission is that in so far as that is concerned, we have now been able to place before the Court the actual evidence on the question.

The next point is that the I.N.A. was a purely voluntary army, and notwithstanding the attempt made, the Prosecution entirely failed to prove that it was not voluntary, because from time to time it has been proved before this Court by the speeches made by the accused and Sri Subhas Chandra Bose, which indicate that at every stage opportunity was given to every member of the I.N.A. to withdraw if he chose to do so. But the strongest evidence is this: It is common ground, apart from actual principles which have not been accurately proved, that only a portion of the volunteers could be armed, equipped and trained, because of the paucity of material, and that there was a large number of people who could not be trained and could not be armed for want of resources—what is called the surplus volunteers. But I put it to you, Sir, as men of commonsense that it would require very much effort on the part of my learned friend to say that when they had more than enough men already, that they coerced more people to join the I.N.A. Or, in the language of Lord Shaw, I think it is a statement that stultifies itself because it is stated that 'we have enough men and we cannot arm them,' and yet it is alleged that you go on coercing people to join. I think it is a folly of which no decent human being would be guilty if he had a grain of commonsense. What has actually happened is that people have been punished for crime of their own, and in order to appear glorious before this Court, they attributed it to pressure by the I.N.A. It is a very clever half-truth, which is not uncommon.

You get a fact which occurred. Then in order to appear virtuous he would say that he was punished to be coerced to join the I.N.A. A more ludicrous story could not have been presented to the Court, because in one case the witness admitted the reason why that took place. They were sent to the Detention Camp Having been sent there, they were asked to surrender their ringleaders. When they did not, ten people came and there was a free fight—300 on one side and 10 on the other. And for the Government to put forward this sort of half-backed story in order that the Court may swallow it passes one's understanding.

This is Lt. Nag : "I heard Subhas Chandra Bose state at a meeting held soon after the meeting of the 21st October, 1943, that anyone who wished to leave the I.N.A. was permitted to do so."

P.W.5: "Prior to my arrival at Port Doxon in Kuala Lumpur—at that time I was in the custody of the Japanese-the bad conditions were due to the Japanese. In January—February 1943, I saw Capt. Shah Nawaz for the first time when he came to collect volunteers. I am quite clear that Capt. Shah Nawaz Khan left it open to everybody to join the I.N.A. or not as they chose. I remember that he wanted staunch men who were prepared to lay down their lives for the freedom of India. I never saw Capt. Shah Nawaz after that lecture."

P.W.24: "I reached Popa on the 25th or 26th February. Col. Sahgal said at Popa that those who did not wish to stay in the I.N.A. and wished to gooverto the enemyshould tellhim today. Hewill then makearrangements to send them in one party to the enemy, but they will not be permitted to take any arms or papers with them. 'I do not want that men should desert in driblets.' As far as I understand it was Sahgal's intention that after the party went over, men should not go over on driblets and so cause demoralisation,"

P.W.6: "The recruitment was absolutely voluntary. We had surplus volunteers whom we could not train or arm."

P.W.7: "The Indian National Army was purely voluntary. As far as I am aware no coercives methods were used in recruiting. I am aware as a member of the Provisional Government that we declared war on Britain and America."

Then, Sir, there is one more statement referring to Lt. Dhillion, to which I wish to call attention. My submission to the Court is that in so far as the accused before the Court are concerned, they by their open speeches gave everybody to understand that it was entirely their own choice whether to join the I.N.A. or not.

That brings me next to the evidence about the alleged coercion for the purpose of compelling men or inducing men to join the I.N.A. The position, Sir, is this with reference to that. At the time when the question arose as to the admissibility of the evidence, it was candidly stated by the Advocate-General that he did not rely on Sec. 10 but the way in which it is sought to make it relevant is this. He said that the accused did not participate in it, did not do it, did not encourage it. But that they knew about it.

The matter did not rest there. When they asked other people to join the I.N.A., they gave a veiled threat : "Remember if you do not join, what hardships exist." And the matter was further strained before this Court bu saying—meaning thereby among other things— that there would be personal coercion. It was on that statement that this honourable Court was pleased to admit the evidence. The attempt was made to show that the accused made this veiled suggestion. That attempt has completely failed because Capt. Dhargalkar who was called to give evidence in support of this, fell through. I shall read that part of his evidence to show that he completely collapsed on what he came to prove. He came to prove that the three caused, or some of them, went with the other officers. He came to support what the Advocate-General was instructed to put forward, namely, that he was given the alleged veiled threat. When we came to cross-examine Capt. Dhargalkar, he said : "I was never asked by anybody. I was never addressed by anybody" and the more significant thing is, he ended by saying : "I cannot state to the Court who said what to anyone." The net result of his evidence amounts to this that the Government having undertaken to this Court to prove that the veiled threat was given in that form, and that meant evidence possible relevant in the eyes of the court, the evidence was allowed to be given. But in the light of the evidence of Capt. Dhargalkar, there is none in which any allegation of veiled threat exists. I therefore ask the Court to hold that evidence as completely irrelevant because it was admitted on this provisional promise, namely, that it would be proved that there was a veiled threat given by the accused, because there is no other way in which it could be made relevant. There is no charge against the accused of any personal cruelty of any kind. There was no charge that they encouraged it, and the mere fact that they had knowledge would not be anything—even that, they have failed to prove. When I pointed out that mere knowledge was not enough, my learned friend added a further point, which I presume induced the Court to allow that and that is when they used the words which they are alleged to have used- "If you do not join remember the hardships"—meaning thereby that inasmuch as they knew that wrong methods were being adopted, they threatened the men by saying wrong methods would be adopted in their case. That I submit is the only process of reasoning by which he attempted to make his evidence relevant. My learned.friend has completely failed to establish either the knowledge or alleged threat and for these reasons, Sirs, I submit that this evidence should not be excluded, and I have prepared a petition so that it may remain on record for my submission.

The learned Judge-Advocate told the Court on the occasion of the question of admission of the evidence:

The learned Advocate-General really bases his case on the speeches of the accused which he will prove showing, as he says, that the accused referred to the hardships which would be inflicted on prisoners of war unless they joined, and thereby implying that they had knowledge of the methods by which he alleges that recruiting for the I.N.A. was being carried on.

At the same time, now we have arrived at a stage when I respectfully ask that the Court should rule that that evidence should be entirely disregarded, because there is no proof of the promise on which that evidence was submitted. That is the formal application I make to the Court.

Judge Advocate : Do you mean that you are asking us to make a decision on this now?

Counsel for Defence : On this point.

Judge Advocate : I am afraid it is not at all the procedure to make piecemeal decision on parts of the case, without hearing the learned Advocate-General and without hearing me. That decision will be made in due course, but I must ask the Court that they should go on now without making any piecemeal decision at this present stage.

Sri Desai : I shall leave it at that. I thought that I would save the Court, and perhaps incidentally myself, the necessity of having to go through that evidence, to show how utterly useless it is. But that being the view of the Court, I will not pursue it.

That brings me to the next question. My submission is that the basis on which that evidence was admitted has completely disappeared; and inasmuch as it has disappeared it should not be taken into considered in this case at all.

The only reason why I thought it my duty to call the attention of the Court at this stage was that you might have to go through the evidence and think if it is relevant.

The first witness, to whose evidence I think it necessary to call the attention of the Court, is Capt. Dhargalkar. This is what Captain Dhargalkar said in his examination in chief:

"I do not remember Lt. Dhillion being there, but I remember Capt. Shah Nawaz Khan and Capt. Sahgal coming there. I recognise both these officers as accused before the Court. Neither of the two accused ever spoke to me, but discussions usually took place and nearly all the discussions were concerned with our joining the I.N.A. I was present at these discussions. It is very difficult for me to quote the exact word which Capt. Sahgal and Capt. Shah Nawaz Khan said, but the gist of the thing was : 'Why don't you all join the I.N.A. rather than waste yourselves living under these conditions'."

That is really the whole point. Let me examine whether the promise is fulfilled even in the examination-in-chief. If "conditions" merely meant conditions as prisoners of war, whether for the time being under the I.N.A. or the Japanese, that is not a matter of charging the accused. But I suppose my learned friend will use the word "conditions" to mean almost anything, meaning thereby that "some people did something to somebody else and that will be your condition." I submit it does not carry the matter far enough.

I would then call attention to the cross-examination of this witness. He says:

"I saw all the three accused on several occasions. I saw them anything between 20 to 50 times. I only spoke to Capt. Sahgal a couple of times; I do not remember having spoken to Capt. Shah Nawaz Khan or Lt. Dhillon. I spoke to Capt. Sahgal in Col. Bhonsle's house. I cannot remember any other occasion. I was present at fifteen occasions at which discussions took place. Capt. Shah Nawaz may have been present about twice and Capt. Sahgal was present about the same number of times. This was in a

Separation Camp at Bidadari. There was one huge Camp at Bidadari and also a Separation camp. I was in the Separation Camp. The whole of the Bidadari Camp was the Indian National Army Camp. We were taken by Capt. Mohan Singh. There were about sixteen of us living in the room. I did not take part in the discussion nor was I addressed by Capt. Shah Nawaz or Capt. Sahgal. That is all that happened during the discussion."

Then he goes on to say:

"Capt. Shah Nawaz Khan came there, but I do not know whether he came to see Capt. Sher Dil Khan. I was not invited to a discussion, I was living in the room and I overheard certain conversations. I cannot remember the words of these discussions accurately but I remember the gist of them. The gist of the conversation included many other subjects other than the Indian National Army. I was addressed but not by any of the officers present there. Capt. Shah Nawaz Khan was speaking to 16 other people. The gist of his conversation was : "Why do you join the Indian National Army?" I remember that occasion to the best of my knowledge. It may have been any time in that month. I cannot remember all that he said. I cannot say exactly what he said."

(You will see, Sirs, a change in the gist. There was no question of what consequences would follow.)

"I cannot remember exactly what he said. I cannot single out from the others what Capt. Shah Nawaz Khan said. My answer is the same with regard to Capt. Sahgal. What I told the Court is the generel impression without knowing who said what."

This is the evidence of Capt. Dhargalkar, and I respectfully and emphatically submit to the Court that the promise on which that evidence was admitted remains unfulfilled: and inasmuch as it remains unfulfilled, my submission is that the evidence should be disregarded completely.

Now, with that submission and in view of the record, it is my duty very briefly to examine the evidence which has actually been given, and I will preface the examination with this remark. This is a case where in some instances what is called a half-truth implies an untruth : e.g., there was a Detention Camp where people were taken if they were guilty of acts of insubordination or any other act contrary to the discipline of an army. Having been taken there, there was no doubt a certain amount of tasks and fatigues they were asked to do. That is perfectly true, but that having been done, the man wants to make a martrydom of it. I will tell you why. He says he was taken there and he was asked to join the I.N.A. It is all, I submit, embroidery of the case, and I will ask the Court to examine that evidence in that light, and in one or two instances I shall be able to show that reluctantly he almost admitted the case I put to him, that he was sent there because he was guilty of insubordination. People very picturesquely said they were asked to pick up one end of a pole and every time a man followed them or hit them—I think the very exaggeration defeated its own purpose. I do not think any Court will believe such an absurd story. True, he was taken there, and no doubt he had to do a certain amount of fatigue. No doubt it may be that a noncommissioned officer thought it was below his dignity to pick up things which were necessary. In fact you might remember with what amount of reluctance the witnesses gave the kind of evidence before the Court—I would recall a picture of one of the witnesses when I told him that this was only for the purposes of manure and there was the evidence of a garden—it almist taxed one's patience to be able to get out of him that evidence, and get him to admit those facts; and even then he kept on saying "Oh, there was a road there and in between there was something and if you call it a garden it is wrong and so on". The fact remains that the witness was taken there for some act of insubordination; he was put to a certain amount of task, but then in order to glorify himself as a martyr, he now comes forward before this Court and says "I was taken there because I did not join the I.N.A." And when I cross-examined him as to what distinguished career he had, he ultimately collapses and admits he was an ordinary soldier. To think therefore that stories of this kind would pass muster before a Court composed of men of affairs and experience, I submit, will not do.

I call attention first to Wolit Bahadur, P.W. 14. The kind of picture he gave—this method of carrying baskets at the end of a pole—I do not suppose it is any great innovation or torture, unknown in India. The way in which he described it, and if he was not giving evidence before men of experience in this country, was almost insulting to one's intelligence. After all it is common method of carrying a load on bars with a man at each end; and if he objects to carring a load like that I am very sorry for him: but I am afraid he has to labour, and if he has to work, he has to work ; and the more we learn to do manual labour, I think, the better for men of my country.

And then he said—it was a ridiculous story—he carried out the order and picked up the cow-dung. There came a road. There were six men who stood just for the purpose of giving a stroke as he lifted the load. That I submit defeats itself. In cross-examination—that is where I wish to call attention to a few passages—this is what he says : "He said that we had now fallen from the English into the Japanese hands and we have to carry out their orders and do their fatigues. He told us that the British had run away and left us there. He said that our home was in India and we have to join with other Indians to fight for India. He also said that for this reason we should join the I.N.A. He also said that the I.N.A. was being formed to set India free. He said that for this reason we should join the I.N.A. About one or two men said that they did not know anything about the I.N.A. and they were not going to join it. At that time we did not know what this I.N.A. was. I know Jamadar Til Bahadur Adhikari." This is a very important thing. They are the people who are said to have come in this party to attack this gentleman and his friends in order that they may be coerced to join the I.N.A. It would be fortunate if one can think a little in advance. He admitted that every single one of them who took part in this raid to induce this gentleman and his friends to join the I.N.A. were all men respected in their Regiment and respected in the parts of the country from which they came. If he had only realised what it involved, he would probably not have admitted it. "I came to know that the I.N.A. was being formed. I knew Jamadar Til Bahadur Adhikari. Jamadar Puran Singh Khawas was a man who was respected by our unit and so was Jamadar Til Bahadur Adhikari. Jamadar Til Bahadur delivered only one lecture at which I was present. He also told us about the object of the I.N.A. which was the same as Puran Singh had told us. When Til Bahadur delivered the lecture there were about 600 men present." He admitted to me that they were being asked in the ordinary course to join the I.N.A., asked by people whom he admitted to be respectable and the point in asking for the admission is this, that those were among the people who came armed with a view to attack these innocent men in order that they may join the I.N.A. I make a present of that kind of story for your acceptance.

Then, Sir, comes in very common parlance the cat out of the bag. "Those who did not join the I.N.A. were required to do fatigues for the Japanese. Those who joined the I.N.A. were not required to do fatigues for the Japanese."

Prosecution Counsel: I am afraid my learned friend is under a misapprehension. He gave no names.

Defence Counsel: In his examination-in-chief he gave the names of the people who formed the party of attackers. It comes in cross-examination.

Prosecution Counsel: He does not say that these were the people who came to assault him. I know my learned friend put those names to him. No such questions were asked that these were the people who were in the firing party.

Judge Advocate: That certainly was not said, Mr. Desai.

Mr. Desai: The point of the argument will be perceived, name or no name.

"Those who did not join the I.N.A. were required to do fatigue for the Japanese. There was dispute when we refused to do fatigue duties for the Japanese. The leaders whom I have named told us not to object to the fatigue. In spite of their persuasion some of us did not obey. We reported that we will do fatigues for the Japanese but we have nothing to do with the I.N.A. The guard was sent because some of us did not obey". That is the point. The point is that it was not because they were to be persuaded to join the I.N.A. that the guard was sent. On his own admission they did not obey to do the task they were sent on and that destroys the whole of that evidence, names or no names. His whole purpose was that these people came on their own with a view just to educate them, because they would not join the I.N.A. If my learned friend will follow the process of cross-examination and the admission made by Wolit Bahadur, I only point out that it was up to the witness to say that they were not in the firing party.

Judge Advocate: It is you here who is in the wrong. You have said that these men were in the firing party, whereas it was pointed out that they were not.

Mr. Desai: There is the evidence in chief. I took the names from the summary of evidence. Because of that ruling the names were not allowed to be given. Whether the witness proved or failed to prove that the attack took place, because they would not join the I.N.A. that is the true issue, and remembering that to be the true issue, I beg leave to read where I left, and that is this: "There was a dispute when we refused to do fatigue duties for the Japanese. The leaders whom I have named told us not to object to do fatigue. In spite of their persuasion some of us did not obey. We reported that we will do fatigues for the Japanese but we have nothing to do with the I.N.A. The guard was sent (that is the material point) because some of us did not obey." You cannot get out of that. In other words the story that the guard was sent with a view to shoot them because they did not join the I.N.A., is entirely destroyed by this evidence. "The guard was sent because some of us did not obey. The guard came to seize the ring-leaders." That is precisely my point. I said they were all guilty of one or other offence against discipline, and hence action was taken against them, and this is the best illustration. Of course people get warned: after one man has been cross-examined you may not get the same type of actual admission. But here you have the clearest possible admission, the negation, the complete negation that any attack was made on them, because they did not join the I.N.A. Of course, they always repeat like parrots, when it becomes necessary : that is what happens. But occasionally there are lapses. "The guard was sent because some of us did not obey. The guard came to arrest the ring-leaders. We were about 550 men. Some of the men had a dispute with the guard stopped us from doing this and then fired in the air." What possible course forsooth—it was sent for the purpose of asking them to join the I.N.A. and they should have fired in the air! The whole point is that these were recalcitrants, a disobedient crowd. They were asked to surrender. As a warning they fired in the air. They would not obey. Of course the trouble took place. "When we did not obey the order of the guard, they fired. The guard did not prevent us from young fatigue but they spoke to us about I. N. A. which we did not obey." All this rubbish is difficult to understand. "First they fired in the air, and when we did not obey ultimately they fired at us. About two or three men were injured after the firing. Then we pursued the guard. The dispute between the guard and ourselves was that we resented the appearance of the guard during the lecture time." I do not know what it means. Whatever that means, they know better. As I said here, it is a complete demolition and the best illustration of how the false is mixed up with the true. There is no doubt that there was a scuffle. That is not denied. But they want to annex the scuffle to something else. That is a piece with all the evidence with which I am familiar. You get hold of a known fact which is not disputed, and then put it on to something else. My submission to the Court is that this evidence alone is sufficient to discredit the kind of evidence the Government has put forward with a view to show that atrocities were inflicted for the purpose of joining the I.N.A. As to the tortures, they were of two kinds. Regarding one, I have got definitely out of the mouth of the witness himself that they objected to the fatigue. They were persuaded not to do it. The very leaders whom they respected, persuaded them not to object to do fatigue. They were again asked to surrender their ring-leaders. These people would not. They fired in the air and ultimately they fired at us. Three people died and there were 550 of them. Such evidence, can my learned friend or any gentleman in his very high position ever place before the Court, name or no name?

Prosecution Counsel: I only corrected a statement which was not justified by the record.

Mr. Desai: I admit that I was in the wrong. I say the point of the argument is really this that the witness who came to swear false to the fact that the party was sent armed with a view to fire at them in order to compel them to join the I.N.A., here stands on his own evidence self-condemned. He admits that the purpose was different. The occasion was difficult, and that disobedience was the only cause. My case is that the cases which they have selected are cases of a similar kind where people undoubtedly were dealt with for breach of discipline, but which they now attribute to a false cause, namely, their refusal to join the I.N.A. The next is the case of Mohammed Hayat. That is the case in which we said that because they killed some cows, a quarrel arose and hence a scuffle. It is true a scuffle took place. The question is—was it with a view to compel them to join the I.N.A. That is where I say they get hold of an admitted event, or a more or less admitted event, and annex it to a false cause. He said:

"The Camp Commandant was Captain M.Z. Kyani, who was succeeded by Col. Shah Nawaz Khan. I heard Col. Shah Nawaz Khan lecturing to the Camp. I was not present at the lecture he delivered in the camp, but I was present at the lecture he delivered in the mosque. He said that Sikhs and Hindus have already volunteered, and that the Mussulmans should also join." He said: " Muslims must join the I.N.A. because when the Hindus and Sikhs go, they will trouble you in your homes in India. He did not threaten us with force but he said that we ought to join the I.N.A. He did not say that he only wanted sincere men. He said: 'I will not give any sort of trouble to you, but you should volunteer. I want true volunteers. After *Dua Khair,* we said that we will not join the I.N.A. We meant by that that none of us who were present there had a right to join the I.N.A. There was no charge against the men of my unit of having committed theft of seven cows belonging to civilians, and of having slaughtered and eaten them. I deny that. That charge is a lie and that the cows were eaten is also a lie. I am shows my additional statement in the summary of evidence I admit that I said in the summary of evidence that Major Aziz Ahmed told us that we were to go to the Concentration Camp because we had killed a cow."

That was at the time they were sent. Remember what was the contemporaneous statement made. I want you to remember that. The Court would have no doubt that that was the real cause of the dispute, and that joining the I.N.A. or not joining the I.N.A. was not the cause.

"No skins or bones were found, and no investigation was made. I never volunteered for the I.N.A. The Bidadari camp was a mixed Camp of volunteers and non-volunteers in July 1942. Neesoon Camp was also a mixed camp...... There was no difference in rations for the volunteers and non-volunteers. In July 1942 there was no separate treatment for volunteers in the Bidadari Camp. I was carrying on anti-I.N.A. propaganda. There was no charge against me of killing or stealing a cow when I was removed from the Bidadari Camp to the Concentration Camp. Aziz Ahmed never told us that we were being sent to the Concentration Camp because we had killed a cow. I am again shown my statement in the summary of evidence. I signed my statement. It was read over to me. I made this statement about Major Aziz Ahmed having told us that we were all to go to the Concentration Camp because we had killed a cow."

In other words, at the time when he was taken, it was proved from his own mouth that he was definitely told that the reason for his being sent was the killing of the cow.

"On the day I went to the Concentration Camp there were approximately 60 or 70 men there....... I said that after two or three days men of my unit were sent away from the Concentration Camp. I and1 1 other men were kept there. After our people went away, there were approximately 60 or 70 people left. They were all non-volunteers. I am talking of the month of July 1942."

Then comes the most tell-tale thing which any man of commonsense will understand:

"I was released from the Concentration Camp after 21 days because I had become very weak."

The whole point is this. Any man reading between the lines will be able to see that these people were taken to the Concentration Camp because they were charged with having stolen and killed a cow. He himself admits that it was a charge made at the time. Major Aziz Ahmed said 'you have to go to the camp, because this is the charge against you'. After investigation, he was released after 21 days. Is that the real story, or what he now says is the real story? It does not show that they were oppressed or coerced to join the I.N.A.

There is one ordinary canon of reasoning and commonsense. Is the court to accept the story he said at that time or is it to accept the story told now? I submit that at that time nobody imagined that anybody was going to make anything out of this incident for the trial against some people in future. The question is, which of the two stories is likely to be true, and I respectfully submit to the Court that there can be only one conclusion. The story he told then is the true story, and not the story he tells now. That is my submission with respect to this witness.

The next witness I take is Ahmed Nawaz, P.W.10. Every man has to undergo some sort of punishment for an offence. This witness is taking the story as it occurred, and adding to it so as to make out that what was done to him was a punishment to induce him to join the I.N.A. The only grievance of this gentleman is that he was asked to carry cow-dung. It was not after all such a serious punishment as he tried to make out. When I asked him whether he was asked to mix cow-dung with soda-ash, he said that in his part of the country they did not do so. The time has not yet come in this country for the use of every kind of mineral manure, of any other kind of manure except cow-dung. I asked him whether it was not intended to be used for the purpose of manuring the garden, and it took a very long time before we could get anything at all from this witness. The demeanour of this witness and his behaviour to the Court stands condemned.

I am now reading part of the cross-examination.

"I do not know what the cow-dung was taken for. I only know we were made to take it as a punishment. We stacked the cow-dung near a road in the camp and on both sides of the road was the garden. We were never told to powder the cow-dung for manure. It is correct that we mixed ash with the cow-dung but I do not know for what purpose it was used. I only did as a punishment."

To this man everything is a punishment. When this gentleman was asked to mix some soda-ash with cow-dung for manure, he thinks it is by way of punishment. He is indignant when he is asked to do something and thinks he was asked to do it as a punishment. He says :

"As a farmer, in our own home, we only use cow-dung as manure and we do not mix ash with it. Only for three hours on the first day I did this work of carrying cow-dung and stacking it near the garden. It was stacked at a distance of about 10 or 12 yards from the garden. For the remaining five days we were digging and levelling earth and preparing garden plots."

When you come to analyses the facts, the indignity this witness comes to nothing. He was asked to do the ordinary work of preparing garden beds for the vegetable garden and mixing some manure. So far as the manuring is concerned, it only lasted three hours of his life time. If this is what is called an atrocity, I submit to the Court, it is a ridiculous type of atrocity. A man is asked to make beds in a garden and prepare some manure, and he imagines it to be a punishment. He may think so, but it is for the Court to say whether it is so. Does the Court believe that it was an ordinary piece of work, or it was an oppression, coercive methods, and I do not know what other language is used to describe it. Is it a torture to prepare beds and to prepare manure? I submit with great respect it is a ridiculous kind of evidence which is put forward as an item of torture, and for what purpose?—for the purpose of making this gentleman join the I.N.A.! Does this stand to reason and commonsense? I submit with great respect that, in spite of the picturesque language used, the Court will not accept the version of the witness. It is a ridiculous thing. He was asked to do ordinary fatigue. This is legitimate work which ought to have been done willingly and it is ridiculous to suggest that this was a kind of torture used to induce or coerce the witness to join the I.N.A. That, Sirs, is the evidence of Ahmad Nawaz.

Then, take the next witness, Havidar Mohammed Sarwar. He said : "Every—body refused to join the I.N.A. The *Jamadar* and Subedar were armed with pistols and they took them out and started firing on us, and ordered the guard also to fire on us. The guard consisted of approximately 14 men. They started firing. Two of us were killed ..... Everybody said Allah-o-Akbar." Now I will read from the cross-examination of this gentleman. He said : "I was for three weeks in No. 4 hospital. It was a very big hospital. There were patients of all kinds there. I was taken to the hospital. I do not know who took me, because I was unconscious. There was an officer to whom I said that I was willing to join the I.N.A. The only force that made me join the I.N.A was that I wanted to escape this bad treatment and bad food. When I joined the I.N.A., I came to know that they were trying to free India. "And this is the gentleman who says that there was a regular firing in order to make him join the I.N.A. He goes on : "I knew I was expected to go and might. I knew it was a question of life and death. I thought that death was better than these troubles. I had no faith that they would set India free. I had every faith that if I went to the front, I might be able to go to the other side, because we had so many hardship otherwise. At the place where we were first, there were numerous other people besides the 300. I do not know the Camp Commander's name. The Unit Commander was Lt. Purshotam Dass. That was the Japanese Prisoners of War Camp. We were split up into parties for the purpose of fatigues. On the day prior to the firing accident, we were not divided into parties of 323 for fatigue purposes. We were not asked to form a party of 323 men. We were not given an order. I do not know anything about being asked to surrender our leaders. I never heard of it. It is not true that Lt. Purshotam Dass advised us not to resist. In the party which came to the Camp there was one Mohammedan Jamadar. He was second-in-command of the guard. There was a scuffle between the men of my unit and the guard after the firing had taken place. Only one man of the guard was killed. The guard consisted of about 300. The name of the guard who was killed was Sardar Singh, who belonged to the Kapurthala Regiment. "That will show who attacked first. I leave it to you, Gentlemen, to judge who was the attacker and who was the attacked. And remember this that they were in a party of a few hundred, whereas the guard consisted, as he puts it, of 300 men. "Because we refused to join the I.N.A., they started firing." That is the picture which we are asked to accept. I submit with very great respect that the story is a most incredible story. There was no conversation and they at once started firing!

Now, Sirs, that is the story which is presented to you for acceptance, and I ask the Court not to accept it because it is a ridiculous story. What is the idea of firing at the men whom they ask to join the I.N.A.? What do you gain by it? You gain this kind of soldiers with a view to fight! My submission to the Court is that there was this scuffle which he reluctantly admits, and evidently they were the first attackers. But they have employed a little story by means of which they say that there was firing on them. If the Counsel thinks that he can walk away with this story, I submit he is mistaken. But when you come to torture, I ask, is it supposed to be a torture? It was an ordinary fatigue duty. In this connection, I would like to call the attention of the Court to the Geneva Conventions, Articles 27 to 34, with reference to the work of the prisoners of war on page 298. I am talking of 1929. "They should be kept according to their rank and if they are physically fit they may be employed by private individuals, but the captors must assume entire responsibility for their maintenance."

Prosecution Counsel : I am afraid I must interrupt. The evidence is not as my learned friend reads it. The evidence is not that the guard was killed first.

Mr. Desai : What he said was : "The name of the guard who was killed was Sardara Singh. There was no other member of the guard who died before Sardara Singh was killed." I had not the least doubt about it.

The point that I submit to the Court is this. The witnesses fall into three types of classes. The first category belongs to the cow-killing incident. The second that the incident was with reference to refusal to do fatigues. The third relates to the incident of refusing to form parties for fatigues as required by the Japanese, whose prisoners they were. As a result of these three incidents, certain accidents occurred. I submit to the Court that the Government had definitely failed to prove any torture for the purpose of joining the I.N.A. Each of these accidents is attributable—in two cases almost—to an admitted fact. In one case it is due to the form which the attack took. With reference to the other witnesses, the less said the better. All that they have said was that they were asked to do certain duties which they thought was an indignity, which they were asked to do, which, I submit, is ordinary decent labour. I know many men of higher rank who do gardening as a matter of honourable occupation, and as a change of occupation from ordinary work. What these gentlemen were really asked to do was gardening, and they seriously come here and say what an indignity it was to ask a soldier to do gardening. And that is why he refused to join the I.N.A. The Counsel has entirely failed to prove what he set out to prove, and I feel the Court should hold if it were necessary—according to my submission it is not necessary at all—that it has not been proved, apart from what is read or stated or alleged, beyond any reasonable doubt, that any torture was inflicted in order to join the I.N.A. That, Sir is my submission on that count.

That is all that I wish to say about the evidence on the subject of atrocities alleged to have been committed on these men to join the I.N.A. With reference to the point that I mentioned in the morning as regards cases which might possibly be relied on, I will give you a list of the three cases which may be relied upon and give you my remarks on them. Before that I wish to make a submission. I will make a request at a later stage but I wish to mention to the Court in so far as any new authority is cited by my learned friend I do not want a general right of reply but I will ask the Court in the end that on any new law that may be cited I may be allowed to give a reply because I could have no opportunity even by anticipation of doing it. I will make that request more formally towards the end. The three cases which may be relied upon are Regina vs. Lynch (1903) I King's Bench Regina vs. Jaegrae (1907) Appeal Cases. p. 346 and Regina vs. Casement (1917) I King's Bench. I do not wish to address you as if you were a high court, and therefore what I will do is this. There are two points which distinguish these cases which I will briefly state. They are cases of an individual being charged under the English law for an act of treason; they were not cases of men who were members of an organized army and of an organized Government. The second distinguishing ground is that in these cases there was no question of what I have submitted shortly as double allegiance. Therefore my submission will be that if these cases are relied upon this is the answer that I have got with reference to them. I will now go on with the regular trend of my argument.

The next point which I have to deal with before the Court is the evidence relating to the charges of murder, but I will take them all together without attempting to distinguish them. But I distinguish them under two heads : one is with reference to the four persons alleged to have been shot on one occasion and Mohammed Hussian, the person shot on the second occasion. I will first briefly state the case as I desire to present to the Court, and then deal with the evidence. It is a matter in which with due submission I probably will call attention in some greater detail to the evidence of three or four witnesses. As to the others, I will only make a submission as to what they said.

The position with reference to that is this. As regards the four persons there is a crime report and therefore up to the point of punishment there is evidence before the Court. As regards Mohammed Husain there is no crime report. In fact as regards Mohammed Husain there is no document whatever relating either to the sentence being passed or the sentence being carried out. Further, there is not even a casualty record in either case that I find on the record. As to Mohammed Husain the only answer given by one of the witnesses as to why a casualty report was not made was that they were moving from Popa that day, and then when I further cros—examined him which you will find in the cross—examination when I come to it—he has given no adequate explanation for the absence of the casualty report. There is this further evidence—I am only anticipating it that in the case of Mohammed Husain there are three persons who are alleged to have shot—Jagiri Ram and two others, whom Jagiri Ram himself did not know. I do not wish to enter into details at this moment except when I read it, but I wish to point out the salient features. It is said in the evidence that Mohammed Husain had three shots on his heart or near thereabout. It is further said in the evidence—he said this—that there was a tear in the shirt; and further in answer to the Court, which is most material point, he said there was no blood of any kind or sort. That is the state of evidence with reference to Mohammed Husain.

And now I will deal with the two sets of cases. There is one other ruling which I should have mentioned and that is that there is in evidence before the Court that Lt. Dhillon who is said to have signed and watched the sentence carried out was in a state of complete collapse of health and on that the document before the Court is Exhibit VVV. And the date of that document is 6th March 1945, the date on which it is alleged this execution was carried out. I am reading this relevant part of that document which is at the bottom.

"Jai Hind—I think most of your queries have been answered in this order. Others I will answer when I come tomorrow. I ought to have come today but last night I went to check certain defences and on my arrival back I felt very weak, so weak that I have never felt before throughout my life. Major Shankar gave me an injection today though for a complete course I must get 12 here when there are none available. I will get one tomorrow."

My case is that so far as carrying out the sentence on the four persons is concerned, though in fact the order was passed, it was never carried out. Not only that, but I will be able to point out from the evidence on record that there are many other similar instances, sworn to and admitted by the witnesses for the Prosecution. That is in outline why I submit that the case in so far as the execution of the sentence is concerned, is no proved. I may go a little further and state to the Court that there is no presumption that because sentences were passed they were therefore carried out. The charge of murder has got to be proved by proving completely what is called the *corpus delicti* of that particular person. And I will say that if there is a reasonable doubt in your mind that the prosecution has failed to prove the actual execution of the sentence, my clients are entitled to the benefit of that doubt.

That is the position with reference to the executions. There are four witnesses with reference to Mohammed Husain. As regards the first witness Havildar Ghulam Mohammed the evidence need not be read to the Court because all that he says is that he was brought up before Capt. Shah Nawaz, which in fact is not denied. There is this in Ghulam Mohammed's evidence:

"I know Havildar Ganga Saran. The first Battalion Commander reported that he (Ganga Saran) had refused to obey his orders. He was a sub-officer in the I.N.A. He was prodiced before Col. Sahgal for this offence and was tried and sentenced to death. He was afterwards pardoned and released." Havildar Ganga Saran himself in his cross-examination has admitted that as a fact.

The next witness is Sepoy Allah Ditta (P.W. 24). He deals with the earlier part of the story, namely, his intention to desert. This is what he says:

"Mohammed Husain said : 'I had a few difficulties and therefore I intended to desert'. But no inquiries were made into his complaints. Mohammed Husain was told by Col. Shah Nawaz : 'You are sentenced to death by shooting because you intended to desert yourself and were persuading others to do the same. Therefore you are not pardoned.' I heard Col. Shah Nawaz say : 'Put off the case to the Regimental Commander'. (Note by Court : Witness used the words in English). Then we all three of us were sent out. I recognise Col. Shah Nawaz Khan as an accused before the Court. We waited there for ten minutes and were brought back to Brigade Headquarters. Mohammed Husain, Jagiri Ram and myself came together back to Brigade Headquarters. Mohammed Husain and myself were put back in the same cell in which we were before and Khazin Shah took away Jagiri Ram. The same day at about 5 p.m. Sardar Mohammed, Adjutant of our Battalion and Aya Singh took away Mohammed Husain. I have never seen Mohammed Husain since then."

Then, Sir, in cross-examination he said :

"No decision was arrived at either in my case or in the case of Jagiri Ram."

The Court will remember that there were three people, and it is common ground that as regards two the sentence was not carried out.

It is true that all that Col. Shah Nawaz Khan said was : 'You deserve to be shot.' Col. Shah Nawaz Khan said that rebels like you will be sentenced to death by shooting. Col. Shah Nawaz Khan told Mohammed Husain: 'You yourself wanted to escape; secondly, you have tried to persuade others to escape; therefore, you are a rebel to the I.N.A. and sentenced to death by shooting.' 'I saw Col. Shah Nawaz Khan write something on the crime report. How could I read the crime report without picking it up from the table. I do not understand English.'

I come to the part of the story which in itself has not the same importance as what it indicates, showing that the witness was a completely factual witness. The man does not know English and yet he says "he was writing a crime report", and the object of the cross-examination is to show that he told a set story which he himself could not have possibly seen or done, and that is the kind of witness he is. That is the object of that part of the cross-examination.

"I saw Col. says he does not know what is crime, but he was told what is a crime report. Yet he is asked to tell a set story that there was a crime report which Col. Shah Nawaz Khan was actually writing, because he was called upon to prove that it was a crime report and sentence was written on it.

"I saw Col. Shah Nawaz Khan write something on the crime report. How could I read the crime report without picking it up from the table? I do not understand English. I do not know what he wrote and where, because I do not know English and I was not reading the crime report at that time."

And the only re-examination is :

"The crime reports were lying on the table and Col. Shah Nawaz Khan read them out as he spoke to us individually. He wrote on the crime report which had already been drawn up."

That is his part of the story. Then we come to the actual evidences of persons by whom sentence is said to be carried out—Jagiri Ram. You have seen him in the witness box. He is in the Nursing Department. He admitted to the Court that he had never handled a gun in his life, or a rifle, or any shooting instrument. But in order to give the colour of truth, Jagiri Ram is made to say this : "I was unwilling; I do not know how to shoot; I have never handled a shooting instrument, but a gun was put on my shoulder..." I ask you, Sirs, to give me the benefit of any description on his part rather than attempt to construct the story for him as if he did so. Then he put the gun here and the trigger was pulled and it seems that this untutored rifleman was extraordinarily accurate, that along with the others all the three shots lodged in the chest of the deceased. Sirs, it will be for you to judge the story. I am going to read out only that part of it which is material:

"I knew Mohammed Husain and Allah Ditta. Mohammed Husain, myself and a Garhwali talked about escape when we were in Popa Hill area. While we were talking of escape, Khazin Shah sent an orderly and ordered us to report to Battalion Headquarters.

Mohammed Hussain said that he had mentioned to Jagiri Ram and Alla Ditta jokingly about an escape. Khazin Shah questioned me and asked if they mentioned this jokingly. I replied that I had no proof of his intention to escape, but he mentioned it jokingly to me. Mohd. Husain and myself were tied to a tree near the Battalion Headquarters, while Khazin Shah was questioning us. Khazin Shah questioned me as to who was trying to escape and I said that I did not know the name of any one who was trying to escape. Then Mohd. Husain was questioned. He also said that he did not know anything. After sunset Khazin Shah took Mohd. Husain and myself to Brigade Headquarters. When I was taken to Brigade Headquarters, Mohd. Husain, Khazin Shah and one sentry were with me. Brigade Headquarters were near a nullah. On arrival at Brigade Headquarters, Khazin Shah went to a telephone and after that Allah Ditta also arrived at the nullah. After that all three of us, Mohd. Husain, Allah Ditta and myself, were put in the Quarter Guard and our hands were tied. On the following day, we were brought before Col. Sahgal. Col. Sahgal questioned me as to whether I intended to escape. I said "no". I did not intend to escape. During this conversion with Col. Sahgal, other people present were Major Negi and Khazin Shah. Col. Sahgal asked me if I had reported to any one after Mohd. Husain had mentioned to me about escape. I said I did not know anything about Mohd. Husain, and I did not reply to any N.C.O. I worked with my Medical Officer. Then we came out of the room and went back to the Quarter Guard. Then Lt. Aya Singh of Brigade Headquarters gave each one of us a beating and said that he would release us if we would tell him the names of the people who intended to escape. I continued to say that I did not know. Next day we were taken to Divisional Commander, Shah Nawaz Khan. We were accompanied by Major Negi, Khazin Shah and a sentry. All three of us, myself (Jagiri Ram), Allah Ditta and Mohd. Husain were lined up before the Divisional Commander. The Divisional Commander asked me to speak the truth whether I intended to escape. I said "no". I did not intend to escape. Capt. Shah Nawaz Khan asked up why we did not report the matter. I said that I did not know anything about it, and I did not intend to escape. He asked if there was any officer or N.C.O. near me. I said no, I was working with my medical officer. Then Captain Shah Nawaz Khan asked Allah Ditta: "When Mohammed Husain had talked to you about escaping, did you report to any one ?" Allah Ditta said : 'I do not know anything about Mohd. Husain's escape; I thought it was a joke, I do not know anything about it. " Capt. Shah Nawaz Khan then said to Allah Ditta : "You are an N.C.O. Why did not report?" Allah Ditta begged his pardon and said that he did not know anything about Mohd. Husain. Then Capt. Shah Nawaz Khan questioned Mohd. Husain, and Mohd. Husain replied that he was in difficulties and that the intended to escape and asked to be forgiven. Capt. Shah Nawaz Khan then told him: "You are not for our country; you are our enemy. I will give you death by shooting." Then Mohd. Husain asked for forgiveness and said that he was prepared to go anywhere he was ordered. Capt. Shah Nawaz said nothing to this.

The whole importance of the question is, whether in fact any sentence was actually pronounced. But, whether or not it was pronouned, the ultimate issue is, whether it was carried out. Like the case of the other two có-accused—Jagiri Ram and the other man—he said that nothing was decided, and "all three of us were then sent out, and taken to Brigade Headquarters accompanied by Major Negi and Khazin Shah."

I need not read the rest of it.

Then comes the next material part of the story :

I moved towards the Battalion with Khazin Shah and Sub-Officer Barfi Singh. When I reached Battalion Headquarters, Khazin Shah told Barfi Singh to take me to Company Headquarters. In the evening an ordeal took me to Battalion Headquarters. Mohd. Husain was there. Khazin Shah and Aya Singh were also there when I arrived."

The most important point is—and which appears from the evidence of witness—that both Khazin Shah and Aya Singh are alive, and they are the only real proper witnesses to that particular transaction. Neither of them has been produced. The story continues:

"Khazin Shah told me, 'You will shoot Mohd. Husain, because you are one of the men who were trying to escape with him'. I declined and said I will not shoot him....."

I have understood many psychological problems but this particular one is curious, namely, that a who does not know how to shoot and cannot shoot, is made to shoot just as a sort of punishment, which I do not understand, and which I trust you will not be able to understand even if you set a problem to yourself.

Khazin Shah told me: "You will shoot Mohammed Husain, because you are one of the men who were trying to escape with him." I declined and said I will not shoot him and that I did not know how to fire a rifle. Khazin Shah told me again : "If you do not shoot Mohammed Husain, you will be shot yourself. I still refused and he drew his pistol."

I can only express my inability to understand this particular psychology except a very foolish invention.

"I refused again and Aya Singh get hold of a rifle. He put the rifle to my shoulder and put my finger round the trigger. Khazin Shah told Aya Singh to give the order to fire. Ther were three of us, one Singh, one Tamil and myself. Mohd. Husain was blindfolded by Aya Singh he was made to sit on the ground with his back against a tree stump and his hands were tied behind his back. Aya Singh ordered me to fire and all three fired. Mohammed Husain died there. Khazin Shah ordered Aya Singh to give the order to fire and Aya Singh gave it. Khazin Shah told me to report to my company and not to come to the Battalion Headquarters. That evening we marched off to Logyi. Then we stayed at Logyi two or three days. Then I went over to the British".

The cross-examination is further continued:

"After I had made the statement it was read over to me and I was asked whether it was the correct version of my statement and I said : 'Yes,' it was. I was again shown my statement day before yesterday and I was asked if the contents were correct and I said : 'Yes.' It was translated to me in Hindustani and read over to me, and I also repeated my statement once again and they both tallied. I have had no training in the use of weapons. I joined the army, I worked as a servant and a labourer. On joining hospital, I was trained in the work of bandaging patients and making their beds. I had nothing to do with the fighting part of the army. Except when the patients were sent to the hospital I had nothing to do with the men of the fighting units....."

The point which I wish to make is that not one of the persons is able to identify any of them by even the remotest possible description, and you cannot prove the death of "A" by saying that I saw somebody shoot someone whom I cannot identify. Continuing be said :

"Mohd. Husain and the Garhwali I have referred to were members of the fighting units. At that time of the conversation they were not sick. I did not know them before the conversation, but they were living in the same company. I had no talk with them before, but when they came to my company I was in company headquarters. When this conversation took place I was in Popa Camp. I had never been to Burma before. Before joining the I.N.A., we were given very hard fatigues by the Japanese in connection with the loading of coal at the ports day and night... I do not know the name of the Garhwali to whom I have referred."

The test is whether the other alleged conspirators were known to him.

"I know he was a Garhwali because he lived with us and he spoke Garhwali. I had never talked either to the Garhwali or to Mohammed Husain before the day Mohd. Husain joined company headquarters. I had never spoken to the Garhwali before that day in the nullah; and from that day's conversation I say that he was a Garhwali. I do not know any language or dialect beyond the dialect which I speak.

"I came to know Mohammed Husain in company. He used to live with me at headquarters. He used to sit in my company. I know he was a Mohammedan. I do not know anything more about him. He used to speak in Punjabi with me. He used to live with me, surely I knew him. I cannot give a long description of him except his physical description. I do not know anything else about him. It was by chance that Mohd. Husain and I got together and the Garhwali arrived in the meantime.....

"When I was arrested I said that I never intended to run away because I would have been also shot otherwise. I knew Lt. Aya Singh because he was in my company. I know he is alive. I saw him in Jigargacha and Chittagong. The last time I saw him was at Chittagong where he arrived two or three days after my arrival there in about May last.

"I saw Capt. Shah Nawaz Khan at Divisional Headquarters. There were other orderlies and sepoys there. I do not remember having seen any officers other than Capt. Shah Nawaz Khan. I do not know the English word "crime" I know the word "report" in the sense of making a report to somebody. I do not understand the words "crime report' which are written on a piece of paper now shown to me. There was no need for anybody to teach me the meaning of crime report when I was about to be produced."

I put it to him to ascertain if he understands the explanation. There cannot be any other explanation except tutoring.

"I was told that a crime report would be put up against me and that we three men would be brought before Capt. Shah Nawaz Khan. No announcement was made before me in respect of anybody except Mohd. Husain being ordered to be shot. Capt. Shah Nawaz Khan did not say anything about myself and Allah Ditta. Allah Ditta was not present with us when we conferred in the nullah...

"Mohd. Husain admitted that he had intended to run away; that he wanted to run away because he was in trouble; and asked to be forgiven and said that he was prepared to go anywhere that he was ordered to. After that Capt. Shah Nawaz Khan said that he (Mohd. Husain) was not for his country: that he was an enemy, and that he would give him death by shooting. We were then marched out. I am quite clear that nothing else happened.

"I was given a rifle at the time of the shooting of Mohd. Husain. I do not know any weapons other than a rifle was put on my shoulder in the aiming position by Aya Singh. I do not know the names of the Tamil and the Sikh who were present at the shooting of Mohd. Husain, but they were both present on the scene when I arrived. I do not know anything else about them or what they did. I do not know their names but I have seen them in Battalion Headquarters. I cannot say anything more about them than what I have said. I was not myself then. The rifle was put into position and I was told to hold it. I held it with the help of Aya Singh. The rifle was pointing to Mohd. Husain. He was sitting on the ground about five yards away. I pressed the trigger when one, two, three was said. Three shots were fired but I do not know which shot shots him down. I did not go to Mohd. Husain's body to see how many shots had penetrated it. I did not go near Mohd. Husain's body after the firing. The last time I saw it, it was lying there."

This is the account given by Jagiri Ram and the most important points are these : First, that he did not know his fellow shooters and he cannot identify them. Secondly, he admits that Khazin Shah and Aya Singh are both alive. The third thing that he says is that I do not know Mohammed Husain and there is no intelligible ground given why a man who did not know how to shoot was made to go through this process and it is for the Court to give some explanation. I can only submit that I can find none, and under these circumstances, I ask you to say that this witness's evidence is evidence which falls short of proof of the death of a particular individual otherwise not described, and in the absence of two persons who have not been produced before this Court.

Then, Sir, there is one more witness on this point, and that is witness L/Naik Sardar Mohammed. I will read the evidence which relates to this matter.

"I knew Mohammed Husain. On the 27th March, Lt. Khanzin Shah sent for the runners. On arrival of the runners he ordered them to bring the following men to the Battalion Headquarters : Sepoy Mohammed Husain, Lance Naik Alla Ditta, Lance Naik Mohammed Shafi, Sepoy Jagiri Ram and Sepoy Gobbru Singh... Khazin Shah told me that these men intended to run away. He further told me that he was going to Brigade Headquarters that evening to talk about these men, and he went away... I met Lt. Khazin Shah on the way and I handed over these men to his charge. He let off Lance Naik Mohammed Shafi on the spot, because his platoon commander had recommended him, and I came back. He said that Mohammed Husain had been sentenced to be shot."

I submit with due respect that it is not good evidence.

To be shot : Nothing was said about others, but Jagiri Ram was with him at the time. He asked me to go to Ghulam Mohammed, the Brigade Adjutant and ask him whether Mohammed Husain was to be shot under Battalion arrangements or Brigade arrangements .... I was also asked to bring sepoy Mohammed Ibrahim who had been released from the quarter guard. I received instructions that Mohd. Husain was to be shot under Battalion arrangements and on the same day. I brought him back with me to Battalion Headquarters..... I conveyed these orders to Lt. Khazin Shah. Lt. Khazin Shah then ordered me to arrange for the execution of Mohammed Husain ... He asked me to detail to men with pickaxes and shovels. I detailed these men to dig a grave. I know that a grave was dug. I was then ordered by Lt. Khazin Shah to take Mohammed Husain to the edge of a nullah. Mohammed Husain was taken to edge of the nullah, Lt. Khazin Shah, 2nd Lt. Aya Singh and Havildar-Major Govind Singh, some sepoys and myself went with Mohammed Husain to the nullah. Lt. Khazin Shah ordered Mohammed Husain to be tied to a tree and also ordered that he should be blindfolded. I passed on the orders to Sub-Officer Govind Singh who carried them out with the help of two other sepoys. After this Lt. Khazin Shah called two men out of the fatigue party to shoot Mohammed Husain. They were both sepoy, one was a Tamil and the other was a Sikh. After the arrival of these men, Khazin Shah ordered that Jagiri Ram would also fire on Mohammed Husain. The three men stood in a line facing Mohammed Husain and Khazin Shah told Aya Singh to give the order to fire. Aya Singh gave the order, "Kneeling Fire." All the three sepoys fired a round each on Mohammed Husain. Mohammed Husain was killed. His body rolled over sideways. Khazin Shah then ordered me to send Abdul Hakim to arrange for his burial.... No casualty report was sent. The sending of a casualty report was part of my duties. I did not make a casualty report because night had fallen and we had to march the same night. On the 3rd April I escaped and reported to the allied forces....

"The night that Mohammed Husain was shot we moved to Logyi. That was on the 29th March, 1945.

That question was put with a view to find out the connection between that day and the day of escape.

".... I did not have the time to prepare a casualty report of Mohammed Husain's death. On the 1st April 1945, I did not take a casualty report to Capt. Sahgal. I do know if any was sent. I knew Jagiri Ram from the day he was arrested and taken to Brigade H.Q. I had been posted to the regiment only three or four days previously, and that is why I did not know Jagiri Ram. I knew that he was a non-combatant nursing orderly. Aya Singh was helping Jagiri Ram to fire the rifle. He was standing near him. Jagiri Ram fired with help. Lt. Khazin Shah ordered that Jagiri Ram will also be one of the firing squad. I could not see very well but the firing squad had been ordered to adopt the kneeling position and they did kneel a bit. I do not remember whether jagiri Ram was standing or in the kneeling position. I was between 12 or 15 yards away when Mohd. Husain fell. I went away after giving orders to Abdul Hakim. I went near Mohd. Husain and found that he was dead. He had three shots in him. The shirt covering his left breast was torn and from the amount of tear I considered there were three shots. I was not present at his burial.

(Question by the Judge-Advocate) :

"When I found that three shots had gone into him and that he was lying on a side I inferred that he was dead. The firing was about 8 to 10 yards away from Mohd. Husain. The shooting of Mohd. Husain occurred at about dusk. I did not see any blood on Mohd. Husain.'

This is the whole of the evidence that you have before the Court and with the absence of Khazin Shah and Aya Singh, with the inexplicable alleged joining of Jagiri Ram, with the complete unidentification of the other two persons who joined in the shooting, and with the most extraordinary story of three shots having gone into the body of this man in one and the same place and not a single drop of blood was found, I submit to the Court that the evidence falls short of any proof of the execution of this sentence.

Though it is a small point Jagiri Ram himself said that he fired the rifle standing and I have a vivid recollection that later on, when he was asked to say where his muzzle was pointing he was completely at sixes and sevens to answer the question or to explain the position, or to answer where and how he held the riffle and where he aimed and how he shot. That is the position in so far as the record is concerned.

Then to the evidence relating to the alleged shooting of the four persons. The first and the most important point in reference to that shooting is the exhibit 3V which I have read to the Court. If you had such clear evidence it is obvious that the other evidence must be rejected. You have the evidence about the condition in which Lt. Dhillon then was. The submission I am making to the Court is that this event did not take place because the whole of the story hinges around order after order being given by Lt. Dhillon. I am able to show, as I submit I am able to show, that document was written at a time when there was not the remotest occasion of making up any document whatsoever as to the condition of his health. But the fact remains that the previous night he had gone out on reconnoitering and he came back, and I ask you to pay attention, 'in a condition so weak that he had never felt like that in his life before.' He was actually given an injection by the doctor, that 11 more had to be given, and it was difficult to find any more medicine. For that reason alone, if there were no either reason, the picturesque account given by the two witnesses, whose evidence I am going to read as to the company being called out and Lt. Dhillon standing and giving orders and calling each man, is a story entirely untrue. More than that, the story of the location of it all seems to be completely upsetting.

As to one of the two witnesses a comment is necessary. He had no intelligible reason to be there; and he had medicines to give as I shall presently point out. He also happens to be one of the members of the nursing staff and he said he had no reason to remain there. But the still more important thing is that the second person says—his evidence shows—that the first witness was not there. What do you make of that?

Counsel for the Prosecution : He does not say that he was not there. He only says, "I did not see any other man.

Mr. Desai : I say that the true inference is that he was not there, because he said he saw nobody, no stranger. The evidence suffers from such grievous infirmities; first, the practical improbability of the person who gave orders for shooting being there. Of course one can disregard anything; but after all you are to judge by human standards and not by possibilities. In fact, I do go as far as this : supposing a charge of his kind had been brought—apart from a trial of this kind—and evidence had been given as to the improbability of the person who is alleged to have given orders for shooting being there, no jury would ever venture to convict him. You may say : "Oh, yes the man was ill but we still believe he went there." Of course you are entitled to do so; you are judges; I do not deny that. But I ask you to be judges on material before you; and the material before you is such that as judges of fact it is impossible at all events, as I respectfully put it then and put it now—if you had a reasonable doubt that Lt. Dhillon could not have been there that day, I submit there is an end of the case. Any other picturesque description in immaterial. What is material is that the man who is alleged to have given orders for the shooting was not there and whether he was there or not depends on the state of his health, as to which there is a contemporaneous report; and I submit to the Court that it would be highly dangerous to accept, in the state of that man's health, the story of these two men. As to both of them I will be able to point out inherently from their own evidence that they are not witnesses of truth; and that you prefer that evidence and act on your own peril. I submit that is the real issue before the Court. I will read the evidence of the other two persons who said they were there.

There is another point which also comes out. There is no identification of the persons alleged to have been shot with the persons mentioned in the crime report. I do submit to the Court that if you find a Crime Report and on the strength of that document it is quite easy to have two willing witnesses of this kind—people who, I submit on their own confession (and I can show it by examination of their evidence) ought not to be believed. I say the strongest piece of evidence in my clients' favour is the evidence of his state of health that day, and you cannot disregard it. You can say : "Oh, no; never mind how his health was; we still believe he was there". But I submit that that is a process of reasoning which is not, what I may call, founded on justice or will be accepted by this Court. I will read the evidence of the first witness on this point :

"One day I was carrying a patient and saw four men near a nullah whose hands were ties behind their backs and who were escorted by two sentries. When I was coming back after leaving the patient in hospital, I noticed some men assembled near the nullah. Seeing this assembly of men, I went up there. When I reached there, one company was fallen in, and a trench had been dug there. The four men were made to sit in the trench. Then Major Dhillon asked for volunteers to shoot these men. Two men from that company and one man from Brigade H.Q. came up. Their names were Naik Sher Singh, Kalu Ram and Hidayatullah. Two carried rifles and one a pistol : Sher Singh had the pistol. Then Major Dhillon called out the name of one of the four men in the trench. Major Dhillon told the Company present that these four men had gone over to the enemy and had been caught, and therefore their punishment would be death. Then Major Dhillon ordered Hidayatullah to shoot the prisoner who had been called out to the trench first. But this time this prisoner had come out of the trench. He was standing on the edge of the trench. This prisoner was then shot by Hidayatullah and he fell down. The prisoner was not blind-folded. He was about 20 yards from Hidayatullah when fired upon."

Then there is the description about the other three men in the same way. Then he says :

"I did not see them moving after Sher Singh had fired. Then I saw Capt. Lee, the Medical Officer of the Battalion examine them. Capt. Lee said something to Major Dhillon."

Capt. Lee is another witness who should have been called to prove this :

"Afterwards Major Dhillon ordered the dead bodies to be buried. I did not see them being buried .... I went over to the Gurkha Regiment a fortnight after these men were shot. These four men who were shot were Jats. I know nothing else about them."

It is most extraordinary. You have A, B, C and D condemned to death, and you are asked to believe the one man who did not know who they were. In a trial for murder, if you are told that A was ordered to be shot and some one says: "I saw somebody shot and therefore I come to the conclusion that A was shot," I think one would be shocked to hear such a thing. I submit we have made our points quite clear in cross-examination. This witness said :

"I have never seen these men before. I did not know where they had come from."

It is not the charge at all that any four men were shot for any other crime or for no reason whatever. You are not called upon to say whether some other men were shot or why they were shot. That is not the charge.

Having dealt with the first part, which I do not want to repeat again, you will see how many infirmities are there. First, the improbability of Lt. Dhillon being there, according to the description in the sick report : next, no identification of any of the four man, never having been seen by these two men before. I do not say merely the cumulative effect of the whole thing—but even if any one of them was wanting you cannot say it is proved.

Then I have tried to prove from this evidence as far as it is possible to do so, as to whether or not he was required to go back to his duties, and he ultimately had to admit that he could not be there in the proper discharge of his duties; and after all the way in which you will judge a man is not by merely saying what they did, but by the probabilities of circumstances. If a man is expected to be on duty, and he says he stayed away out of sheer curiosity, would you rather prefer to believe that he went to his duty and was not there, or are you prepared to say, just because he said so, that he was there ? He says further :

"I stopped there for about half an hour." It is rather important from the point of view which I submit is of a man in that condition which as I said, is a fact which you cannot possibly disregard. In that condition, according to him, this process took half an hour. Then he says:

"I had nothing to do with either the men who were present there or the incident which took place there. I cannot tell the date or the week or the month on which this incident happened. I went over to the Gurkha Regiment which was in nearby village, the name of which I do not know. The incident to which I referred happened in 1945. I did not mention this incident at all in the Gurkha Regiment. I did not talk to anybody out to the assembly in the *nullah.* The company assembled in the nullah was about 100 strong."

The next witness will tell you there were about 25 men there :

"I did not see any outsider apart from the officers, the company and myself."

If in the teeth of that, the Advocate-General still insists that my interpretation of the evidence of the other man that he was no stranger is not correct, I ask the Court not to accept such an argument, because he may be plain and tell us who were there. I cross-examined the other witness and asked him whether besides the officers and the Company there was any stranger, and he said 'No'; and if after that I am to be told that I have not proved from the mouth of the other witness that the first witness was not there, it is an untrue interpretation of the evidence. He further says :

"I knew the names of Hidayatullah, Sepoy Kalu Ram and Naik Sher Singh because they belonged to my Battalion. My duty was to render first-aid. I never preferred first-aid to the three men I have mentioned. While at Popa, the Battalion consisted of 200 to 250 men. The three men do not come from the same place in India as I do. Ido not know where they come from. I had no personal contact with these three men before that date. I had nothing to do with them after the incident."

I say the probability is one in a thousand—the man knows nothing before, knows nothing afterwards; does not shoot and does not know how to shoot; has no business to be there; and yet you are asked to believe that the shooting took place. I submit it is a story which men of reason, just as we have on this tribunal, will not accept. The evidence goes on—

"They used to be in my Battalion ad I knew them. I cannot give the nominal roll of all the men of the Battalion. I knew the names of some but not of all men in the Battalion. I can give the names of 10 or 12 people in the Battalion ...... I did not talk to any of these men before that date. I have never seen these three men since."—(that is with reference to the person alleged to have been shot).

"I was 10 or 12 yards away form Major Dhillon. Nobody asked me why I was standing there. I had nothing to do with what Major Dhillon said on that occasion. I am not a poet. I am not a writer either. I swear and say to the Court that I remember every detail of what I have told the Court. I remember very well that none of the first men nor any of the other men were blindfolded. I omitted this detail in my evidence because I was not asked. I said that three volunteered to shoot these four men. The whole Company was armed. Most of them had rifles and a few of them had not. I knew at that time the name of the man whom Major Dhillon selected to shoot first. I do not know the names of any of the four men who were shot nor do I know their identity. After the shooting, Major Dhillon went away and so I went away as well. At the beginning I did not know what was happening there, but when I came to know what was happening there, I stayed on to see the end. I was 12 to 13 yards away from the place where these men fell. This occurred at about 4 o'clock in the afternoon. I did not have a watch."

The next improbability is that at the time there were sudden air raids, and this process which , according to the witness went on for half an hour is a matter for you to consider. But the important points are those which I mentioned first. This witness himself says:

"The place was subject to air attacks during those days..... Aeroplanes used to come over us frequently. There were trenches about and the nullah was a sheltered area. I do not know the persons who chose the *nullah*.... I am shown my statement of the Summary of Evidence. I signed that statement and identify my signature. It was read over to me before I signed it. My attention is drawn to the passage. As far as I remember, I said that Major Dhillon had ordered Sher Singh to fire a pistol, but it was not taken down."

I mean, he is quite willing to improve on any story so long as you ask him to do so.

"I was not interested in Captain Lee's examination or his Report. I was not interested in their burial either. Darbans Singh gave orders for their burial in my presence."

Questioned by the Court he said :

"This Company in the *nullah* was properly fallen in. These men were in front of the Company. The Company was about 10 or 12 yards from these men and I stood near the Company on one side. Major Dhillon gave orders for the fourth man to be shot."

Sepoy Gian Singh : "I remember four men being shot there. At about 4 o'clock one evening our Company got orders to fall in a *nullah*. On arrival there I saw four men whose hands were tied behind their backs. They were in a trench. Major Dhillon said that these four men had tried to go over to the British and so they were sentenced to death." Then he gives the names and details of the shooting of each man. "These four men who were killed were Jats. I do not know anything more about them . " For all I care any four Jats were killed, that would be the proof. That this particular sentence was carried out would be, I submit, the height of improbability, and unless there is definite evidence that the four particular individuals named in the crime report were shot, as having been identified as having been shot, I submit to the Court that you cannot possibly hold that these particular four persons were shot. The charge is aiding or abetting or the committing of the crime of shooting, and by proving that a Jat was shot, I submit with very great respect, nothing is proved. My case is honestly and deliberately that this is a false story. The sentence was not carried out. But taking everything against myself, and standing before a Court of law I say you do not establish a charge of shooting A by saying that you shot a Hindu. A Hindu may have been shot for all I know one same day.

Then, Sir, we come to the cross-examination of this witness. "The nullah to which I have referred was about five feet wide." Imagine the picture as this man gives, and of course it cannot possibly agree with the other picture. The other picture was one hundred people were present. This man's picture is that "from where I stood to where the trench was, it was about 25 feet, 20 feet deep and five feet wide." Few would believe that the company had fallen in such a place for such a purpose. I cannot imagine that a company would be asked to fall into a kind of well as this gentleman has described. Then he says that the height of the room was about 20 feet. "There were about 30 men in this space. Such men of the company as were in the lines were present there. Some men had gone out on fatigue. The trench was dug at one end of the nullah. I do not remember how many officers were there. Capt. Dhillon was in front of the company. The trench was below the nullah bed. I did not see the depth of the trench. The trench was between 20 and 25 yards from where the company had fallen in. A person in the trench could hear what was said from the place where the company was, if it was spoken loud enough to be hard. In that narrow space it is impossible to suppose that the other gentleman if he was there could ever have escaped detection. The man says that the whole process took half an hour, and hence the value of the submission that I make. "I do not remember any person not belonging to the company being there." I say that it requires a lot of conviction to submit to a court of law that this does not prove what I say it proves, namely that the first witness is proved by the second witness not to have been there. After all he said that there were thirty people. He knew that they were members of his company. Others had gone out on fatigue duty. This man says definitely : "I do not remember any person not belonging to the company being there." I submit with great respect that it has only one and one result, and that is that at all event the second witness says that the first witness was not there at all. Remember that within that five feet space you could not escape noticing any man. You could not help it if he was there. "We were standing in a place like this room except that it was not so broad. At some places it was wider but the place where we were standing in the nullah was about 5 feet broad. Of these three men who volunteered to do the shooting, two belonged to the company and one to Brigade Headquarters Police. Those three men who did the shooting were fallen in with the rest of the company when they volunteered to shoot. Because of air raids men used to go and hide themselves in the nullah bed and Naik Sher Singh was hiding in the nullah at the time. At that time there were constant apprehensions of air raids. The trench was about 20 yards away from where I was standing. The trench was at right angles to the bed of the nullah. I did not notice at the time what the length of the trench was. I did not notice whether the nullah was any wider at the point where the trench was. We were standing in two lines in the nullah facing the end of the nullah and I was in the middle of the company. All the men were facing towards where the men were shot. The men were in two groups. Major Dhillon was standing in front of the two groups, about 2 paces away from me. I heard Major Dhillon order the four men out one by one. I do not know their names. I had been in the company for a long time and that is how I knew the names of Kalu Ram and Hidayatullah." I submit that this again falls completely short of the proof of anything whatever like the death of an individual with whose death a man is accused. Remember that you have got to be satisfied, not in a vague sort of way, that some people were ordered to be shot, that some people were shot and those who were shot were those who were ordered to be shot. It is a process of absolutely vicious reasoning which I hope will not be resorted to or made use of by the Prosecution. Merely because the names of four persons whom you say were shot were there, you cannot prove that they were shot by saying that some people were shot.

Therefore, to summarise the evidence, it suffers from the worst infirmities, and much more so in a case where a man is charged with murder. First, it is improbable that the person who is alleged to have given orders was there or could have been there. It is improbable that in that state of health he could have been there for the period of time alleged for the process. Next, neither of the two witnesses is able to identify in the least degree who was shot. Then, the second witness say that the first witness was not there, and the second witness gives a picture which it is for you to believe to what extent it is correct. And then in addition to that, I am going to call attention to the evidence of witnesses, where in many instances of that kind, people were sort of sentenced but the sentence was never carried out.

The evidence to which I am referring is the evidence of P.W. 5 and it belongs to the same period to which this particular alleged shooting refers. The evidence of P.W. 5 in cross-examination is :" I know Captain Rab Nawaz. He was the commander of one of the P.O.W.'s Camps at Port Dixon, and the other camp was commanded by Capt. Karam Chand Bias of the first Bahawalpur Infantry. Capt. Rab Nawaz did not volunteer for the I.N.A. nor did Captain Bias. After Capt. Sahgal's conference on the 1st of March, within the next two weeks, there were several people arrested. After investigation all were released except Capt. Bedi. The reason for my remembering the date on which Capt .Sahgal commanded No. 2 Division was that on 28 February 1946 five officers deserted and on that occasion Capt. Sahgal arrested Captain Bedi. Captain Sahgal arrested Captian Bedi on the 1st or 2nd of March 1945 as a Divisional Commander. I do not remember the exact date on which Capt. Sahgal began to act as Divisional Commander."

Then, Sir, you have then the evidence of Gangasaran, to which I have already called attention, and this belongs to the same period as the date of the alleged execution of this sentence. Considering the evidence on record, I would submit to the Court that there is such a lacuna of evidence of identity, of improbability, that the Court should hold that there is at least a reasonable doubt whether this particular event took place. I of course put it more affirmatively myself, but feeling as I do in a case of this kind, it is my duty to put the case at the very lowest, and I say that there is want of evidence that is sufficient for my purpose. It is not enough that A should have been ordered to be shot, that by any process of reasoning therefore he must have been shot. That is a process which I submit is wrong and not permissible. The actual execution of the sentence has got to be proved with complete identity between those against whom the sentence was passed and those whom it is alleged were shot on this occasion. The thing has got to be proved by affirmative evidence and the burden of proof is completely on the Prosecution, hundred witnesses notwithstanding. In this case there are only two. One of them says that the other was not there. The point really is not how the deficiency of evidence arises. The question really is that the burden of proof being on the Prosecution to show that a definite person, A, B, C or D was killed, and died as a result of the action of a person who ordered the shooting is a fact, which must be proved.

All that is proved is, taking the allegation at its face value, that four shots were fired, and the identity of the persons shot is not known. My submission to the Court on that is that the evidence on this point suffers from infirmities which I have detailed to the Court in dealing with the evidence.

Therefore, with reference to this charge dealing with murder, my submission is that the Prosecution has entirely failed to prove the charges. The alternative submission is, assuming that the Court agrees with me that this was done in due course of the execution of the duty of an office in the I.N.A. governed by its own code, there is no question of any liability.

I say that Kalu Ram and Sher Singh who are said to have fired the shots are alive, and there is not that sufficiency of evidence either on facts or identity. Therefore I ask the Court not to run away with the idea that a sentence was passed on A, B, C and D, some people were shot on that day, and thereof the persons shot were those identical persons. This is a point which I cannot too often submit for the consideration of the Court. To say that A was shot because some persons were shot, is indeed a piece of logic which ought not to be allowed in a case of this grave magnitude. It is not permissible even in an ordinary case. The question says : Did you see A? The answer is : I do not know, but I saw somebody going into the fort and he was expected to go there. In a case of his kind, to say that he did go, would be the height of wrong reasoning. That is all I have got to say on the question of the sentence.

I submitted in the beginning of this case that this army of the I.N.A. was an organised army. The actual sections of the I.N.A. Act have been cited, as the Court will see from the crime report, and the Court will see that there can be no liability for any acts done in due prosecution of the war in the execution by officers of their respective duties. That of course is a complete answer. I was submit that even if the case is laid against A as a private individual, even then the evidence on the subject of having caused death, falls short.

Then there is a small point. I come to the evidence of Col. Kitson and Ghulam Mohammed with reference to the circumstances of Captain Sahgal's surrender. It is a point of substance, because under the terms of the surrender which were offered and accepted, the accused are entitled to all the privileges of prisoners of war on the cessation of hostilities. I shall now read the evidence of Col. Kitson, P.W. 29. He says:

"I then went forward myself up to the east corner of his village, when I met my leading Company Commander together with Captain Sahgal, the accused. With him were a number of other officers of the Indian National Army and approximately a hundred Indian troops of the I.N.A. at that particular time. More appeared late. My leading Company Commander handed me a note which he had received from a surrender party under a white flag. I am afraid I have not preserved the note. I destroyed it about two months later when I was going through some papers, and I am afraid I saw no importance of this note which I threw away. The note was addressed to the Commander of the British Forces, or may have been addressed to the Allied Forces, and it said that approximately 30 officers and 500 troops of the I.N.A. wish to surrender as prisoners of war. I then talked to Captain Sahgal, and he gave me his name and his regiment. He said 'I am Captain Sahgal', and I asked him what his unit was both in the I.N.A. and in the Indian Army, and he told me then that he had been in the 5/10th Baluch and that he was then commanding a regiment of the I.N.A., and that he had with him there at his Regimental Headquarters a 1st Aid attachment and one Battalion of his Regiment. I then made arrangements for the collecting of all the arms of the prisoners and arranged with Captain Sahgal about their feeding. We had no food for them."

You have to read this evidence in the light of what Ghulam Muhammad said. He has given evidence before you to this effect that all non-commissioned officers collected together, they were give an hour's time to consider the question of surrender as prisoners of war, and that if that was not accepted they were prepared to fight. A letter to that effect was written and despatched, and you have the evidence of Col. Kitson as to what happened. Under these circumstances I submit that in so far as the surrender of Captain Sahgal is concerned, it has been on the terms on which the offer was made, and I submit he is entitled to be released.

There are one or two small matters which I should like to deal with before I raise three points of law. You must have heard the evidence of the last defence witness, Captain Arshad. He gives you a truthful account of what occurred prior to the surrender of Rangoon, and the reoccupation of Rangoon. I have produced four documents which clearly show the recognition on the part of the British officers of the existence of an organised army called the I.N.A. The men in charge have been addressed by their proper designation and they have been entrusted with definite duties, and there is ample evidence to prove that the I.N.A. was an organised army, and it was treated as an organised army. I would draw your attention to Exhibits 5 Us. 5Vs. and Ws. You will find instructions there regarding the address of officers. This includes a document by Brigadier Lauder.

So, I submit that right up to the time of the surrender there has been recognition on the part of the opposition armies, that the I.N.A. was an organised army and it was so referred to an addressed through its proper officers. They were also recognised as officers for the time being. That, Sir, is practically the whole of the case regarding the documents and the recorded evidence.

I now come to certain submissions regarding further points of law. They are three in number and they are founded on a true interpretation of the Indian Army Act and of the rules thereunder. Under Section 41, this Court is authorised and is given jurisdiction to try among others civil offences.

The word 'civil offence' is defined in the Act itself. Section 7, Sub-section (18) reads : "A civil offence means an offence which, if committed in British India, would be triable by a Criminal Court." The question really depends on the true construction of the words 'triable by a Criminal court.' I know and I am fully aware that the Criminal Procedure Code has not been applied to the proceedings of this Court. But that is irrelevant to the issue that I am now going to submit to the Court. If, by the definition under Sub-Section (18) you have to find out what is triable by a Criminal Court, you cannot just do it in the air. I defy my honourable friend, or anybody else, to say what it is unless you go to the appropriate Act which shows what things are triable by a Criminal Court. That is not saying that the Criminal Procedure Code is applied here. That is where there is a likelihood of false reasoning. The point is this. In order to understand one statute, and where the statute expressly refers to what is triable by a Criminal Court, you must go to the statute which defines what is triable by a Criminal Court. It would be an extraordinary thing if the whole thing were left in the. Therefore, if there is another statute which shows what is triable by a Criminal Court, you have got to go to it, notwithstanding that the statute is not applicable to the proceedings of this Court. What I do say is this. If you have to find out what is triable by a Criminal Court, you must go to the statute which shows what is triable by a Criminal Court, and that Statute, so far as one is aware, is the Criminal Procedure Code. On that two points arise. One is that under Section 196 of the Criminal Procedure Code it is laid down as follows :

"No court (meaning no criminal court) shall take cognizance of any offence punishable under Chapter VI (which is this offence) unless upon the complaint made by the order or under the authority of the Provincial Government or some officer empowered by the Provincial Government in this behalf." If merely for the purpose of finding out what is it that is given to you for trial you have to go to another statute, then it is a wrong argument to say that you will not. Let me put it in plainer language. When you say that my terms of engagement are the same as those of Major Preetam Singh's, it is not enough. I must ascertain my terms from the contract. That is the simple illustration which will bring home to even a layman's mind the point that I am intending to make. The point that I am making is this that the civil offences which are committed to you for trial are those which will be triable by a Criminal Court. Therefore, my first submission is that what offences are triable by a Criminal Court you can only discover by looking at another law which is appropriate to the purpose and not by shutting your eyes to it. When you go and look into that law, what do you find? That law requires that that offence would not be triable by that Criminal Court except upon the complaint of an officer of the Local Government, etc. It has nothing to do with Captain Mead's case or any other case. That was a case of Section 270 of the Government of India Act and has got no bearing on the question. The point is this : How do you discover or where do you discover that the offence is triable by a Criminal Court. That you must discover because you cannot say that anything that is brought to you for trial, you will try. You will yourself ask : "What is it that I am entitled to try and if I am only entitled to try that which is triable by a Criminal Court, I must necessarily go to the statute which gives me that power." My submission to the court is that by reason of Section 196, no complaint having been made by a Local Government or an officer in that behalf appointed by them, this Court may not try an offence under Section 121, Chapter VI. My next point is again a point of construction, a point which, I submit, is of commonsense. If I am given a power to try offences within a certain limit, then I must find out what is being triable by a Criminal Court. If I find that a Criminal Court is incapable of trying an offence, then you must come to the conclusion that a Criminal Court of its own motion and of its own authority is incapable of trying that offence. If a Criminal Court is incapable without more of trying the offence, equally this Court is incapable of trying the offence. In other words, there are two alternative arguments before the Court. One is that within this sphere of the offences triable by this Court, this particular offence does not fall, in that it is not triable by a Criminal Court without more. In other words, a Criminal Court of its own motion could not possibly take cognizane this charge. Until the Local Government by itself or through its proper officer, does not move, the Criminal Court is incapable of trying it. Therefore, the question is two-fold. Firstly, that the Criminal Court being incapable of trying, this Court is also incapable of trying it. Secondly, if you put the point that the Criminal Court is capable of trying, but with a condition satisfied. There fore, in either view of the case, this Court is not competent to try the charge before it. My submission is that, in so far as the charge of alleged murder by Shah Nawaz or Dhillon are concerned, they are really part of it and nothing else. It is not suggested on the record that either of them wanted to shoot anybody for personal enmity or for any other cause of any other kind. It is patent on the face of the record that they were part of the actions which they took as officers of the I.N.A. Therefore, my submission is that the Court is not competent to try the two sets of offenses before it. *Per contra* if the Court is of opinion or hould it come to be of opinion that the charges of murder or abetment of murder are independent charges, then my submission to the Court is that under Rule 24 of the rules of conduct of trial in this court, the joint trial is completely illegal on a decision of the Privy Council in Indian Law Reports, 25 Madras, Subramaniam's case. (Rule 24 was read out and the Judge Advocate pointed out the amendment to it). That does not fall within the Rule because as to the murder and abetment of Mohanmmed Husain all the persons are not there. So that whether you call up this rule or any other rule, that is what you my call in the plain language of the section, a complete misjoinder of the charges and of the accused. Shah Nawaz has nothing to do with the alleged murder nor has Dhillon anything to do with the murder of Mohammed Husain. I submit to the Court confidently that if you treat the second set of charges as independent charges, this trial is wholly illegal.

I will now give to the Court the judgement of the Privy Council in Law Report 25 Madras, on page 61.

"The appellant was tried at the Criminal Session of the High Court, and convicted on an indictment the first count of which contravened the provisions of Sections 233 and 234 of the Code of Criminal Procedure (which proved that every separate offence shall be charged and tried separately, except that three offences of the same kind may be tried together in one charge if committed within the period of one year), and did not fall within the provisions of section 235 (I) which provides that if, in one series of acts so connected together as to form the same transaction, more offences than one are committed by the same person, he may be charged with and tried at one trial for every such offence. On a case certified under article 26 of the Letters Patent and heard by the Full Court, it was held by the majority of the Court that the union of the first count with the others made the whole indictment bad for misjoinder, but that it was open to them to strike out the first count, rejecting the evidence with regard to it, and deal with the evidence as to the remaining counts of the indictment. This was done with the result that the conviction was upheld on one count only, the sentence being reduced:

Held, by the Judicial that the disregard of an express provision of law as to the mode of trial was not a mere irregularity such as could be remedied by Section 537 of the Criminal Procedure Code. Such a phrase as 'irregularity' is not appropriate to the illegality of trying an accused person for more different offences at the same time, and those offences being spread over a longer period than by law could have been joined together in one indictment.

"Nor could such illegal procedure be amended by arranging afterwards what might or might not have been properly submitted to the jury. To fallow this would leave to the Court the functions of the jury, and the accused would never have been really tried at all upon the charge afterwards arranged by the Court. The trial having been conducted in a manner prohibited by law, was held to be altogether illegal and the conviction was set aside."

The judgement of the Lord Chancellor is on P. 96.

"In this case the appellant was tried on an indictment in which he was charged with no less than forty-one acts, these acts extending over a period of two years. This was plainly in contravention of the Code of Criminal Procedure, Section 234, which provides that a person may only be tried for three offences of the same kind if committed within a period of twelve months. The reason for such a provision, which is analogous to our own provisions in respect of embezzlement, is obviously in order that the jury may not be prejudiced by the multitude of charges and the inconvenience of hearing together such a number of instances of culpability and the consequent embarrassment both to judges and accused. It is likely to cause confusion and to interfere with the definite proof of a distinct offence which it is the object of all criminal procedure to obtain. The policy of such a provision is manifest and the necessity of a system of written accusation specifying a definite criminal offence is of the essence of Criminal Procedure. Their Lordships think that the course pursued and which was plainly illegal cannot be amended by arranging afterwards what might or might not have been properly submitted to the jury."

It means that it is too late for even this Court to say, " We will either strike out the charge of waging war or strike out the charges of murder and abetment of murder in which some of the persons are uninterested and not charged with reference to offences charged against others."

Then the judgment proceeds—

"Upon the assumptions that the trial was illegally conducted it is idle to suggest"—I am glad I am not using those words by the Lord Chancellor uses them—"that there is enough left upon the indictment upon which a conviction might have been supported if the accused had been properly tried. The mischief sought to be avoided by the Statute has been done. The effect of the multitude of charges before the jury has not been averted by dissecting the verdict afterwards and appropriating the finding of guilty only to such parts of the written accusation as ought to have been submitted to the jury.

"It would in the first place leave to the Court the functions of thc jury and the accused would never have really been tried at all upon the charge arranged afterwards by the Court.

"Their Lordship cannot regard this as cured by Section 537."

They do not say that any irregularity has not caused injustice and so does not matter. But even that does not exist, because he must be held to the consequence in both ways. My learned friend says that the Criminal Procedure Code does not apply, and as such we proceed. So he cannot have resort to Section 537. And then you get back to a very narrow point that the trial, as I submit, is clearly in contravention of Rule 24 of the Rules of Procedure. It is a complete irregularity and there is no way of curing it. Their Lordships proceed :-

"Their Lordships are unable to regard the disobedience to an express provision as to a mode of trial as a mere irregularity."

In other words, you cannot in one trial charge people collectively unless they have committed all the offences collectively, which admittedly they have not done. Even on the extended words which the judge-Advocate read they would not apply because one thing is quite clear in relation to the charges and that is this, that some of accused are not in any manner liable for the offences alleged to have been committed by others. Therefore, I submit that this trial is wholly illegal. The judgment proceeds:-

"Such a phrase as irregularity is not appropriate to the illegality of trying an accused person for many different offences at the same time and those offences being spread over a longer period than by law could have been joined together in one indictment. The illustration to the section itself sufficiently shows what was meant."

The remedying of mere irregularities is familiar in most systems of jurisprudence, but it would be an extraordinary extension of such a branch of administering the Criminal Law to say that when the Code positively enacts that such a trial as that which has taken place here shall not be permitted that this contravention of the Code comes with in the description of error, omission or irregularity.

"Some pertinent observations are made upon the subject by Lord Herschell and Lord Russel of Killowen in *Smurthwaite* vs. *Hannay*, where in a civil case several causes of action were joined. Lord Herschell says that 'If unwarranted by any enactment or rule it is much more than an irregularity', and Lord Russell of Killowen in the same case says, 'Such a joinder of plaintiffs is more than an irregularity; it is the constitution of a suit in a way not authorized by law and the rules applicable to procedure.'

With all respect to Sir Francis Maclean and the other Judges who agreed with him in the case of In the Matter of Abdur Rahman, he appears to have fallen into a very manifest logical error in arguing that because al irregularities are illegal, that therefore all things that may in his view be called illegal are therefore by that one adjective applied to them become equal in importance and are susceptible of being treated alike. But the trial was prohibited in the mode in which it was conducted, and their Lordships will humbly advise His Majesty that the conviction should be set aside."

And I submit it does not require much argument. It is therefore wrong on the face of the charges with which these men are charged, and I submit that this trial is wholly illegal and I ask you to hold it so.

That is as far as I will go on the record on the points which arise for your decision, and there are very few points indeed. I will plainly and briefly state to the Court the points on which I really, so that there may be no room for mistake or equivocation about it. I say that this is a case of men not acting on their own in any struggle or waging war at all. This is a case of men as part of a regular organized army, accepted as such by their opponents, fighting a war under the directions of a regularly formed Government. That being so, I submit that they are subject to the ordinary laws of war with which I have troubled you at some length, namely, they are entitled to all the rights and immunities of belligerents. My submission is that to the extent to which this is a matter pertaining to war and the conduct of war it is outside the municipal law. But I am afraid sometimes in the narrow precincts of a Court like this, one may say : "What have I got to do with international law ?" But fortunately for myself I am fortified in this case so that I can fall within the four corners of the Indian enactment, i.e., Sec. 79. I say that if my first submission as to the jurisdiction or municipal law and its non-application is not upheld by this Court—though I submit is should be—I say that within the meaning of Sec.79 it is quite plain—you are bound to give effect to it and I have submitted authorities—that the word "law" as ministered in Britain and Indian recognises the principles of international law. And therefore , if a thing is justified by law, I can plead justification before this Court under Sec. 79. That is my first point.

My second point before the Court is that as regards questions which were incidental, I do not wish to repeat them here, though I wish to submit to the Court that the question of allegiance is irrelevant to the issue, but to the extent to which it is relevant I have already submitted that when the time arrives in relations between the Crown and the Colonies, the Colonies are entitled to throw off their allegiance on the outbreak of war for the purpose of their liberation. And I have given you the most classical instance of those who are now the friends of Britain and , if I may say so, their warmest and greatest supporters in the task of saving civilization. You could not have a stronger instance than that.

Then the next point which I ask the Court to hold is that on a question of fact entirely, in so far as the Indian National Army was concerned, it was voluntary organisation. Even if there were conscription, it does not make any difference in this case, because there are countries where there is conscription and punishment attached to it even today. But it has become fashionable to says : "Oh, there was torture and coercion" and all the rest of it, and I ask the Court to hold that it was entirely free from any such complaint. At all events, apart from any hearsay, on the evidence recorded before this Court, I have already submitted that the people who complain of torture fall into four classes : there were those who prove that in two cases it was for reasons which are self-confessed in one case and practically admitted in the second case. The first was refusing to do fatigue and the second case was cow-killing. As to the other cases of an isolated character, they are exaggerated, and deserve nothing else but contempt at your hands. If men were asked to do fatigue duty, merely because they have to carry baskets or make beds for the purpose of sowing vegetables, if they say it was torture, I hope my learned friend will not use that word in connection with that conduct.

Then I ask the Court to hold that in any event this evidence is totally irrelevant for the purpose of this case, for the reasons which I have submitted, namely, that the ground on which that evidence was attempted is entirely proved not to exist.

The next thing that I submit to the Court is that the evidence with reference to the alleged charges of murder would be really covered, if I am right in my first submission, by the fact that they are part of the prosecution of the war, in that these people were sentenced by Court Martial to be shot under the proper law. The next thing I ask the Court to hold is that there was an organised Government, that a very large number of Indians in the

Far East owned allegiance to this Government, which was recognised, having had ceded to it territories which are mentioned, and it was by this Government that war was declared, and the Indian National Army fought this campaign.

I will hand over to the learned Judge Advocate the list which I offered to give him yesterday on the point which my learned friend on the other side attempts to make, in that as if there was some provision as to flogging, intending possibly thereby to argue that the whole of that Code was an uncivilised Code. I think he was snatching at a complete straw, because as to the rest of the Act he admitted that it was in consonance with the Indian Army Act. And the only thing that he referred to is corporal punishment. I am therefore handing to the Judge Advocate provisions of the law in which the same thing appears under a different head, in force when the Indian Army Act was in operation.

Judge Advocate : Are you referring to Sec. 22 of the Indian Army Act?

Mr. Desai: My learned friend tried to make out as if whipping was a punishment which was abolished with reference to the army in this country, and I submit that he was entirely mistaken.

Judge Advocate : The very first sentence in writing that you have given is wrong. You have got flogging under the Act as it stands. Punishment of whipping can be inflicted on menial servants up to a maximum of 20 scores—that is what is written here, and the correct thing is 12 strokes on active service.

Mr. Desai : If I am wrong, I must correct myself.

Judge Advocate : I have corrected it now.

Mr. Desai : The point, Sirs, which I am trying to labour before the Court is this : In addition to the provisions in the Indian Army Act, there are provisions under the Defence of India Act and in the Ordinances. All of them have got to be taken together to see whether or not, and what punishment is permissible.

By Ordinance 3 of 1942—if necessary we will produce the actual copy of the Ordinance before you —whipping was ordered as a punishment.

Let me get back to the point : The point really is that in so far as the governance of the Army is concerned, it was governed by an Act which except for the purpose of whipping, has been practically or tacitly admitted to be the Indian Army Act. As regards whipping, I submit to the Court that that kind of punishment exists, though not in the Army Act wholly, in the there ordinances which are reproduced. Supposing to the extent to which there was an excess of the number of strokes, I submit with very great respect that it is not going to make an uncivilised Army because of that. Therefore, substantially the point is, there is an army governed by a Code which is substantially, if not actually, word for word, the same as the Indian Army Act.

I next come to the question that, in fact, the alleged atrocities—that is the mildest word that can be used from the point of view of my learned friend—which are said to have been exercised for the purpose of getting enrolment to the I.N.A. are in fact not true. The accused are not charged with it, nor have they anything to do with it. They neither did it, nor permitted it, nor encouraged it, nor have they any knowledge of it. That, Sir, is the actual position so far as that charge is concerned.

Then, coming to the alleged charge of murder and abetment, I have dealt with that and I have satisfied that Court that the execution of the sentences has not been proved.

My next submission to the Court is that this trial is wholly illegal.

My next submission to the Court is that so far as the construction of the words 'offences triable by a Criminal Court' is concerned, the Court must have reference to the only enactment which says what are the offences triable by the Court, and you cannot do by saying that the Criminal Procedure Code is not applicable—and if it has to be resorted to, then it has to be stated : First, this charge is not triable at all. Alternatively, in any case, this charge is not triable except on the complaint of a Local Government or an officer authorized in that behalf, and such a complaint does not exist. And for this reason my clients should be declared innocent of the charges against them.

The last thing that I wish to say is that if any new or fresh authority is cited by my learned friend which I had no opportunity of meeting, I should be permitted to hand in a very short statement, covering a single page, as to why those authorities if they are relied upon are not applicable to the facts of this case or to the decision in this case.

Finally, Sirs, I acknowledge with appreciation the courtesy and attention that has been given to us, and I hope that when I hand over a signed transcript to each member of the Court, it will receive such attention as it may deserve.

Judge Advocate : With regard to your last submission, under what rule are you applying to make another address?

Mr. Desai : I do not pretend that there is a rule. It is a matter of common Justice. If any authority is cited by one side which the other side has never had any opportunity of seeing or meeting, with the best of imagination he could not possibly deal with it. Therefore, common fairness demands that he should be given a chance to explain. All that is forbidden is an address to the Court. But surely for your own assistance, if we may pretend that we are able to give any assistance, if anything is cited by the other side which is not seen by me, surely I should be allowed to present to the Court a very short resume of my grounds on which it is not applicable.

Judge-Advocate : Would that not apply to any case in which your opponent had the last word?

Mr. Desai : Then the law is accepted. My learned friend will not contradict it. Even when a man has no right of reply and a fresh authority is cited, he has a right to answer. I hope my learned friend will agree with me there. It is a rule of common fairness. You do not need a rule for this: that a thing which is never urged before this Court, is urged before this Court, and no reply is allowed.

Judge-Advocate: As I have often told you, gentlemen, a Court Martial is bound by very rigid rules outside which they cannot go. The rule is laid down for your strict obedience by the Indian Legislature, and whether rightly or wrongly you cannot go outside that rule. Rule 48 of the Indian Army Act is the only rule I know with regard to the right of address, and it reads as follows.

(Reads Rule 48 of the Indian Army Act).

That rigid rule is for your strict compliance.

Mr. Desai : There is one point I would like to urge. The words are : "The Prosecutor may reply." If the Prosecutor confines himself to merely replying to what I have said, I have nothing to say. Let him be confined completely to what I have argued by way of reply, and I am quite content. I am glad that thought the ruling is partly against me, it is partly in my favour also. Let that ruling be strictly followed, namely that it will be enjoined on the Prosecution that he does nothing more than reply to what I have argued. Then I am quite content.

Judge-Advocate : The Court regret they are unable to permit a further address by the Counsel for the Defence after the address of the Counsel for the Prosecution.

Mr. Desai : Would the Court direct that the Prosecutor would only reply what I have argued and nothing more? You cannot have it both ways.

Council for the Prosecution : That is not the meaning of the word 'reply', I submit.

Mr. Desai : If my friend thinks that he is supporting the cause of justice by saying that I cannot reply to a new matter in case law, that is a new law. Unless he is prepared to submit to this restriction, I submit the law lays on him the duty merely to reply to what I have said. I have nothing more to say, justice or no justice. I hope my learned friend cited nothing that is not strictly relevant to what I have said.

Counsel for the Prosecution : My submission is that it is not replying to what you have said but it means addressing the Court on the case. I ask for an adjournment for my address and I have to ask for an adjournment up to Saturday. What I intend to do is to give my address in writing, if not the whole of it, at least the largest part of it.

President : The whole of your address on Saturday?

Counsel for the Prosecution : I think so. But I would suggest that an extra hour might be thrown in. If I have in writing, it will not take so long.

Mr. Desai : I have no objection.

The case was adjourned to December 22.

13

Prosecution Address at I.N.A. Trial, Red Fort[1]

22 December, 1945

Mr. President and Members of this Honourable Court :

I will first deal with the charge relating to the waging of war. The evidence shows that all the accused recruited men for the I.N.A., took part in the organization of the I.N.A. gave directions and orders for fighting against His Majesty's Forces and themselves fought against them. Capt. Shah Nawaz Khan was promoted to the rank of 2nd Lieutenant in the I.N.A. with effect from September 1, 1942, On September 9, 1942, he was made a Major with effect from September 10, 1942. On October 15, 1942, he was promoted to be Lieutenant Colonel. On November 30, 1942, he was appointed to be Officer Commanding Cadets Training School with effect from November 26,1942. On April 10,1943, he was transferred from Reinforcement Group to the Office of Directorate of Military Bureau. On April 17,1943, he was appointed Chief of General Staff. In February 1945 he was promoted to be Colonel in the I.N.A. Capt. Sahgal was made a 2nd Lieutenant in the I.N.A. on September 1, 1942, and he was promoted to be Captain with effect from November 10, 1942. On October 15, 1943, he was promoted to be a Mahor. On October 10, 1943, Capt. Sahgal was transferred form the Headquarters of Hind Field Force, G.P. to the D.M.B's office with effect from February 26, 1943. On April 17, 1944, he was posted as Military Secretary. Lt. Dhillon was appointed 2nd Lieutenant in the I.N.A. on September 1, 1942. He was promoted to be a captain with effect from September 10, 1942. On October 15, 1942 he was promoted to be a Major. On April 17, 1943, he was posted to "O" Branch as Deputy Quarter Master General.

1. *Ibid.*, The above address was delivered by Sir. N.P. Engineer, Advocate-General of India, Council for the Prosecution.

The evidence establishes beyond doubt not only that all the three accused joined the I.N.A. immediately after the fall of Singapore but that they also tried, by means of lectures, to make other prisoners of war forsake their allegiance to the Crown Capt. Shah Nawaz Khan lectured in March 1942 when he was in the Neesoon Camp to all the V.C.Os. and N.C.Os. who were collected for the purpose.

This is provided by the evidence of Subedar Major Baburam. Witness Jemadar Mohammed Hayat also deposes to Capt. Shah Nawaz Khan having given lectures in Neesoon Camp after the fall of Singapore. Witness Jemadar Iltaf Razak desposes to the fact that Capt. Shah Nawaz Khan went to Port Dickson in January or February 1943 and gave a lecture there to the Indian Officers asking them to join the I.N.A. Witness Nayak Santok Singh says in his evidence that Capt. Shah Nawaz Khan lectured in April 1943 in Saletar Camp which was for non-volunteers, saying that it was the duty of every Indian to join the new I.N.A. Witness Lance-Naik Gangaram says in his evidence that he saw Capt. Shah Nawaz Khan in port Swettenham at the end of April or beginning of May 1943 and that he delivered a lecture to the prisoners of war in the camp.

Witness Naik Santok Singh says in his evidence that Capt. Sahgal in January 1943 came to the men of No. 1 Signal Company and told them that the I.N.A. which was going to be formed would be the new Indian National Army and that every Indian should join it.

Subedar Major Baburam in his evidence says that at the end of February or the beginning of March, 1942, Lt. Dhillon delivered a lecture at Neesoon Camp to the V.C.Os. and N.C.Os. and to the men of the Battalion; asking every one to join the I.N.A. Witness Subedar Asal Nur Khan says that he saw Lt. Dhillon in Neesoon Camp at the end of February or the beginning of March 1942, and he delivered a lecture asking the prisoners of war to co-operate with the Japanese. Witness Havildar Suah Singh says that in June 1942, Lt. Dhillon came to Jitra accompanied by Major Dhara and that Major Dhara delivered a lecture asking the prisoners of war to join the I.N.A. Lt. Dhillon spoke after Major Dhara and asked them to join the I.N.A. Witness Sepoy Kaka Singh said in his evidence that Lt. Dhillon delivered a lecture in Taiping in March 1943 to the prisoners of war who were there, asking them to join the I.N.A.

All the accused admit having fought against the Forces of His Majesty the King. In view of that admission, it is not necessary to deal at length with the evidence establishing that fact. The entries in the diaries of Capt. Shah Nawaz and Capt. Sahgal are themselves sufficient to prove the part which they took in the fighting. Witness Sepoy Dilasa Khan who was in the Third Battalion Bose Brigade commanded by Capt. Shah Nawaz deposes to the fighting on the Falam Haka Front. He was instructed to try to contact with a company of Punjabi Mussalmans. In a scuffle which took place, his company captured a party of Chin Levies. Witness Havildar Nawaz Khan who was attached to No. 1 Guerilla Regiment, deposes to Capt. Shah Nawaz giving directions for the fighting in April 1944.

Witness Hanuman Prasad who was in the Seventh Battalion Nehru Regiment, which was commanded by Lt. Dhillon, deposes to the fighting which took place on March 16, 1945, when some Gurkha troops attacked his Regiment at Myingan. Witness Gunner Bhal Singh who was in the First Battalion of the Fifth Guerilla Regiment deposes to the encounter with an Allied Patrol on March 3, 1945, near Popa Hill. That was an encounter when two Allied soldiers were killed and two jeeps were captured with a wireless set by the I.N.A. Battalion, One of these Jeeps was in fact, thereafter, used by Capt. Shah Nawaz Khan. An entry in the diary of Capt. Shah Nawaz corroborates this incident.

Witness Sepoy Sadullah Khan who was in the seventh Battalion of the Nehru Brigade deposes to the fighting near Popa Hill under the command of Lt. Dhillon. Witness Lance Naik Mohammed said who was in the Fifth Guerilla Regiment, which was afterwards called the Second Infantry Regiment, deposes to Capt. Sahgal taking over the command in December 1944 and to the attack on Pyinbin and to the fighting near Legyi village at the end of March 1945. Witness Havildar Ghulam Mohammed was posted to No. 2 Battalion as adjutant. Lt. Dhillon was second in command. The Regiment Commander was Capt. Sahgal and the Divisional Commander was Capt. Shah Nawaz. This witness desposes to the fighting with the Allied patrol on the occasion when the two jeeps were captured by the Battalion. The witness also deposes to the fighting which took place immediately before the surrender of Capt. Sahgal on April 28, 1945.

As regards the Defence application to exclude the evidence of coercion, it is submitted that no such application can be entertained. The Prosecution tendered this evidence on the ground that the Prosecution was entitled to show that the accused tried to win over other prisoners of war from their allegiance to the Crown in order to join them in waging war against His Majesty the King and to show the conditions under which they did this recruiting work. It is true that the Prosecution case is that in the speeches which the accused made they referred to the conditions prevailing and to the hardships which they were undergoing and they held out promises that, if the prisoners of war did join the I.N.A., they would avoid those hardships and the treatment and that the accused also held out various threats as to what happen if they did not join the I.N.A. This, however, is by no means essential to make the evidence relevant. As I said, when I argued the question of the relevancy and admissibility of this evidence, "it will be sufficient for my case to show that atrocities were committed openly and notoriously and that they (the accused) were aware of them, and with knowledge of that they continued to press the Indian prisoners of war to join the I.N.A." Of course, it will be for the Court to decide after considering the whole evidence :—

(a) whether in fact atrocities were committed in order to make the prisoners of war join the I.N.A.;
(b) whether the accused to press the Indian prisoners of war to join the I.N.A.; and
(c) whether they held out veiled threats as to what would happen if they did not join the I.N.A.

The Court will come to its own conclusions on these questions, at the proper time ; but the question of excluding the evidence cannot arise and the application cannot be entertained.

There is ample evidence to prove that not only men of Indian Army but the officers also were brutally treated if they refused to join the I.N.A. Several witnesses despised to the fact that while they were being tortured they were told that they would continue to be tortured unless and until they joined the I.N.A. Capt. Dhargalkar in his evidence deposed to his experiences in the concentration camp in August 1942. He says that the conditions were very bad and he was not treated as an officer. For the first seven days he and others with him were kept in a tent which was full of white-ants. They were then removed from the tent to a hut about 500 yards away. They had to fall in with the other prisoners to collect their food. There was a lot of wire fences in which lots of Indian ranks used to be kept throughout rain and sun. On several occasions he saw a good number of Indian ranks being beaten. He and others with him had to salute the I.N.A. sentries and if they did not wear head gear they had to bow to them. When he developed some sort of body rash and went to the hospital and asked for medicine, he was told that he could not have any.

Jemadar Mohammed Nawaz deposes to the treatment which he and his companions received in the concentration camp on September 13, 1942. According to this witness, they were first deprived of all their belongings and then they were taken to a tent which was surrounded by barbed wiring and guarded by an armed sentry. They were told that as they were undergoing troubles and were educated people, it was better for them to volunteer for the I.N.A. They were also told that they had been asking Mussalmans not to join the I.N.A. This witness was asked to join the I.N.A. but he refused. The next day all those who refused to join the I.N.A. were made to fall in and they were asked to double march. They were then beaten with lathis and made to do fatigue work consisting of carrying dung heaps. While carrying them, were beaten by the sentries who were with them. He further deposes to the fact that there was a roll call every evening and if anybody reported sick and the doctor said that he was not sick, he would be given 12 strokes by the cane. He deposed to having seen while he and his companions were doing fatigue a man clad in khaki uniform whose hands were tied to a stick and his feet to iron pegs from behind and two sepoys were beating him. He further deposes to the fact that at the roll call every evening they were told that they were foolish people because the Japanese had promised that they would hand over India to Indians after conquering it. This witness in his evidence said that he never joined the I.N.A.

Capt. Arshad, one of the witnesses for the defence, said in his evidence that sometimes in October or November 1942 he was sent for by the V.C.O.s. of his unit who had volunteered and the V.C.Os., including Jemadar Mohammed Nawaz and about 400 other ranks, signed their names on the form. When Jemadar Mohammed Nawaz was in the witness box this was never put to him. The summary of evidence of Jemadar Mohammed Nawaz was furnished to the defence a long time before the trial commenced and the defence had also interviewed Capt. Arshad as a contemplated witness on their behalf.

Capt. Arshad also in his evidence said that Subedar Ahmed Khan had been arrested and taken to the detention camp for stealing, and that there was a protest against his arrest. Jemadar Mohammed Nawaz and a few other V.C.Os. also went to the detention camp.

According to Capt. Arshad he was instrumental in getting them out of the detention camp. It is submitted that this version of the story cannot be accepted. It is impossible to conceive that the Commander of the concentration camp would admit into it all these people simply because they wanted to go in. The evidence of Capt. Arshad on this point, it is submitted, is very unsatisfactory. He himself cannot explain how it was possible that these people could have been taken in. He did not go into the alleged charge of theft which, according to him, was preferred against Subedar Ahmed Khan, and it is difficult to accept the statement that without making any enquiries into the matter he could have asked for the release of these persons.

Witness Havildar Mohammed Sarwar deposes to the incident of the firing in Kranji Camp. According to him, he and the Punjab Mussalmans refused to join the I.N.A. One day a Jemadar and a Subedar with a guard came to them and the Jamadar delivered a lecture asking them to join the I.N.A. All of them refused to do so and the guard then started firing on them and two of the prisoners of war were killed. Thereupon, the prisoners of war attacked the guard and the guard continued firing on them and many of them were wounded. One of the guards was killed on the spot.

Later on, some Japanese officers accompanied by I.N.A. officers came and the witness and his companions were told by the Japanese officer that if they continued behaving like that they would be all killed. The Japanese officer told them that if they killed one I.N.A. man they would kill a hundred of them in return. The witness and his companions were then taken to the concentration camp and they were beaten with canes. The witness was rendered unconscious and taken to hospital. He remained in hospital for approximately three weeks. When he was discharged from hospital he was taken to Kranji Camp. After that he joined the I.N.A. because of those troubles. But he had made up his mind that when he was detailed to the fron the would desert.

In the cross-examination of this witness, it was suggested that all this treatment was given to them because on the previous day they refused to obey an order to be divided into parties of 323 for fatigue purposes. The evidence of this witness remained unshaken and it is submitted that there is no reason why this evidence should not be accepted.

Jemadar Mohamad Hayat said in his evidence that the Mussalmans of his Battalion did not join the I.N.A. The Hindus and Sikhs of the Battalion joined it and a few Mussalmans also. He was ordered to join the I.N.A. but he refused. He was of the idea that he should not join the I.N.A. He always told his officers and his soldiers that they should not join the I.N.A. and he always carried on propaganda against the I.N.A.

In July 1942, the unit of this witness was at Bidadari Camp. In that month he was taken with 500 men of his unit to the concentration camp. They were stripped of their belonging and they were ordered to take off their Indian Army badges. The officers, N.C.Os and sepoys were then taken separately to separate places and imprisoned in separate cages. Among the prisoners there were four I.C.Os. and 12 V.C.Os. The witness then describes the beating given on the next day to 12 of them, the witness being one of them. They were made to lie flat on the ground and beaten with sticks five feet long and two inches thick. Witness became unconscious by reason of the beating. The other 11 men were also injured by the beating. They were then made to do fatigue consisting of carrying sacks filled with earth. While they were doing this, they were beaten by the sentries who were posted along the way. At night they were not allowed to sleep. One after another of the inmates of the cage had to do duty as sentry in the cage and every five minutes a report was called for by the I.N.A. sentry outside. The inmates of this concentration camp were made to salute every member of the I.N.A. including sweepers. The food which was given to them was absolutely bad.

The witness and his companions complained to the Camp Commandant but he replied that they would continue receiving the same type of food. The wetness then told him to shoot him but the Camp Commandant replied that he would not be shot, but that he should volunteer for the I.N.A. He said that if they volunteered they would be taken out of the concentration camp and all good things given to them. He further said that if they did not volunteer they would continue to be beaten like that until they died.

They remained in the concentration camp for 17 days on that occasion. After that they were taken to Saletar Camp. There they were repeatedly given lectures urging them to join the I.N.A. The witness did not join the I.N.A. and carried on propaganda against it. They were then put in an enclosure which was enclosed with barbed wire and after that sent back to the concentration camp, after being in Saletar Camp for about 15 or 20 days. The same 11 men were taken with the witness to the concentration camp and they were given the same treatment as before. On the day following that on which they were taken to the concentration camp they were asked by the Camp Commandant to volunteer saying that, if they did not volunteer, they would get the same treatment as before. The witness and his companions refused to volunteer. The same fatigue was given to them as before. This time they were in the concentration camp for 21 days. They were beaten and no medical treatment was given to them. On one occasion when the witness asked for a drink of water he and another companion of his were given 18 strokes. When they called upon God and his Prophet, the persons torturing them replied that the Prophet and God were not present in those enclosures. They added: "If there is a God he is outside these enclosures ; inside the enclosures the concentration camp authorities rule".

This time they were in the concentration camp for 21 days and then they were sent to Saletar Camp. They were kept in the portion called D. I which was for non-volunteers. From there witness was taken to the hospital. He remained in the hospital for seven or eight days. In the hospital volunteers and non-volunteers were kept separate. Some fruit used to come from the Supreme Headquarters and it was given only to volunteers.

The non-volunteers did not get anything. From the hospital he was again taken to Saletar Camp. He was again asked to join the I.N.A. but he and his party refused to do so and they were kept in the D. I Camp for about one month. They were then sent to the concentration camp where also they were lectured to join the I.N.A. For a third time they were sent to the concentration camp where again they received the same treatment as before.

The witness then describes an incident which he saw of two Sikhs close by being beaten. They were beaten from 9 p.m. to 1 a.m. and then they were put in the hospital closeby and the sweeper who was there was told to report to them if the two persons died. The next morning the witness saw them in the hospital tent lying with their faces to the ground and fetters on their legs. This time they were kept in the concentration camp for 24 days, after which they were again taken to the D.I camp at Saletar.

Ultimately, the witness and his party were sent to New Guinea on May 1, 1943. There were about 2,400 persons who went with the witness to New Guinea. The witness never joined the I.N.A.

In his cross-examination the witness related an incident of a lecture given by Capt. Shah Nawaz Khan in a mosque. He said that Capt. Shah Nawaz Khan did not treat them with force, but said that they ought to join the I.N.A. He said : "I will not give any sort of trouble to you but you should volunteer".

He further said : "I do not want to press the men, but I want true volunteers". After that 11 Mussalmans said "Dua Khair" and decided in the "Dua Khair" that they would not join the I.N.A. It was suggested in the cross-examination that there was a charge against the men of this unit of having committed theft of seven cows belonging to civilians and of having slaughtered and eaten them.

It was put to the witness that in his summary of evidence he said that Major Aziz Ahmad told them that they were to go to the concentration camp because they had killed a cow. Even if that be so, it was merely an excuse for sending them to the concentration camp. Witness denied that any skin or bones were found and denied that any investigation was made.

The fact that the witness and his companions were taken to the concentration camp on three different occasions as stated by him in his evidence refutes the suggestion made in the cross-examination of the witness. Obviously, the witness and his companions were tortured in the camp for several days at a time and then taken back to Saletar Camp and again taken to the concentration camp because such a course was likely to weaken the resolution of the witness and his companions not to volunteer.

The evidence of this witness also should, it is submitted, be accepted as true.

The next witness was Havildar Wolit Bahadur. He related the incident which happened in Bidadari Camp on September 24, 1942. Prior to that the witness and his companions had been exhorted to join the I.N.A. They had often been told that they should join the I.N.A., otherwise it would have bad results for them. Subsequently about 14 officers and N.C.Os from the unit of the witness were taken to the concentration camp. The witness and his companions were told that if they did not volunteer it would have bad consequences for them.

The incident which happened on September 24, 1942, was, according to him, as follows : An I.N.A. officer delivered a lecture and said? "We have already informed you about the I.N.A. You people have not accepted what we said in the lectures. With reference to this I am going to show you one result of your conduct".

The witness belonged to the 2/9th Gurkha Rifles but the followers of this unit were Indians. The followers were asked whether they were prepared to join the I.N.A. They, however, said that they would stick to their unit and would not join the I.N.A. The followers were then cruelly beaten. Thereafter the I.N.A. officer called out six or seven people by name from among the men of the unit. He said that they were the ringleaders who did not allow the 2/9th Gurkha Rifles to volunteer for the I.N.A. He then ordered two I.N.A. men to beat those six or seven people and one of them fell down. Thereupon the unit stood up to protest and said : "Even if you beat us like this we are not going to join the I.N.A. but we are ready to do fatigues for the Japanese".

One of the I.N.A. officers then said : "Whilst you were gathered at this meeting on whose orders did you stand up?" The men from the unit replied that they were not getting justice and they stood up to make a report. Thereupon one of the I.N.A. officers ordered the guard to fire. At first they fired in the air. Another I.N.A. Officer said : "Are these Gurkhas your fathers that you are not shooting them?" The Gurkhas then started moving forward. The guard fired on them and one or two of the Gurkhas fell on the ground. The witness himself received a bullet in his left knee and fell down. Nine people were wounded, eight by rifle fires and one by being struck by a lathi. The unit was then made to fall in and march off. The witness was taken to the hospital. According to the witness, I.N.A. officers came to him in the hospital several times and they told him to sign in the I.N.A. books. They said : "If sign the I.N.A. books, you will get good medicines and the bullet will be taken out from your left knee". The witness, however, did not agree to volunteer for the I.N.A. The witness remained in the hospital for about five months. Witness never joined the I.N.A.

In the cross-examination of this witness, it was put to the witness that there was a dispute about fatigues and that they were required to do fatigues for the Japanese. The suggestion was that the firing was done because the unit refused to do fatigue duty. If the passage relating to this point in the cross-examination is taken as a whole, it becomes clear that the attitude of the witness and his unit was that they were prepared to do fatigues for the Japanese, but would have nothing to do with the I.N.A. The whole of the relevant cross-examination on this point is as follows : "There was a dispute about the fatigues, that they were required to do fatigues for the Japanese. Those who did not join the I.N.A. were required to do fatigues for the Japanese. There was a dispute when we refused to do fatigues for the Japanese. The leader whom I have named told us not to object to the fatigue. In spite of their persuasion, some of us did not obey. We reported that we will do fatigues for the Japanese but we have nothing to do with the I.N.A.". The interpretation of the question put to the witness and answers given by him were not quite satisfactory and at this stage Major Pritam Singh was sworn as interpreter. The answers in further cross-examination were as follows : "The guard was sent because some of us did not obey. The guard came to arrest the ringleaders. We were about 550 men. Some of the men had a dispute with the guard. The guard stopped us from doing this and then fired in the air. When we did not obey the order of the guard, they fired. The guard did not prevent us from doing fatigue but they spoke to us about the I.N.A. which we did not obey. First they fired in the air and when we did not obey ultimately they fired at us. About two or three men were injured by the firing. Then we pursued the guard". In his re-examination the witness said that the dispute between the guard and him was that they resented the appearance of the guard during lecture time. In answer to a question by the Court witness said that the bullet was taken out of his knee after one or one and a half months.

The next witness Rifleman Rabilal also deposes to the same incident. He mentions the lectures in the Bidadari Camp in which it was said that those who did not join the I.N.A. would be put in danger later on. Witness further said that an I.N.A. officer told him that if he did not join the I.N.A. he would be sent to the concentration camp and would be given a beating. It was thereafter that the V.C.Os. and N.C.Os. were taken away to the concentration camp. This witness also describes the incident of the firing. Witness said that before this firing took place some men in the Bidadari Camp were doing fatigues for the I.N.A. and others being ill-treated.

Witness said that he never refused to do this fatigue work and he was certain that none of this company refused. This witness was one of those who were taken to the concentration camp after the firing and he describes the hardship and torture suffered by them there. According to this witness, an officer in charge of the concentration camp separated 14 men from the party saying that they were doing propaganda against the I.N.A. and stopping the personnel from joining the I.N.A. The rest of the party were sent back to Bidadari camp. Thereafter, the battalion to was sent for a second time to the concentration camp. Witness went along with them. On the day following their arrival in the concentration camp the I.N.A. guard there started beating them and making them do fatigues. This continued for five days. After five days they were sent back to Bidadari camp. The witness was then taken to hospital and ultimately he and his unit were taken to River Valley Camp and the Japanese kept them for digging trenches in the jungle. The witness and his party were released from the Rivery Valley Camp when the British Army arrived there. There is nothing in the cross-examination of this witness to throw any doubt on the veracity of the deposition. It is submitted that there is no reason why this evidence should not be accepted by the Court as true.

Another witness examined on this point was Subedar Ram Sarup. According to this witness, as he refused to volunteer he was taken in about July 1942 to the concentration camp with five other men. He was told that he was doing anti-I.N.A. propaganda and that was why he was there and that he would now suffer the consequences. He then gave the details of the cruel beating given to him by an I.N.A. man following the instructions given to him by one of the camp staff in Punjabi in these words: "Guests have come, given them a good reception". The witness became unconscious by the beating. The next morning he and several others were made to do fatigue. In the evening one of the camp staff officers with another man came and asked him how he was. The witness replied he was all right. The officer then asked him if he was willing to volunteer to which the witness replied that he had already suffered and was ready to suffer more, but he was not going to volunteer under those conditions. Thereupon the officer abused him and told the other fellow to show him how they treated those who did not agree to volunteer. They then tied hands of the witness at his back, gave him a blow on the face, kicked him and beat him with a stick. Witness again became unconscious. When he regained consciousness the other fellow asked him whether he was still unwilling to volunteer. This time he gave his consent under the impression that it was better to become a volunteer than to die there of beating etc. In the cross-examination of this witness it was suggested that he had invented this story in order to save his skin when he went back to the Indian Army. It was put to the witness that under the instructions of Capt. S.A. Malik, he infiltrated into India and that on his arrival in India he reported to his Depot. It is submitted that there is no substance in the suggestion made in the cross-examination. On the contrary if a man was forced to join the I.N.A. under circumstances related by the, witness, it is quite natural that at the first opportunity he would report back to the authorities of the Indian Army. The numerous desertions which took place in the I.N.A. are very significant. As soon as men and even officers of the I.N.A. got an opportunity to leave the I.N.A. they did so and reported to their authorities. It is submitted that the inference to be drawn from these significant desertions is that a large part of the I.N.A. had been made to join the Army under compulsion.

Lance Naik Fitter Mohinder Singh originally volunteered for the I.N.A. in the Saletar Camp in September 1942. After the December crisis, he did not volunteer and he also communicated his ideas to his companions. Sometimes afterwards he and two of his communions were taken to the concentration camp where he was beaten. Before he was beaten, he was informed the beating was given to him because he had done anti-I.N.A. propaganda. After the beating he was put into a barbed wire cage six feet long and three feet wide and he was kept in the cage for 15 days. From the third day he was made to do fatigues. The rice which was given to him and his communions was mixed with lime and grit. He became very weak. He enquired from the sentry how he could escape from there. The sentry advised him not to do propaganda against the I.N.A. but to volunteer. He then became a volunteer. In March 1944, witness was sent to the front. He was detailed to bring rations from a nearby hill. When he went there he found a British Regiment to whom he surrendered. I may add, the evidence given by Col. Loganadan in which he says that one case that one case of atrocity came to his notice when a man with gangarene was admitted to the hospital. Col. Loganadan made a report about it but received no reply.

It is submitted that there is ample and trustworthy evidence in support of the fact that gross atrocities were perpetrated by the officers and men of the I.N.A. who were in charge of the concentration camp in order to make persons who were unwilling to join the I.N.A. and those who were advising others not to join the I.N.A. to change their minds and to compel them to join the I.N.A.

A very significant corroboration of this fact appears in the leaflet styled. Our Struggle (Exhibit 5C) by Rash Behari Bose. The relevant paragraph in this pamphlet is as follows: "Prior to election, Mr. Mohan Singh in his speech made statements which now appear to be misrepresentation of facts because he solemnly gave us to understand that the majority of the Indian Army personnel were prepared to join this movement without any threat or force and that they had acclaimed him as their military leader. I was horrified at a later date to learn of the atrocities meted out to officers and men of the Indian Army for which the blame naturally falls on Capt. Mohan Singh. Many of our poor brethren were shot while many were tortured, humiliated or sent to concentration camp and thus by sheer threat and violence he demoralized the majority of officers and men and compelled them to become volunteers, which is against our principle. I for one will be the last man to see my countrymen shot in cold blood. This is what we are fighting for against the British and I personally cannot afford to see Indians tortured in this manner".

The document was published under the authority of the Indian Independence League. That this pamphlet was widely circulated is borne out be the fact that an Urdu translation of this pamphlet was also published at the same time by the Indian Independence League. The profession made in this pamphlet that the same thing was not going to happen as regards the Second I.N.A. is to be taken for what it is worth. Even as regards the First I.N.A. several witnesses said that those who made speeches for recruitment said that they did not intend to use force or coercion. The question, however, is not what was said but what was done. Mr. Ayyar who was in charge of the Publicity Department of the Headquarters of the Indian Independence League in East Asia asserted that the Army ws raised voluntarily. When confronted with this pamphlet he said that he did not remember having read this passage and that he might not have read the whole of this pamphlet but might just have seen it. He also said that he did not remember whether the pamphlet was published in Urdu. He, however, admitted that he had no reason to doubt that the pamphlet was published by the Indian Independence League Headquarters at Singapore. In the evidence of Capt. Arshad, he said that the relations between Mr. Rash Bihari Bose and Capt. Mohan Singh were not too cordial. The suggestion was that Mr. Rash Behari Bose in this pamphlet made allegations against Mohan Singh which were not true. Mr. Ayyar, however, admitted that so far as he knew no protest was made against this passage by anybody. The evidence makes it clear that Mohan Singh had a large number of friends and followers in the I.N.A. It is impossible to conceive that, if this passage contained an allegation which was not true, no protest should have been made by any of Mohan Singh's friends.

In view of the above facts, the statements made by the defence witnesses that no compulsion was used to make prisoners of war join the I.N.A. cannot be accepted as correct. It was not part of the Prosecution case that the accused themselves committed or helped to commit any atrocities on prisoners of war; but it was the case of the Prosecution that the accused held out veiled threats meaning thereby that the threats convoyed were that, unless the prisoners of war joined the I.N.A., they might have to suffer tortures and be the victims of atrocities.

As Counsel for the Crown, it is my duty to concede and I concede, that the evidence does not support this averment. The question, however, remains whether the accused themselves had knowledge of any atrocities that were committed in the concentration camp. The duty of proving this is on the Prosecution. It has to prove it beyond reasonable doubt. There can, of course, be no presumption that the accused had any such knowledge; but knowledge might be inferred from such evidence as there is on record. If the Court comes to the conclusion that the atrocities were committed and that such atrocities were a matter of public notoriety, and that the accused could not have been ignorant of them, the Court may come to the conclusion that they had no knowledge of such atrocities. On the other hand, there is a considerable body of evidence to show that while delivering lectures in order to persuade prisoners of war to join the Indian National Army the accused said that they did not want anybody to join the Indian National Army. It is for you, Sirs, to arrive at your conclusion on the evidence before you.

There is no doubt, and in fact it has not been attempted to deny, that the accused recruited men for the Indian National Army by delivering lectures asking them to join it. The further fact as to whether they did it with knowledge of any atrocities that might have been perpetrated can only be a matter of aggravation.

International law does not come into this case at all either as regards the jurisdiction of the Court or as regards the law to be administered by it. The question is between the State and its subject. The accused hold commissions in the Indian Army as Indian Commissioned Officers. They became subject to the Indian Army Act and they remain subject to that Act under Section 2 until duly retired, discharged, cashiered, removed or dismissed from service. They have not so retired or been discharged, cashiered, removed or dismissed from service. In fact, there is evidence which I will point later to show that the officers and men of the Indian Army who, when they were prisoners of war, joined the Indian National Army at first but subsequently did not agree to continue in it after December

1942 were to revert to their position as prisoners of war. The argument for the Defence amounts to this that Section 121 (a) of the Indian Penal Code must bear different meanings where the offender is an Indian and where he is not an Indian. They want to read into the section a proviso that waging war against His Majesty the King is not an offence if it is accompanied by a declaration of Provisional Government and a declaration of war with Great Britain. In fact, a declaration of Provisional Government is itself an offence and such an act cannot give immunity to the offender. The object with which the war is waged is entirely immaterial. The act is an offence, whatever the motive for it may have been.

In Halsbury's Laws of England (second edition), Volume 6, page 504, paragraph 623, the following propositions are laid down: "The rules of international law are part of the law of England, but only in so far as they can be proved by legislation, judicial decision; or established usage to have been received into English law. A consensus of international jurists even if unanimous does not make a rule of international law a part of the law of England. To the extent that rules of international law are part of English law, they are applied by municipal courts so long as they are not in conflict with an Act of Parliament or a rule of common law; but the Courts have no jurisdiction over acts of State. "In Halsbury (second edition), Volume 31, page 509, paragraph 959, we have the following proposition of law: "Statutes are to be interpreted provided that their language admits so as not to be inconsistent with the comity of nations. International law, however, being mainly conventional can, it seems, only be administered by the courts when it forms part of the law of this country. If, therefore, statutory enactments are clearly inconsistent with international law, they must be so construed, whatever the effect upon the rights of aliens not within the jurisdiction may be". In footnote (s) at page 504 of Volume 6 of Halsbury, after mentioning that the wider view concerning the incorporation of international law in the law of England is seen expressed in the cases mentioned there, it is stated that it was also the view of Blackstone, and that the modern more limited view was first enunciated clearly by the majority of the judges in R. Vs. Keyn, 2 Ex. D., page 63, at page 202 and though the Territorial Waters Jurisdiction Act which gave effect to the opinion of the minority was declaratory in form, the view of the majority has since been upheld in West Rand Central Gold Mining Company Vs. R. (1995) 2 K.B., page 391. In that case, at page 408, it is stated as follows: "The expression the law of nations forms part of the law of England ought not to be construed so as to include as part of the law of England opinions of text writers upon a question as to which there is no evidence that Great

Britain has ever assented and *a fortiori* if they are contrary to the principles of her laws as declared by her courts!"

In the Zamora (1916), 2 Appeal Cases, the Privy Council in giving the judgment stated as follows: "A court which administers municipal law is bound by and gives effect to the law as laid down by the Sovereign State which calls it into being. It needs to inquire only that law is; but a court which administers international law must ascertain and give effect to a law which is not laid down by any particular State, but originates in the practice and usage long observed by civilized nations in their relations towards each other or in express international agreements".

This court is not sitting as an international court. It has not to decide questions between different States or between one State and a subject of another State. In Pitt Cobbett, Volume I, page 4, international law is described as the sum of the rules accepted by civilized States as determining their conduct towards each other and towards each other's subjects, and in the footnote it is stated that this definition save for its concluding words is virtually that put forward by Lord Russell of Killowen in 1896 which was judicially adopted in the West Rand Central Gold Mining Company V. Rex (1905) 2 K.B., page 391.

This court is sitting as a court duly constituted under the Indian Army Act to try persons who are subject to the Indian Army Act for offences which are made punishable under the Indian Army Act and the Indian Penal Code.

It was then argued that the word 'law' in Section 79 of the Indian Penal Code includes international law. My submission is that the term 'law' in Section 79 means a law in force in British India. In this connection, reference may be made to the definition of special and local law in Sections 41 and 42 as follows: "A special law is a law applicable to a particular subject"; and "a local law is a law applicable only to a particular part of British India".

There is a decision of the Bombay High Court which reports my submission. In re Ram Bharashi (I.L.R. 47 Bom. 907), Section 191 of the Indian Penal Code which gives the definition of giving false evidence is in these terms: "Whoever being bound by a rule or by an express provision of law to state the truth or being bound by law to make a declaration upon any subject makes any statement which is false and which he either knows or believes to be false or does not believe to be true is said to give false evidence".

The charge against the accused in that case was under Section 193 for giving false evidence, and in delivering the judgment the court said as follows: "As regards the offence under Section 193, India Penal Code, it is not suggested that the accused was legally bound by oath, that his oath was administered under the provisions of law in force in British Indian or by any express provision of law that is law in force in British India to state the truth before the Vyara court". In that case, the change was for giving false evidence in a court in Baroda territory.

While repeating the submission that no question of international law can or does arise in this case, it is further submitted that even according to principles of international law there is no obligation on the part of a State to give recognition of belligerency to insurgents. Unless such recognition is given by the State itself, there is no immunity for the persons taking part in the insurgence. Further, the recognition of insurgence by another State does not affect in any way the parent State so far as its own subjects who are insurgents are concerned.

I will cite only a few passages from Oppenheim's International Law, sixth edition, Vol. II, at page 173, paragraph 59, we have the following statement:

"In the proper sense of the term a civil war exists when two opposing parties within a State have recourse to arms for the purpose of obtaining power in the State or when a large portion of the population of the State rises in arms against the legimate Government. As war is an armed contention between States, such a civil war would not be war from the beginning nor become war at all in the technical sense of the term. But it may become war through the recognition of the contending parties or of the insurgents as a belligerent power. Through such recognition a body of individuals receives an international position in so far as it is for some parts and in some points is treated as though it were a subject of international law. Such recognition may be granted by the lawful Government and the other States will, in most cases, although they need not, likewise recognize a state of war as existing and assume duties of neutrality. But it may happen that other States recognize insurgents as billigerents power before the State on whose territory the insurrection broke out recognises them. In such a case, the insurrection is war in the eyes of these other States, but not in the eyes of the legitimate Government".

At page 197, Par. 76, we have the following passage: "The distinction between legal qualification and actual power to make war explains the fact that insurgents may become a belligerent power through recognition. The principles governing recognition of belligerency are essentially the same as those relating to the recognition of States and Governments. Certain condition of facts, not stigmatized as unlawful by International Law—the law of nations does not treat civil war as illegal—create for other States the right and the duty to grant recognition of belligerency. These conditions of fact are the existence of a civil war accompanied by a state of general hostility: occupation and a measure of orderly administration of a substantial part of national territory by the insurgents; observance of the rules of warfare on the part of the insurgent forces acting under a responsible authority; the practical necessity for a third State to define its attitude to the civil war. Without the latter requirement recognition of belligerency might be open to abuse for the purpose of gratuitous manifestation of sympathy with the cause of the insurgents. In the absence of these conditions recognition of belligerency constitutes illicit interference in the affairs of the State affected by civil disorders—an international wrong analogous to the premature recognition of a State or a Government. Refusal to recognize belligerent status, notwithstanding the existence of these conditions, must be deemed contrary to sound principle and precedent".

In Oppenheim's International Law, sixth edition, Volume II, at page 200, in footnote (2), it is stated as follows : "See also case concerning certain German interests in Polish Upper Sillies where the Permanent Court held in regard to claims put forward by Poland under the Armistice Agreement that the recognition by the principal Allied powers of the Polish Armed Forces as an allied, autonomous and co-belligerent army could not be relied on as against Germany which had not granted such recognition".

The next passage which I will refer to is that which has already been cited by learned counsel for defence. That is Para. 76a at page 200. The passage runs as follows: "Recognition by a third State is not as a rule binding on the parent State. Notwithstanding such recognition, it is entitled to treat insurgents as traitors. But the position is controversial with regard to recognition as a belligerent power granted to separate armies which comprise subjects of the enemy who are fighting to free their nation from his rule and which are responsible to an authority recognised as representing the nation in question. It has been maintained that as in the case of insurgents in a civil war the enemy is entitled to disregard such recognition and to treat the members of the insurgent army when they fall into his hands in accordance with the provisions of his criminal law. The better opinion is probably that when such recognition is granted by the adversary to large bodies of men effectively organized on foreign soil in anticipation of independent statehood a point is reached at which the belligerent confronted with the disaffection and desertion of a considerable number of his subjects engaged in hostilities against him can no longer, without exposing himself to justifiable retaliation, assert the provisions of his own criminal law as the only legally relevant element in the situation". This passage does not mean that it is obligatory upon a parent State to grant recognition to the insurgents because the State which was at war with it granted recognition to the insurgents as a belligerent power.

The passage in question refers to the position as between the parent State and the State at war with it, and not the position as between the parent State and the insurgents who are fighting on the side of the enemy State. Further, the only effect of the parent State not granting recognition would be that it might expose itself to justifiable retaliation. There is one more passage to which I will refer on the point of recognition as a State. I refer to the first volume of Oppenheim, page 125, paragraph 74: "Recognition is of special importance in those cases where a new State tries to establish itself by breaking off from an existing State in the course of a revolution. And here the question is material whether a new State has really already safely and permanently established itself or only makes efforts to this end without having already succeed. That in every case of civil war a foreign State can recognize the insurgents as a belligerent power if they succeed in keeping a part of the country in their hands, set up a Government of their own, and conduct their military operations according to the laws of war. But between this recognition as a belligerent power and the recognition of these insurgents and their part of the country as a new State, there is a broad and deep gluf. The question is precisely at what exact time recognition as a new State may be given instead of the recognition as a belligerent power. For an untimely and precipitate recognition as a new State is a violation of the dignity of the mother State, to which the latter need not patiently submit. It is frequently maintained that such untimely recognition comprises an intervention. This is, as a rule, not correct, unless such recognition is accompanied by active assistance rendered to the rebellious party.

"In spite of the importance of the question, no hard and fast rule can be laid down as regards the time when it can be said that a State created by revolution has established itself safely and permanently. Indication of such safe and permanent establishment may be found either in the fact that the revolutionary State has utterly defeated the mother State, or that the mother State has ceased to make efforts to subdue the revolutionary State or even that the mother State, in spite of its efforts, is apparently incapable of bringing the revolutionary back under its way. Of course, as soon as the mother State itself recognizes the new State, there is no reason for other States to withhold their recognition any longer, although they have even then no legal obligation to grant it".

This passage deals with the right of recognition by a third State of a revolutionary State which tries to break off from the parent State. So far as the parent State itself is concerned, unless recognition is granted by the parent State to the insurgents, no belligerent rights accrue to the insurgents.

Further in the present case there was no revolutionary State and no civil war. There was no contention between two States. There was no recognition by the parent Government of the insurgents as a belligerent State or as having belligerent rights. There was no war in the eyes of the legitimate Government. There was no occupation of national territory by the insurgents, no administration by them of a substantial or indeed of any part of national territory. No part of the country was in their hands which they could call their part of the country. There was no revolutionary State, much less any safe and permanent establishment of any such State. The so-called revolutionary State did not defeat, much less utterly defeat the mother State, nor can it be said that the mother State ceased to make efforts to subdue the revolutionary State or that the mother State was incapable of bringing the revolutionary State back under its sway.

As regards the authorities cited by learned counsel for the Defence, most of them are American authorities. This court is not concerned with what the law in America is or even with the view of the American courts on questions of international law. In fact, the law in America is different from that in England. The law in America is that international law overrides previous municipal law of a State. In America there is a digest of the International Law of the United States consisting of documents relating to that subject issued by Presidents and Secretaries of State, of the decisions of Federal Courts and of the opinions of Attorneys-General.

The propositions laid down in those volumes have all been accepted by the American Federal Government. One of the propositions there laid down is "the law of nations is part of the municipal law of separate States. The intercourse of the United States with foreign nations and the policy in regard to them being placed by the constitution in the hands of the Federal Government, its decisions upon these subjects are by universally acknowledged principles of international law obligatory on everybody. The law of nations unlike foreign municipal law does not have to be proved as a fact. The law of nations makes an integral part of the laws of the land".

The above appears from Maine's International Law, published in 1888 at page 36. Again, at page 37, the author says : "Here you see that according to American doctrine international law has precedence both of Federal and of municipal law, unless in the exceptional case where Federal law has deliberately departed from it".

The authorities I have cited above show clearly the great difference between the law in America and the law in England. All American authorities whether in text-books or in decided cases are, therefore, irrelevant.

I will, however, deal briefly with the authorities cited for the defence. A passage in Pitt Cobbett's Cases on International Law was cited in connection with the case of the Paquete Haband which case is reported in 175 U.S. Reports, page 677. It was laid down in that case that international law formed part of the law of the United States and must be ascertained and administered by courts of justice of appropriate jurisdiction as often as any question of right dependent on it duly presented itself for determination, and for this purpose where there was no treaty and no controlling executive act or judicial decision, resort must be had to the custom and usages of civilized nations.

As a matter of fact that case was one in a Prize Court. Prize Courts are those set up by the respective different States in which they exist and they administer international law. No question of administering municipal law arises in those cases. But even as regards Prize Courts, it has been held in England that if there is a statute which lays down a principle of law in contravention of international law that statute must be given effect to. In the present case, the court which has been duly constituted according to the law of this country, namely, the Indian Army Act, is trying persons who are subject to that Act, and no question of international law arises.

While dealing with this authority, it may be pointed out that at page 21 in Volume I of Pitt Cobbett, it is stated, while dealing with the relation of international law to English law, that notwithstanding some statements to that effect made by text-writers, and some dicta to be found in the decisions, it can scarcely be said that the law of nations is adopted in its full extent by the common law, or that it is deemed to be part of the law of England. It may also be pointed out that at page 61 of the same volume (Vol. I of Pitt Cobbett's Cases on International Law) in connection with recognition by a third State of the belligerent character of the subjects of another State, that the question whether such recognition should be accorded or not is a question for the political or executive department of Government, by whose action the courts will be bound. It goes on to say : "It would seem that such recognition cannot be demanded as of right for the reason that it is strictly a question of policy and not of law".

The question in the present case is as to whether the British Government recognized the belligerency of the insurgents. As submitted above, the parent State is not affected at all by the recognition of belligerency by other States. At page 246 of Vol. II of Pitt Cobbett, while dealing with Prize Courts, the decision in the Zamora, which has been cited above is given as regards the international character of Prize Courts and the fact that what it administers is international law.

Wheaton's International Law, Vol. II, was also cited by the learned Counsel for the Defence and the passage at page 101 on civil war was referred to. It may be pointed out that the question between a State and its suzerain is entirely different from the question between a State and its subjects. The passage cited expressly states that the Government of the State may recognize its subjects as belligerents in which case other States do normally but need not follow the same course. I submit that it is clear that there is no obligation on the part of the parent State to recognize insurgents as belligerents and there is no right on the part of the insurgents to claim such recognition. The passage goes on to say that the rule of General Grant that the question is one of fact is opposed by the doctrine that the matter is one of unfettered discretion.

The next authority cited was Lawrence on International Law, page 309. The passage in question deals with contests between States or between States and communities having with regard to the contest the rights of States. In the same passage it is stated : "War is a contest, not a condition; and moreover, it is restricted to contest carried on under State authority directly or indirectly given". Then follows the sentence : "Private war has long ago disappeared from civilized societies". But the author goes on to say : "If individuals now attempt to redress their real or fancied wrongs by the might of their own hands, they are regarded by the law as disturbers of the public peace, and their act is an offence in itself, however gross may have been the injury that brought it about". At page 310, after saying that all war is now public war, the author goes on to say : "Even the military and naval operations of revolted provinces or colonies have a public character impressed upon them by the process known as recognition of belligerency". It is clear that the public character impressed upon such a contest is by reason of recognition of belligerency".

The really relevant passage in this book is at page 328, Par. 141 : "Every independent State decides for itself whether it shall make war or remain at peace. If it resorts to hostilities it obtains as a matter of course all the rights of a belligerent. Other States have no power to give or to withhold them. But the case is very different with regard to such communities as are not already States in the eye of international law, though they are striving to become independent, and to have their independence recognized by other powers. Technically they from portions of old-established States. Practically, each is in revolt against the State organisation to which it belongs in law, and is endeavouring to set up a separate State organization for itself or to gain control of the existing organisation. By the municipal law of the country of which the community is still legally a part its members are traitors and liable to punishment as such. Yet they are carrying on open war under the orders of authorities analogous to those of recognized States. How then are they to be treated? International law gives no answer to this question as far as the Government against which they are in revolt is concerned. Questions between it and its rebels are domestic questions to be resolved by internal authority".

Moore's Digest of International Law, Volume I, which was cited is, as the title of the book says, a Digest of International Law as embodied in diplomatic discussions, treaties and other international agreements, international awards, the decisions of municipal courts, and the writings of jurists and especially in documents—published and unpublished, issued by Presidents and Secretaries of State of the United States, the opinions of the Attorneys-General and the decisions of courts, Federal and State. The passage cited at page 2 in fact expressly states that "the Government of the United States has, on various occasions, announced the principle that international law as a system is binding upon the nations not merely as something to which they may be tacitly assumed to have agreed but also as a fundamental condition of their admission to full and equal participation in the intercourse of civilized States." I have pointed out above the difference between the doctrine prevailing in America and that prevailing in England. I have cited authorities which, I submit, are conclusive on the question of the relation of international law of England.

As regards Oppenheim, I have already referred to the relevant passages.

Hyde on International Law was next cited. The title of the book is "International Law chiefly as interpreted and applied by the United States". The passage refers to a man being armed by a sovereign State. It has no relevance at all to the question as to whether the subjects of a State taking up arms against the State have any right of belligerency.

The case of *Underhill* vs. *Hernandez*, United States Supreme Court Reports, Volume 168, page 250, was cited and an isolated passage was read which says that whether the political revolt fails or succeeds, still effectual war has been waged and acts of legitimate warfare cannot be make the basis of individual liability. Apart from its being an American authority, and having no relevance to the question before the Court, it is necessary to consider what the case was and some salient facts thereof. The third headnote of that case is as follows : "This court is bound to take judicial notice of the facts that flagrant civil war existed in another country, that the revolution was successful, and that the revolutionary Government was recognized by the United States as the Government of the country and for information as to those facts this court may consult the Department of State". The action was brought to recover damages for the detention caused to the plaintiff by reason of the refusal to grant a passport and for the alleged confinement of the plaintiff to his own house. The case was tried in the Circuit Court of the United States for the Eastern District of New York. The acts which were alleged to have been wrongful had taken place in Venezuela.

The facts stated above are sufficient to show how irrelevant the authority is to the present question. There was no question in that case as between a State and its subjects. The second paragraph of the headnote of the case of Ford vs. *Surget,* 97 United States Reports, 594, is as follows: "destruction of cotton under the orders of the Confederate military authorities for the purpose of preventing it from falling into the hands of the Federal Army was an act of war upon the part of the military forces of the rebellion for which the person executing such orders was relieved from civil responsibility at the suit of the owner voluntarily residing at the time within the lines of the insurrection." The defence was that at and before the time the alleged trespasses were committed, the people of Mississippi and of Virginia, North Carolina and South Carolina, Floria, etc., had confederated together for revolt against the United States and within their territorial limits, had entirely subverted the Government of the United States and in place thereof and within and for their territory and people had created a new and separate Government called the Confederate States of America having executive, legislative and judicial departments. From pages 605 611 of the Report it appears that to the Confederate Army was conceded in the interests of humanity and to prevent the cruelties of reprisals and retaliation such belligerent rights as belonged under the laws of nations to the armies of independent Governments engaged in war against each other. This is sufficient to show how irrelevant this case is to the question now before the Court. Further, as stated above, the Court is not concerned with what the law is in America. Reference has already been made to authorities and textbooks showing what the law is in England.

Blackston's Commentaries, Volume II, were then cited. As regards this, it is sufficient to point out that in Halsbury, Second Edition, Volume 6, page 504 in footnote(s), dealing with the statement of law set out in paragraph 623, it is mentioned that there was a wider view held originally concerning the incorporation of international law in the law of England and that such was also the view of Blackstones; but the modern more limited view was enunciated in *Reginas* vs. *Keyn,* and the view of the majority has since been upheld in *West Rand Central Gold Mining Co.* vs. *R* : (1905), 2 K.B. 301, which has already been cited above.

Hershey, which has also been cited, is also an American authority. The more appropriate reference should, I submit, be to the English authorities on the point which have already been cited. 159 U.S. Reports, page 113, stands on the same footing. The case reported in 1939 Appeal Cases page 160, is really not against the Prosecution. The passage cited from the judgment is as follows; "It must be always remembered that so far at any rate as courts in this country are concerned, international law has no validity save in so far as its principles are accepted and adoppted by our domestic law. There is no external power that imposes its rules upon our own code of substantial law and procedure. The courts acknowledge the existence of a body of rules which nations accept among themselves. on every judicial issue, they seek to ascertain what the relevant rule is and having found it they will treat it as having been incorporated into the domestic law so far as it is not inconsistent with the rules enacted by statute." This enunciation of law is in no way different from the propositions laid down in the authorities I have already cited.

The British Year Book of International Law, 1937, page 18, contains an article on some problems of the Spanish Civil War. It deals with the recognition by a third state of belligerent rights of insurgents and their parent state. Whatever the views of the author of this article may be, I have mentioned above the authorities on the question. It is submitted that it is beyond dispute that the recognition by a third State of belligerent rights in a conflict between a parent State and its insurgents is :-

(a) a matter of policy; and

(b) does not affect the parent State at all.

The quotations from "Hansard" of the speeches made by various English politicians on the occasion of recognizing the belligerent rights of insurgents in other countries are not authorities on the point. If, as submitted by me, recognition by a third State is a matter of policy, the recognition by England of belligerent rights on the part of its insurgents against their own parent country does not affect the question whether, without such recognition the insurgents are entitled to any immunities. In fact, in some of the speeches it was actually stated that the act of recognition by England was based upon the interests of England and was necessitated by the impossiblity of treating the insurgents as pirates. It is entirely incorrect to say that the same point arises for decision by this court. It is incorrect to say that it is not necessary that the Provisional Government of Free India should have been recognized by Great Britain. A third State may find it necessary or may choose to grant belligerent rights to the parent state as well as to the insurgents; but that does not mean that the insurgents are entitled to any immunity for their acts, so far as the parent State is concerned, unless the parent State has recognized or granted such rights. The illustrations given of Belgium and other countries are entirely out of place. Those countries were in military occupation. So too as regards France. There was a Free French State which refused to recognize the Petain Government. The proclamation of Eisenhower was directed against Germany and not against France. The Berlin reply is relevant to show that the recognition by other states is not binding upon a State which considered itself a parent State. It is not correct to say that the Prosecution asks the Court to adopt the view of Germany on the point. In any event, no such prodlamatiou affects the rights of a parent State against its insurgents if the parent state has not granted belligerent rights to the insurgents or has not recognized a Government formed in opposition to itself . The communique published by the Government of India and the statement made in the House of Commons are absolutely irrelevant to the question. Even if they were relevant, they do not amount to an admission of justification as regards the conduct of those who joined the I.N.A.

Many, if not most, of the considerations urged on behalf of the defence may be appropriate to be urged before a legislative body which enacts legislation, but are entirely irrelevant before a court administering law.

Learned Counsel for the accused referred to the *communique* published by the Government of India and the statement in the House of Commons. This is not evidence in the case, but since mention has been made of it, I may be permitted to mention that, according to another statement made by His Excellency the Viceroy, 45,000 Indian Prisoners of war did not join the Indian National Army and out of those 45,000, 11,000 lost their lives as a result of disease, starvation and murder. Twenty thousand prisoners of war joined the Indian National Army and the casualties from that Army were only about 1,500—of course, all these considerations are irrelevant in this trial.

Much has been said on behalf of the accused as regards the activities of the Provisional Government of Free India. The defence witness, Mr. S.A. Ayyar, who was in the Publicity Department of the Headquarters of the Indian Independence League in East Asia, said in his evidence that the Provisional Government used the machinery of the Indian

Independence League as its own executive. This statement is by itself significant. He then goes on to say that the Provisional Government collected donations from Indians throughout East Asia and that in Burma the Provisional Government opened a National Bank of Azad Hind. The position occupied by Mr. Subhas Chandra Bose was that of the President of the Indian Independence League and he took over the command of the I.N.A. Mr. Ayyar then states that there was a school for training civil administrators. He further said that the Azad Hind Government in Malaya and Burma took care of social welfare through the Indian Independence League branches in the matter of education, medical and other relief and relief of air-raid victims. As regards himself, he said that he was appointed to take charge of the Publicity Department in July 1942. and that later he become a Minister of the Provisional Government. As regards his own duties as a Minister of the Provisional Government, he said in his cross-examination that they were to give publicity to the activities of the Provisional Government and of the I.N.A. and to carry on propagand directed to the people in India through the short wave radio, to arrange public meetings with the help of the machinery of the Indian Independence League and generally to do the publicity and propagand activities of the Provisional Government. In further cross-examination he said; "The Indian Independence League had various departments and the Provisional Government got its policy executed through the staff and the other machinery of the Indian Independence League. The Indian Independence league had various department which were in the charge of secretaries—these were secretaries of departments—and whatever policy was laid down by the Provisional Government was put into actual execution by the secretary with his staff. From time to the instructions were sent from the Headquarters of the Provisional Government to the secretaries of the Indian Independence League branches. By policy I mean any decision taken by the Provisional government; it was immediately communicated to the secretaries of the departments concerned by the minister and they put it into execution. In my own department, apart from the ministry of Publicity and Propaganda, there was a Press Publicity and Propaganda Department of the Indian Independence League which was in the charge of a secretary and whatever we decided about propagand, for instance of starting a new broadcast or a newspaper, was communicated to the secretary of the League and he took the necessary measures to carry out that decision. As an instance, in Burma when we decided to have an additional broadcast on the short wave radio, I communicated the decision of the ministry to the secretary of the Propaganda Department and he arranged for the additional broadcast session. I know instances relating to my own department and I know other Ministers did the same. I cannot give you instances relating to other Ministries. "In regard to my own Ministry, I can give other instances, Secretary of Publicity Department of the League communicated to the secretaries in the branches of the League about carrying on propaganda in their territories. That is a typical example. Another instance was when we decided to hold a celebration of Netaji Bose Week, that is, on the arrival of Netaji Subhas Chandra Bose in in Singapore and his taking over the presidentship of the Indian Independence League. The Ministry communicated to the secretaries of the Publicity and Propaganda Department of the League and we issued instructions to the Secretary and he communicated these instructions to the League branches throughout Burma to observe that week. Similarly, the decision about the celebration of the first anniversary of the Provisional Government of Azad Hind in October 1944 was communicated to the secretaries, on the lines of the instructions given by the Ministry through the Secretary of the Propaganda Department. Similarly, when we celebrated February 4, 1944, when the I.N.A first went into Indian on the Arakan Front, instructions were issued in the same way. I cannot think of any other decision as much immediately as far as the Propaganda Department was concerned." The above evidence is sufficient to give an idea of the scope and extent of the functions of he Provisional Government of Free India.

This witness also purported to say in his evidence-in-chief that he heard about the famine in Bengal and that Netaji Subhas Chandra Bose offered 100,000 tons of rice for relief of the famine in Bengal and that it was not accepted. In his cross-examination, he said that the offer to send rice to Bengal was made through the radio to the people of India for information and to the British authorities in India so that they could consider the offer. This broadcast was, I believe, made either in July or August 1943. The offer was made by broadcast from Singapore. Rice was to be sent from any port in Burma, I believe. I could not tell you whether it was said on the radio that the rice was to be sent from any port in Burma but I believe that it could be sent from any port in Burma if the British authorities in India could vouchsafe safe conduct. The people of Burma were not starving for want of rice ". This evidence is extremely unsatisfactory and by no means proves the allegation made: but even if it be true, it does not advance the defence case any further.

Col. Loganadan in his evidence-in-chief said that he was present when the Provisional Government of Azad Hind was formed, that he was one of the Cabinet Ministers and that he was also the Director of Medical

Services, I.N.A. In his cross-examination, he said : "On the day on which exhibit 4 F was proclaimed the functions of officers were as stated in the proclamation. I was the Director of Medical Services of the Provisional Government form the time the Government was formed until I left for the Andamans. Each officer performed his duties as laid down. As D.M.S. I carried out my functions in the Provisional Government. We held Cabinet meetings. Various details were discussed, e.g., about the National flag, the National Song, Marching Songs, Declaration of War, language to be used in the I.N.A., various things concerning the Indian Independence League branches and their functions, the recruitment of the Army, training and such other subjects. The subjects were inter-linked."

Mr. Dina Nath said in his evidence-in-chief: "I was a member of the Indian Independence League, Rangoon Branch. I know of the formation of the Provisional Government of Azad Hind. There was an Azad Hind Bank. I was one of the Directors of that Bank. " Further on in his evidence-in-chief he said : "There were branches of the Indian independence League all over East Asia. The activities of the Indian Independence League so far as I personally know of them are these : they worked as an executive body to carry out the instructions of the Provisional Government of Azad Hind. Each branch had various departments dealing with various activities. For example, it had a Finance Department, a Recruiting Department, Training Department, Propaganda Department, Welfare Department, A.R.P. Section, Women's Section, and Boys Scouts Section. The League branches looked after the interests of the Indians and one of the main functions in this respect was to look after the absentee-Indian properties, to provide relief to the suffering people to do A.R.P. Service and each branch had also opened schools for the education of children". In cross-examination, he said; "When I mentioned recruiting, I meant recruiting for the I.N.A. by propaganda I meant propaganda for the Provisional Government of Free India and I.N.A When I mention protection, I meant protection against air attacks and helping the victims. When I mentioned women's section, I meant an organisation of women who gave their support to the movement and used to collect funds for the movement and enlist ladies for the Rani of Jhansi Regiment. The main job of Boys Scouts used to be welfare work during air-raids and other periods.'

One may ask oneself the question as to what it was that the Provisional Government of Free India governed. It did not own nor was it in occupation of an inch of territory. Not a pie of tax or revenue was recovered. It was supposed to be a Provisional Government of Free India. Such activities, there fore, if any, as it pursued in Malaya cannot be said to be in exercise of any function as regards the Government of Free India. In fact, as the name itself indicates, it was supposed to come into existence as a Government if and when the Japanese, after conquering India, handed it over to the Indians. It was a Government only on paper. There was in fact no Government.

As regards the defence application to the court to take judicial notice of a magazine called "Stamp Collecting" published in London by a philatelist, it is submitted that the application cannot be entertained. Section 57 of the Indian Evidence Act says that the court shall take judicatio notice of certain facts. The defence asks the court to take judicial notice of this magazine. There is no provision in the section for this. The document in question cannot be brought within any of the 13 items in Section 57. It is only if a fact of which judicial notice is requested to be taken comes within any of the 13 items and further on all matters of public history, literature, science or art the court may resort to appropriate books or documents of reference. Further, the magazine in question is not an appropriate book or document of reference. Moreover, the application itself shows that what the defence want to do is to prove that the Provisional Government of Free India had got prepared to issue and were about to issue postal stamps of a particular character and that the designs were prepared under the direction of the Japanese. There is this further objection against the defence application and that is that the evidence, if admitted, would be hearsay of the worst character. The magazine says that its correspondent informs them that he has seen proof of impressions in the hands of the man who was responsible for the printing in Rangoon. If this is not hearsay, it is difficult to imagine what is hearsay evidence.

As regards the recognition of the Provisional Government of Free India by Japan and her allies, the evidence clearly establishes that the recognition by Japan was for its own object in order to enable it to win the war. It was Japan who made arrangements with Germany for getting Mr. Subhas Chandra Bose to come from Germany to Malaya. Mr. Shunichi Matsumoto in his cross-examination says as follows : "Japan made arrangement with the German Government and he (Mr. Subhas Chandra Bose) was sent to Japan. He was asked because they knew that he was working for the independence of India and he thought that it would help Japan's war aims and at the same time Japan wanted to help this man to obtain independence for India. The Japan Government did this at its own instance. It was done to help the Japanese war aims. As far as I am concerned, I understand that Mr. Subhas Chandra Bose came to Japan in about April 1943. I heard of the intended Provisional Government of Free India in or April 1943. I think Mr. Subhas Chandra Bose remained in Japan for about one month on that occasion. I knew officially that the Indian National Government was going to be formed and that Mr. Subhas Chandra Bose was to be the head of it and that Japan would recognize and help that Government. I think the only reason why the Japanese Government wanted to recognize the Provisional Government of Free India was to help the Japanese war efforts. Japan had asked all her allies to recognize the Provisional Government of Free India and they did recognize it." Later on, the witness said that Mr. Bose asked Japan's allies through the Japanese Government to recognize the Provisional Government of Free India. He, however, could not mention any document containing such a request. But whether it be so or not, there is no doubt that it was Japan who got her allies to recognize the Provisional Government of Free India. He further says : "I think that Japan recognized the Provisional Government because she thought that it was going to help her war effort. I think that Japan asked all her allies to recognize it because she thought that it would be a good thing for Japan." In the re-examination of this witness, he said that Japan's war aim as regards India was to make it independent. This statement is, of course, to be taken for what it is worth. Japan had to win the war first and defeat Great Britain and her allies. The professed desire of Japan to hand over of the estate was donated India to the Indians after it was conquered has also to be taken for what it is worth. It may be pointed out here that Mr. Ayyar who was the Publicity Officer says : "I am not aware that the Japanese ever made a formal clarification of the attitude of Japan towards India". What the Japanese did in countries conquered by them is a matter of history. As regards the other countries which are said to have recognized the Provisional Government of Free India, he had to admit and it is an undisputed fact that they were all in the Military occupation of Japan. The witness, of course, said that the countries were independent and not under Japanese control. He had to admit, however, that Japanese troops were in all these countries but he said they were not in occupation.

As regards Japan sending her Minister to the Provisional Government of Free India, he said that the decision to appoint a Minister was taken in November 1944 and that Mr. Hachiya was appointed Minister and that he arrived at Rangoon in March 1945. In cross-examination this witness admitted that no letters or credentials were given to Mr. Hachiya when he went to Rangoon. The credentials were not issued solely because the Government was Provisional. He went on to say that at the instance of Mr. Bose a decision was arrived at to issue credentials and they were issued and sent to Mr. Hachiya about the middle of May. In fact, no credentials ever reached Mr. Hachiya. The witness further said in his cross-examination that Mr. Hachiya actually acted as Minister in this sense that he paid an official visit to the Foreign Minister of the Provisional Government and the Foreign Minister paid a return call to him. He admitted, however, that Mr. Bose refused to have anything to do with Mr. Hachiya because he had no credentials.

Mr. Hachiya himself in his evidence said that he did not bring any credentials when he went to Rangoon and that he never received any credentials; but that he received a telegram stating that the credentials had been sent. According to this witness, he saw Col. Chatterji twice or thrice and he saw Mr. Ayyar once. He also admitted that Mr. Bose refused to see him because he had no credentials. He said that he sent a telegram to Tokyo asking for his credential because he was told to do so by the request of Mr. Subhash Chandra Bose which was conveyed to him through Col. Chatterji.

As regards the alleged administration of liberated territory, the defence tried to make out in the evidence-in-chief of Lt.-Col. Loganadan that the Andaman and Nicobar Islands had been ceded by Japan to the Provisional Government of Free India. The version given by Col. Loganadan in his evidence-in-chief was deliberately misleading. His own documents put to him in cross-examination showed how far from true were the statements made by him in his examination-in-chief. He said in his evidence-in-chief: "In the Far Eastern Asiatic Conference, the Andaman and Nicobar Islands were ceded to the Provisional Government. On February 17, 1944, I went to Port Blair. After I had been there two to three weeks we had a ceremony at the Indian Independence League Headquarters at Port Blair. The Rear Admiral in charge as well as the Army Commander there, one Major-General, attended the function and the Andaman and Nicobar Islands were handed over to me as Chief Commissioner. Mr. Subhas Chandra Bose appointed me Chief Commissioner.... I took charge of the Administration two or three weeks later at the time of the function which I have described. Major Alvi was in charge of the Education Department in the Andaman and Nicobar Islands. Lt. Subha Singh was in charge of Revenue and Finance and Lt. Iqbal was in charge of Police. With the help of the local administration, I began to administer these Islands. I administered these islands as long as I was there, that is, until September 1944, when I returned to Singapore."

In cross-examination, when it was put to him that the only department which was handed over to him was the Education Department, he tried to make out that it was because he refused to take over the other departments, unless the police Department was also handed over to him. He admitted that the authority for the Statement that the Andaman and Nicobar Islands were ceded to the Provisional Government of Azad Hind was a broadcast from Tokyo; but he did not remember the exact wording of the broadcast. Mr. Subhas Chandra Bose gave a letter to this witness (Exhibit 5 B) appointing him Chief Commissioner, dated January 6, 1944. At the same time he gave him a letter dated November 16, 1943, from the Japanese Vice-Admiral to Mr. Subhas Chandra Bose. In this letter (G5 E) it was stated as follows : "We are already going ahead with preparatory measures necessary for a speedy and smooth transfer of the Islands. In accordance with a statement made by the Prime Minister, a Governor is to be appointed after completion of the transfer. It is to be understood that pending completion of the transfer an official of the Provisional Government bearing some such title as the Chief Commissioner for the Andaman and Nicobar Islands should be despatched to co-operate fully in the military administration of the Islands, under the direction of the Naval Commandant there". When confronted with this letter, Col. Loganadan said that certain verbal instructions were given by Mr. Bose to him. When asked what those instructions were, he said that they were that consistent with the local difficulties he should as soon as possible take over the whole of the islands. Later on, in his cross-examination, Col. Loganadan said as follows: "The word 'minsimu' means civil administration. The head of this was Jochi. The military and naval administration was in the hands of the Rear Admiral. As regards the self-sufficiency programme, I went to the villages and gave lectures. Apart from running schools and the self-sufficiency programme, my administration comprised nothing else. The Education Department consisted of running schools; that is all. There were about 30 or 33 schools. We had our own funds for running these schools. The funds for running the schools were issued by the Japanese to me. All these sums were not repaid by the time I left. I have not worked out how much this sum would come to per month. I never knew what it cost to run these schools. Teachers were there and they continued to work; if a vacancy arose, I filled it. Regarding the self-sufficiency programme, I went about from village to village urging the peasants to grow more food. I did nothing else specially. I was interesting myself in other departments, if you put that way, that is, taking charge of departments. That was the extent of my administration." He admitted that except for domestic purposes, the Provisional Government of Azad Hind incurred no expenses with regard to the administration of these islands, and that other than the loans received from the Japanese, there was no other expenditure by the

Provisional Government of Azad Hind.

The reports made by the witness to Mr. Subhas Chandra Bose from time to time show that it was not true that the other deparments were not taken up because the Police Department was not transferred.

The witness also admitted that the Administrative and Consultative Committees were in existence when he came. He also admitted that the Japanese had a Supply Department and that the self-sufficiency programme was carried out under instructions of the Japanese Supply Department. The witness also admitted that, if he wrote anything which was unpalatable to the Japanese in any of his letters, they would either suppress it or ask him to alter it. He admitted that when he was in the Andamans gross atrocities were committed by the Japanese in spy cases. He said he was aware of that but he was unable to remedy the matter.

The witness admitted that it was true as a general statement that civilians feared to come near any of them and they were not anxious to expose themselves to be seen with them.

When Col. Loganadan left the Andaman Islands, Major Alvi wrote a letter to him (Ex.5/c) in which he stated, among other things, as follows : "I do not know how I can maintain the prestige of the Provisional Government here without either commanding the least respect or confidence of the people or being able to render any co-operation to the Government; for it I cannot help the people in the least in their misfortunes. I cannot expect to work them into patriotic frenzy and make them go all out to help the Government war effort." He also stated that there was absolute insecurity of life and liberty and that if the Provisional Government was merely to watch but not to open its mouth where the question of spying was concerned, he could not stick to a place where he was expected to watch without emotion and without powers of interference in the execution of men whom he believed to be innocent.

In the report which Col. Loganadan made to Mr. Subbas Chandra Bose (Ex. 5/c), he stated, among other things, that the propaganda required by the Japanese Government was carried out and that any propaganda for the Independence movement was ineffective. It further said that the total amount of work done by the staff was so little that their absence would not be missed. "The higher authorities say that we have been helpful but to what extent I cannot conceive. The subordinates think and feel and say that we are a hindrance to their work. This is applicable chiefly to the Police Department. The public have lost confidence in us as we failed to lessen their sufferings. The public feel that the withdrawal of the Provisional Government may improve their lot as its intervention, if any, is likely to stiffen the attitude of the local authorities."

This report, according to the witness, was handed over by him to Mr. Subhas Chandra Bose in December 1944.

The witness was asked whether, before he left the Andamans, he did not tell the Vice-Admiral and the Civil Administrator that he was going to recommend the withdrawal of the Provisional Government from the islands. He denied it. He also denied that he sent any telegram himself to Mr. Subhas Chandra Bose after his arrival in Singapore recommending the withdrawal of the Provisional Government from the Andaman and Nicobar Islands.

He was then confronted with an entry in his diary (Ex. 5.c) under the date, October 25, 1944, in which he had made a copy of the telegram sent by Col. Bhonsle to Mr. Bose to the effect that Col. Loganadan was strongly of opinion that the entire Provisional Government staff should be withdrawn from the Andaman Islands as they had not got any useful work to do there. Col. Loganadan then said that a copy of the telegram was shown to him by Col. Bhonsle after the telegram had been despatched, and that he did not quite approve of the wording of the telegram and that he would have sent it differently. He said that it was not correct that he caused the telegram to be sent. He said that the words which he did not approve of were, "as they have not got any useful work to do here." He added that he did not think it worthwhile taking steps to correct the false impression on a telegram which had already been sent.

It was argued on behalf of the defence that Col. Loganadan in his evidence said that he had re-named the Andaman and Nicobar Islands and that he was not cross-examined on this point. Surely, it was not necessary to cross-examine the witness on a statement made by him which is contradicted by the documents produced by him. All the reports which Col. Loganadan made from the time of his arrival in the islands up to the time of his departure from that place are signed by him as Chief Commissioner of the Andaman and Nicobar Islands. The report which he made on December 23, 1944, also refers in terms to the Andaman Islands and is signed by him as Chief Commissioner of the Andaman and Nicobar Islands.

My submission is that it is abundantly proved that Japan never ceded the Andaman and Nicobar Islands or indeed an inch of any other territory to the Provisional Government of Free India, nor did Col. Loganadan or anybody else on behalf of the Provisional Government of Free India administer it. As a matter of fact, Japan had no right to cede any territory, even if it wanted to. The rights of an army inoccupation are thus set out in Oppenheim's International Law, Vol. II, Page 341, Par. 169 : "As the occupant actually exercises authority and as the legitimate government is prevented from exercising its authority, the occupant acquired a temporary right of administration over the territory and the inhabitants; and all legitimate steps taken by the exercise of rights must be recognized by the legitimate government after occupation has ceased. But as the right of an occupant in occupied territory is merely a right of administration, he may neither annex it while the war continues, nor set it up as an independent State, nor divide it into two administrative districts for political purposes. Moreover, the administration of the occupant is in no wise to be compared with ordinary administration, for it is distinctly and precisely military administration. In carrying it out the occupant is totally independent of the constitution and the laws of the territory, since the occupation is an aim of warfare, and the maintenance and safety of his forces and the purpose of war stand in the foreground of his interest and must be promoted under all circumstances and conditions. But although as regards the safety of his army and purpose of war the occupant is vested with an almost absolute power, as he is not the sovereign of the territory he has no right to make changes in the laws or in the adminsitration, other than those which are temporarily necessitated by his interest in the maintenance and safety of his army and the realisation of the propose of war. On the contrary, he has the duty of administering the country according to the existing laws and the existing rules of administration; he must ensure public order and safety, must respect family honour and rights, private property, religion and liberty. It is clear that these and other obligations of the occupations of the occupant cannot be avoided by dint of the additional illegality of prematurely annexing the occupied territory".

As regards the evidence given by Col. Loganadan, he could not have forgotten the substance of the various reports which he made and the contents of the letter which Major Alvi wrote to him, and the report which he made to Mr. Subhas Chandra Bose in December 1944. He attempted to give an entirely misleading impression to the court in his evidence-in-chief about the administrations of the Andaman and Nicobar Islands by him. His attempt to get out of the fact that the letter of the Japanese Minister to Mr. Subhas Chandra Bose definitely stated that in accordance with a statement made by the Prime Minister a Governor was to be appointed after the completion of the transfer and that it was to be understood that pending completion of the transfer an official of the Provisional Government bearing some such title as Chief Commissioner for the Andaman and Nicobar Islands should be despatched to co-operate fully in the Military administration of the Islands under the direction of the Naval Commandant there was futile.

He attempted to make out that Mr. Bose actually gave him greater authority than what was contained in the letter of the Japanese Minister. Ultimately, however, when asked what those instructions were, he said that the instructions given by Mr. Bose were that consistent with the local difficulties, he should as soon as possible take over the whole of the islands and that the full instructions were to take over the Islands as soon as possible. The witness in his evidence-in-chief tried to make out that his reports were not censored by the Japanese and that he gave them in sealed covers to the Japanese authorities for being transmitted to Mr. Subhas Chandra Bose. He had subsequently to admit that all his reports were seen and that if they contained any passages which were not palatable to the Japanese they would either withhold the report or ask him to alter the objectionable passage. He admitted that, in fact, from one of the reports a paragraph had to be deleted and that that paragraph was never communicated to Mr. Bose. His statement that he refused to take over the other departments unless the Police Department was transferred to him is also shown to be incorrect by the report which he himself made. He denied in the first instance about a telegram having been caused to be sent by him to Mr. Subhas Chandra Bose for withdrawing the so-called Provisional Government from the Andaman and Nicobar Islands. When confronted with the entry in his diary all the explanation that he could give was that he did not quite approve of the wording of the telegram and that he would have sent it differently. He said that the words of which he did not approve were "as they have not got any useful work to do there!" He said that he did not think it was worthwhile taking steps to correct the false impression on a telegram which had already been sent.

The story of the Andaman Islands having been ceded by the Japanese to the Provisional Government of Free India and having been administered by the latter having been exploded, the defence next tried to make out that the Provisional Government of Free India administered a portion of Burmese territory known as Ziawadi Estate. The two witnesses called in connection with this part of the case were Mr. Dina Nath and Mr. Shiv Singh. According to Mr. Dina Nath, this estate was handed over to the Provisional Government of Azad Hind and their representative administered it. In his evidence-in-chief this witness said : "This representative was appointed by the Revenue Ministry of the Azad Hind Government. There was one big sugar factory on the estate. There were yarn factories, blanket making factories, gunny-making factories, hospitals, and in addition to them cultivation was being carried out there. The population was about 15,000 mainly consisting of Indians. The Indian National Army had a base there. They had hospitals and these factories were also being run by the Indian National Army there. They had training camps also there. The produce was all handed over to the Provisional Government to be utilized by them in the manner they thought best." In cross-examination, he said that the estate belonged to a man named Mr. Parmanand, but he did not know personally who was the owner of that estate, and that it was handed over to the representative of the Provisional Government of Azad Hind by Mr. Parmanand. He said that at a public meeting at which Mr. Subhas Chandra Bose spoke and appealed for funds, Mr. Parmanand came up and announced: "I formally hand over the estate to the Provisional Government of Free India today". Mr. Parmanand was Minister of supplies. He added that after this announcement the products from that area were going to the Provisional Government only and the factories there were also run under the control of the Indian National Army. He admitted that the estate was in Burmese territory and he said that the estate was handed over as well as its revenue, income from factories, etc. He understood that it was handed over for the purposes of administration and for looking after the production. He wound up by saying : "All that the I.N.A. did was to sell the produce and whatever produce there was they sold it. The I.N.A. also arranged for further production. As I have said before, factories were also set up and they administered that area. I have no personal knowledge of the administration of that area."

There is nothing to prove that even the estate itself was handed over to the Provisional Government of Free India. What really happened was that the income to the fund of the Provisional Government of Free India, but even if the estate itself was handed over, it did not amount to an administration of liberated territory by the Provisional Government of Free India. The witness, Mr. Dina Nath, said that he did not know what happened to the estate afterwards.

The next witness called on this point was Mr. Shiv Singh. He put forward a ridiculous story of the estate having been occupied by the Provisional Government of Free India and having been administered by it. According to him, there had been agreement between the Japanese Government and the Provisional Government of Free India that the Provisional Government of Free India was to be the master of all that property which belonged to other owners who were not present. Apart from the inherent absurdity of this story and its being contrary to the version given by Mr. Dina Nath, the evidence of this witness is of no value at all. He said that he volunteered to fight for the Provisional Government of Free India in August 1942. He said that when he went to the Bangkok conference he belonged to the Indian National Army. Later on he tried to show that he joined the Indian National Army from the time the Japanese recognized the I.N.A. and the Provisional Government of Free India, and that that was in September 1943. He admitted that he was in the I.N.A. even before also but that he did not start work till September 1943. He further admitted that he went to Rangoon in September 1942 as one of a special party who were sent under Col, Gill, and that he actually proceeded to Arakan to reconnoitre and that he returned and made his report. This witness after joining the Indian National Army gave information about it to the British Army as regards the whereabouts of the I.N.A. He made a flimsy effort to wriggle out of this by saying that in so doing he did a trick to save the Ziawadi estate, the I.N.A. and the Provisional Government. It would be a waste of time and energy to say anything more about the evidence of this palpably false witness.

It was then attempted to show that when the I.N.A. entered Indian territory they administered the area occupied by them. The area referred to is the portion of the Manipur State which is on the border of Burma. The source of information of this witness, viz., Capt. R.M. Irshad, is according to him, reports from Vishnpore area which was commanded by Capt. S.A. Malik.

If the defence wanted to prove this fact they could have called better evidence than the evidence of a witness who deposes to facts from his recollection of certain reports which he saw. The declaration which he deposes to having been seen by him only stated that the administration in the liberated areas would be carried out under the head of the Provisional Government of Azad Hind. All that he says in his evidence-in-chief about the alleged administration of the area is that he came across official documents about the administration carried out on the Manipur Front and that at the time when operations were being carried on in Manipur Area, the administration of the liberated area was being carried on by Major M. Kiani, No. I Division Commander, that there were also units of Azad Hind Dal at More hand that these units came under the orders of No. I Division Camp. He further said that in his official capacity as G.I. He received reports from Vishnupore area which was commanded by Capt. S.A. Malik who came under the command of No. I Division Camp, about the administration carried out by him and by units of the Azad Hind Dal in Vishnupore sector.

In cross-examination, the witness could give only two instances of the administration about which he deposed. He said that Capt. Kiani operating on the left of the road had to settle some land dispute among the Manipuris in that particular area. As regards the other incident, all that the witness said was that he remembered the instructions given to the Azad Hind Dal Unit for collection of supplies, giving medical aid, etc., to the villagers. The witness admitted that at the time when Palel was besieged there were British troops in the operational areas of Manipur and that fighting had never ceased in Manipur and that the areas which had been liberated from Moreh to Chimol—a little this side of Palel—were administered by the I.N.A. He said that there were certain areas where operations had not actually been carried out; there were certain areas where operations had been or were being carried out and there were certain areas where operations had ceased. In other words, where Japanese and the I.N.A. were in military occupation. He added : "That is what I meant by liberated areas. " Finally, he said : " There was, as, I have said before, military administration in those particular parts of Manipur and Vishnupore area where the I.N.A were operating. " As a matter of fact, the Azad Hind Dal, which consisted of a small body of persons trained for civil administration, was, according to the prosecution case, never in Manipur and never went beyond the limits of Burma. Proof of this fact appears in Exhibit 5-L which is a letter dated June 21, 1944, by Subhas Chandra Bose to Col. Loganadan. Paragraph of the letter is as follows : "We have started a new organisation called the Azad Hind Dal. It is a semi-military organisation consisting of civilians and administrators who will be going to India in the wake of our victorious armies. " This letter clearly shows that up to June 21, 1944, the Azad Hind Dal had not gone into India. It will be recollected that from about the end of June or beginning of July, 1944, the Japanese and the units of he I.N.A. that were there began to retreat from the Manipur area.

The evidence given by Capt. Irshad is coloured by a desire to make it favourable to the defence. In his evidence-in-chief he said that Col. Hunt had said : "From now on you belong to the Japanese Army and you will obey their orders as you have been obeying our orders." In cross-examination he admitted that those were not the words used by Col. Hunt and that in the statement which he made to the defence what he said was : "Now you are prisoners of war and I hand you over to the Japanese authorities." His statement about having heard that the Congress was hostile to the Japanese is also without foundation. His statement about Capt. Sahgal having joined the I.N.A. in August 1942 is also not correct. There is abundant evidence to show that Capt. Sahgal joined the I.N.A. long before August 1942 and actually made speeches persuading other prisoners of war to join the I.N.A. He stated that he was not aware of any coercive methods used in making prisoners of war join the I.N.A. This is entirely inconsistent with another statement in his evidence-in-chief to the following effect :" It was also decided that the recruitment for the 2nd I.N.A. should be entirely voluntary." He could not explain why such a decision should be taken if previously the recruitment was voluntary. The explanation which he attempted to give is lacking in sincerity. He admitted that the alternatives before the Indian soldiers who were prisoners of war were either to join the I.N.A. or to be treated as prisoners of war. He however would not admit that the treatment by the Japanese of prisoners of war was brutal. He would not go beyond stating that the treatment was unsatisfactory and that the Japanese were not treating the prisoners of war according to international rules and regulations. He admitted that in February officers were separated from the men but he suggested that he did not know the object of doing so. He denied having seen the pamphlet "Our Struggle" (Exhibit 5A). His statement that he did not know what happened to Capt. Mohan Singh after he was arrested can hardly be accepted. The statements, therefore, of this witness even as far as they go can hardly be taken as carrying any weight.

It was then attempted to show that there was something like a State Bank called the Nationl Bank of Azad Hind. In cross-examination, witness (Mr. Dina Nath) stated that the bank was registered in Rangoon like any other public bank and that there were shareholders in the bank. The capital of the bank was Rs. 50 lakhs. He further stated that the bank acted as the bankers to the Provisional Government just as it acted for its other constituents. He also said that all the money was in Japanese occupancy notes and that there was only about Rs. 50 to 60 thousand in British currency.

An attempt was made to rely on the evidence of Col. Kitson and Ghulam Mohammed in support of the contention that Capt. Sahgal sent a note saying that he and his party wished to surrender as prisoners of war and that as this offer was accepted, there was a recognition of belligerency so far as he is concerned and he is not liable to be tried for the offence of waging war against the King. So far as the evidence of Col Kitson is concerned, it is quite clear that in the conversation which he had with Capt. Sahgal, Capt. Shahg told him that he had fought for what he considered to be right and that now that he had lost he was preprared to take the consequences. Col. Kitson then told him that he would be marched off to Brigade Headquarters on the morrow and that he would be sent back and disposed of by Brigade or Division but that his disposal had nothing to do with him after he had sent him off. In any event, it cannot be suggested that the leading Company Commander to whom Capt. Sahgal surrendered had or could have any authority either to grant belligerency or to recognize belligerent rights. So far as the evidence of Havildar Ghulam Mohammed is concerned , it was suggested in his cross-examination that there was something more written in the letter. No such suggestion was made to Col. Ketson and he was not cross-examined by Counsel for the defence. As a matter of fact, according to the evidence of Ghulama Mohammed after Capt. Sahgal and his party had decided to surrender and before they actually surrendered, Capt. Sahgal asked the officers to communicate to all the men about the decision which had been taken and ordered the pickets on the hills to withdraw.

An attempt was also made to rely upon what happened in Rangoon when the British Army entered it in the beginning of May, 1945, in support of the defence plea of recognition. It is difficult to see how any such contention can be urged. It was admitted that some days before the British entered Rangoon the Japanese Army had evacuated Rangoon and it is in evidence that Mr. Subhas Chandra Bose, while leaving Rangoon, told Capt. Irshad and Col. Loganadan that he was leaving the Indian Army in Rangoon for the sole purpose of looking after Indian civilians in Rangoon. There was no question of resisting the British entry. The evidence also makes it clear that, when the Japanese evacuated Rangoon, they withdrew the sentries from the prison in which the British prisoners of war were kept and according tot he evidence of Capt.. Irshad and the documents put in during his examination, Wing-Commander Hudson, who was the senior officer among the Allied prisoners of war there, gave him certain orders and Capt. Arshad implemented those orders but before the orders were carried out, the British Army arrived in Rangoon. In fact, according to Capt. Irshad himself, Brig. Lander said that he was not in a position to accept Capt. Irshad and the other I.N.A. troops as prisoners of war.

In the statements made by accused, an attempt has been made to give an explanation of their conduct in joining the I.N.A. and waging war against His Majesty the King. Waging war against His Majesty the King is an offence on the part of a person even if he is compelled to do so by threats. Section 94 of the Indian Penal Code which creates a general exception in respect of an act to which a person is compelled by threats excludes murder and offences against the State from this general exception. Waging war against His Majesty the King which is an offence under

Section 121 of the Indian Penal Code is an offence against the State. There might conceivably be circumstances in the commission of an offence, which may be a palliative of the offence but if war has been waged in terms of the section, no reason or explanation can be a defence to the charge under Section 121. In the statements of all the accused it is attempted to be made out that the Indian prisoners of war were left in the lurch to face the consequences of the surrender by themselves. This is not true. It was under the orders of the Japanese authorities that the British prisoners of war were separated from the Indian prisoners of war, it is not suggested and it cannot be suggested that the British prisoners of war expected to receive or in fact received better treatment from the Japanese than the Indian prisoners of war. The statements of the accused attempt to suggest that they were freed from their allegiance to the Crown by reason of what happened at the Farrier Park meeting. As Capt. Shah Nawaz Khan says in his statement, Col. Hunt on that occasion said : "Today I on behalf of the British Government hand you over to the Japanese Government whose orders you will obey as you have done ours." Of course, Col. Hunt said this under the orders of the Japanese authorities : It is difficult to conceive what else could have been said on an occasion like this, When the Singapore army surrendered the whole army came under the orders of the Japanese Government and all the prisoners of war had to obey the orders of the Japanese authorities from that time. Even if no statement had been made by Col. Hunt, the consequences and the result of the surrender would have been exactly the same. There is no justification for saying that the Indian prisoners of war were handed over like cattle by the British to the Japanese. The British prisoners of war were similarly surrendered.

The very fact that immediately after the surrender they were asked to join the I.N.A. shows that the idea of making the Indian prisoners of war to fight against the British as members of the I.N.A. had been conceived and put into train before they fall of Singapore. The evidence shows that at the meeting at Farrar Park there were Indian prisoners of war wearing arm bands with the letter F on them : F stands for Fujiwara Kikan. Capt. Shah Nawaz Khan says in his statement that up to the end of May 1942 he was against the idea of the organization of the I.N.A. coming into existence. This is in consistent with the evidence for the prosecution which is to the effect that Capt. Shah Navaz delivered lectures even before April 1942 asking other prisoners of war to join the I.N.A. Capt. Shah Nawaz Khan further says that from June 1942 to July 1943 he decided in the interests of his men to volunteer for the I.N.A. with full determination that he would do everything possible to break it or to sabotage it from within as soon as he felt that it would submit to Japanese exploitation. This is also inconsistent with the proved facts that Capt. Shah Nawaz Khan took an active part in winning other prisoners of war from their allegiance to the Crown. Capt. Sahgal says in his statement that he joined the I.N.A. in August 1942 and that up to that time he was in the non-volunteer camp in Tangan aerodrome. No question was put to any of the prosecution witnesses suggesting this.

Lt. Dhillon admits that he co-operated with Mohan Singh in the organisation of the I.N.A. till June 29, 1942, when he became ill and had to go to the hospitals. He says that on receiving the assurance that Netaji Subhas Chandra Bose would come to lead the movement, he decided to continue in the second I.N.A. after December 1942.

It is also suggested in the statements of the accused that their object in joining the I.N.A. was that they did not wish indiscriminate looting and raping taking place in India as had happened in Malaya after the Japanese entered the country. The evidence, however clearly establishes the fact that all the accused did everything they could to enable the Japanese to conquer India. In fact, they insisted on the Japanese authorities giving them an active part in the fight at the front. It is also significant that, even after the Japanese began to retreat from Manipur and Kohima, the accused kept on fighting in Burma and in fact were anxious that the Japanese should overrun India.

The explanations sought to be given of their conduct in their statements are inconsistent with their own case that the I.N.A. was raised in order to drive the British out of India; in other words, to help the Japanese to conquer India. The entries in the diaries of Capt. Shah Nawaz and Capt. Sahgal are significant on this point. They have been read to the Court more than once and I will not read them again.

It was argued that, so far as the accused are concerned, there was a question of duel allegiance. This argument overlooks the wording of Section 121. The offence mentioned in that section is that of waging war against the Queen. The word "Queen" is defined in Section 13 of the Indian Penal Code as denoting the Sovereign for the time being of the United Kingdom of Great Britain and Ireland. The cases of the King Vs. Casement (1917) 1 K.B. 98, and the King vs. Lynch (1903) 1 K.B. 444, give a complete answer to this contention. The case of Jeager the Attorney-General for Natal (1907) Appeal Cases, 326, is a complete answer to the contention that the accused no longer owed allegiance because the Crown failed to protect them. As a matter of fact, the British Government did succeed in protecting India against the Japanese. The fact that up to a certain stage the fortunes of war were against Great Britain can make no difference in the question. It is relevant to point out in this connection that the officers and the men of the Indian Army who, when they were prisoners of war, joined the Indian National Army at first, but subsequently did not agree to continue in it after December 1942, were to revert to their positions as prisoners of war. Not only that, but even as regards those men who were willing to join the Indian National Army but who were in the category of B and C men who could not be absorbed in the Indian Natinal Army, it was announced that they would be reverted to prisoners of war and sent to those camps . I am referring to exhibit SS which is a document signed by Capt. Shah Nawaz Khan and addressed to the Headquarters, Indian National Army, and is dated May 27, 1943. It states, *inter alia,* as follows:

"Besides this, the Indian National Army has approximately 2,000 men under-strength and up to date it has been found very difficult to fill up this large gap. All Unit and Formation Commands are, therefore, requested to give their best co-operation and support in overcoming this difficulty .... There is also a likelihood that all category B and C men who can not be absorbed in the Indian National Army will be reverted to prisoners of war and sent to those camps. It is fully realized that it is a very hard and regrettable decision; nevertheless, it may have to be resorted to."

In exhibit which is a document from Mr. Rash Behari Bose, President of the Council of Action, and addressed to officers and men of the Indian National Army, it is stated as follows : "Some of you many be anxious to know what will happen to those rejected from the Indian National Army. Unfortunately, I shall have no control over those who deliberately chose to quit the Indian National Army at the present juncture. I cannot speak for the Japanese, nor say in what manner or at what place they will be employed by the Powers whose prisoners they choose to be". It is also interesting to know that in Exhibit AA which is a Special Order dated September 1, 1942, and refers to the promotion *inter alia* of the accused, their old rank and unit is mentioned. Even as late as March 26, 1944, in a document signed by Capt. Shah Nawaz Khan headed 'security' and which gave the allotment of personal numbers to the officers, the Indian Army Units of the officers are also mentioned.

As regards the contention of the accused that they were entitled to throw off their allegiance to the Crown and that they were justified in doing so, because they were fighting for the freedom of their country, it is relevant to consider some cases which throw light on the subject. In King vs. Casement (1917) 1 K.B. page 98, the report of the case shows that Sir Roger Casement circulated a leaflet which said as follows : "Irishmen! Here is a chance for you to fight for Ireland. You have fought for England, your country's hereditary enemy. You have fought for Belgium in England's interest, though it was no more to you than the Fiji Islands. Are you willing to fight for your own country with a view to securing the national freedom of Ireland? With the moral and material assistance of the German Government, an Irish Brigade is being formed. The object of the Irish Brigade shall to be fight solely for the cause of Ireland and under no circumstances shall it be directed to any German end. The Irish Brigade shall be formed and shall fight under the Irish flag alone. The men shall wear a specially distinct Irish uniform and have Irish officers. The Irish Brigade shall be clothed, fed and efficiently equipped with arms and ammunitions by the German Government. It is to be stationed near Berlin and be treated as guests of the German Government. At the end of the war, the German Government undertakes to send each member of the Brigade who may so desire to the United States of America with necessary means to land. The Irishmen in America are collecting money for the brigade. Those men who do not join the Irish Brigade will be removed from Lumburg and distributed among other camps. If interested, see your company commanders. Join the Irish Brigade and win Ireland's independence". Sir Roger Casement circulated the said leaflet among British subjects who were prisoners of war of the Germans. In delivering judgment Chief Justice Lord Reading referred to the case of William Caundell which was decided in 1812. It was the case of persons who were confined in the Isle of France and who had there fore saken their allegiance to the King and transferred it to the French. In that case a number of British sailors and marines were confined as prisoners of war in the Isle of France. The prison being much crowded was greatly incommoded with dirt and vermin and there being no way of escaping from such inconvenience but that of desertion every art was practised by their keepers to induce the unhappy prisoners to enter the French service. Fifty men among whom were Cundell and Smith had not virtue enough to resist the temptation on the one hand, and the hope of escaping from distress and filth on the other. They forgot their country and their allegiance and put on the enemy uniform acting as sentinels over those who were so recently their companions in captivity. The traitors continued to do the duty with the French until the surrender of the Island to the British forces when Cundell and Smith with ten others positively refused to accompany the ememy and threw themselves upon the mercy of their country, having immediately surrendered to the English, while 38 others marched off to old France. These culprits were then transmitted to England and a Special Commission was issued for their trial. They were convicted and hanged. The Chief Justice, in giving his judgment, said : "I cannot doubt that before the statute, it was treason in a British subject to join the force of an enemy abroad, and that if a British subject had joined the forces of an enemy abroad at war with the country and he afterwards returned or was brought back to the country he could be tried here for that offence. When one has regard to the nature of the offence of high treason I think it is obvious, it must have been so. Foster in his Crown Law page 183 thus describes the offence of high treason: "High treason being an offence committed against the duty of allegiance it may be proper to consider from whom and to whom allegiance is due. With regard to natural born subjects, there can be no doubt they owe allegiance to the Crown at all times and in all circumstances. This is what we call natural allegiance in contradistinction to that which is local. Natural allegiance is found in the relation every man standeth in to the Crown, considered as the head of the society whereof he is born a member and on the peculiar privileges he derives from the relation, which are, with great propriety called his birth-right. This birth right nothing but his own demerit can deprive him of; it is indefeasible and perpetual; and, consequently the duty of allegiance which arises out of it and is inseparably connected with it is in consideration of law likewise inalienable and perpetual." Justice Darling in his judgment after referring to Cundell's case said that he had violated his allegiance which followed him, which remained with him wherever he might be outside the King's dominion, and by which he was bounden even when he was a prisoner of war. In King versus Lynch (1903) I K8. page 444, the accused was a British subject born in Australia. During the Boer War he made a declaration of willingness to take up arms for the South African Republic where he was residing in order to maintain and defend its independence and he became a fully enfranchised burgher of the South African Republic. On March 22, 1900, he published an address to Irishmen inciting them to assist the enemy and he commanded an armed body of men called the second Irish Brigade with intent to co-operate with the military forces of the enemy. He actually fought on behalf of the enemy against the British troops. The defence was that he had transferred his allegiance during the war by becoming naturalised in an enemy country. It was held that he could not do so during the time of war. In his judgment, Justice Wills said at page 459 : "With regard to the rest of this case it is sufficient for me to say that throughout the argument I have never been able to comprehend how an act of treason could give any sort of rights or could exempt a person from criminal responsibility for subsequent acts of treason. If Mr. Sheeny's argument was sound, an army might, if each member of it were individually to accept letters of naturalisation from the enemy, desert in the hour of battle without rendering any of its members liable to the penalties of treason. So extravagant a conclusion shows conclusively that the contention cannot be supported."

In Jaeger vs. Attorney General of Natal (1907) Appeal cases 326, the defence against a charge of treason which was sought to be raised was that when the protection of the State ceased its counterpart, namely, the duty of allegiance ceased also. This was a case of a resident alien within British territory owing allegiance to the Crown. Hc was a burgher of the South African Republic and when the British forces had retired from Waschbank to Ladysmith and the Boer forces occupied that part of Natal in which Waschbank was situated, he joined the Boer Forces and aided and assisted them both as Commandant and as a Commissioner and Justice of Peace. In giving judgment their Lordships of the Judicial Committee of the Privy Council said : "Their Lordships are of opinion that there is no ground for this contention. The protection of a State does not cease merely because the State Forces for strategical or other reasons are temporarily withdrawn, so that the enemy for the time exercises the right of an army in occupation. On the contrary when such territory reverts to the control of its rightful sovereign, wrongs done during the foreign occupation are cognisable by the ordinary courts. The protection of the sovereign has not ceased. It is continuous though the actual redress of what has been done amiss may be necessarily postponed until the enemy forces have been expelled."

Learned Counsel for the Defence put forward two points of distinction : (I) That they were cases of individuals charged with treason under the English law and that they were not members of an organized body; and (2) that in those cases there was no question of double allegiance. I have dealt with both these points in my address. It was further contended that in India there is no such thing as treason and that the whole law is codified in the Indian Penal Code. Treason, never the-less, is an offence against the State. High treason has been defined as an offence committed against the duty of allegiance. The essence of waging war against the King is that the offence is against the duty of allegiance. It is an offence against the State. The principles laid down in the cases which I have cited are applicable to the cases of waging war against the King.

The only other case to which I wish to refer on this subject is Aung Hla vs. King Emperor, I.L.R. 9 Rangoon 494. That was a case where the accused was charged with the offence of waging war against the King. In delivering the judgment, Chief Justice Page at page 413 said : "We propose, therefore, to make clear what is meant by the word 'wage war' in Section 121 of the Indian Penal Code". In his judgment, he quoted from 21 State trials pages 644, 645, from the charge of Chief Justice Mansfield to the jury which deals with two kinds of waging war, one against the person of the King and the other against the Majesty of the King: in other words, against him in his Regal capacity, where it was pointed out that it was treason to attempt to attain by force and violence any object of a general public nature. The learned Judge then quotes from the charge of Lord President Hope in Rex vs. Wilson, 21 St. Tr. 1353. If they rise to effect a general public purpose by force and numbers that object renders the rising treason, be the numbers great or small. The learned Judge then quoted from the charge of Justice Tindal in R. Vs. Frost, 4 St. Tr. at page 93. An assembly of men armed and arrayed in a warlike manner with any treasonable purpose is a levying of war although no blow be struck. And enlisting and drilling and marching bodies of men are sufficient overt acts of that treason, without coming to a battle or action. And if this be the case, the actual conflict between such a body and the Queen's forces must beyond all doubt amount to levying war against the Queen—not necessarily that it should be accompanied with the pomp and pageantry of war. The learned Judge then quotes from page 216 of Foster's Crown cases that joining with rebels in an act of rebellion or with enemies in acts of hostility will make a man traitor.

It is submitted that, notwithstanding all that has been said about the formation of Provisional Government and the immunity which it is supposed to have given to the accused what the accused did was nothing else than joining the enemy in act of hostility against His Majesty the King.

It was argued that there was no charge of desertion or any breach of duty on the part of the accused as prisoners of war. It is submitted that it was not necessary to have any separate charge of desertion. Desertion was the first step taken by them in connection with the offence of waging war against His Majesty the King. Not only did they desert the army, but they actually waged war against the King.

It must be remembered that the accused were not merely civil subjects but Indian Commissioned Officers in the Indian Army. If they waged war against His Majesty the King, it necessarily implies previous desertion by them from the army. They could not have fought against His Majesty's forces without first deserting the army in which they held commissions.

As regards the contention that this court-martial has no authority to try the case because of Section 196 of the Criminal Procedure Code, it is not denied by the defence that the Criminal Procedure Code is not applicable to these proceedings. Section 41 of the Indian Army Act provides that every person subject to this Act who either within British India or at any place beyond British India commits any civil offence shall be deemed to be guilty of an offence against military law and if charged therewith under this section shall, subject to the provisions of this Act, be liable to be tried for the same by court-martial and on conviction be punished. It will be noticed that the section itself gives jurisdiction to the court-martial to try the offence. It is contended that by Section 7 (18) civil offence is defined as an offence which if committed in British India would be triable by a criminal court and it is argued that it cannot be left in the air as to which criminal court is to try the offence. The answer to this has already been given, namely, that Section 41 itself says that the person shall be liable to be tried for the same by court-martial. It was contended that we must go to an appropriate Act to show what is triable. It is submitted that the appropriate Act is the Indian Army Act itself. The Criminal Procedure Code is a Code of Procedure. All offences under the Indian Penal Code are triable by some criminal court or other. The Criminal Procedure Code lays down which particular court shall try which particular offences. In dealing with this procedure, Section 196 of the Criminal Procedure Code says that no court shall take cognisance of an offence punishable under Chapter VI unless upon complaint made by order of or under authority from the Provincial Government or some officer empowered by the Provincial Government in this behalf. The words "no court" in this section, of course, mean no court under the Criminal Procedure Code. There is no prohibition either in the Indian Army Act or in the rules under the Indian Army Act of a nature similar to that contained in Section 196 of the Criminal Procedure Code. It is submitted that the attempt to bring in Section 196 by the back-door is futile.

As regards the contention that the trial is illegal by reason of Rule 24 of the rules under the Indian Army Act, it is submitted that this contention is also unfounded. Rule 24 deals with the joint trial of several accused persons. If that is an offence which is charged to have been committed collectively by more than one person and they are tried together, there is no provision in the rules to prevent separate charges being brought against one or other of the accused and tried at the same trial along with the joint charge. Rule 18 says that a charge sheet may contain one charge or several charges. This is in marked contrast to the provision in Section 233 of the Criminal Procedure Code that for every distinct offence of which any person is accused there shall be a separate charge and that every such charge shall be tried separately except in the cases mentioned in Sections 234, 235, 236 and 239. Rule 39 provides that the accused when required to plead to any charge may object to the charge on the ground *inter alia* that it is not in accordance with the rules. Rule 68, sub-rule (e), says: "Where a charge-sheet contains more than one charge, the accused may before pleading claim to be tried separately in respect of any charge or charges in that charge-sheet on the ground that he will be embarrassed in his defence if he is not so tried separately and in such a case the court, unless they think his claim unreasonable, shall arraign and try the accused in like manner as if the convening officer had inserted the said charge or charges in different charge-sheets. No such objection was taken. It was only in the closing address of counsel for the accused that the objection was taken. Rule 135 of the Indian Army Act Rules provides for validating irregular procedure in certain cases and, omitting the unnecessary part, says that the finding and sentence of a court-martial may be confirmed and shall, if so confirmed and in all cases where confirmation is not necessary, be valid notwithstanding any deviation from these rules, or notwithstanding any defect or objection, technical or other, unless it appears that any injustice has been done to the offender. The case of Subramania vs. the King-Emperor, I. L. R. 25 Madras, page 61, cited by Counsel for the Defence has no relevance in this case.

The tenth charge against Capt. Shah Nawaz is of abetment of the murder near Popa Hill on or about March 29, 1945, of sepoy Mohammed Husain, by Khazin Shah and Aya Singh. The witnesses who disposes to this incident are Havildar Ghulam Mohammed, Alla Ditta, Jagiri Ram and Lance Naik Sardar Mohammed. Hav. Ghulam Mohammed in his evidence said that on or about March 26 or 27 he received the report that three men from No. I Battalian had been placed in quarter guard and he gave the name of one of these three men as sepoy Mohammed Husain. The witness was told that these men had tried to desert and therefore had been placed under orders in the quarter guard. According to this witness, on the evening of March 28 when Capt. Shah Nawaz Khan returned from his duty the Commander of No. 1 Battalion brought these three men before him. Capt. Sahgal interrogated them and Mohammed Husain admitted his guilt and the other two pleaded not guilty. The witness was told by Capt. Shah Nawaz to ask the officer to investigate the case. According to the witness, on the morning of March 29 the three accused were again brought up. He says in his evidence : "On the morning of March 29 these three accused were again brought up. The Battalion Commander read out the same charges to them and Col. Sahgal asked them whether they pleaded guilty to the charge or not. Mohammed Husain pleaded guilty, the other two pleaded not guilty. Three separate charge-sheets were prepared. I read all the three; then these men were sent back to the Divisional Headquarters. I was present at the office and saw them go out accompanied by the regimental second in command and the Battalion Commander. Between 2 and 3 p.m. I was in my hut when the regimental second in command and the Battalion Commander came back. Their names were Major Negi, and Lt. Khazin Shah. They they went away. I saw Mohammed Husain in the evening at about 4 or 5 o'clock when he passed in front of my room. He was accompanied by 2nd Lt. Sardar Mohammed, Adjutant of No. I Battalion, and 2nd Lt. Aya Singh". It will be noticed that this witness was not cross-examined on the statement which he made that three separate charge-sheets were prepared and that he read all the three.

The next witness Alla Ditta said in his evidence that he knew sepoy Mohammed Husain who belonged to a British regiment before. Witness belonged to the "C" Company and Mohammed Husain to Headquarters "C" Company. Witness also said that he knew Jagiri Ram who was also in "C" Company of his battalion. The witness then said that on March 26, 1945, between 2 and 3 p.m. Mohammed Husain came to him and told him that he intended to desert that day. The witness told him that that day was not suitable for escaping and that some other day would be more suitable. He went back. The same day at sunset witness was called to battalion headquarters where he saw Jagiri Ram, Mohammed Husain and Khazin Shah. The further evidence of this witness is in these words. "After that Khazin Shah gave me a beating and told me that I was disloyal to the I.N.A. and that I was one of the men who intended to escape and said : Mussalmans like you betrayed even Turks. Then I was shut up in the quarter guard and taken to headquarters. The next day I was brought before Col. Sahgal and statements were taken individually. Col. Sahgal asked me if I intended to escape. I said "no," I did not intend to escape'. I mentioned to him about Mohammed Husain's visit to me regarding his intended escape. Then I was sent out. Khazin Shah ordered Ghulam Mohammed, the Brigade Adjutant, to inquire and question Alla Ditta and others who wished to escape. Ghulam Mohammed detailed Aya Singh to beat us and question Alla Ditta and others who intended to escape. Ghulam Mohammed told Aya Singh to find out from Alla Ditta regarding the six other persons who intended to escape. On March 25, 1945, I was beaten and interrogated by Aya Singh. I stayed there on March 27 and 28. On March 28, our battalion was to move to Legyi village. Khazin Shah told

Ghulam Mohammed to inform Capt. Sahgal that if these men were not punished he would give up the command of the battalion. I was present then. On March 29, Major Negi and Khazin Shah took me before Col. Shah Nawaz to the Divisional Headquarters. I was put before Col. Shah Nawaz. Three of us were present : myself, Jagiri Ram and Mohammed Husain, besides Col. Shah Nawaz, Major Negi, Khazin Shah and two other sentries stayed out and were sent in.

I saw that three different crime reports had already been made regarding us. Major Negi took the crime reports and handed them to Col. Shah Nawaz who read them out separately to each one of us. First, Jagiri Ram was questioned by Col. Shah Nawaz. There myself and Jagiri Ram were present at the same time. Col. Shah Nawaz inquired from Jagiri Ram if he had intended to desert. He replied "no." I did not inquired from Jagiri Ram if the had intended to desert. He replied "no". I did not intend to desert. I was questioned next and I told that I did not intend to desert. Then Col. Shah Nawaz said that I was an N.C.O. and Mohammed Husain had approached me and I had not reported the matter. I said that it was my fault. Then he questioned Mohammed Husain as follows : Did you intend to desert or make others to desert with you ? Mohammed Husain replied "No". I did not intend to desert. Col. Shah Nawaz told : "speak the truth." Mohammed Husain said : "I had a few difficulties and, therefore, I intended to desert. But no inqueries were made into his complaints. Mohammed Husain was told by Col. Shah Nawaz : 'You are sentenced to death by shooting because you intended to desert yourself and were persuading others to do the same. Therefore you are not pardoned. I heard Col. Shah Nawaz saying put off the case to the Regimental Commander. Then we all three of us were sent out. I recognize Col. Shah Nawaz as the accused before the Court. We waited there for to minutes, and were brought back to Brigade Headquarters. Mohammed Husain, Jagiri Ram and myself came together back to Brigade Headquarters. Mohammed Husain and myself were put back in the same cell in which we were before and Khazin Shah took away Jagiri Ram. The same day at about 5 p.m. Sardar Mohammed, adjustant of our battalion, and Aya Singh took away Mohammed Husain. I have never seen Mohammed Husain since then."As regards the witness himself, he says that he did quarter quard for three or four days; then he was produced before Major Negi. He was reduced in rank and Major Negi said : "You will have to go to Rangoon.." This witness was taken to a concentration camp in Popa and on April 7, 1945, along with 16 other men he was despatched to Rangoon by march route.

In the cross-examination of this witness, it was attempted to be made out that Capt. Shah Nawaz did not sentence Mohammed Husain to be shot. The whole or the cross-examination is as follows : "No decision was arrived at either in my case or in the case of Jagiri Ram. It is true that all that Col. Shah Nawaz said was that you deserve to be shot. Col. Shah Nawaz said that persons like you will be sentenced to death by shooting. Col. Shah Nawaz told Mohammed Husain.: 'You yourself wanted to escape ; secondly, you have tried to persuade others to escape. Therefore you are a rebel to the I.N.A. and should be sentenced to death by shooting.' I saw Col. Shah Nawaz write something on the crime report. How could I read the crime report without picking it up from the table? I do not understand English. I do not know what he wrote there and I do not know English and I had not read what was written in the crime report at that time." In his re-examination , witness said that the crime reports were lying on the table and Col. Shah Nawaz read them out as he spoke to us individually. He wrote on the crime report which had already been drawn up.

It is submitted that this cross-examination does not help the defence in any way. Reading the cross-examination as a whole, it is submitted that, according to the evidence of this witness, Capt. Shah Nawaz sentenced Mohammed Husain to death by shooting. The previous witness deposed to three crime reports having been prepared and his having read them ; the fact that the witness did not know English does not detract from his evidence on this point. In fact, as noted by the Court, the witness used the word 'Put off the case to the Regimental Commander' in English. Even a sepoy who does not know English knows what a crime report is and from the fact that Major Negi gave the papers to Col. Shah Nawaz and he read them out separately to each of the three accused, witness can certainly say that they were crime reports. The questions put by Capt. Shah Nawaz to the accused from the papers before him were sufficient to convey to the witness the fact that the papers were crime reports.

The next witness on this point was Jagiri Ram. He says that he knew Mohammed Husain and Alla Ditta and that Mohammed Husain himself and a Garhwali talked about escape when they were in Popa Hill area. He also deposes to the inquiry made by Khazin Shah in the matter and that Khazin Shah allowed the Garhwali to go. He gives the details of the inquiry by Khazi Shah. Witness then deposes to the fact that at sunset Khazin Shah took Mohammed Husain and the witness to Brigade Headquarters. Alla Ditta arrived later. After that all the three of them, Mohammed Husain, Alla Ditta and the witness were put into the quarter guard and their hands were tied. On the following day they were brought before Col. Sahgal who interrogated them. Major Negi and Khazin Shah were present. Witness then deposes to the fact that Lt. Aya Singh gave each of them a beating and said that he would release them if they would tell the names of the people who intended to escape. Witness continued to say that he did not know.

The further evidence of the witness is in these terms. "Next day We were taken to the Divisional Commander, Col. Shah Nawaz. We were accompanied by Major Negi, Khazin Shah and the sentry. All three of us, myself, Alla Ditta and Mohammed Husain were produce before the Divisional Commander. The Divisional Commander asked me to speak the truth. He asked whether I intended to escape. I said no, I did "not" intend to escape! Capt. Shah Nawaz asked us why we did not report the matter. I said that I did not know anything about it and If did not intend to escape. He asked me if there was any officer or N.C.O. near me, I said No, " I was working with my medical officer! Then Capt. Shah Nawaz asked Alla Ditta : 'When Mohammed Husain talked to you about escaping did you report to any one? Alla Ditta said : I do not know anything about Mohammed Husain's escape. I thought it was a joke. I do not know anything about it.

Capt. Shah Nawaz then said to Alla Ditta " 'you are an N.C. O. Why did you not report ? Alla Ditta begged his pardon and said that he did not know anything about Mohammed Husain. Then Capt. Shah Nawaz questioned Mohammed Husain and Mohammed Husain replied that he was in difficulties and that he intended to escape and asked to be forgiven. Capt. Shah Nawaz then told him : 'You are not for our country; you are our enemy. I will give you death by shooting. Then Mohammed Husain asked for forgiveness and said that he was prepared to go anywhere he was ordered. Capt. Shah Nawaz said nothing to this. All the three of us were then sent out and we were taken to Brigade Headquarters accompanied by Major Negi and Khazin Shah. I moved towards the battalion with Khazin Shah and sub-officer Barfi Singh. When I reached the Battalion Headquarters, Khazin Shah told Barfi Singh to take me to Company Headquarters. In the evening an orderly took me to Battalion Headquarters. Mohammed Husain was there. Khazin Shah and Aya Singh were also there when I arrived. Khazin Shah told me :"Your will shoot Mohammed Husain because you are one of the men who were trying to escape with him ! I declined and said : I will not shoot him and that I did not know how to fire a rifle. Khazin Shah told me again : "If you do not shoot Mohammed Husain, you will be shot yourself." I still refused and he drew his pistol. I refused again and Aya Singh got hold of a rifle. He put the rifle to my shoulder and put my finger round the trigger. Khazin Shah told Aya Singh to give the order to fire. There were three of us, one Sikh, one Tamil and myself. Mohammed Husain was blindfolded by Aya Singh. He was made to sit on the ground with his back against a tree. His hands were tied behind him. Aya Singh ordered me to fire and so I did. Mohammed Husain died there. Khazin Shah ordered Aya Singh to give the order to fire and Aya Singh gave it. Khazin Shah told me to report to my company and not to come to the Battalion Headquarters. That evening we marched off to Legyi. Then we stayed at Legyi for two or three days. Then I went over to the British."

In the cross-examination of this witness, it was suggested that the witness could not know that a man was a Garhwali because the witness did not know the Garhwali language. Surely a man can know that another man is a Garhwali even if the first man does not know the Garhwali language. Witness said that he knew that he was a Garhwali because he lived with him and he spoke Garhwali. Witness further said that he came to know Mohammed Husain in the company. He used to live with him at headquarters. He used to sit in his company. He knew that he was a Mohmmedan and he did not know anything more about him. Witness said : "He used to live with me. Surely I knew him. I cannot give a long description of him except his physical description. I do not know anything else about him." The suggestion in the cross-examination was that the witness did not know Mohammed Husain. But the answers of the witness are, it is submitted, abundantly clear to show that the witness knew Mohammed Husain. The witness was not asked to give a physical descriptio of Mohammed Husain. A man may definitely know many persons by sight and by name without knowing anything more about them. In fact, witness knew Mohammed Husain more than merely by name and by sight as his evidence shows. It was then attempted to shake the evidence of this witness by showing that he did not know the English word crime. Witness said that he knew the word report in the sense of making a report to somebody. Witness was given slip of paper on which the words "crime report" were written and he was asked whether he understood the words written on the piece of paper. Of course, the witness said no. Witness never suggested that he could read English. As stated above, the phrase 'crime report' would be known even to Indian sepoys who do not understand English. In fact, it would be surprising if they did not know the phrase. Witness further said in his cross-examination that Capt. Shah Nawaz said that he (meaning Mohammed Husain) was not for his country, that he was an enemy and that he would give him death by shooting. It was contended on behalf of the defence that no reason has been given why Lt. Khazin Shah ordered Jagiri Ram to be one of the shooting party. The reason has been given by Jagiri Ram in his evidence when he said:

"Lt. Khazin Shah told me : 'You will shoot Mohammed Husain because you are one on the men who were trying to escape with him'. Obviously, this was Lt. Khazin Shah's idea of 'nemesis'. It was also suggested in the closing address of Counsel for the Defence that Jagiri Ram's evidence was to the effect that nothing was decided 'in our' case. The attempt was to read the words 'in our case' as meaning in the case of all the three of them. But if the whole passage is read, it is clear that the witness meant in the case of himself and Alla Ditta. He had already deposed to the fact of Mohammed Husain having been sentenced to death. Then he goes on to say "nothing was decided in our case" meaning thereby in the case of himself and Alla Ditta. The next witness on this point was Lance Naik Sardar Mohammad. He was the Adjutant of the First Battalion. According to his evidence, on March 27, Lt. Khazin Shah sent for the runners. On arrival of the runners he ordered them to bring the following men to the Battalion Headquarters, sepoy Mohammed Husain, Lance Naik Alla Ditta, Lance Naik Mohammed Shah, sepoy Jagiri Ram and sepoy Gobru Singh. Witness said that Mohammed Husain was a sepoy in the Indain Army before he joined the I.N.A. and that he knew it from his own knowledge. Witness said that when he brought him from Brigade Headquarters he asked him what he was in the Indian Army and to what unit he belonged. He said : "I am a sepoy of the H.K.S.R. A. Witness then deposed to the interrogation of the men by Khazin Shah. Lt. Khazin Shah told the witness that he was going to Brigade Headquarters that evening to talk about those and then he went away. Lt. Khazin Shah then ordered him to take those men to Brigade Headquarters. Witness and a sub-officer took them there . Witness met Lt.. Khazin Shah on the way and he handed over those men to his charge. He let off Lance Naik Mohammad Shafi on the spot because his Platoon Commander recommended him and he came there. He said that Mohammed Husain had been sentenced to be shot. Nothing was said about the others, but Jagiri Ram was with him at the time. Lt. Khazin Shah asked the witness to go to Ghulam Mohammad, the Brigade Adjutant, and ask him whether Mohammad hussain was to be shot under battalion arrangements or brigade arrangements.

The further evidence of this witness is in the following terms : "If the orders were for Mohammed Husain to be shot under battalion arrangements, I was to bring back Mohammed Husain with me. I was also asked to bring sepoy Mohammad Ibrahim who had been released from the quarter guard. I received instructions that Mohammed Husain was to be shot under battalion arrangements on the same day. I brought him back with me to Battalion Headquarters. I also brought back sepoy Mohammed Ibrahim and Aya Singh came with me. I conveyed these orders to Lt. Khazin Shah. He then ordered me to arrange for the execution of Mohammed Husain. I then asked him what arrangements I should make. He asked me to detail 10 men with pick axes and shovels. I detailed those men and a grave was dug. I was then ordered by Lt. Khazin Shah to take Mohammed Husain to the edge of a nullah. Mohammed Husain was taken to the edge of the nullah. Lt. Khazin Shah, 2nd Lt. Aya Singh and Havildar Major Gobind Singh, some sepoys and myself went with Mohammed Husain to the nullah. Lt. Khazin Shah ordered Mohammed Husain to be tied to a tree and also ordered that he should be blindfolded. I passed on the orders to sub-officer Gobind Singh who carried them out with the help of two other sepoys. After this Lt. Khazin Shah called two men out of the fatigue party to shoot Mohammad Hussain. They were both sepoys : one was a Tamil and the other was a Sikh. After the arrival of these men Lt. Khazin Shah ordered that Jagiri Ram would also fire on Mohammed Husain. The three men stood in a line facing Mohammed Husain and Khazin Shah told Aya Singh to give the order to fire. Aya Singh hesitated. Khazin Shah once again told him to give the order to fire. Aya Singh gave the order. All the three sepoys fired a round each on Mohammed Husain. Mohammed Husain was killed. His body rolled over sidewards. Lt. Khazin Shah then ordered me to send Abdul Hakim to arrange of his burial. I passed on these orders to Abdul Hakim. The battalion was to move the same day on an operational role and it did so. No casualty report was sent. The sending of a casualty report was part of my duties. I did not make a casualty report because night had fallen and we had to march the same night. On April 3, I escaped and reported to the Allied forces. I escaped from Legyi village."

In cross-examination it was suggested to the witness that on April I, he took a casualty report to Capt. Sahgal. Witness denied this. Witness said that he did not know if any casualty report was sent. No evidence was called by the defence to support this suggestion. Witness said in his cross-examination that he was between 12 and 15 yards away when Mohammed Husain fell. He said that he went near Mohammed Husain and found that he was dead, with three shots in him, 'The shirt covering his breast was torn and from the amount of tear I considered there were three shots." Witness was not present at his burial. In answer to the Judge Advocate the witness said that when he found the three shots had gone into him and he was lying on a side, he inferred he was dead. The firing was about eight to ten yards away from Mohammed Husain. The shooting of Mohammed Husain occurred at about dusk. Witness did not see any blood on Mohammed Husain.

In the statement of Capt Shah Nawaz it is stated that it is in fact wrong that he sentenced Mohammed Husain to death or that he was shot in execution of a sentence passed by him. According to the witness' statement, Mohammed Husain and his companions were only informally produced before him, there being no crime report drawn up. Capt. Shah Nawaz said that he only very strongly admonished Mohammed Husain and told him that he had committed an offence for which he could and should be shot. Capt. Shah Nawaz says that he left the matter there and asked the case to be put up again before him or the regimental commander, who had in the meanwhile been vested with the power to try such cases if the men concerned attempted to misbehaviour a second time and that the case never came up before him, presumably because the contingency never arose.

It is submitted that the evidence clearly shows that Mohammed Husain was sentenced to death by Capt. Shah Nawaz, that the sentence was to be carried out under battalion arrangement and that Lt. Khazin Shah as the battalion commandant ordered Aya Singh to give the order for firing and that Mohammed Husain was shot dead pursuant to such order. It is submitted that the evidence leaves no doubt as to the identity of Mohammed Husain. It is also submitted that as the result of the shooting Mohammed Husain died. The detailed evidence of the prosecution on this point is more than sufficient to prove the above facts. Havildar Gulam Mohammad who was the adjustant actually saw the crime reports, and the statement of Capt. Shah Nawaz that no crime reports were drawn up cannot be accepted as correct. Havildar Ghulam Mohammad's statements that the crime reports were drawn up and that he read them was not challenged in his cross-examination. The fact of the shooting is, it is submitted, also proved beyond doubt. As also the fact that Mohammed Hussain died as the result of the shooting. The evidence shows that a grave was dug for Mohammed Husain before the sentence was carried out and after he was shot orders were given for him to be buried. It is submitted that the proof of death is beyond reasonable doubt; but even if there is any doubt left in the mind of the court, the only consequence would be that the conviction of Capt. Shah Nawaz would be that of abetment of an attempt to murder instead of abetment of murder.

I will now deal with the charges two to nine which are against Capt. Sahgal and Lt. Dhillon, of the murder, as far as Lt. Dhillon is concerned, of the four sepoys and abetment of murder, so far as Capt. Sahgal is concerned, of the four sepoys. So far as these charges are concerned, there is documentary evidence which, it is submitted, is conclusive. There are two crime reports both dated March 6, 1945, exhibits K K K and W W W. We do not know why and how there came to be two such reports. They are identical except that in exhibit W W W the service is stated to be "years 3," whereas in exhibit K K K the servioce is stated to be " years 4-8 months." The only differsnce therefore is that in exhibit W W W the figure "4" before the letters "years" is omitted, but both these documents are original crime reports and the evidence as regards these documents which has not been challenged in cross-examination is that given by Lt. Nag. He says : "The words remanded for Divisional Commander's trial' under the column punishment awarded are in the handwriting of Lt. Dhillon and the signature below it is that of Lt. Dhillon. The words "sentenced to death": are in the handwriting of Capt. Sahgal and there is the Signature of Capt. Sahgal under the column by who awarded and date and at the bottom of the crime report there is the signature of Lt. G.S. Dhillon as "Commander of Unit No. 420.' He could not recognize the handwriting of the words after the words 'sentenced to death' which is before the signature of P.K. Shagal. As regards exhibit W W W, witness says "under the column head punishment awarded. The words ".remanded and signed by him. the words sentenced to death' are in the handwriting of Capt. Sahgal and signed by him. At the bottom of the crime reports conclusively prove that Capt. Sahgal passed the sentence of death on these four persons. In the statenebt of Capt. Sahgal he admits that they found guilty and sentenced to death, but he says that the sentence was not carried out, and the convicts like many others who were similarly tried and sentenced about the time had been pardoned on their expressing regret and giving an assurance not to misbehave in future. He says that the fact of a sentence having been passed was used for its propaganda value in order detector others from deserting. Lt. Dhillon in his statement says : "It is true that I committed four men for trial witht the charge of desertion and attempt to communicate with the enemy. It is, however, quite untrue that these men were shot at my instance or under my orders. On the day and at the time they are said to have been shot, I was confined to bed and unable to move. In fact, the sentences of death passed on these men were subsequently remitted by the Divisional Commander and were never executed." In making this statement both Capt. Sahgal and Lt Dhillon seem to have overlooked exhibit W W which is a special order of the day dated March 19, 1945, signed by Capt. Shah Nawaz Khan who was the Divisional Commander. This document was also not referred to by Counsel for the Defence in his address. This document has also been proved by the evidence of Lt. Nag which has not been challenged in cross-examination . In this document it is clearly stated as follows : "The sentence of death was carried out at 19-00 hours on March 6, 1945, and then goes on to say : "This order will be read out to all troops."

As regards the actual shooting of the four sepoys we have the evidence of Nursing Sepoy Abdul Hafeez Khan. He says in his evidence as follows: "After I came back from Rangoon I saw four men being shot. They belonged to No. 8 Battalion. There was a company fallen in to witness this shooting. This Company belonged to No. 7 Battalion. One day I was carrying a patient and saw four men near the nullah whose hands were tied behind their backs and who were escorted by two sentries. When I was coming back after leaving the patient in hospital I noticed some men assembled near the nullah. Seeing this assembly of men I went up there. When I reached there one company was fallen in and a trench had been dug there. The accused Major Dhillon and a few other officers were collected there. The four men were made to sit in the trench. Then Major Dhillon asked for volunteers to shoot these men. Two men from that company and one man from Brigade Headquarters came up. Their names were Nayak Sher Singh, Kalu Ram and Hidayatullah. Two carried rifles and one a pistol; Sher Singh had the pistol. Then Major Dhillon called out the name of one of the four men in the trench. Major Dhillon told the Company present that these four men had gone over to the enemy and had been caught and, therefore, their punishment would be death. "Then Major Dhillon ordered Hidayatullah to shoot the person who had been called out of the trench first. By this time this person had come out of the trench. He was standing on the edge of the trench. This person was then shot by Hidayatullah and he fell down. The person was not blindfold. He was about 20 yards from Hidayatullah when fired upon. Then Major Dhillon called out the name of another person who also came out of the trench. As in the first case, this person was also told his punishment and this person also was shot by Hidayatullah. Then Major Dhillon called out the name of the third man who was also told his sentance like the previous ones and Kalu Ram shot him under Major Dhillon's orders. Major Dhillon then similarly called to the fourth man and this man was also shot by Kalu Ram. I saw the four persons after they had been shot. They where not dead because I saw them move. Major Dhillon then ordered Naik Sher Singh to put one or two bullets into those who had not died . Sher Singh then went up to them and fired putting one or two bullets into each one of them. I did not see them moving , after Sher Singh had fired. Then I saw Capt. lee, the medical officer of the service battalion, examine them. Capt Lee said something to Major Dhillon. Capt. Lee told Major Dhillon that these men were dead. Afterwards Major Dhillon ordered the dead bodies to be buried. I did not see them being buried. I then came away from the scene."

In the cross-examination of this witness it was suggested that his conduct in stopping to see what was happening was extraordinary, and that instead of waiting to see what was happening he should have gone back straight to his unit after admitting the patient. It is submitted that there is nothing unnatural in the witness stopping to see what was happening. It was only human and natural on his part to stop and see the tragedy. It was then suggested in the cross-examination that he could not have known the names of Hidayatullah, sepoy Kalu Ram and Naik Sher Singh because he never rendered first-aid to these three persons. The witness said that he knew them because they belonged to his battalion. He was, of course, attached to No. 7 battalion hospital. That, however, does not mean that for that reason he could not have known them. It was also put to the witness and the witness admitted that he had no personal contact with these three men before that day and he had nothing to do with them after the incident. But he added : "They used to be in my battalion and I knew them." He also said : "It was part of my duty to know the names of as many men as I could in the battalion. When a few men live together they know the names of each other. I had not talked to any of these men before that day. I have never seen these three men since. Witness said that he was 10 to 12 yards away from Major Dhillon at the time and that he remembered every detail of what he had told the Court. He said he did not know the names of any of the four men who were shot nor their identity. It was then put to him in cross-examination that in the summary of evidence which he gave he did not say that Major Dhillon had ordered Sher Singh to fire a pistol. The answer of the witness was that as far as he remembered he said that Major Dhillon had ordered Sher Singh to fire a pistol, but that it was not taken down. In answer to the Court the witness said: "This company in the nullah was properly fallen in. These man were in front of the company. The company was about 10 to 12 yards for the men and I stood near the company on one side. Major Dhillon gave orders for the fourth man to be shot."

The next witness examined on this point was sepoy Gian Singh. He corroborated the version given by the previous witness including the firing and said that Major Dhillon ordered Sher Singh to shoot and finish off those of the four who were not dead and then Sher Singh fired an all the four with a pistol from a distance of about five yards. He further said : "Before Naik Sher Singh had fired on them, they were shrieking but I do not see them. They were lying near the nullah. Mjor Dhillon then said that anybody who did what these men had done would be dealt with similarly. The four bodies were buried in a trench. I saw them being buried. These four men who were killed were Jats. I do not know anything more about them." The witness was cross-examined in detail as regards the size of the nullah and the position of the four sepoys and of the persons who were present there. It is submitted that the answers given in the cross-examination, throw no doubt on the veracity of his evidence. The statements made by him in cross-examination did not show that there was anything improbable or inconsistent in the evidence given by him. Even if there is any ambiguity, it was completely removed in the answers which he gave to the Court at the end. Witness also stated to the Court that Maj. Dhillon read out that these men were Jats from No. 8 Battalion.

On behalf of Lt. Dhillon it was argued by counsel that he was ill on the date in question, namely, March 6, 1945, and that he could not have been present at the shooting as deposed to by the witnesses for the prosecution. For this reliance is placed on exhibit V V V which is an operation order signed by Lt. Dhillon and dated March 6, 1945. What is relied upon is the letter at the foot of this operation order in which Lt. Dhillon says that the previous night he had gone to check certain defence and on his arrival back he felt very weak, so weak as he had never felt before throughout his life, and that Shankar gave him an injection that day and that he would get one the next day. But the same letter says as follows : "I hope most of your queries have been answered in this order, others I will answer when I come tomorrow." I submit it is not possible from this document to come to the conclusion that Lt. Dhillon could not have been present at the shooting as deposed to by the prosecution witnesses.

It was further contended that there was no proof of identity of the four persons who were shot. I submit that hte identity has been sufficiently established by the two crime reports exhibits K K K and W W W and by the special order of the day dated March 19, 1945, exhibit W W W There is the further fact that according to the prosecution evidence, Lt. Dhillon stated at the time of the execution that these men had attempted to desert and they were, therefore, being shot.

It was also contended on behalf of the defence that the fact of nursing sepoy Abdul Hafiz Khan having been present at the incident has been contradicted by the next witness (Sepoy Gian Singh) because Gian Singh said : "I do not remember any person not belonging to the company being there." This is entirely incorrect. It is not the second witness Gian Singh who says that he first witness nursing sepoy was not there. The answer in question was given by nursing sepoy Abdul Hafiz Khan and not by the second witness Gian Singh. What nursing sepoy Abdul Hafiz Khan said is as follows : "I did not see any outsiders apart from the officers of the company and myself ."

But even if the answer had been given by the several witnesses as stated by Counsel for the defence and not by the first witness as appears from the record of the evidence it does not follow that a person could not have been there because somebody else did not see him there.

There is, therefore, nothing in the point sought to be made by my learned friend.

Section 302 of the Indian Penal Code provides the punishment for murder. According to Section 299 of the Indian Penal Code, whoever causes the death by doing an act with the intention of causing death commits the offence of culpable homicide. Section 300 provides that except in the cases therein excepted culpable homicide is murder if the act by which the death is caused is done with the intention of causing death. The exceptions mentioned in that section have no relevance to the present case. Section 109 of the Indian Penal Code provides for the punishment of abetment if the act abetted i committed in consequence. Section 107 of the Indian Penal Code says that person abets the doing of a thing who, among other things, instigates any person to do that thing or intentionally aids by any act or illegal omission to the doing of that thing. As Capt. Sahgal was not present when the four sepoys were shot, he is charged only with abetting their murder and not with the murders itself. Section 144 of the Indian Penal Code says "whenever any person who is absent would be liable to be punished as an abettor is present when the act or offence for which he would be punishable in consequence of the abetment is committed, he shall be deemed to have committed such act or offence." As he was not present at the shooting, he can only be charged with abetment of the offence. For the same reason as Captain Shah Nawaz Khan was not present at the shooting of Mohammed Husain, he is charged with offences of abetment of murder.

It has been contended that there is only one charge, namely, that of waging war because murder is a part of the first charge. I was argued that the first charge would cover every charge of firing a second shot. It issubmitted that this contention is not correct. The prosecution has not charged the accused with more than one charge in respect of waging the war. The charge of murder is distinct and separate from that of waging war because waging war involves fighting against and it might be killing the persons in the opposing army. Waging the war does not necessarily involve killing a man who is on the same side as the person charged with the offence.

If it is conteneded that the accused were justified in passing the sentence of death and in shooting the persons mentioned in the charges because they were authorised under the Indian National Army Act which is said to have been passed under the authority of the Provisional Government of Free India, the answer to the ergument is that the Provisinal Government of Free India was itself and illegal body an the formation of that body was itself an offence against the State and neither that body nor any tribunal constituted under it nor any order or authority derived from such a body can be recognised by this court, all of them being unlawful. In the case of R. Maguire and O'Sheil reported in 1923 second Irish Reports, King's Bench Division, page 58, the question of such a body and authority derived under it came up for consideration. The question arose on an application for a writ of *certiorari.* Certain persons in Ireland were attempted to be deprived of their land under certain orders or judgements of the judges and commissioners of Land Court and Land Settlement Commission of Dail Eireann. Jurisdiction of those courts was said to be derived from a decreed of An Dail. In dealing with the question, Justice Molony at page 63 said : "In the present case, far from there being any right or duty in the tribunal to decide the matter, their assumption of authority was illegal from the beginning and consequently they are not subject to the writ of *certiorari.* "In further dealing with the point, he said : "The answer is that this court while it prohibits and quashes the orders of inferior tribunals which exceed their jurisdiction does not take notice of bodies which act openly and avowedly in defiance of the law. The court has never issued a writ of prohibition of *certiorari* to an illegal body which challenges the authority of the Government and with which it is the duty of the Government to deal. "Justice Dodd said : " I extract from all the authorities that the only courts that can be restrained by prohibition are courts established by the Legislature who are usurping a jurisdiction of a judicial character not within or in excess of powers conferred upon them by the Legislature.... I do not ground my decision on the proclamation: I base it upon the fact that the courts were not established under any legislative enactment. Their orders are without sanction. They cannot protect any sheriff, jailor or other officer acting upon them.":

Justice Samuels in his judgement at page 66 said: "These tribunals whether of first instance or of appeal were not courts in any sense known to the law. They had no jurisdiction either by common law or by statute to sit, decide or decree. Further they purported to act as tribunals of a Republic claiming to have been established in Ireland within a Dominion of His Majesty the king. At common law and by the statute law of the Realm, those who instigated or took part in the proceedings of this court were themselves liable to indictment." Further on at page 69 the learned Judge said: "The so-called court that we have to consider, however, never had any legal powers and was never entrusted with any jurisdiction which it might exceed. It operations were not merely extra-legal, but anti-legal." At page 70 the learned judge said : "The tribunal we have to consider in the case was not so created. It acknowledged no such authority. It was not a court within the British constitution. It was set up as the court of a Republic and in repudiate of any such allegiance as is inherent in all court hitherto known as court within the King's Realm."

My submission is that charges two to nine have been proved beyond any reasonable doubt.

In conclusion, I submit that all the charges against all the accused have been proved beyond any reasonable doubt. There is no defence in law to the charges against the accused. There is a good deal of evidence to the effect that what the accused did was done by them not with any mercenary motive, but out of what the accused *bona fide* consider to be patriotic motives and impelled by a sense, whether wise or misguided, of doing service to India. This, while not affording any defence to the accused in law, may legitimately be taken into consideration on the question of punishment, if the court's findings on the charges are against the accused. So far as the court is concerned, its hands are tied in the matter of punishment. The minimum punishment which this court can give is transportation for life. If the court's finding is against the accused, but the court feels on the evidence before it that the case is fit one for mitigation of punishment, it is open to the court to add a rider to its finding and sentence to that effect for the consideration of the confirming officer.

The court reopens : the accused is brought before the court. Counsel for the prosecution addresses the court. Transcript of his address is marked 6 A, signed by the President and attached to the proceedings.

Note by the Court

The Judge -Advocate requests an adjournment until December 29, to enable him to prepare his summing up. The court grants this application.

At .... hours the court adjourned until 10 a.m. on Saturday, December 29.

15

Report by Military Intelligence on Hikari Kikan, Japanese Liaison Agency Dealing with I.N.A.[1]

2 January, 1946

1. **Introduction**—The Hikari Kikan was the Indian Affairs of the earlier Fujiwara and Iwakuro Kikans. The Fujuwara Kikan itself had its roots in No. 8 Sec of the Second Bureau (M. I. Dte) at Imperial H. Q. Tokio where its Commander Major Fujiwara was working for some years before the war.

   The name Hikari was selected for in Sanskrit its means "Help". Relations, however, between Indians and Japanese were by no means as good as the choice of nomenclature would suggest, and the history of the Kikan is one which they sought to control. The attitude of the I. N. A. towards the Hikari Kikan is well illustrated by the nickname which they give to it MURGHI (Chicken) Butai, for its propensity for assimilating the rations intended for its "allies".

2. **Sources of Interrogation**—The sources available for interrogation in Rangoon are on the whole disappointing. None had any connection with the Kikan before the end of the 1943, during the interesting period of the despatch of agents by the land route into Indian and the arguments over the control of such organisations as the S.Y.T.I. All were posted away by the beginning of 1945. This has rendered interrogation on stay behind activities completely inconclusive. The whole of the Hikari Kikan as constituted in 1945 evacuated to Bangkok where the most interesting personalities such as Lt. Gen Isoda, Col. Kagawa, Lt. Kunizuka and the earlier Chief Col. Kitabe were recovered at the time of the Japanese surrender.

   The following should, however, in the opinion of the interrogators be despatched to S'Pore for D. I.

1. War Office, 203/808. P.R.O.

Col. Kadomatsu	–	for his pre war work in No. 8 Sec, Second at Burma.
Col. Komtasubara	–	for his connections with the Spy-schools at Penang
Capt (now Major) Kawaji	–	who is co-operative under i nterrogation.
Major Fumio Miura	–	Evasive under interrogation. It is considered that under D.I. he might part with more information.

3. **Pre-War Jiffery**—Col Kadomatsu, although head of Chinese intelligence before the war was also a member of No. 8 Sec (Co-ordination) under Col Nishi in the Second Bureau. In the same section were working Maj Fujiwara and Major Ozeki (Both in Japan at the end of the war) who concentrated on Indian affairs.

The organisation of Lt. Gen Arisue's Second Bureau has already been given in detail in Kadomatsu's preliminary interrogation issued separately. The various Secs were organised on regional basis e.g. Intelligence on China, Intelligence on Russia, Anglo-American intelligence, Southern Regions intelligence, Kadomatsu was, however, very vague about the demarcation between Southern Regions and Anglo-American intelligence with reference to Siam, Malaya, Burma and India, claiming that he himself was only interested in the China Section.

Sources of intelligence were

(a) M. I. Channels which fed the appropriate Sec of the Second Bureau.

(b) Naval Intelligence,.There was in Naval H.Q. a parallel organisation to the Second Bureau. Copies of Intelligence summaries were exchanged and weekly conferences of Army-Navy opposite numbers were held to ensure liaison.

(c) The Deptt. of Foreign Affairs which received intelligence through diplomatic channels,. Col. Kadomatsu opines that pre-war agents were sent out to contact Indians by the Military Intelligence Bureau. Information and dealings with Indians in countries like Siam, Malaya etc. would be the responsibility of the local consuls. Copies of Intelligence reports were sent by the Foreign Affairs to the Military Intelligence Bureau but NOT vice versa.

When questioned about the responsibility for the organisation of puppet movements to support Mily oprations (such as that of Wang Ching Wei in China), Col Kadomatsu stated that to the best of his knowledge this belonged to the Mily Affairs Bureau of the War Ministry.

This Mily Affairs Bureau was divided into 2 main Secs.

Gumo – Dealing with political movements and agitation.

Gunji – Dealing with the 'Q' side of local suppllies and requisitioning of food and material from the local population.

Both these Secs were divided into a number of Sub Secs on a regional basis comparable to the Second between the Second Bureau and the Mily Affairs Deptt of the war Ministry by the replacement of Maj Fujiwara by Col Iwaguro in May 42.

4. **The Fujiwara Kikan**—Major Fujiwara had been dealing with Indian Affairs from the Mily-Intelligence angle in No. 8 Sec of the Second Bureau. Just before the outbreak of war he was summoned to a direct interview with the Chief of Staff who briefed him personally for his mission to Bangkok and despatched him to work under the command of H.Q. 15th Army. Fujiwara himself was responsible for the selection of Lt. Kunijuka as his deputy and for the formation of his Kikan which included about 10 Ind Agents from Bangkok. Col Kadomatsu believes that Fujiwara's aim was stricIty limited and tactical in scope-fifth column activity to aid the Japanese advance and ensure co-operation from Indians residents. to Malaya for the occupying troops. Branches of the I.I.L. were formed during the advance probably with this latter end in view on the Japanese side rather than with any ideas of harassing the Indian population for a large scale mobilisation to achieve Indian Independence. It was only after the Fujiwara Kikan's initial outstanding success, the capture of Captain Mohan Singh, his discussions with Major Fujiwara and the really spontaneous welcome which the Indian population gave in the first few days at least of their "liberation" that the larger air took shape.

It was at this stage that the War Ministry took a hand and Col. Iwaguro who was head of the “Adjutant Sec” of the Ministry was deputed to attend the TOKIO conference in Mar 42. He was afterwards removed from his former post and transferred to work directly under the Chief of Staff in the formation of the Iwaguro Kikan which took over from the Fujiwara Kikan the organisation of Indians throughout E. Asia. Iwaguro set up his H. Q. in Bangkok and the famous Bangkok Conference was one of the first results of his activities.

5. **Indian in Prewar Japan**—As regards Indians who co-operated with the Japanese before the war, Col Kadomatsu remembers only 3

(a) Rash Behari Bose. The Japanese had implicit faith in him and regarded him as "a Japanese amongst Indians" unlike A. M. Sahay whom they regarded with some suspicion as an "Indian amongst Japanese" who might learn their secrets and later betray them. Col Kadomatsu himself saw R. B. Bose in the 8 Sec office a number of occasions before the War - he used to attend conferences (matter under discussion unknown) with Major Fujiwara and with a Lt. Col. Kato from the Anglo-American Sections of the Ministry of War. This officer is now in Tokyo. Kadomatsu impression is that R. B. Bose was not in the regulars pay of the Japanese but was advanced money on an "as required" basis for propaganda and publishing work. He heard that Bose was a close friend of Toyama, the old statesman from the Black Dragan Society.

(b) A. M. Sahay—A free-lance amateur who was well known in with the monied classes.

(c) Baba Osman[2]— Col. Kadomatsu remembers hearing "vaguely" of the San Francisco Party. In his work on Chinese Intelligence he came across Osman's name. Osman, however was not working directly under the Second Bureau but under a Commander Hidaka of the China Intelligence Sec. of the Japanese Navy in Shanghai Hidaka's present whereabouts unknown.

None of the officers or men in the Jail know anything of the Pre-war activities of Giani Pritam Singh, Baba Amar Singh, Deb Nath Das, Endo etc. etc.

2. Baba Hari Singh alies Osman khan has an old revolutionary, who worked with the Germans during the first world war for India's freedom. After the war lived in Indonisia before joining the Japanese Intelligency agency in China

Col. Kadomatsu has denied the story of G. A. Qureishi (vide C.S.D.I.C. (I) No. 2 Sec Report No. 1053). He states he has never heard of Qureishi, knows of no Indian answering to his desciption and never had anything to do with the briefing of Ind agents for Bangkok. He claims that Qureshi may have mistaken him for another Col possibly Iwaguro whom he resembles. This is a point of considerable importance. If Qureshi's story is true Col Kadomatsu was himself directly involved in Indian affairs before the war and will be able to furnish even more important information. Kadomatsu should be subjected to D.I. on this question and if necessary confronted with Qureshi (Now in Delhi).

6. **Tokyo Foreign Languages School**—Both Cols. Kadomatsu and Komatsubara (himself a student of Russian) remember a Tokio Foreign Languages School before the War which was attended yearly by 10 officers selected by the personnel Sec (Honinka) of the Imperial H.Q. No knowledge of any officers who studied Hindustani.

7. **Iwaguro and Hikari Kikan in Burma Prior to move of HQ to Rangoon**—No information worth recording. None of the sources came to Burma before the end of 1943 and even their hearsay is limited to well known facts such as the arrival of Capt Tsumimuchi with his Kikan on the heels of the adv tps, the early quarrels with Indians in Burma the friction between Col Kitabe and the INA/IIL and his replacement by Col Yamamoto.

8. **Organisation of Hikari Kikan-Jan 44**—As below, the organisation was believed to be slightly different in Dec 44 but the differences are not known to the sources present in RGN Central Jail.

   H. Q. Hikari Kikan
   Staff Deptt. Mily Affairs Deptt. Political Deptt. Admin Deptt.
   Finance Deptt. Ordnance Section. Medical Sec. Sigs Sec.
   In addition there were "agencies" at Kalewa, Homalin, Myiktyina, Maymyo and Akyab of which more hereafter.

   Staff of the various deptts are listed at Appendix "A".[3] The functions of each Deppt are in most cases self-explanatory, with the notable exception of the Staff deptt which from the names of some of its more well-known members would appear to cover a multitude of aims.

9. **Chain of Command**—H. Q. Hikari Kikan come directly under H. Q. Burma Area Army and through them under Jap H. Q. at Shonan.

3. Not printed

There was no direct contact with the Second Bureau in Tokio and no and no references were ever made to Tokio.

10. **Hikari Kikan as an Intelligence organisation**—The sources deny that there was any regularly Joho Han (Intelligence Section) in Burma or that the Hikari Kikan was anything but a purely liaison "organisation". They plead ignorance of the Tokumu Han. Their contention is that strategic infiltration of agents into India was an extremely high level affair organised by Neta ji Chandra Bose himself in direct contact with the Penang Branch of the Hikari Kikan. Local tactical intelligence was the responsibility of the I. N. A. Intelligence and Bahadur Groups and although Hikari Kikan personnel were attached to their parties, the Hikari Kikan did not organise or control the work of the parties, this being responsibility of the local Commanders INA or Japanese. The Hikari Kikan attached staff were responsible for (1) Liaison with Japanese Units. (2) Reporting of information received by Indian intelligence parties to the local Jap Commander just as HQ Hikari Kikan in RGN was responsible for passing all "Indian" information of military intelligence value to the Intelligence Branch of H. Q. Burma Area Army. (3) Supply of rations (I.O.'s Comment:— This state of affairs although certainly not true of 1942-1943. I find more acceptable when applied to 1944. The earlier situation whereby Tsuchimuchi could direct the operations of Ram Sarup, Tsukamoto organised separate W/T courses in conjuction with G. S. Pardesi and Awata sent away trainees from the S.Y.T.I. to Japanese forwarding agencies at Sagaing, Monywa etc in rather amateurish attempts at infiltration into India had by then been largely resolved by the establishment of the P. G. A. H. in RGN and the insistence by Bose of Indian control over Indian affairs.

Capt Kawaji who was in the political Deptt from Feb. 44 - Dec. 44 states that the administration regarding the despatch of agents, if any, would be done by the Staff Deptt. He and all others in the Jail plead ignorance on the subject of the "Bats" dropped by parachute in Assam.

11. **Political Deptt.**—The Political Deptt besides being responsible for liaison with the P. G. A. H. on important issues between the Japs and the Indians also dealt with propaganda. This was confined to the provision of paper, priniting and propaganda facilities to the P.G.A. H. whose publicity branch under S.A. Ayyar actually issued all propaganda. Propaganda lines and thesis were sometimes supplied

with relevant extracts from Domei News to this Deptt but actual commentaries were always written by Indians.

There had formerely been pre-censorship by the Hikari Kikan but after a vigorous protest from Subhas Chandra Bose a tacit arrangement (Not a formal agreement) was Subhas Chandra Bose copies of all publications were sent to the Kikan. Capt Kawaji knows of no instances where the Kikan had occasion to suppress or alter any articles. He remembers an incident which took place in early 44. Some person or persons unknown on the Japanese side had on their own an initiative printed propaganda leaflets directed at Indian tps describing Subhas Chandra Bose and his movement and asking the I.N.A. to join them. These leaflets were signed by the local Japanese Commander and never submitted to Netaji for approval. When a copy finally found its way into his hands, he collared the unfortunate, Gen, Isoda who had recently arrived in Maymyo and indignantly demanded an explanation saying that the pamphlet being signed by a Japanese would have exactly the opposite to the desired effect upon the I.A.

12. **Komura Kikan**—An offshot of the political deptt was the Komura Kikan. Function - liaison with the local administration in the occupied areas of India. The Kikan moved from Rangoon to Maymyo in Apr., to Tamu in July and thence retreated via Shwegyin. Sources think that it worked in close liaison with the Azad Hind Dal but never had an opportunity to function. Capt Kawaji met (Lt Col) Ehsan Qadir in Maymyo and describes him as a "man of soldier bearing". He did not know of Ehsan's reputation with the rest of the INA.

Officers of Komura Kikan
Major (now Lt.–Col) Komura
Lt. Komohara
Lt. Nishiyama

The Mily Affairs Deptt was a straightforward liaison organisation to ensure adequate co-operation between the Japanese Army and the I. N. A. in the field. Notes on the activities of individual Hikari Kikan personnel attached to INA Units are attached in Appendix "B".

Unions of INA and P.G.A.H.

The general Hikari Kikan impression of the I. N. A. was that it was not up to much . Chandra Bose, as they call him, obviously impressed them a great deal and they speak with considerable respect of him and of a few of his subordinates including let it be said Shah Niwaz who had such a tussle with them in the Manipur Campaign. I. N. A. Div they considered not all bad; of 2 Div (apart from its Commanders) they had a very low opinion. At that stage of the Campaign as one officer put it "INA" meant only one thing "Hands up". The incident which stuck most in their minds was the surrender of such a large body of men under the Bde Comd (Lt Col) S. M. Hussain at Magwe without fight.

None of the sources would volunteer any opinion on why 1 INA Div whose morale and discipline they admitted was high on the Indian frontier. They pleaded surprise when told of the tenor of Shah Niwaz famous letter to Netaji from his Bde. H. Q. at Myittha Haka complaining that the I. N. A. was being treated as a labour Corps.

Col. Komatsubara opined that had the invasion been successful, Indian would have been given her "independence important communications." The other sources merely replied that it was a question of high policy to be decided between Chandra Bose and the Imperial Govt in Tokyo. It is perhaps significant that they all refer to negotiations with "Chandra Bose" and do not with the Provisional Govt of Azad Hind.

The only names in the Provisional Govt which excited any comment were,

(a) 'Maj–Gen' Bhonsle—for his corpulence.

(b) A.M. Sahay – who was considered to have made an unmitigated nuisance of himself over building material for barracks in Thingangyun.

(c) One O-Rakshmi San commanding a "Strange" (source Capt Kawaji) organisation known as the Jhansi Butai, This lady and/or her Butai in one of their more plighty moments also caused much heartburning over their insistance that a Ry should shift out of its quarters to make room for them. The Ry Regt finally shifted!

Finance Dept.—My Miura has been interrogated at some length on the distribution of "M.I. Funds". He disclaims all knowlege of these, a disclaimer which coming from a man in his position. I find extemely difficult to accept especially considering the fact that numbers of

Indian agents despatched from Burma have been arrested with counterfelt Indian Currency in their possession. He first for feigned surprise when confronted with this fact but later suggested that one of his officers Lt. Miyake, Gintaro now believed to be in Rankok was actually in charge of the distribution of funds and might be able to elucidate.

O.C. of the Finance Deptt, Hikari Kikan in S'PO was Lt. Col Murata, Maki, present wehreabouts unknown and under him were two officers - one a Lt. Koga: One of his own officers from RGN Capt Unoki, Taro he now believes to be in Bangkok.

Other Deptts.—The Admin Deptt, the ordanance and Med Secs were internal organisations served Hikari Kikan personnel only and had no dealing with Indians.

O. C. of the Med Sec was a Maj Kochi who was transferred to S'pore in 1944 and relieved by Maj Kawamura. Sources impact that this Maj Kawamura's activities were purely medical.

None of the sources was ever in the Sigs Sec and can give no information about it.

15. **Homalin & Myiktyina Agencies.**—There are in RGN Jail 3 men who were attached to agencies.

Homalin—Med orderly, Civ Ujino Tokiyoshi. Arrived Homalin Dec 43. Found that the agency was an intelligence Unit of 20 Men. A Lt Kubo form HQ Hikari Kikan, RGN was L. O. At this time there was no "Indian" activity as the agency was employed on the collection of rations for Retsu Butai then moving up for the attack on Manipur. After a visit to Maymyo as med orderly to Lt. Kaneko he retuned to Homalin found that the agency had moved so followed it up to join 58 Inf Regt with in the Kohima Ops. Knows nothing about (Lt) N. D. Sinha, the hoisting of the Indian National Flag or the capture of the B. C. R." who is alleged to have broadcast propaganda after capture.

Myiktyina.

Sgt–Maj	Kamezawa Shoichi
Sgt	Satake Tsuzuku

Object of Myiktyina agency liaison between 18 Div and local Indians. In Myiktyina there were 20-30 INA Sikhs and Gurkhas under (Capt) Harka Singh Bahadur. One of them name unknown, could speak Japanese. Their activities were recruitment for INA and supply of rice to Indians. There was a fwd post at Sinkaling Hkamti which sources heard was visited by an Indian name Durga Mali into organised at 1(S) F.I.C. No infiltration parties despathced to India. Agency retreated 25 Mar 44 to Mogaung and to Hopin 20 June 44. The 'Nippon Guerrilas' were caught by the Chindit Ops in the ry-corridor and only 3 eventually reached Maymyo. Sources do not have a high opinion of them. Disclaim any knowledge of espionage activities by these Gurkhas against Chindit Columns.[4]

4. This note was prepared by the Forward Interrogation unit after interrogating many Japanese officers, who were available in Rangoon at that time.

16

Reception to the I.N.A. Officers at Lahore after their Release[1]

5 January, 1946

We have no words to describe adequately and fully the scene that we, along with over a lakh of people, witnessed at the Lahore Railway Station on the arrival of Col. Shah Nawaz, Col. Prem Sahgal and Col. Gurbakhsh Singh Dhillon here to day. The least that one can say is that Lahore has never seen ever before such crowds, bubbling with enthusiasm.

The Frontier Mail, by which the three I.N.A. officers arrived was late by about three and a half hours. At every stoppage of the train from Delhi to Lahore, there were crowds shouting "Jai Hind" and "Shah Nawaz, Sahgal and Dhillon Zindabad".

Crowds at the Lahore railway station, which began gathering from early morning, even before the dawn, continued expressing their joy by raising slogans of "Jai Hind" "Sanghal Dhillon Shahnawaz Lal Qila se ho gai Azad". But what was even more exciting was the enthusiasm among the students. They sang and danced. There were students "Bhangra" parties and one cannot do full justice to the enthusiasm that prevailed by trying to describe it. These dances and singing of songs went on outside the railway station and on the station platform itself.

All roads, that lead to the railway station premises were full, and while pedestrians began to march their way to every available space at the railway station, traffic remained almost suspended for over four hours so far as going to the railway station was concerned.

In spite of the best efforts of the railway authorities, which gave their full co-operation to the Lahore District Congress Committee, which organised the reception, thousands—and their number cannot be mentioned correctly—secured entry into the railway station and occupied

1. *Tribune*, 6 Junuary, 1946

every available space on the station platforms, and on the bridge. Outside the railway station every inch of space within the area surrounded by the octroi posts was occupied and the whole area looked like a seething mass of humanity.

The Qaumi Sewa Dal volunteers of the District Congress committee, the volunteers of the Azad Hind Fauj Brigade of the Lahore Students' Congress, the Khaksars in their characteristic dresses, the scouts, the Patel Sewa Samti volunteers and the Police did their utmost to keep the crowds under control and regulated entry to the premises of the railway station. But it required yeoman's effort to keep such tumultuous crowd under control for about five hours and naturally therefore these control arrangements collapsed towards the end. The volunteers of all the organisations and the Police did their utmost to maintain order.

The one flag at the occasion which was seen being waved at hundreds of places, was the National flag and the one slogan that people were not tired of raising over and over again was "Jai Hind" when a special train carrying soldiers passed through Mughalpura the crowd which had gathered there shouted "Jai Hind" and this was enthusiastically responded to by many of the young and enthusiastic officers and men in the train who shouted "Jai Hind" and waved their hands to the crowd at the platform.

Outside the Lahore Station the District Congress Committee had provided an improvised platform on a lorry from where speeches continued to be made by Shrimati Amar Kaur, Mr. Ram Nath and others to keep the people busy.

The organisers succeeded in maintaining secrecy about their plans and in order to avoid any mishap at the Lahore Station and the "mobbing" by people of their heroes they detrained Shah Nawaz, Prem Saighal and Dhillon at the Mughalpura railway station and then brought them by motor cars to the lawn outside the Lahore Railway Station.

While the crowd at the Lahore railway station kept waiting for the Frontier Mail to come the organisers with the co-operation of the Railway authorities had the train stopped at Moghulpura railway station where Col. Shah Nawaz, Col. Dhillon were detrained. At Moghulpura the three were received by Prem Sehgal's father, Mr. Justice Acchru Ram and Mrs. Acchru Ram, Mr. Amrik Lal Budhwar, his brother-in-law, Raizada Hans Raj, M.L.A.(Central), Maulana Daud Ghaznavi, President P.P.C.C., Dr. Gopi Chand, Lala Bhim Sain Sachar,. M.L.A., Mr. Virendra, M.L.A., Mr. Ram Krishan Secretary , P.P.C.C. Maulana Habib-ur-Rehman, Malik Jeewan Lal Kapur, Comrade Ram Chandra, President and Mr. Hem Raj, General Secretary of the Lahore District Congress Committee.

In spite of the fact that this arrangement was kept a close secret about 500 people gathered at the Moghulpura station also getting their clue from the presence of the Congress leaders there. As the train stopped Shah Nawaz, Sehgal and Dhillon were greeted with slogan of "Jai Hind" as they appeared at the door of their compartment which was loaded with garlands and flowers which had been offered to them the whole way long from Delhi. The three jumped out of the compartment on being told that they were to be detrained there and they bowed to the mother of Prem Sehgal who blessed them and Prem's sister applied 'Tilak' on the foreheads of the three, a ceremony which in ancient Indian history used to be performed by the sisters when their brothers came back victorious from the battlefield. Maulana Daud Ghaznavi, on behalf of the Provincial Congress Committee, garlanded the three I.N.A. officers whom Mr. Justice Acchru Ram embraced in paternal affection.

The train steamed off to Lahore and as it entered the distant signal at the Lahore Railway Station rows of men standing along the whole route from the distant signal to the other end of the platform No. 2 where the Frontier Mail was specially taken, cheered and raised slogans of "Jai Hind."

From platform No. 1 to platform No. 2 there was hardly any space left vacant by men who were eager to have a look at the heroes. But they were all disappointed when they were told by men in the train that the three had been detrained at Moghalpura. The crowds, however, rushed out to the open space outside the station where the three I.N.A. officers were brought by cars from Mogulpura.

There was an outburst of "madness" as Shah Nawaz, Sahgal and Dhillon standing on the roof of the car appeared before the multitude. There were deafening cheers and sky-rending slogans of "Jai Hind" and "Zindabad" as they approached the improvised platform on the lorry to which place they were taken up from the car. They stood saluting the mass of humanity sitting and standing around them in the area that looked like a vast ocean of human heads. Joyous outburst and gladness of heart found expression in slogans being raised and "Jai Hind" being shouted. Shrimati Shanno Devi, Shrimati Amar Kaur and some other lady workers applied 'Tilak' on the foreheads of the three as they stood on the lorry saluting the crowds.

After silence had been restored as a result of appeals made by Prem Sahgal himself, the three addressed the gathering and were heard with the utmost respect and attention which they deserved.

Col. Prem Sahgal said that he wanted to reiterate the pledge that he and his comrades gave to Netaji, that pledge being that they shall consider no prize too big for the freedom of their country. He said that he and his comrades stand by that pledge even today. Amidst deafening cheers Prem Sahgal said, "Let me assure my countrymen that every man and officer of the I.N.A., including my comrades and myself, will be prepared to shed the very last drop of blood in us for the freedom of our motherland. The struggle for freedom which commenced in the Far East has not ended. Under the guidance of the Congress leaders we will now continue the struggle for the freedom of India and her teeming millions up to the time there is even one drop of blood left in us."

Thanking for the honor which the people had done to his comrades and to himself Prem Sehgal said: "Let me say that this honour which you has done us is the honour done to our Netaji who had nothing nearer to his heart than the freedom of India."

Col. Shah Nawaz, who received a warm ovation, said that he was glad that every organisation and community, including the Congress and the Muslim League, the Hindus, the Muslims and the Sikhs, Jains, Christians and others had demanded their release with one voice. He wanted to thank every body not for the fact that he and his two comrades had come out alive but for the fact that British imperialism had for the first time yielded to pressure of public opinion. Amidst prolonged cheers Shah Nawaz added : "Let me say to you and to the people of India that it is wrong that Netaji Subhas Chandra Bose ever thought of helping any foreign power to come and invade India.

Netaji's Last Message

With a voice full of feelings Shah Nawaz referred to what he described as Netaji's last message, given to the Indian people through Col. Habib-ur-Rehman who, he said, was unfortunately still behind the stony walls of the Red Fort. Shah Nawaz mentioned how at the time of the crash of the plane in which Subhas Chandra Bose travelling along with Col. Habib-ur-Rehman, Netaji received five serious injuries on his head and Col. Habib-ur-Rehman, got burns on his forehead and arms. Col. Habib-ur-Rehman at great risk to his own life succeed in extricating Netaji from the plane which had caught fire. It was at this time that Netaji asked Col. Habib-ur-Rehman to convey his message to his countrymen. Netaji's message was:

> "I have been injured rather seriously and I do not know if I will survive these injuries. Let my countrymen however know that I have fought upto the last minute of my life for the freedom of my Motherland and I want them to continue that fight till India is free."

Shah Nawaz commending the message of Netaji to the people exhorted them to continue that struggle for the freedom of India.

Lt. Col. Dhillon speaking said that they were being honoured for the brave and courageous acts of the men of the I.N.A. who were lying dead, cold in the battlefields of Far East where India's battle for freedom was fought. He was sorry that the fathers, mothers and the sisters of those brave men would never see their faces but all honour to them who laid down their lives in that heroic manner. He said that after the speech of Major-General Shah Nawaz and Prem Sahgal he as their junior officer had nothing further to add. He, however, said "Let me request you, my countrymen, whether you are Hindus, Muslims, Sikhs or member of any other community you should all regard me as your humble servant and my life is at your disposal in the service of mother India. I only appeal to you to learn discipline : for discipline and sacrifice combined can result in great achievements."

A touching scene was witnessed when the old father of Lt. Col. Dhillon came up and embraced his own son and two comrades and patted them on their backs with tears of joy in his eyes.

17

Note by C.S.D.I.C. Red Fort, Delhi on the Number of Indian PW who Joined the INA[1]

8 January 1946

1. This report is an attempt to give statistical information regarding the number of Ind PW who, on the one hand volunteered for the INA., or on the other resisted its propaganda.

2. A clear distinction must be made between the first and the second INA. While there was much spontaneous enrolment in the first INA., there was also considerable compulsion. In this connection, the words of Mohan Singh, the founder of the whole movement, are considered substantially correct. (CSDIC(I) 'S' Sec Report 1007, Appx B para 7 on Capt. Mohan Singh)[2]

   "Of about 55,000 Indian prisoners of war, about 45,000 voluntered for India's cause, although the Japanese did not allow me to raise an army of more than 20,000. (CSDIC (I) Note: 15,000 only). These volunteers included men from all classes recruited into the Indian Army, including a large number of Gurkhas as well. Out of the remaining 10,000 nearly half were such who were prepared for India's cause, but who did not trust the Japanese".

3. Thus of the original 55,000 PW,

15,000	were enrolled in the first INA. Of these about 4000 resigned, became ex-volunteers, and were sent to the South West Pacific.
25/30,000	were 'surplus' volunteers.
15/10,000	were non-volunteers.
55,000	

1. W.O. 208/818. P.R.O. See also F. No. 601/13097/H.S.
2. These reports are available with the I.N.A. Papers in the National Archieves of India and some amogest the War office at the Public Record office, London.

4. The 25/30,000 'surplus' or unabsorbed volunteers were in 1942 administered by the Japanese and not by HQ I.N.A. The 'surplus' volunteers received treatment little better than that of the non-volunteers and were employed on fatigues. The Japanese organised many of these surplus volunteers into Fatigue Parties (including the well-known 323 parties), which were sent to various places on the Malaya mainland and elsewhere (Sumatra etc). The remainder of the 'surplus' volunteers were kept in Singapore. In Jan 43, the 'surplus' volunteers reverted to genuine PW status but about 20 per cent (approx) later volunteered for the second I.N.A. A large number of these original 'surplus' volunteers have returned to India as RAPWI. (See also the Note on page 9 of this Report).

5. In the second I.N.A., the element of compulsion was very largely removed, and large number of civilians were recruited to reinforce the depleted ranks of the I.N.A., and later served to make possible the raising of 2 and 3 Div. I.N.A.

6. The information is based on interrogation and should be assessed accordingly. The degree of reliability with which the information given should be accepted is shown in the first column, thus:—

   (a) Reliable: generally provided by KCOs. The following units fall into this category:—

      (i) 3 Cav

      (ii) HKSRA (Singapore only)

      (iii) Inf units

      (iv) Mil Accts Dept

   (b) Fairly reliable

   (c) Uncertain. Requires Confirmation from other sources.

7. The information given is incomplete. Of the 55,000 Indian PW captured in Malaya, it has been possible to obtain figures for only approx 31,000. The statistics cover infantry units only and a few units of other arms.

8. As sub-units in the RIASC/IACC/IE/IAMC, etc. were mostly small, figures for these arms of the service are very incomplete. It is well known that the Japanese desired troops from combatant units to form the backbone of the early I.N.A., and such units were therefore

subjected to much more persistent propaganda than the "non-fighting" troops such as RIASC/IACC/IE/IAMC etc. of which only a very small number were selected for the first I.N.A., and then mostly for Bahadur and Intelligence Groups. The bulk of the remainder served as surplus volunteers during 1942, and large numbers reverted to PW status from 1943 onwards.

9. More exact details of non-volunteers, volunteers and surplus-volunteers from non-combatant units might be available or obtainable from the Depots of these respective arms of the service.

For the following arms of the service, only partially complete figures are available :—

RIASC	Figures are available only for :
	12 SPC Coy
	8 IBT Coy
I.E.	Figures are available only for :
	46 Army Tps Coy, Madras S &M
	6 Bdg Sec Madras S &M
	14 Bdg Sec Madras S &M
	13 Fd Coy Madras S &M
	15 Fd Coy Madras S &M
	23 Fd Coy, Royal Bombay S & M
	17 Fd Coy, Royal Bombay S & M
	19 Fd Coy, Royal Bombay S & M
	22 Fd Coy, Royal Bombay S & M
	42 Fd Pk Coy " "
	45 Army Tps Coy " "
	3 Fd Coy, Bengal S & M
	43 Fd Park Coy " "
	54 Eng Sec " "
IMS/IAMC/IHC	Figures are available only for :
	19 IGH
	5 CCS
IAOC	No reliable figures available.

	FIRST I.N.A.												SECOND I.N.A.												
Unit and degree of reliabilty	**No of man alive on 15 Feb 42**			**Vol in First INA**			**Surpluse Vols in First INA**			**Non-Vols in First INA**			**Vols in Second INA**			**Non-Vols & Ex Vols sent to SW Pacific**			**Ex Vols Ex Surp Vols/Non-Vols Sent to PW Camps in Malaya Singapore**			**No. of RAPWI up to 10 Dec 45 (through Madras only) all rank.**
	ICO.	VCO.	IOR.	ICO.	VCO.	IOR.	ICO.	VCO.	IOR.	ICO.	VCO.	IOR.	ICO.	VCO.	IOR.	ICO.	VCO.	IOR.	ICO.	VCO.	IOR.	
(d) 6/1 Punjab	Total 900 all ranks			Total 900 all ranks						NIL			810-Jat & Sikh Coys			Total 90 all ranks			Jat & Sikh Coys (whereabouts after Jul 42 not know)			391
(A) 5/2 Punjab	11	23	1400	9	10	450	0	12	700	2	1	250	6	6	250							208
(A) 1/8 Punjab	6	27	1250	4	2	20	0	12	650	2	13	580	3	12	550	2	11	550	1	4	140	329
(A) 7/8 Punjab	2	19	800	1	8	420	0	1	20	1	10	360	0	5	330	0	4	110	2	10	360	
(A) 2/9 Jat 4/9 Jat	7	35	1100	6	20	600	0	1	50	1	14	450	5	15	750	0	9	220	0	11	130	138
(A) 2/10 Baluch	7	28	1320	3	0	10	0	2	90	4	26	1220	4	0	30	1	2	80	2	26	1210	133
(A) 5/22 Sikh	5	0	750	3	0	350	0	0	30	2	0	100	2	0	400	0	0	275	3	0	75	228
(A) 2/12 FFR	2	28	1125	2	16	515	0	0	50	0	12	660	0	3	288	1	16	484	1	9	235	236

Unit and degree of reliabilty	FIRST I.N.A.												SECOND I.N.A.										No. of RAPWI up to 10 Dec 45 (through Madras only all rank.
	No of man alive on 15 Feb 42			Vol in First INA			Surpluse Vols in First INA			Non-Vols in First INA			Vols in Second INA			Non-Vols & Ex Vols sent to SW Pacific			Ex Vols Ex Surp Vols/Non-Vols Sent to PW Camps in Malaya Singapore			
	ICO.	VCO.	IOR.	ICO.	VCO.	IOR.	ICO.	VCO.	IOR.	ICO.	VCO.	IOR.	ICO.	VCO.	IOR.	ICO.	VCO.	IOR.	ICO.	VCO.	IOR.	
(A) 1/13 FF Rif	3	54	1300	1	16	600	0	4	100	1	14	600	1	4	200	0	20	800	0	10	300	267
(A) 1/14 Punjab	8	21	650	8	15	600	0	0	10	0	6	40	8	9	480	Officers Nil, VCOS 12, IORs 170						1718
(A) 5/14 Punjab	1	23	750	1	8	300	0	12	350	0	3	100	0	8	100	1	6	350	0	9	300	
(A) 6/14 Punjab	3	19	650	3	13	350	0	6	300	Nil			1	7	100	1	6	300	1	6	250	
2/15 Punjab	1	18	750	9 VCOs, 225 IORs Stayed in Balikpapan/Kuching/Miri. 25 IORs sent to unknown destination. 1 Offr, 9 VCOs, 441 IROs brought to Singapore—details as under																		357
				1	0	10	0	4	240	0	5	190	1	0	235	0	0	148	0	0	57	
(A) 2/16 Punjab 3/16 Punjab	8	36	1350	5	10	550	0	0	175	3	26	625	4	3	150	0	17	700	3	16	500	610
(A) 2/17 Dogra 3/17 Dogra	6	48	2600	5	33	1390	0	15	100	1	0	110	1	10	1000	3	29	950	2	9	650	514
(A) 2/18 R Garh Rif 5/18 R Garh Rif	5	45	1850	5	30	1375	0	10	200	0	5	275	5	30	1375	0	5	425	0	10	50	149

Unit and degree of reliabilty	FIRST I.N.A. No of man alive on 15 Feb 42			Vol in First INA			Surpluse Vols in First INA			Non-Vols in First INA			SECOND I.N.A. Vols in Second INA			Non-Vols & Ex Vols sent to SW Pacific			Ex Vols Ex Surp Vols/Non-Vols Sent to PW Camps in Malaya Singapore			No. of RAPWI up to 10 Dec 45 (through Madras only) all rank.
	ICO.	VCO.	IOR.	ICO.	VCO.	IOR.	ICO.	VCO.	IOR.	ICO.	VCO.	IOR.	ICO.	VCO.	IOR.	ICO.	VCO.	IOR.	ICO.	VCO.	IOR.	
(A) 4/19 Kumaon	7	20	1000	6	9	650	0	5	225	1	6	125	3	6	650	1	3	4	3	10	340	373
(A) 1 Bahawalpur Inf	13	19	900	11	10	200	Offrs 2, VCOs 9, IORs 700						5	6	100	2	6	180	6	7	620	322
(A) Kapurthala Inf	12	18	698	10	18	612	0	0	40	2	0	46	11	17	290	0	1	340	1	0	68	16
(B) 1 Mysore Inf			700*			50*			500*			150*			50*			107*			543*	405
(B) 1 Hybad Inf			650*		Nil			Nil				650*		Nil				650*		Nil		489
(B) Jind Inf			650*		Nil			Nil				650*		Nil			Nil				350*	592
(A) S Cav	2	19	606	0	5	140		Nil		2	14	466	0	5	295	0	3	64	2	10	247	99
(A) BKSRA			4240*		1300* (jats)			*400 (PMs)			* 2540 (PMs)			1450* (1300 Jats, 150 (PMs)			*375 (PMs)			*2415 (PMs)		2078

* All ranks

Unit and degree of reliabilty	No of man alive on 15 Feb 42	Vol in First INA	Surpluse Vols in First INA	Non-Vols in First INA	Vols in Second INA	Non-Vols & Ex Vols sent to SW Pacific	Ex Vols Ex Surp Vols/Non-Vols Sent to PW Camps in Malaya Singapore	No. of RAPWI up to 10 Dec 45 (through Madras only) all rank.
	FIRST I.N.A.				SECOND I.N.A.			
	ICO. VCO. IOR.	ICO. VCO. IOR.	ICO. VCO. IOR.	ICO. VCO. IOR.	ICO. VCO. IOR.	ICO. VCO. IOR.	ICO. VCO. IOR.	
HONG KONG	4700 ?	Exact figure for HKSRA Hong Kong are not known.						
HKSRA		Volunteers for Gd duties Hongkong /Swatow etc				600		
		Semi-Volunteers (Hainan Islands etc)				800		
		Joined INA at Singapore Jan 44				1300		
		Non- Volunteers				?	(Depend on total strength of Hong Kong HKSFA which is not known)	

If has not been possible so far to make any reliable assessment of the figures for HKSRA (HONG KONG) because

(a) Exact degree of collaboration of the Hainan and other "Gurard parties is not known.

(b) The only men who actually volunteered for service in the INA (about 1000) were shipped to Singapore in Jan 44 after the recruiting tour by Lt. Col Loganadan to Hong Kong/Shanghai etc. They were posted to Rft Gp at Jobore Bahru from where they were allotted to INA units. Mostly units of 3 Div.

(c) Total strength of HKSRA (Hong Kong) is not known at CSDIC (i).

18

General Auchinleck to Army Commanders Explaining the Reasons for Changing the Policy Towards I.N.A.[1]

12 February, 1946

1. I have now been able to study a large number of reports from higher and unit commanders and other sources on the effect of the action taken in respect of the first "I.N.A." trial on the Indian Army as a whole.

   It is most important that we should study and analyse carefully these effects, as they may influence very greatly our ability to maintain the solidarity and reliability for the Indian Army in the difficult times which undoubtedly lie ahead of us. It is for this reason that I am writing this letter to you. I have considered the desirability of making a personal public statement in explanation of my action in commuting the sentences of transportation passed by the Court on the first three accused, but I have decided that this would not be in the best interests of discipline or the maintenance of my influence and authority as commander-in-chief.

   I feel, however, that we should do all we can to remove the feelings of doubt, resentment and even disgusts which appear to exist in the mind of quit a number of British officers, who have not the knowledge or the imagination to be able to view the situation as a whole or to understand the present state of feeling in India.

2. As I see it, the commutation of the sentences of transportation on Shah Nawaz, Dillon and Sahgal has had the following effect in India :

   (a) *On the general public, moderate as well as extremist, Muslim as well as Hindu*

1. Aruchinleck Papers. The above memorandum was sent to all the senior British officers, who were deadly against the I.N.A. and wanted that they should be punished.

Pleasure and intense relief born of the conviction that confirmation of the sentences would have result in violent internal conflict.

This feeling does not, in my opinion, spring universally from the idea that the covicted officers were trying to rid India of the British and, therefore, to be applauded, whatever crimes they might commit, by from a generally genuine feeling that they were patriot and nationalist and that, therefore, even if they were misled they should be treated with clemency, as ture sons of India. In this connection, it should be remembered, I think that every Indian worthy of the name is today a "Nationalist", though this does not mean that he is necessarily "anti British". All the same, where Indian and her independence are concerned, there are no "pro-British" Indians.

Every Indian Commissioned Officers is a Nationalist and rightly so, provided he hopes to attain independence for India by constitutional means–

(b) *On the Indian officer of the Indian Army*

Except for a few recovered prisoners of war who have suffered much at the hands of their fellow countrymen who joined the so-called "I.N.A.", the vast majority, almost without exception, however much they may like and respect the British, are glad and relieved because of the result to the trial. Most of them admit the gravity to the offence and do not condone it, but practically all are sure that any attempt to enforce the sentence would have led to choose in the country at large and probably to mutiny and dissension in the Army culminating in its dissolution, probably on communal lines.

The more senior and intelligent undoubtedly realize the implications of our having established in Principle the seriousness of the crime of forsaking one's allegiance and the wisdom of meeting it with a heavy banishment such as "Cashiering" which carries with it the stigma of disgrace.

They realize that their future is to be at all secure, discipline and loyalty must be maintained, but they, too, are nationalists and their feelings are much the same as those of the public at large.

(c) *On the V.C.Os.* and rank and file of the Indian Army

In very many units apparently little interest was displayed in the "I.N.A." trials, especially in the more illiterate and educationally backward arms of the service, such as the infantry and artillery.

In the technical units and amongst clerks, etd., however, interest was keen and widespread.

Some of the V.C.Os. and rank and file had suffered like their officers at the hands of their former comrades who joined the "I.N.A." and perhaps feel correspondingly bitter and disgusted at the leniency shown. This is inevitable and cannot be helped, regrettable though it may be. This section of opinion is relatively small.

The great majority are, I think, pleased that leniency has been shown for a variety of reasons.

Many of them have relations and friends from the same villages amongst the "I.N.A." Many think that, as the war is over, bygones should be bygones and a fresh start made.

Others are genuinely nationalistic in outlook and have been affected by agitation and propaganda. The great majority feel, I think, that the whole episode is unpleasant and discreditable to them as a class and to the Army as a whole, and would wish it forgotten and decently buried as soon as possible.

Under all this, there is, I think, an uneasy feeling as to the future and doubt as to whether their interests will be as well watched in the days to come as they have been in the past.

(d) *on the British officers of the Indian Army*

As I have already said, the effect on many British officers has been bad, and has led to public criticism, which has not been in accordance with the traditional locality I am entitled to expect. To these officers, perhaps not always very perceptive or imaginative, an officer is an officer, whether he be Indian or British, and they make no allowance for birth or political aspirations or upbringing, nor do they begin to realize the great political stresses and strains now affecting this country. They are unable to differentiate between the British and Indian points of view.

Moreover, they forget, if they ever knew, the great bitterness bred in the minds of many Indian officers in the early days of "Idealization" by th discrimination, often very real, exercised against them and the discourteous, contemptuous treatment meted out to them by many British officers who shold have known better.

These facts constitute the background against which the decisions should be judged, always keeping before one the object, which is to preserve by all possible means in our power the solidarity of the Indian Army, and of the R.I.N. and the R.I.A.F. as well. I have not specifically mentioned the two younger services, but everything I have said in this letter applies to them just as much as to the Army, and perhaps more so, as the ratings or other ranks of these services are better educated and perhaps more politically minded than those of the Army.

3. I would like you also to consider and to impress on others, especially those British officer who have been upset by the result of the first "I.N.A." trial, the effect of the capitulation of Singapore on the Indian troops involved in it, from amongst whom the "I.N.A." was subsequently formed.

Those who have served for many years with Indian troops, as I have done, have always recognized that the loyalty of our men was really to the officer of the regiment or unit, and that although there may have been some abstract sentiments of loyalty and patriotism to the Government and to the King, the men's allegiance for all practical purpose was focused depended for the (i) welfare, advancement and future prospects.

In these officers, their faith and trust was almost childlike, as events have proved time and time again. It is true to say that in almost every case of serious discontent or indiscipline, and there have been remarkable few of them, which has occurred in the past fifty years, the cause could be traced to indifferent officers and bad man-management.

4. The terrible tragedy of Singapore following on the fall of Hong Kong must have seemed to the great majority of the V.C.Os. and rank and file to be the end of all things, and certainly of the British "Raj" to whom the Army had been used for so many years of war and peace to look to as its universal provider and protector, acting through their own regimental officers.

Their British officers were at once taken from them and they were at once assailed by traitors who had been kept in readiness by the Japanese to seduce them from their allegiance. Their Indian officers in many instances proved false to their trust and used their influence to suborn their own men, skillfully aided and encouraged by the Japanese.

The strain and pressure to which these men, the majority of whom were simple peasant farmers with no cultural or educational background, were subjected is very difficult for any British officer, however experienced, to visualize. Nevertheless it is quite impossible for any British officer to judge them fairly unless he does try to visualize it and realize what these men must have thought and felt.

It is quite wrong to adopt the attitude that because these men had taken service in a British controlled Indian Army that therefore their loyalties must be the same as those of British soliders. As I have tried to explain, they had no real loyalty or patriotism towards Britain as Britain, not as we understand loyalty.

5. So much for the rank and file. The officers who went over present a much more difficult problem. Owing to their presumably superior education, knowledge of the world and experience generally, it is not possible to apply the same reasoning to them, except possible to the vary junior and to those who had been promoted from the ranks, whose background was more limited and whose knowledge was less.

There is no excuse for the regular officers who went over, beyond the fact that the early stages of "Indianisation" from its inception to the beginning of the late war were badly mismanaged by the British Government of India, and this prepared the ground for disloyalty when the opportunity came.

There is little doubt that "Indianisation" was at its inception looked on as a political expedient which was bound to fail militarily. There is no doubt also that many senior British officers believed and even hoped that it would fail.

The policy of segregation of Indian officers into separate units, the differential treatment in respect of pay and terms of service as compared with the British officer, and the prejudice and lack of manners of some—by no means all- British officers and their wives, all went to produce a very deep and bitter feeling of racial discrimination in the minds of the most intelligent and progressive of the Indian officers, who were naturally nationalists, keen to see Indian standing on her won legs and not to be rules from Whitehall for ever.

It is no use shutting one's eyes to the fact that any Indian officers worth his salt is a Nationalist, though this does not mean, as I have said before, that he is necessarily anti-British. If he is an anti-British this is as often as not due to his faulty handling and treatment by his British officer comrades.

It is essential for the preservation of future unity that this fact should be fully understood by all British officers.

No Indian officers must be regarded as suspect and disloyal merely because he is what is called a "Nationalist" or in other words—a good Indian!

6. This aspect of the business, though it cannot excuse the action of those officers in going over to the enemy, must be considered as it does provide the background against which we must view the present and the future.

We have very full evidence of the mental processes which these officers went through and many of them hesitated for a long time before they finally succumbed to circumstances and the persuasion of the Japanese and their extremist fellow-country men. Many of them having joined the first so-called "I.N.A." under Mohan Singh refused to join the second under Bose and spent the next three years as prisoners of war in the islands of the Pacific. This does not excuse their original lapse but does show that they were subjected to conflicting stresses and strains mentally.

7. There remains the matter of the decision to commute the sentences of the first three officers (Sahgal, Dhillon and Shah Nawaz) from "Transportation" to "Cashiering". If, as we have admitted, they were guilty of the worst crime a soldier can commit, then it may well be asked—"why be lenient with them?"

In taking the decision to show clemency, the whole circumstances past, present and future had to be considered and was (were) so considered most carefully and over a long period.

The overriding object is to maintain the stability, reliability and efficiency of the Indian army so that it may remain in the future a trustworthy weapon for use in the defence of India and, we hope, of the Commonwealth as a whole.

It was essential to establish the principle that falseness to his allegiance is a crime which cannot be countenanced in any officer under whatever Government he may be serving. By confirming the finding of the Court and the sentence of "Cashiering" which carries with it the highest degree of disgrace to an officer, we have done this. To have added imprisonment to the sentence would not in any way have helped to emphasise the principle we were concerned to preserve.

On the other hand, having considered all the evidence and appreciated the best of my ability the general trend of Indian public opinion and of the felling in the Indian Army, I have no doubt to all that to have confirmed the sentence of imprisonment solely on the charge of "waging war against the King" would have had disastrous result, in that it would have probably precipitated violent outbreak throughout the country, and have created active and widespread disaffection in the Army, especially amongst the Indian officers and the more highly educated rank and file. To have taken this risk would have been seriously to jeopardise our object.

Always keeping before one the difference in outlook between British and Indian, which I have tried to explain in this letter, I decided, therefore, that in the interests of the future of both India and British and because of the unprecedented circumstances of the case, the only proper course to pursue was to confirm the finding and so establish the principle but to show clemency in respect of the sentence. Some bewilderment has been caused, I believe, by the fact that Shah Nawaz who was found guilty of "abetment of murder" as well as of "waging war" received the same treatment as the other two accused who were found guilty of "waging war" only. Shah Nawaz's offence, which was committed by him as an officer of the "I.N.A." in the alleged execution of his duty, in that he ordered a sentence authorised by a higher I.N.A. authority to be carried out, did, in the circumstance, flow from his basic offence of "waging war" as a member of the I.N.A. The punishment for this—the principle offence—Was "Cashiering" in the case of all three officers. Shah Nawaz did not himself commit any brutal or violent act against any person, but passed on the orders of a superior authority which he claims to have believed to have been properly constituted.

It is necessary also to remember that some 20,00 officers and men joined the so-called "I.N.A." and that, even if it were desirable, it would have been a physical impossibility to bring all these men to trail within anything approaching a reasonable period of time.

8. The situation now is that the principle that the for sake of his allegiance by a soldier is a crime in any circumstances has been established, and that no further trials on this account alone will be held. Those against whom there is adequate evidence of murder and brutality will be tried and punished in the ordinary way.

In the second, third and fourth trials the charge of "waging war" has been included in addition to the other charges because trials were commenced before the finding of the Court in the first trial was known. If the accused in these three trials are found guilty on this charge the court will pass the sentence of "Transportation of life" which is the minimum admissible under the Army Act for the offence of "waging war".

When it comes to confirmation of the sentence, however, the facts in respect of the other charges of brutality will be the guiding factor.

In any subsequent trials, the charge of "waging war" will be omitted as our object is now to punish those who may have been guilty of brutal acts towards their former comrades.

9. As to the great mass of rank and file of the so-called "I.N.A.", these are now being examined by Courts of Inquiry as rapidly as possible with a view of finding out whether they are to be classified as "White", "Grey" or "Black". I realise very well and so does everyone else at G.H.Q. and in the War Department, the urgent need for disposing of these men at the earlier possible moment, so that the whole affair may have a reasonable change of being forgotten, which is I am sure the ardent desire of the Army as a whole. At the same time, it is quite certain from the evidence at our disposal that if this enquiry is not carried out with reasonable thoroughness, great injustice may be done to innocent men. The temptation, therefore, to discharge or dismiss all and sundry summarily and without more ado must be resisted.

10. There is one other criticism which is often made. If is said that we ought to have dealt with the accused summarily in forward areas; that if the men were to be brought to India we should have avoided

publicity, and in particular trial in the Red Fort; and that we ought to have put out counter-publicity from the start. The answer to the first point is that we had to deal with 45000 men, in one instance a whole I.N.A. division surrendering without firing a shot. It was obviously impracticable for forward areas to deal with men on this scale summarily and it was the obvious course to send them back to India where the records and Intelligence organisation existed for interrogation. As to publicity, I am sure it was right to decide not to hold trials in secret because it would have been thought that the men were not getting a fair trial. Once it was decided that the trials could not he held in secret, it would have been wrong to tuck them away somewhere where defence counsel, relations, etc., could not conveniently attend; and the Red Fort was the most convenient place from nearly every point of view. We avoided counter-publicity because it was practically certain that a big publicity drive would be represented as prejudicing the accused in their trial; but in any event it is not possible for us to force papers to publish anything which they regard as propaganda and with which they do not agree. We have no control over them in this respect.

11. This letter has become very lengthy, but I make no apology for this as I consider it essential that the full facts of this sad business should be put before you, so that you in your turn can put them before the officers serving under you, as and when it appears necessary to you.

You should not, in explaining the matter to your officers, quote me as Commander-in-Chief but should use the material I have tried to give you in this letter in any way you think suitable to the purpose as if it came from yourself.

12. Finally let me again state the object : it is to maintain the reliability, stability and efficiency of the Indian Army for the future, whatever Government may be set up in India.

This can be done only if the British and Indian officers of the Army trust and respect each other and continue to work wholeheartedly together for the common cause as they have done in war.

It is your task to do your utmost to bring this about and I am sure you will ? You have excellent material on which to work.

13. If your are still in doubt on any point or have any suggestions to make in furtherance of our common object, I will be glad if you will let me or the Adjutant-General know.

C.J. Auchinleck,
General

19

Wavell's Report of his Interview with Jawaherlal Nehru Regarding I.N.A.

2 May, 1946

1. I had asked Nehru to come and see me because of letter he had written to the Commander-in-Chief about certain proposed I.N.A. trials. I told him that after discussion with the Commander-in-Chief and consideration of the evidence, we had decided that these particular men would not be tried. I asked him not to make public the fact that he had written to the Commander-in-Chief and sought to influence him in the matter, as it would cause the Commander-in-Chief some embarrassment. He promised not to do so, but said he could not entirely guarantee that the Press might some embarrassment. He promised not to do so, but said he could not entirely guarantee that the Press might not attribute the matter to his intervention.

2. I then told him my views on the I.N.A.; and that I thought it was an act of folly on the part of the political parties to have glorified the I.N.A. men, who were for the most part the weakling and softlings of the prisoners of war in Malaya; by far the greater percentage of them had joined to obtain better treatment and rations or to avoid hardship. The real heroes were the 45,000 men who had remained staunch; in spite of starvation, ill-treatment, and torture; 15,000 of them had perished as result of this, while the casualties of the I.N.A. had been relatively very small, and they had done little real fighting.

   Nehru listened quite quietly, and said that any body of men were a mixture; but that while he realised that some of the I.N.A. men had not joined from the best of motives and were not the best type of men, he had met many of them who were of a good type. He said that the attitude taken by the Congress Party towards the I.N.A. trials

1. Wavell Papers. Indian office Library & Records. London.

was not simply from political motives but in response to the real feeling in the country. I said that the feeling in the country had been largely worked up by agitation in the press and on the platform. He said that nevertheless the feeling was a very genuine one. He said there was no intention to withhold admiration from the regular Indian Army, though they had hitherto felt that this was a foreign instrument of repression.

I think, from what he said, that Congress has begun to realise that the I.N.A. is not entirely a creditable asset.

20

Nehru to Claude Auchnileck Pleading for Leniency Towards the I.N.A. Soldiers[1]

4 May, 1946

Dear Sir Clude,

I want to think you for your decision to withdraw all trial of I.N.A. personnel. I am sure this decision will be widely welcomed and will help in producing an atmosphere which we all desire.

It has been said sometimes that the regular Indian army has been largely ignored while the members of the I.N.A. have been lionised. To some extent this may be true, but I do not think it is fundamentally true. All Indians are proud of the courage and capacity of the Indian army. They are splendid material, but inevitably they have been looked upon in the past as agents of foreign authority and so long as political conditions in India do not change completely, this approach will remain. As a matter of fact do not change completely, this approach will remain. As a matter of fact various factors during the past few months have gone towards breaking down, or at any rate lessening, the barriers between the army and the civil population. This is all to the good. Nevertheless the final barrier will remain till the army can consider itself, and is in fact, a real national army. I hope the day is not distant when this will happen. You must know that most of us have friends and relatives in the Army, the Navy and the Air Force and so, apart from wider national considerations, even personal factors make us interested in the future of the defence services.

We know that large numbers of officers and men of the Indian army, who were taken prisoners by the Japanes in Malaya, suffered terribly. Thousands did not survive this ordeal. Those who underwent this suffering certainly deserve our full sympathy. We know also that every person who joined the I.N.A. did not necessarily do so for patriotic motives, but, having personally come across a fairly large number of I.N.A. officers and

1. Nehru Papers, Nehru Memorial Museum and Liberary, New Delhi. Also Printed in Auchinleck (London, 1959) pp. 817-819, by John Connell.

men, I must say that I have been struck by the high calibre of many of them. I have no doubt that basic motive for many of them was patriotic and the desire to help in achieving India's freedom.

It is sometimes said that we have exploited this I.N.A. situation for political purposes. Almost everything in India fits in somewhere into the political picture because the fact of India's subjection dominates life here. But I can say with some confidence that there was no desire or even thought of exploiting the I.N.A. issue for political purposes when this matter first came before the public. I believe I was the first person to mention it is public. The sole thought before me was that thousands of my countrymen, whom I believed to be patriotic, were in grave danger. I did not then know the full story of the I.N.A., but knowing my countrymen fairly well I could understand how they must have felt in a difficult situation. I realised also the repercussions on them of events in India. I had not appreciated the political and international approach of some of the leaders of the Indian independence movement in South East Asia. I had differed from them in the past on international and national issues. Nevertheless I felt kinship and sympathy for these people and I knew well what the reaction of the public mind in India would be. The possibility that some swift action by courts martial might be taken against large numbers of them filled me with apprehension not only because of the persons involved, but also because of the inevitable consequences in India. Sensing all this I made my first public reference to the I.N.A. and followed this up with subsequent reference. It did not strike me at all at the time that political advantage could be taken of this affair. Then a strange and surprising thing happened, not strange in itself but very surprising because of its depth and extent. Though I had sensed the mood of the Indian people, I had not fully realised how far it went in the direction. Within a few weeks the story of the I.N.A. had percolated to the remotest villages in India and everywhere there was admiration for them and apprehension as to their possible fate. No political organisation, however strong and efficient, could have produced this enormous reaction in India. It was one of those rare things which just fit into the mood of the people, reflect, as it were, and provide an opportunity for the public to give expression to that mood. The reason for this was obvious. Individuals were not known nor were many facts known to the public. The story as it developed seemed to the people just another aspect of India's struggle for independence and the individuals concerned became symbols in the republic mind. Whether one agrees with this or not, one should at least understand how things happen and what forces lie behind them. The widespread popular enthusiasm was surprising enough, but even more surprising was a similar reaction of a very large number of regular Indian army officers and men. Something had touched them deeply. This kind of thing is not done and cannot be done by politicians or agitators or the like. It is the fundamental aspect of the I.N.A. question that has to be borne in mind. All other aspects, however important, are secondary.

I suppose everyone who has given thought to the matter realises fully that it is a dangerous and risky business to break the disciplines of an army. It would obviously be harmful to do any injury to a fine instrument like the Indian army, and yet at every step, till major changes take place converting it into a real national army, we have to face the political issue which governs every aspect of Indian life today. Risks have to be taken sometimes, more especially when existing conditions are felt to be intolerable. You will forgive me for writing this rather long letter. It was my intention only to think you; but then I felt that I should say something also on this subject, something that might give you a glimpse into my own mind.

Sincerely yours,
Jawaharlal Nehru

21

Note by the C.S.D.I.C. (I). on the Part Played by the INA in Active Operations Against Allied Forces[1]

12 May, 1946

Note: This Note has been prepared at 12 hours notice and does not purport to be either an exact or a comprehensive account of the subject dealt with.

1. **The First INA, 1942—**

The INA of Mohan Singh comprised of

16000 Absorbed volunteers.

30000 Surplus volunteers.

The maximum allowed by the Japanese.

Men who had signed volunteer forms but who could not be absorbed into Mohan Singh's organisation. The Japanese declared on 1/1/42 that all surplus volunteers would thenseforth be regarded as PW/- itself a sign that the Japanese did not intend to allow the INA to become too strong.

The first INA was organised, trained and disbanded in Singapore. Its officials life was from 1 Sep. 42 to 28 Dec. 42. 400 men left Singapore for Burma in Nov. 42 as an Advance Guard.

In Burma in 1942 a group of about 400 men captured during the Burma Campaign volunteered for 5th Column tasks, were taken from Rangoon Jail and trained by Capt. L.S. Misra 5/17 Dogra and Jem Ram Sarup. These 400 men were trained in line contact work and propaganda.

2. **1943, The Second INA**—The INA in Singapore languished after Mohan Singh's arrest, when R.B. Bose announced that in future only willing and enthusiastic volunteers were required. 4000 men resigned from the INA, leaving only 12000 members. The DMB took

1. W.O. 208/868. P.R.O.

charge until S.C. Bose arrived in July 43 from Germany to infuse new life into the moribund INA. The Japanese, however, knew exactly how they intended to use the INA, and pushed ahead with the training of the SS (Bahadur), Intelligence and Reinforcement Groups. These units were intended to spearhead the Japanese invasion of India, and they moved to Burma in Sept./Oct. 1943 to link up with the other large group of trained saboteurs and fifth columnists under Jem Ram Sarup and Capt Misra.

S.C. Bose immediately reorganised the INA, secured an unlimited ceiling for recruitment, and initiated a large programme of training schools for civilians. Thousands of civilians flocked to join the Training Centre and the OTS 1943 was thus the year of training for the INA, whose strength was then about :-

Military	-	15000
Civilians	-	5000
		20000

Towards the end of the year, the INA units began to move to Burma (1,2,3,4, Guerrilla Regts) in anticipation of the forthcoming Japanese all out offensive of early 1944.

In Burma, throughout 1943, there was nothing but frontier patrolling and skirmishing. Small Groups of trained JIFS from Rangoon were sent to numerous towards posts (Paungbyin, Kalewa, Mawlaik, Homalin etc.) to carry out recces for Japanese units and to disseminated propaganda leaflets. There was however no real fighting and a large numbers of these JIFS seized the opportunity to return to India and surrender.

3. **1944.**

1944 was the year planned for the Japanese all-out offensive. Unfortunately for them, owing to the earlier crisis in the INA, the INA was still an embryo organisation and though the training schools were full of recruits and cadets. Only No 1 Div (Comd M. Z. Kiani) of the INA was fully trained by early 1944 and sent to Burma. Its composition was:-

1 Guerrilla Regt (Bose Regt)	–	2000 men
Guerrilla Regt (Gandhi Regt)	–	2000 men
2 Guerrilla Regt (Azad Regt)	–	2000 men
2 Guerrilla Regt (Nehru Regt)	_	2000 men

HQ 1 Div	-	400 men
HT Coys	-	800 men
SS Gp	-	600 men
"I" Gp	-	400 men
Rft Gp	-	400 men
Rear details/L of C	-	2000 men
	Approx.	12600 men

The above force was purely a Guerrilla Force, lightly armed and really intended as skirmishers for the Japanese Divisions. The INA force had no aircraft, no artillery, no heavy mortars, no tanks or AFV's. They were equipped with British rifles and equipment of 1941 issue, and were consequently outmoded and out-weaponed.

4. **The Kohima/Imphal Campaign of 1944**

(a) **General**—The massive Japanese offensive opened with the unsuccessful drive in the Arakan, followed in March by the advances on Kohima, Imphal and Tiddim These advances were made by purely Japanese forces to which had been allotted a quota of trained JIFS of Bahadur and "I" Gp. Thus, during the early and sweeping phases of the advances many reports were received of JIF activity, particularly in the Sangshak fighting and the siege of Kohima when broadcast exhortations were made to subvert British/Indian troops. In the wider picture of INA history, however, the activities of these small bands of specialist JIFS can be disregarded as they were essentially part of the enemy "I" offensive and not part of his armed offensive. The JIF Sector or Butai Commanders were:-

Capt	Maghar Singh	(Imphal Area)
Lt.	Ajmer Sing	(Kohima Area)
Capt.	S.A. Malik	(Imphal/Tiddim Area)

The first two met with practically no success in their attempts to subvert Allied personnel. Capt S.A. Malik enjoyed a certain measure of suceess, mainly because much larger numbers of Allied PW and Stragglers were captured in his Sector.

(b) **The Guerrilla Regts in Action**—The INA Guerrilla Regts followed up behind the Japanese thrust which was levelled at Imphal along the Term/lale Rd. Whereas the siege of Kohima took place in Apr 44, it was early. May before the leading Grla Regt (Ghandhi) arrived in the Tamu area. After much argument, the Japanese agreed to allow the Regts of 1 Div INA to operations Regts and not as sub-units of Japanese formations. Gandhi Regt was ordered to pursue allegedly retreating British elements along the Tamu/Palel road. Flushed with enthusiasm but without adequate reconnaissance, a special raiding force of about 20 men under Lt Pritam Singh (Kapurthala Inf), set out on the night of 2/3 May to capture the Palel Landing Strip. Unbeknown to this force, path of advance, on a hill near Litan village (Point RK 4018 1/4" map. Five miles from Palel and three miles north of Purum Khulan). This Gurkh a picquet was No. 11 platoon of 'B' Coy 4/10 Gurkhas (10 Ind Inf Bde), and comprised 26 men commanded by Jem Bharta Singh Rai. At 2230 hrs the INA force was discerned approaching, talking and smoking. It was allowed to proceed into an ambush position before fire was opened upon it. During the next hour seven separate attacks were made on the Gurkha picquet position, but each attacks was repulsed. The INA force then withdrew in disorder having suffered considerable casualties. The Gurkha picquet lost only two men killed.

The above action was the first recorded and concerted action undertaken by INA troops under their own commanders. Its utter defeat and discomfiture must have spread incalculable pessimism and defeatism amongst the INA troops then massing in the Tamu area. The action served to remind the INA troops who had fed on stories of mutiny and disintegration in the Allied forces that:-

(a) British/Indian troops would not hesitate to shoot on the INA

(b) British/Indian troops would not throw down their arms when attacked by INA.

(c) British defences were soundly organised, with overwhelming fire-power support.

After the above action, operations became largely static owing to the monsoon. There were no pitched battles but a certain number of patrol clashes. 2 Guerrilla (Gandhi) Regt (Comd Capt I.J. Kiani) was deployed on either side of the Tamu Palel road. 3 Guerrilla (Azad) Regt (Comd Capt Gulzara Singh) was deployed north of the road in the Mintha/Narum area. Malaria and sickness took heavy toll and when the Japanese supply system broke down, starvation and disease overtook the Japanese and the INA. Of the 6000 INA troops on the Tamu front.

250 were killed in action/by bombing
1000 died form starvation/disease
600 deserted to join the British.

1. **Guerrilla (Bose) Regt was known as the "Crack" Regt.**

In Mar 44 one of the Batallions moved via Prome to the Arakan, under Lt P.S. Raturi, whilst the other two Batallions moved via Kalewa/Myittha Haka to the Chin Hills above Falam.

The Bn in the Arakan operated on the Kaladan against west African troops and took part in about a dozen patrol clashes. The West Africa forces withdrew during the monsoon and the INA force advanced to occupy Mowdok at the head of the Sangu River - just inside the Indian frontier. This advance was extensively used in Japanese/ INA propaganda but at the end of the monsoon the West Africans advanced again and the INA force retraced its steps to Paletwa and eventually to Myohaung. In INA circles 1 Bn Bose Regt was reputed to have put up one of the best performances against Allied troops, for the return to Rangoon in Nov 44 it was earmarked to become No 1 Bn of a new unit known as "X" Regt.

2 and 3 Bns Bose Regt under Capt Shah Niwaz (Comd Bose Regt) moved to the Falam area of the Chin Hills and remained there from March to June doing nothing but patrols and keeping its L of C (via Kalewa/Natchaung) in repair. In Mar the famous "Manning Incident" took place when 20 British Chin levies were captured by a ruse: this was followed by the abortive attack on Klang Klang. Decimated by malaria and disease 2 and 3 Bns Bose Regt were moved up in June 44 to the Ukhrul/Humine area, to assist in the extrication of Japanese/INA remnants from the Kohima/Imphal disasters.

From July onward the Japanese/INA withdrawal degenerated into a route. Thousands of Japanese and hundreds of INA perished en route from Tamu to Kalewa. Throughout the campaign (March-July 44) after the first fiasco at Palel the INA was never again entrusted with any really independent combat task. Its strength was dissipated by patrol actions, the maintenance of a precarious L of C, and the constant loses caused by sickness, disease, starvation and desertion.

Of the total of 8000 INA troops who crossed the Chindwin

300	-	were killed in action
600	-	deserted to the British
1000	-	were captured or picked up by the Advancing British Forces.
1500	-	died of sickness or starvation.
3400	-	(Figures approx. only).

It is to be noted here that 4 Guerrilla (Nehru) Regt never moved North of Mandalay as it arrived too late to take part in the Imphal operations.

The failure of the INA in the 1944 campaign sent S.C.Bose to Tokyo to secure greater independence and autonomy in the INA Command, and freedom from Hikari Kikan. This bore fruit in the campaign of 1945 when INA Regt took orders only from HQ Supreme Comd and from INA Div HQ and when INA Regt 1/Bn Commanders were authorised to exercise initiative and independent command within the areas allotted to them. In 1945 the INA became more of a fighting force and fought more as Allies of the Japanese rather than as an appendage of the Japanese Army.

It was to rely more on its own strength of arms and military virtue than on hopes that the British /Indian forces would crumble at the first shout of front-line propagandists. It is indicative of the campaign of 1945 that the sedulously trained men of Bahadur and SS Groups (whose work in 1944 had been zealous but fruitless) were sent to the rear and never used. For the 1945 campaign propaganda was abandoned as a weapon - perhaps because it was appreciated that propaganda has less affect on an advancing than on a retreating enemy.

The INA failed in 1944 because

(a) It grossly underestimated the strength and determination of Allied resistance, and sadly overestimated the military efficiency of the Japanese Army.

(b) It had beguiled itself by its own propaganda, and thought it could win battles by propaganda alone. It relied on the Japanese to win battles and territory and its own intended task was to consolidate the territory so won.

(c) It was not present in sufficient numerical strength to make any real impression on the Allied Forces opposed to it.

(d) It was outdated in its weapons and its tactics. It was David against Goliath but a David without a sling. It had enthusiasm and revolutionary ardour, but locked most of the other military requisites. S.C. Bose devoted too much of his energies to delivering propaganda lectures, rather than insisting on better military equipment etc.

(e) Its "commisariat" was part of the Japanese "Q" organisation- which failed radically, and was one of the chief reasons for the Japanese defeat.

The actual fighting performed by the INA in the 1944 campaign was negligible. It spent the bulk of its time fighting hunger and disease and the inefficiency or inadequacy of its own organisation. Even as a propaganda weapon it was over-rated because it achieved practically nothing. In every recorded clash between British and INA troops the latter were worsted. From the sorry tale of the 1944 campign there emerges no name from the petty hierarchy of INA Commanders which can be said to be even mediocre, let alone great.

5. **The Pause between The Campaigns**—From July 1944 to Feb 45 the INA was withdrawing and reorganising and practically all contact with it was lost. The remnants of 1 Div 1, 2 and 3 Grla Regts (about 4000 men) were finally sent back to Zeyawaddy Rest Camp. Meantime units of 2 Div INA were being hurriedly brought up from Malaya. These units were :-

5 Guerrilla Regt (later named 2 Inf Regt)	2000 men
Hind Fd Force (later named 1 Inf Regt)	2000 men
HQ 2 Div	400 men
Miscellaneous units	2000 men
INA AA Coy (5) stationed in southern Burma and Siam	1000 men

To the above fresh troops were added the 1000 men of 4 Guerrilla (Nehru) Regt of 1 Dev, which had not been committed in the 44 fighting. Thus in early Feb 45 the INA front-line set-up was : -

4 Guerril la (Nehru) Regt	- South bank of Irrawaddy between Nyaungu and Pagan.
2. Inf Regt	- Moving up to Mt Popa/ Kyaukpadaung area.
1 Inf Regt	- Movilng up to Magwe area.
Remnats 1 Div	- Zeyawaddy (Toungoo)

By the begining of Feb 45 the Allied Divisions had advanced through Shwebo, Monywa, Sagaing and Pakokku and stood poised for the assault on Mandalay and for the thrust across the Irrawaddy. The ensueing period 15 Feb to 30 April was a period of heavy and constant fighting and these 2/1 months include the entire INA 1945 campaign of front-line fighting. The period opens with the British thrust across the Irrawaddy at Nyaungu and ends with the total disentegration of all INA forces.

6. **Outstanding Events of the 1945 Campaign**

(a) On 15 Feb 45 British forces in the Pakokku area opened there attack on the INA forces (1000 men of Nehru Regt) who lined the Southern bank of the Irrawaddy in the Nyaungu/Pagan area. The weight of the Allied bombing, mortaring and shelling demoralised the INA defenders and on 18 Feb over 300 men of Nehru Regt surrendered voluntarily to British forces. The remaining 700 men under Regt Comd Lt G.S. Dhillon retreated in disorderly confusion to the Mount Popa area. By that time however, the 2000 men of 2 Inf Regt under Capt. P.K. Sahgal had reached the vital Mount Popa positions and entrenched themselves there where they were to remain for the next six weeks. Shortly after Nehru Regt had settled down at Popa the British airborne landing at Meiktila was flown in and the British bridgehead forces at Nyaungu/Nyingyan moved across country to link up with the Meiktila garrison. These moves brought the British bridgehead forces into contact with the Screen of INA positions covering the northern approaches to Mount Popa. A number of hard-fought engagements resulted, in which for the first time INA troops fought with mettle and determination.

(b) By the end of Feb 45, HQ 2 Div INA had set up its HQ MT Pop,. Within a few days of arrival, and by means of a brilliant subterfuge, four of the five staff officers of HQ 2 Div deserted and escaped to the British lines. This joint desertion severely rattled the INA High Command and S.C. Bose was obliged to inaugurate a "hate campaign" against all traitors. The gaps in th staff of HQ 2 Div were filled by second rate officers.

(c) The remnants of Nehru Regt were allotted the defence of an area between the Irrawaddy and Mt Popa, and were based on Kyaukpadaung. On 15 March 45 a newly arrived company of reinforcements under "Lt" Gian Singh (and comprising 75% civilians) moved forward to village Kunywa (or Kazaung) and took up position inside a dry water tank. This position was attacked by Gurkha troops and British tanks. The INA Coy stood its ground, and after 45 men had been killed the remainder surrendered. "Lt" Gain Singh was killed. This action was made much of by the INA Rangoon propagandists and a newsheet was published called : "The Charge of the Immortals" which was an idealised version of the action referred to above.

(d) On the 10th March 45 all Bns of 2 Inf Regt were in position et Mt Popa. Capt Shah Niwaz had taken over command of 2 Div and capt. P.K. Sahgal reverted to Comd 2 Inf Regt. To cover an intended move by Japanese forces under General YAMAMOTO up the Irrawaddy, 2 Inf Regt under Sahgal made a night attack on 15/16 March on the village of Pyinbyin, but withdrew to its positions at Popa when met by Allied MG fire.

(e) On 16 March a coy of INA troops of 2 Inf Regt, under Sub Khan Mohd attacked Sade Village and fierce hand-to-hand fighting took place, the INA troops fighting well.

(f) On 25 March a second attack was made on Pyinbyin Village by 2 Inf Regt, in conjunction with Japanese troops. This operation was intended to assist Japanese troops at Maiktila who were counter attacking the British.

(g) From 26/31 Mar 2 Inf Regt was ordered to attack northwards to assist the Japanese counter offensive towards Myingyan/ Mandalay. Moving from Popa to Seiktein with 1 Bn 2 Inf Regt Capt P.K. Sahgal was rambushed and narrowly escaped and drew back to Legyi to dig in.

(h) One the three Bns of 2 Inf Regt were in position at Legyi on 30 March, there developed the biggest pitched battle of the campaign. For four days the INA positions were shelled and mortared and attacked by Allied troops, but the INA stood their ground well. Capt. P.K. Sahgal wrote a long appreciation of this battle and named Nk (2/Lt) Kanwal Singh as a men who distinguished himself. However, men were deserting every day, and by 4 April over 400 men had deserted, mostly in large groups led by officers. Heavy casualties had also been suffered and 2 Inf Regt (which had fought extremely well, mostly due to Sahgal's leadership) withdrew and gradually disintegrated. Nehru Regt and 2 Inf Regt joined their depleted forces on 8 April but by then British tanks were forging ahead towards Magwe, from Meiktila. The INA in the Popa area therefore withdrew via Yenangyaung to Magwe. There were no more pitched battles. The INA in Burma had shot its bolt.

(i) During the period 15 Feb-8 April 45 there was a constant stream of desertions from the INA and it was this flow of desertions which weakened and disorganised 2 Inf Regt and rendered it incapable of further effective resistance. Many of the desertions were assisted by the dropping of Allied surrender leaflets singed by the recently escaped Staff Officers of HQ 2 Div.

(j) The three battalions of 1 Inf Regt (previously Hind Fd Force) under Capt S.M. Hussain were stationed in the Magwa area in an anti-paratroop role. 2 Bn (650 men) were at Megwa and when British Tanks arrived (650 men) were at Magwe and when British tanks arrived on 19 April 45 the 650 men surrendered without firing a shot. 1 and 3 Bns disintegrated on contact with British forces and surrendered in numerous parties, some large some small. Only a small number of die-hards attempted to make their way across country to Pegu and thence to Siam. In the end, only one party led by Lt. S.N. Gupta finally reached Bangkok.

(k) Thus the Fiercest resistance by INA troops was put up by 2 Inf Regt under P.K. Sahgal, but ever his men deserted him. Eventually Sahgal himself was compelled to surrender near Allanmyo with 600 of his men, when overtaken and surrounded. Comparatively, Nehru Regt and 1 Inf Regt offered no resistance whatsoever to Allied troops.

(1) Meantime, S.C.Bose had formed "X" Regt under Capt Thakar Singh, Kapurthala Inf from amongst the fit personnel of 1 Div INA from Zeyawaddy Rest Camp. Three Bns were formed.

No 1 under "Capt" Suraj Mal	(from 1 Bn Bose ex-Arakan)
No 2 Lt Ran Singh	(600 men)
No 3 Civ (Major) Abid Hussan	(600 men)

2 and 3 moved forward from Zeyawaddy but disintegrated at first contact with Allied forces. They moved eastwards from Tougoo/Mawchi/Papun/Moulmein/Bangkok, disdaining even to join combat with the small parties of Forces 136 guerrillas which occasionally tried to bar their way and the bulk of the men reached Bangkok - the only formed bodies of INA troops to do so.

(m) Thus the story of the INA 1945 campaign in Burma is one of half-hearted resistance and constant surrenders relieved only by the few battles fought with determination by 2 Inf Regt. The reasons are many, and include general demoralisations, superior to Allied weapons, tactics, air-power etc. But one of the reasons is also the poor leadership exhibited by the great majority of INA officers - with one or two notable exceptions only. The INA lacked real officers: it had a number of good Nks - cum- Lieuts, the majority of INA officers though suitable for propaganda parades, were not suitable for the battle field. The INA had an excellent paper organisation but its foundations were inherently weak and insubstantial. There were thousands of INA troops in Rangoon in April 45 but they all surrendered without firing a shot.

(n) the following points emerge from the INA's 1945 campign :-

(i) It fought as an ally of the Japanese to hold Burma for the Nippon Empire. It on longer fought as the Indian Army of liberations. Inspite of this, S.C. Bose by his propaganda and personality kept alive in the minds of the INA the illusion that they were fighting for the freedom of India.

(ii) 2 Inf Regt fought with courage and determination from 15 March 45 to 15 April 45, inspired by the personal example and leadership of capt. P.K. Sahgal. All other INA unit collapsed at first contact with British forces and mass surrenders followed. First contact was joined on 15 Feb 45 and during the next two months over 3000 "fighting troops" of the INA surrendered.

(iii) With one or two notable exceptions, the INA officers proved poor leaders. The "Officers" who distinguished themselves were mostly ex-NCOs. The bulk of NCIO/ IECO officers in the INA retained jobs on the L of C and in rear areas, and hoped for a comfortable journey from Rangoon to Delhi.

(iv) INA medical and evacuation arrangements were rudimentary. There was an ample supply of doctors but organisation was poor because the senior IMS officers discarded medicine for politics. (Lt Col Chatterjee, Lt-Col Loganadan, Lt Col Alagappan etc), and left medical organisation in the hands of men of mediocre ability.

(v) On Paper, the INA had an impressive organisation, but when this was reduced to terms of fighting potential, the inherent feebleness of the INA was revealed. At no time was the INA properly equipped to wage war on modern lines.

(vi) Though as a fighting force the INA was a negligible factor it cannot be denied that the political (or spiritual - as it was called) indoctrination given to the troops had a more potent and lasting effect. The patent sincerity of S.C. Bose was made clear to all ranks for Bose shared the dangers of the battle fields with them.

7. **The INA in Burma**—Thus, in the two campaigns of 1944 and 1945, a total of approx 15000 men served with the INA in Burma. Of those :-

750	were killed	}	
1500	died of disease	}	Figures
2000	escaped to Bangkok	}	
3000	"Surrendered"	}	approx
7000	"captured"	}	only

8. **The INA in Malaya (3 DIV)**—Malaya remained the Trg ground for the INA. Strengths in Malaya in Aug 45 were :-

HQ 3 DIV	800
3 Inf Regt (6 Grla)	2250
7, 8, 9 Grla Regts	6000
AHF Trg Centres	3000
AFV Bn	1000
Pack Tpt Unit	1000
Animal Tpt Unit	1400
Rft Gp	1000
Miscellaneous	2200
	19000

(* About 60% Civilians). The above men all surrendered without firing a shot, after S.C. Bose had instructed "Maj Gen" M.Z. Kiani to order capitulation.

The total strength of the INA in 1944/45 was from 35000 to 40000 of whom about 20000 were ex-military and 20000 were civilians. Of those 40000 only about 10000 were ever engaged on active operations against Allied Forces, and on not more than 10 or 12 occasions were pitched battles fought. The INA was 95 per cent "ballyhoo" and 5 per cent "Serious business". In 1944 it failed as a propaganda weapon, and in 1945 it failed as a fighting weapon. It was never a cause of real trouble or annoyance to the Allies: the most trouble it ever gave was in giving the British the problem of handling thousands of its men as recovered PW when the Allied L of C in Burma was littered by thousands of surrendered JIFS.

Note—The above does not purport in any way to be a complete or meticulously accurate statement of the case. Most of the paragraphs could be amplified and much additional material introduced.

22

Fujiwara's Observations on INA. and Subhas Chandra Bose[1]

9 July, 1946

My experience of the INA. is limited to the main force of I Div.[2] which took part in the Imphal operations. It cannot be positive or accurate judgement.

1. **General Observation**—As a revolutionary army, its morale was high and it was quite well organised. But the standard of its tactics, training and leadership was low. These together with other shortcomings and weaknesses mentioned below contributed to make the fighting strength of the INA. not what it might have been. It lacked in particular offensive strength and tenacity.

2. **Morale of the INA.**—The revolutionary spirit, organisation and discipline which was the foundation of the INA. morale, was low and maintained by all officers and men of the INA. on their enthusiastic respect and pledge of loyalty to Subhas Chandra Bose. Had they not had Mr. Bose as their leader, their morale certainly would have been considerably lower than it was and during a crisis when they would have been shaken and divided. During the most distressing and difficult period of the Imphal operations about June and July 1944, the great majority of the I.N.A. answered the urgent appeals of Mr. Bose and followed the leadership of their superiors maintaining discipline and otherwise carrying out their respective duties. Even during the retreat they overcame overwhelming difficulties and retreated in an orderly fashion. This won for them the admiration even of the Japanese army.

3 **Leadership**—The leaders were quick to observe enemy intentions and generally speaking they were competent in their leadership. But with the Div. as the strategic unit of operations, they lacked experi-

---

1. S.E.A.T.I.C. Bulletin No 240. This Bulletin consists of the translation of essays written by Fujiwara on various topics when he was in prison in Singapore in 1946.
2. Col. M.Z. Kiani was commander of this Division.

ence and training and not infrequently they failed to see the picture in its correct prospective. I have the·impression that the officers were incompetent when faced with unforeseen difficulties, but this can be attributed to their lack of experience.

4. **Technical Training**—Technical training of INA. troops in jungle and mountain warfare was lacking and they had little imagination or experience in the construction or fortification. As a result when faced by Allied forces superior in equipment and numbers although they pushed ahead ferociously, if those advances met a counter off sure they were unnecessarily heavy. Having once suffered a set-back the psychological effect was great and they were always inclined to on the defensive.

5. Other than the attempted advance made by the INA. to the area south of Palel, they did not participate in any major battle. Their main job was to guard the flank of the Yamamato Force and prevent the Indian Army from outflanking this unit i.e., their job was a defensive one.

Difficulties met by INA Division

(a) Civil volunteers were mixed with military and they lacked the proper housing.

(b) Personnel arrived piecemeal and had to be employed separately for instance I infantry Regiment arrived in Haka and Falam in March 1944 as 2 Inl. arrived at Palel front in April whereas the 3 Int. did not arrive until June 1944.

(c) They were short of equipment especially guns.

(d) They lacked organisation and means of supply and during the monsoon season, when supply lines were cut, they had to rely on manpower alone for movement of supplies.

(e) The Chins and Shans on the frontier were not sympathetic to the Indians.

On S. C. Bose

I would like it to be mentioned that what I shall state below is from my observations not very profound. Bose was a man who fought body and soul for independence. He was by nature a revolutionary. He had a zealous fighting spirit, though in outward appearance, he was very gentle. His earnest and precise mind, his vigorous actions, and his initiative together with his love for the masses showing no discrimination between classes won him the respect which was later transformed into reverence from all those who came into contact with him.

As a revolutionary, his political abilities were great as his record from July 43 shows, but he had not the capacity for constructive political projects.

When contacting the Japanese, it was his policy to give as his motto "Freedom and Equality" when and if there was any fear of being apprehensive of the Japanese taking advantage of him, he was quick to refuse, however, slight the matter may have been.

As a leader of the Army, he became the fountain head of spiritual strength and was the pivot of the INA. organisation. However, the standard of operational tactics was, it must be said with regret, low. He was inclined to be idealistic and not realistic. For instance, without being familiar with the actual fighting power of the INA., he was always demanding that the INA. be employed in a separate and decisive operation on Imphal front, and in July 1944, when the tide of battle had turned and the Japanese Army had retreated, he urged that although the Japanese might retreat the INA. should continue to confront the Allies until their aim was attained. He was temperamental and had strong likes and dislikes. It is also said that although stubborn he would adhere strongly to his arguments on matters which were slight in importance. This is so and it cannot be said that he possessed an extraordinary magnanimity of mind or very tolerance for the opinion of others.

23

Statement of Yoshimi Taneyoshi, Captain (Medical) of the Imperial Japanese Army regarding the death of Subhas Chandra Bose in the Air-crash

19 October, 1946

Taneyoshi Yoshimi, Captain (Medical) of the Imperial Japanese Army at present at Stanley Gaol, Hong Kong, having observed a statement in a Japanese newspaper, requesting information regarding the death of Chandra Bose, wish of my own free will to place any knowledge I have of this matter at the disposal of the Authorities requiring it. To the best of my ability and memory I hear state the events surrounding the death of Chandra Bose.

In August, 1945, I was the Senior Officer at the Nanmon Military Hospital, Taihoku, Formosa. At about 1700 hrs on the 18th day of August, 1945, a truck driven up before the hospital contained several men who had been injured in an aeroplane crash. Two of the men were Indians, and the remainder, about five or six in number were Japanese. One of the Japanese, a Staff Officer with the rank of Lt-Colonel whose name I cannot properly recall but believe was Ishii-something, informed me that one of the Indians, pointing him out, was Chandra Bose and that I was not to spare myself and must give him very best of treatment. I immediately gave instructions for some medical orderlies to go and prepare a bed, and for other to carry in the injured man.

When he was laid on the bed, I personally cleaned his injuries with oils and dressed them. He was suffering from extensive burns over the whole of his body, though the most serious were those on his head, chest and thighs. There was very little left on his head in the way of hair or other identification marks. During the first four hours he was semi-conscious, and practically normal, speaking quite a good deal. The first words I remember him speaking were in Japanese, when he made a request for

1. W.O. 208/3812. Public Record office London

water, which had to be fed to him through a hospital cup with a spout. As most of his speaking was in English, a request for an interpreter was made, and one was sent from the Civil Government Offices named Nakamura. He informed me that he had very often interpreted for Chandra Bose and had many conversations with him. He appeared to have no doubt that the man he was speaking was Chandra Bose. During the treating of his injuries, I twice inquired of Chandra Bose if he was in any pain and neither time did he make any answer. After about four hours, I inquired whether there was any statement, will, or such matter he wished to make. He answered "Nothing". After the fourth hour he appeared to be sinking into unconsciousness. He murmured, and muttered in his state of coma, but never regained consciousness. At about 2300 hrs. he died. There was apart from the injuries mentioned above, abrasions on his elbows and knees. There were no fractures.

The other Indian was Chandra Bose's Adjutant, a Colonel of the Indian National Army, who was suffering from burns to the sides of his head, arms, hands and knees. I do not remember this man's name, but recall that it was a very long one. He was a very tall man, about six feet or over, medium build, and clean shaven.

It was the wish of this Colonel, and also that of the authorities that the remains of Chandra Bose should be transported to Tokyo, and to facilitate this I injected Formalin into the body, and also had the coffin partly filled with lime. The whole was put in a box, and on the 20th August, was taken to Taihoku airport for transporting to Japan, in charge of Warrant Officer Nishi. W.O. Nishi returned later and informed me that the body could for some unknown reason, not be taken to Japan, and was to be sent to the crematorium for cremation. I therefore made out a Death Certificate, stating the cause of death to be extensive burning and shock. The orders for this change of plans came from the Adjutant's Department, Taiwan Army.

On the morning of the 19th August, Colonel Miyata, Staff Officer of General Ando came to the hospital to express mourning on behalf of General Ando and his staff, and as is our custom brought gifts of flowers, fruits and cakes for the deceased. The news of the death of Chandra Bose was kept a secret, and I and my staff were warned not to divulge that we know who it was that had died.

Statement of Yoshimi Taneyoshi Continued

From the other passengers of the aircraft I have some direct and some information which was told to me. As far as I could make out, the aircraft, carrying Chandra Bose, his Adjutant and about ten or twelve others (Japanese), took off from the Taihoku Air Port, and after rising to a height of about thirty feet, suddenly burst into flames and crashed to the ground. A Major-General Shidei and two others escaped or were rescued, and were brought to Nanmon Hospital. The two pilots, Warrant Officer (later 2/Lt.) Adyagi and a Sergeant Major, were both burned, but after remaining in my care for about two or three weeks had practically recovered and were transferred to the Hokuto-Military Hospital here. I later heard they had died, about three weeks after admittance.

The Indian Colonel, Adjutant to Chandra Bose, remained in my care for about 10 days, and was then sent to the Hokuto Military Hospital. The interpreter Nakamura went up there with him, and I have no knowledge of what became of either of them. I do know, however, that the ashes of Chandra Bose were handed over to the Indian Colonel.

There is nothing more I can remember of this matter, at the present, but will give thought to it, and anything of importance I later remember I will disclose. Signed at Stanley Gaol, this 19th Day of October, 1946.

Yoshimi Taneyoshi.

Certificate of Interpreter

I, Hanagaki Yoshio, state that I truly and correctly translated the above statement made by Yoshimi Taneyoshi, into English, and saw it taken down by Captain A.R. Turner. I later read over the whole of the above statement in the Japanese language, and Yoshimi Taneyoshi agreed and then signed the above statement. Signed at Stanley Gaol, this 19th Day of October, 1946.

Hanagaki Yoshio.

I, Alfred Raymond Turner took the above statement of Yoshimi Taneyoshi, with regard to the death of Chandra Bose, and the Certificate of the Interpreter Hanagaki Yoshio at Stanley Goal, this 19th day of October, 1946, duly witnessing their signatures.

Captain,
A.R. Turner.
War Crimes Liaison Section (Formosa).

Appendix-I

Memoirs of Anand Mohan Sahay Regarding his Activities in Japan and his Role in the Indian Independence Movement

Early in 1923, when the Gaya Session (1922) of the Indian National Congress, held under the Presidentship of Desbbandu Chitranjan Das, could not offer any dynamic programme resulting in an atmosphere of uncertainty regarding the future of Gandhiji's Non-violent Non-Co-operations Movement, I decided to leave for U.S.A. to complete my study of Medicine there and then return to continue my part in the struggle for Indian's freedom. I did not get a passport for U.S.A. from the Government of Bihar and, after consulting my well wishers, decided to proceed to Japan. I sailed from Calcutta for Japan by an Indo-China steam Navigation Company's ship, KUMSANG, on 6th May, 1923, with the blessings of Deshratna Rajendra Prasad and Deshbandhu Chitranjan Das.

I landed in Kobe, an international port in Central Japan, where a large number of Indian merchants were settled in export and import trade, just Rs. 75/- (Seventy-five) in my pocket and without any letter of introduction for any one except one from Prof. Pearson of Santiniketan of Dr. Rabindra Nath Tagore, for a Japanese Christian Social worker of Tokyo, Mr. Ogawa. Being interested in politics of my country, I naturally wanted to know if there was any awakening among the Indians in Japan regarding our freedom struggle at home. To my great disappointment, I found that although most of the Indian merchants in Kobe were from Bombay and Gujarat, they did not take any interest in Indian politics. I learnt that they were keeping aloof from Politics out of the incurring the displeasure of the local representatives of the British Government who might have cancelled their passport.

I learnt that the Indian revolutionary, Rash Bihari Bose, of 1912 Delhi Lord Hardinge Bomb Case fame, was living in Tokyo in exile under the protection of famous Black Dragon Society leader, Toyama Misturu of Japan, Toyama had saved him from being handed over to the British

Embassy by the then Japanese Government. Those were the days of Anglo-Japanese Alliance and Treaty of Friendship. Most of the Japanese political leaders of intelligentia class were under the influence of Western Political Schools.

I failed to obtain a passport for U.S.A. from the Consul of Britain even in Japan. Thus, I had no choice but to return home or to continue to stay in Japan and do some publicity work for Indian independence movement there. I consulted Pandit Jawaharlal Nehru, Deshratna Rajendra Prasad and some other leaders who knew me. They encouraged me to stay on in Japan and work as I suggested. However, to do publicity work for our freedom movement in Japan in those days was not any easy job. No Japanese newspaper would accept any materials that would openly or directly speak of British aggression in India, however truthful the story might have been. I had to be contented with within about the life history of various nationalist Indian leaders like Mahatma Gandhi, Rajendra Prased, Deshbandhu Chit Ranjan Das or Jawaharlal Nehru.

Rash Bihari Bose visited Kobe early in 1925, with Toyama Mitsuru, to see off the great Chinese revolutionary leader, Dr. Sun Yat Sen, known as the father of the Chinese Republic. I met Rash Bihari Bose in the Oriental Hotel and he introduced me to Toyama and Sun Yat Sen and invited me to join the banquet given in honour of the Chinese leader. Later, we had extensive discussions about some work in Japan for Indian independence. He informed me that Indians in Japan would not even invite him to visit them or dine with them due to British influence and no political activities on behalf of the Indian National Congress against British would be tolerated by the Japanese authorities that time.

Same year, later, Raja Mahender Pratap, well known Indian revolutionary, who had attempted to liberate India during the first World War of 1914-18, by organising the first free India Government in Exile with the help of Germany, Turkey and visited Japan as an Afghan national and with an Afghan passport. I met him when he came to Kobe. He was staying in a Buddhist Temple called Gokurakuji, in Kobe. Ostensibly, he was more interested in his World Federation Movement. However, I found in him the fire of Indian patriotism very much burning. Later, we become very good friends and whenever he visited Japan and came to Kobe, stayed with me. My relations with Rash Bihari Bose was also very close and whenever I visited Tokyo, I invariable stayed with him.

I realised by coming in close contact with Rash Bihari Bose that, being completely cut off from Indian scene for such a long time, he had no idea, much less appreciation, of the great mass upheaval in India after the

Jallianwala Bagh tragedy of 1919. Being active in secret societies revolutionary movements, he did have the opportunity to work in a mass struggle and could not imagine how the peaceful and non-violent movement of Mahatma Gandhi could be helpful in driving the powerful British Raj from India. Naturally, he did not support the N.C.O. Movement of the Indian National Congress. Being in Japan and living and moving in the circle of feudal politicians, who protected him from the arm of the British agents, he was largely influenced by the type of feudal politics of Black Dragon Society of Toyama Misturu, known as Robin Hood of Japan.

I, therefore, felt an urge to do something to primarily make the Indians in Japan conscious of their duty towards their motherland. I worked in Indian firms, as assistant, to come in close touch with the youthful assistants and gradually impressed them of the need to study India's N.C.O. Movement and the happenings there through Indian newspapers. I also came in contact with the young Japanese students and youth through the local Y.M.C.A. where I had established friendly relations with the Secretary, Mr. R Okumura, and had rented a room for my abode in its dormitary. I also secured a job as English teacher in the night school of the same Y.M.C.A. that offered me golden opportunity to come in close contact with the young men. Gradually both Indian Assistants of Indian firms and the Japanese students become more and more interested in India's Gandhiji and his unique non-violent struggle. Young assistant of Indian firms and another reason close to me. They were treated not too well by their bosses who did not permit them even to go to Indian Club and mix with them even socially.

In August 1926, some prominent Japanese politicians in cooperation with Rash Bihari Bose and myself, organised an Asian Youth Conference in Nagasaki, Southern Japan. Some Indian friends of Rash Bihari Bose like K.R. Sabarwal and Vidyadhar Bakshi also attended the Conference. Raja Mahendra Pratap, who was then touring North China and Manchuria, rushed to Nagasaki to attend the Conference. I believe, he was invited by some Japanese friends-organisers of the Conference. But, when the ship arrived, the Japanese authorities did not permit him to land although he held valid Afghan passport. Perhaps he did not have proper entry or landing visa on the passport. We felt much disappointed; but, the Port Police of Nagasaki said they had orders form Tokyo and they were helpless. The ship carrying Rajaji proceeded further to Osaka, its destination. We learnt later that the British Embassy in Tokyo had brought pressure on the Japanese Foreign Office to prevent him from attending the Conference.

However, through the efforts of the Japanese friend, Rajaji was allowed to land in Osaka and remain there so long as the ship remained in the port. He was lodged in a hotel but not allowed to go out. In the meantime, after the conclusion of the Nagasaki Conference, Rash Bihari Babu and myself reached Osaka and met Rajaji. Efforts were made to secure the permission of the Japanese Foreign Officer to enable Rajaji to stay on. But we did not succeed. When time come for the ship to leave the port on return journey, the police asked Rajaji to return to the ship. But, he refused to leave the hotel and claimed that he was a follower of Mahatma Gandhi and would not obey unjust orders. The police had to physically remove Rajaji from the hotel and carry him on their shoulders to the waiting car and thence to the ship.

When the ship arrived at Kobe Port, where I resided, some Japanese young men came to me and expressed resentment at their Governments timidity and for the refusal of permission to Rajaji to stay in Japan due to British pressure. They asked me to persuade him to accompany them to a waiting launch and they would escort him to a safe place and would not allow the Police to find out. I did not like the ideas, but on their pressure told Rajaji about their plan. Rajaji did not comply. He was, he said, not prepared to run away and hide like a thief. The ship sailed back to North China with Rajaji, to our great regret. But, before the ship sailed I got plenty of Indian delicacies prepared by my Sindhi and Gujarati merchant friends for him so that he could have them on the way.

At Nagasaki Conference important secret plans were prepared to organise the youth of enslaved Asian countries for revolt. It was decided that, as I held a valid passport for East Asian countries, I undertake a tour of these countries and meet nationalist youth and establish contact for further activities. To do this secretly, I had to travel in the guise of the trader. I organised an Export/Import concern and named it "International Traders", collected varieties of textile and other kinds of samples that Japan was exporting to East Asian countries at that time, collected some addresses of traders of different countries, wrote to them informing them that I was visiting their respective, centres to establish business relationship and negotiate business. All this done, I started on my adventure by sea route on 6th November, 1926. I visited Hong Kong, Canton, Saigon, Thailand, Malaya, Singapore, Sumatra, Colombo and then crossed over to South India, staying in each place for a week or less according to need. I arrived in Calcutta towards the end of December or early in January, 1927, when the Gauhati Session of the Indian National Congress was in progress.

I was tempted but decided to keep away from anything that might have created suspicion in the mind of the Indian Government about my political intention. I remained in India for several months and also got married in Calcutta with Sm. Sati Devi, niece of Deshbandhu Chittaranjan Das and daughter of Smt. Urmila Devi, well known woman leader of Bengal Congress. I visited other parts of the country to meet some of the revolutionary leaders, like Jawaharlal Nehru, Maulana Azad, and others.

On the eve of my departure for Japan, with my wife, in September 1927, I learnt that Subhas Chandra Bose had been released from Mandalay jail and was brought to Calcutta in a very bad state of health. I learnt that doctor did not allow any one to meet him. Yet, I with my wife called at his home and when he was told about me he immediately called us and we had about fifteen minutes to talk when I confided in him the real purpose of my tour. He expressed great satisfaction at my plan and asked me to keep in touch with him and keep him informed about our efforts.

On our way back, we had to change ships at Singapore. We stayed with a South Indian friend, Mr. Dharma Rajah, during the sojourn. During our sojourn, the Indian Association of Singapore came to know about us and its Secretary, Shri Abid Ali, invited me to an Association Meeting and dinner. At that meeting I spoke on duty of Indians towards their motherland. Unconsciously, having forgotten that I was visiting Singapore as a merchant, I put myself in a trap that might have undone all my plan, because next day I had to go to the Police Commissioner's office and face prolonged interrogation. They had asked me to leave Singapore only after informing them. However, by sheer luck, I managed to escape from Singapore with my wife on a French ship within a few days after the investigation.

Back in Japan, I met Rash Bihari Babu and the Japanese leaders and reported the result of the tour. I also told them about my meeting with Subhas Chandra Bose in Calcutta and other leaders like Jawaharlal Nehru and Maulana Azad, who had directed me to establish a Congress branch in Japan. I set about organising the Congress Committee. But in this I did not receive any co-operation either from Rash Behari Bose or from those Japanese leaders who had helped and sponsored the Nagasaki Conference. They were rather opposed to the propagation of the ideals of non-violent NCO. However, when Raja Mahendera Pratap visited Japan, I received wholehearted cooperation from him at the India Club, I proposed the formation of the Congress Committee, with the support of some young Sindhi and Gujarati merchants. Rajaji himself offered to become its member and the resolution was passed.

In 1930, I started publishing a monthly journal by the name of the "Voice of India", in English with Japanese translation side by side, for publicising the Congress struggle at home. The publication proved very popular among the college and University students because it helped them in learning English, I also started a home for Indian students coming from Indian for educational purpose. This proved very useful for accommodating such Indian revolutionaries who escaped from India and needed safe shelter. It was called "India Lodge". Simultaneously, Rash Bihari Bose had also started a similar home in Tokyo, calling it ASIA JIKU, where our youngmen stayed when going to Tokyo for similar purposes. Gradually, several Indo-Japanese Youth Associations, Indo-Japanese Buddhist Associations and Indo-Japanese Students Associations were also formed in various parts of Japan; and, I regularly visited those centers and gave talk on India's struggle for freedom Large gatherings of students heard such speeches with keen interest and offered moral support to the cause.

In due course these activities gave satisfactory dividend. The younger generations, particularly University students and members of the Buddhist Associations became considerably interested in our struggle at home. On the other hand, trade rivalry between the British and Japanese industries in Indian Market, and imperial perference to British goods, encourged discontent among the Japanese commercial community in Japan and the Indian exporters in Japan found a common ground for them because their trade was equally affected. This helped us in encouraging anti-British sentiment among the Japanese.

I had kept Subhas Babu constantly acquainted with these developments, and our plan to take advantage of the situation if and when the opportunity came, through letters carried by same Indian crew of the British Indian Steam Navigation Co. ships that plied between Calcutta and Japan. I sent my wife to Calcutta with more important secret informations regarding Japanese preparations in Feb. 1939, declaring that she had returned home separated from me, due to serious differences, and she was in Calcutta when Subhas planned SATYAGRAHA at Holwell Monument on 3rd April, 1940 and was arrested and imprisoned. When our emissary, Atul Sen, was sent to Bombay with some secret documents to meet the Indian leaders, Subhas was in prison and Sen contacted him there with the help of a relative, Bela Bose.

Soon after the declaration of War in Europeon 1st September 39, in consultation with Raja Mahendra Pratap and Rash Behari Bose, a Council of Action was formed to prepare for active support to our struggle in

India. I had long considered Thailand to be the only country from where external aid to Indian could be possible. I had some young. Indian merchants there who were prepared to co-operate. We, therefore, decided to send my nearest intimate colleague, Deb Nath Das, to Bangkok to organise a centre there. Funds were collected from Indian merchants. I was already in contact with the Japanese Army Headquarters (ASMBO-HAMBU) through Captain (now a Retired General I. Fujiwara). They were helpful in sending Das to Bangkok with plans and documents, and Atul Sen to Bombay.

In 1935, due to some foreign branch of the Congress having acted against the creed of the Congress, the working Committee decided to withdraw recognition to all foreign branches. I received a letter from Jawaharlal Nehru informing me that, as our Japan branch has been working in line with Congress creed, we should continue our activities as usual, though we could no longer claim to be an official branch. After that we decided to change the name of our organisation to "Indian National Association of Japan" from the "Indian National Congress Committee of Japan". As the Indians in Shanghai had expressed their desire to work for the country under our organisation, when I visited Shanghai in 1933. I started an organisation known as the "Indian National Association of China". Shanghai, in pre-War days had a large Indian population. The Shanghai British Police Force consisted mostly of Sikha. There were some Pathans also. And, there was an Indian Mercantile community consisting of Sindhis, Punjabis, Gujaratis and Parsis. I enrolled a large number of members from all sections of Indians. Sikhs of the Police Force were particularly enthusiastic to join the Association, but, I explained to them the implication that because they were in the British Police Force, the British authorities would immediately take steps against them. They were ready to risk that but agreed to wait till time for their open co-operation came. However, our meetings were generally held in the Gurdwara.

In December, 1941, when Japan declared War, and when Rash Behari Bose was declared President of the Movement, it was necessary to bring all Indian national activities under one organisation. Rash Behari Bose had already started his Indian Independence League. I therefore decided to abolish the branches of Indian National Association both in Japan and China and let all Indians join the League. This was also desirable from another point of view. Indian National Association, although no more a branch of the Congress, was still considered as an associate organisation I did not want to betray the trust of the Congress leaders and misuse that name. I consulted my colleagues and decided to declare that Congress had nothing to do with the new movement.

When Subhas Bose disappeared from his home and arrived at Kabul, he informed me through Japanese Embassy there. Captain Fujiwara informed me that Mr. Bose wanted to go to Japan. But, he told me, Japanese High Command were not prepared for that because they were afraid that his arrival in Japan would make the British suspicious of Japan's war intentions. After Netaji's arrival in Germany, in October, 1941, the German Embassy informed me that Netaji wanted me to proceed to Germany for consultations. The Ambassador told me that I could go on a Japanese ship to Brazil, as a Japanese citizen with Japanese passport, and thence I could fly to Germany by air. The preparations were under way, when on 8th December 1941, Japan attacked Pearl Harbour and Malay Peninsula and declared War against the Western Powers.

For some time I was feeling that Japanese did not like my contact with the Germans. I had lent the services of some Indian youngmen in Shanghai for German Broadcasting in Indian languages, who were paid by them. I had also got them publish Will Durant's well known, "CASE FOR INDIA", for free distribution among the English knowing people in China and Japan. I did not consider anything undesirable in such activities because we were fighting a common enemy . But, the Japanese wanted me to be exclusively in their camp and I was not prepared to mortgage my liberty of action, or to follow their dictate. The Japanese Kempaitai (Gestapo) interrogated me for hours to fine out I had any financial transaction with the Germans. When I told them frankly and they realised that neither from them nor from the Germans I received any funds either for the Indian freedom movement or for an personally, they left me alone. But, since then, I decided not to cooperate with them more than absolutely necessary to avoid a break and unpleasantness.

When, on 8th December, 1941, Japan declared War, we had to organise our active efforts and select a leader, I knew, the Japanese wanted Rash Bihari Bose to be the leader because he was a naturalised Japanese national and would be more amiable to their ideas and plans. When they consulted me, I promptly suggested Rash Behari Bose on the ground that he was senior to me; and I assured them of my co-operation wherever necessary. I considered that period to be a temporary phase because I had in mind the ultimate leadership of Netaji Subhas Chandra Bose. Raja Mahendra Pratap did not join. I had constantly kept Netaji informed of these developments through the German Embassy in Tokyo.

Rash Behari Bose was a revolutionary of old days when our activities consisted of secret sabotage and sporadic attack on British and pro-British Indian officials. With all his zeal to serve the cause of freedom he could not have been expected to lead a mass struggle during a war in 1942. Much less control or command a regular army. Our armed forces of ex-British Indian Army were well-trained and well-disciplined hardened soldiers and they would not have liked to fight under a virtual Japanese command. Japanese Army Officers, generally speaking, were of medieval mentality. They were brave fighters and commanders but they had very little knowledge of the training land habits of our soldiers of British Army. They were devoted to their Emperor and were ready to die for him because he was the symbol of their country and God. Japanese Naval officers were somewhat different in the scheme of War except where Naval warfare was concerned.

Japan High Command, i.e. the Japanese Army wanted to control and guide our freedom's fight. Naturally, they welcomed Rash Behari Bose with open arms. I considered it necessary in the interest of our struggle to continue to cooperate with the Japanese sponsored set up. After the British surrender at Singapore on 15th Feb. 1942, a preliminary conference of some Indian officers of surrenedered British Indian Army and Indian civilians of different East Asian regions was held in Tokyo from 28th to 30th March, 1942. I kept out of it to the great relief of the Japanese. But, most of the delegates expressed their astonishment at my absence. They came for lunch at my residence and I explained to them Why I did not attend. Then Mohan Singh secretly gave me a letter form one Swami Satyanand Puri, a devoted Indian revolutionary who was residing in Thailand and who was one of the delegates to Tokyo Conference. The plane carrying him and other two delegates (Capt. Akram and Sardar Pritam Singh) from Shanghai, was reported crashed in a mountain in south Japan, in danger and that he would explain everything when he met me. He never met me. I have a copy of terms and conditions on which I had offered to co-operate with the Japanese and of which one copy was forwarded to Netaji and other Indian leaders through Atul Sen, to Mr. Raghavan.

Tokyo Conference decided, among other things, to hold a larger conference in Bangkok in June, 1942. When Lt. Col. Kadomatsu, the Japanese incharge of Indian Affairs, came to request me to accompany Japan's Indian delegation to Bangkok, as its leader, I agreed in order to avoid bitterness and with future plan in view. Rash Behari Bose was to be the President and the leader of the whole conference. Debnath Das was already in Bangkok and was the Chairman of the Reception Committee of Bangkok branch of the Indian Independence League, and with the help of Mr. Raghavan of Penang, we got a resolution passed at the Conference, requesting Netaji to visit East and asking the Japanese and German Governments to facilitate his journey. This was not liked by the Japanese and the Rash Behari group of Tokyo Indians. No steps were taken to implement the resolution. I had already informed Netaji through German sources about the resolution. I, later, learnt that the Germans had consulted to send Netaji to Japan. But, the Japanese, reportedly, replied that as there was already a revolutionary Indian leader in the East, there was no need for another.

Japanese attitude in this matter was intelligible. They wanted a leader who would be guided and controlled by them and would not create any problem for them. They were aware of Netaji Subhas Chandra Bose's calibre. When Netaji defeated official candidates of the Congress for Presidentship and defied even Mahatma Gandhi, I had written in my paper, VOICE OF INDIA, "Subhas would gladly give his life but would not submit to any suggestion of compromise on the question of Indian independence, not even to Mahatma Gandhi, whom he respects as his father-"Japanese knew that they would not be able to control him, and they could not tolerate defiance of their operation. However, after the Bangkok Conference when the Council of Action was formed and the Headquarters moved to Singapore, within a short period it was clear that Rash Behari Bose could neither impress his colleagues in the Council nor the Indians of East Asia as a leader. There were constant differences between the Army officer and civilian wings of the council and neither of them respected President's opinion. Mohan Singh , who was designated as General and was Commander-in-Chief of Armed Forces, and his own ideas and ambitions. At last the climax came in January 1943 and the I.N.A. broke up and Gen. Mohan Singh was arrested. Japanese High Command at last realised that it was a folly to depend on such a leader and to conduct a war depending on the Indian Army of liberation that they could not control. And then they agreed to approach the Germans to arrange for Netaji to go to the East. When Netaji returned form Rangoon to Bangkok withdrawing his Head Quarters towards the end to the war, I told him that it was my greatest regret that, due to the folly of the Japanese, we could not secure his presence in th East before "QUIT INDIA" declaration of the Congress on 9th August 1942. Had the Japanese agreed to invite Netaji to go to Japan directly from Kabul or even a little later, and had we been able to enter

India with I.N.A. Forces simultaneously in August or September, 1942, the history of Indian freedom might have been written differently. That opportunity was lost due to the narrow minded and selfish attitude of the Japanese.

However, only after the collapse of the first I.NA. in January 1943, the Japanese realised that they had to request Netaji to visit East and take over the leadership of the I.N.A. They approached the Germans and the latter arranged for the hazardous journey of Netaji to the east by submarine. German sources informed me about Netaji's departure though they would not tell me the means of journey. The Japanese kept mum. At last, about the middle of June, I learnt that Netaji had arrived in Tokyo. My wife had met him. I heard his voice on Radio Tokyo, perhaps, on 21st June, 1943, I felt Japanese had deliberately kept me out of picture because they were afraid that, if I met Netaji before reaching Tokyo, I might have poisoned his mind by giving him facts of past developments. Or, perhaps, they were ashamed that they could not manage the things without Netaji, and had kept him out against our wishes.

Netaji arrive at Singapore on 2nd July, 1943. I was one of the first Indians to be with him at tea on arrival at his residence. He wanted to know facts about the happenings during the past months. We discussed various problems including our approach to Mahatma Gandhi, Jawaharlal Nehru and the Indian National Congress as a whole. We discussed our programme and plan for future move. He told me he heard everything from my wife in Tokyo regarding Japanese treatment to me and added, "they were sadly mistaken if they thought they could mislead me. I have seen enough of such games in the past in my life". He also told me about his plan to form a Provisional Government of Free India as soon as possible and to reorganise the I.N.A. and the India Independence League on modern lines. I promised him whole hearted co-operation under all circumstances. and dedicated myself to the cause under his leadership. I enjoyed his confidence to the last.

Rash Behari Bose handed over the leadership of the Movement to Netaji Subhas Chandra Bose formally on 4th July, 1943, at a conference of the Indians of East Asia, at the Cathay building of Singapore. Netaji, assuming the leadership, made a very impressive and emotional speech that touched the heart of the audience. The next day, 5th July, 1943, Netaji addressed the I.N.A. jawans and officers and again on 6th July, Netaji addressed them in the presence of Gen. Tojo. His talk to the jawans impressed rank and file of the I.N.A. as deeply as Gen. Tojo himself. The officers of the fauj regained their self-confidence and the civilians realised that atlast they have found a leader in which they could place their confidence unreservedly. Indian merchants all over East Asia began contributing to Azad Hind Fund liberally . Young Indians started pouring in to enrol as volunteers.

At the very first Press Conference arranged by the Japanese, when the Japanese Army Chief of Press Bureau welcomed Netaji, he assured him of all out Japanese aid to I.N.A., and asked him to let them know what help would be expected from them . Netaji with his usual politeness expressed his gratitude for the offer of help that he said was necessary and indispensible for the fight and said "For the present I want to make one request and that is that not to give us any help so long as we did not ask for it. I request that no propaganda or publicity be done on our behalf. We know that mind of our people and we shall address them ourselves in a way that would be conducive to our mutual interest I know, you need publicity for Japan to be directed to India. For this I would lend you some young men who would speak on your behalf as you desire. That would be your voice not ours. When we need your help I will certainly not hesitate to ask for it...." Language may not be exactly as mentioned. But, in substance that is what he said. And, the Japanese had no difficulty in realising the calibre of the leader they had to deal with.

Japanese had taught the Indian volunteers to salute their superiors in Japanese fashion, i.e. by taking off their cap and bowing. Netaji told the Japanese that the Indians had bowed to their alien rulers for centuries. "I want them now to learn to stand erect and look straight into the face of the officers when saluting and not top take off their head gear." Japanese agreed. Netaji gave us a new way of greetings, "Jai Hind". He gave the Azad Hind Fauj a new slogan, "Chalo Delhi" just as the old French Forces were given "Al Sa Ce Lauran" of German slogan "on to Paris".

All preparations complete, the Provisional Government of Azad Hind was formed on 21st October, 1943. And, at a very impressive ceremony in the same spacious hall of the Cathay Mansion of Singapore, in the presence of a large gathering of the representatives of Indians of different regions of East Asia, Netaji declared the establishment of the *Arazi Hukumate* Azad Hind, and took Oath of Allegiance and Loyalty to India and the cause of Indian fight for freedom. All the members of the Cabinet, then, took Oath of Allegiance, one by one, to Netaji under whom they promised to fight for the freedom of India. Besides being the Secretary to the Azad Hind Government, due to my knowledge and close contact with the Indians in East Asia, I was also later appointed Minister of Revenue and Man Power.

We needed both men and money and I had to tour all the countries east of Thailand where Indians were residing. I visited the territorial branches of the Indian Independence League; sent written appeal for men and appointed influential Indians 33 in each region to take up the work earnestly. The response was spontaneous and very encouraging. Even young women volunteered to be enrolled in Rani of Jhansi Regiment. Shanghai had a large population of Punjabis and in recruitment both men and women vied with each other.

At the very first meeting of the Cabinet on 21st October; 1943; we declared war against the Anglo-American Allies. Some members were of opinion that; as India was only under British domination, we should declare war only against the British. Netaji told them that "all those powers who were working for the helping our enemies were our enemies and we must declare war against all of them : He said "Our enemy's friends were our enemies. Our enemy's were our friends." The same evening it was also decided that a delegation of our Government should attend the GREATER EAST ASIA CONFERENCE in Tokyo in November, to which we were invited. Our delegation consisted of Netaji, the leader, Maj. Gen. J.K. Bhonsle, the chief of staff and, A.M. Sahay, Secretary to Netaji and Lt. Col Dr. D.S. Raja, Personal Physician to Netaji, were the two personal staff of Netaji.

In reply to the proposal that we should attend as full-fledged Delegation of the Greater East Asia Co-Prosperity Sphere Conference, as the Japanese called it, Netaji made it clear to the hosts that India was not yet independent land we had no territory of our own. Ours was a Government in Exile, and it was a Provisional Government. To join the Co-Prosperity Sphere or not could be decided only by the people of India when India was free. The Japanese appreciated our contention and we attended as Observers, although the Indian Delegation was given all honour and were treated at par with other delegations. In fact Netaji received much greater attention and commanded much greater respect than other leaders of the Conference, both by the Government and the people of Japan, almost to the point of Netaji becoming an object of envy.

The Conference being over, we sat down for business negotiations. We had quite a few important subjects to discuss and secure Japanese concurrence. Most important of them all was the transfer of Andaman and Nicobar groups of islands to our Government. We had to face certain difficulties in achieving this. The islands were, naturally, under Naval Command, They were very important because they were the first line of defence against any attack from Indian mainland. We had no Navy of our own . Thus, clearly, the presence of Japanese Navy was unavoidable in our mutual interest. Another difficulty was that the Burmese Government claimed it as their territory because the islands were far separated from India, were straight sougth of Burma, and there was a sizable population of Burmese settled there. We had prolonged discussions with Admiral Yamamoto, the Navy Minister of Japan. However, our contention was that for India it was impossible and totally unacceptable any party's claim on those islands because they were the symbols of our very struggle for freedom, Netaji told them that hundreds of our patriots were sent to the islands as political convicts for the fault of their love for India. Many of them died there. For those who were fighting for freedom, Andamans was symbolic of a shrine as Yasukuni or Ise Shrines were for the Japanese. This immediately touched Japanese sentiment and they agreed to our demand. However, we had to agree that we could not undertake the defence of the islands. So an arrangement was mutually made according to which some departments of Civil Administration like, Education, Agriculture etc. were to be undertaken by our Government and Defence and allied subjects were to be under Japanese control. We were engaged in a life and death struggle on the mainland and, even if allowed, we could not have been able to spare much, either in men or in money, for the territory thus transferred to us. However, it was of great importance for our prestige in international and constitutional realm. This gave us the status of a dejure Government with our own territory. I had every reason to feel proud because I had played an important part in getting the Japanese to agree to it due to my very friendly relations with some of the Japanese Naval senior officers who were negotiating on th side of the Japanese. I had also given hint to Netaji about the sentiment of the Japanese regarding their two Shrines mentioned above and Netaji took full advantage of that. Those shrines in Japan are of Imperial ancestors of the Japanese, and they hold them in highest esteem. Even, when declaring a war, they go to those shrines to pray for their blessings, to begin with.

Other subjects we had to discuss were about the printing of our own currency. I had to stay on in Tokyo to get the designs of our currency prepared according to the direction of Netaji. I had also to get all other stationaries of the Government printed in Tokyo. In this the German Embassy in Tokyo was of great help. They introduced me to their printers who supplied very high quality of papers for the purpose and the printing was equally of very high standard. Netaji was very pleased and satisfied when I presented the currency to him at Singapore on my return. He also liked the final designs of the currency notes, of our government. It was decided in Tokyo that after returning to our Headquarters at Singapore, Netaji would visit the Andamans to formally take over the administration and to unfurl our National Flag of Free India.

Netaji returned to Singapore, after visiting the Philippines. Shanghai etc. I returned later by the end of December after finishing the work assigned to me. Immediately after my arrival I was told that we had to proceed to the Andamans on 29th December, 1943. We took off early in the morning. Besides Netaji, the party consisted of Lt. Col. D.S. Raju Personal Physician to Netaji. We arrived in the Andaman in the afternoon, and were received by a large crowd of Indians, Burmese and Japanese officials. We were received by the Naval Commander of the Islands and escorted to the palatial residence of the Chief Commissioner of British Raj of old days. At an impressive ceremony Netaji formally took over the charge of the islands of Andaman and Nicobars. The Flag of Free India, the tricolour, was unfurled by Netaji in the presence of a large gathering amidst prolonged cheers. 30th December was full of engagements. Most important one was a visit to the notorious Cellular Jail where so many of our brave patriots were detained by the alien rulers of India for their fault of loving their motherland and died as martyrs. We visited Defence establishments of the Island, agricultural farms, children school etc. addressed large public meeting where the citizens presented purse to Netaji, interviewed some prominent Indians settled there and enquired about their problems and grievances and finally discussed the details of transfer of administration with the commander of the Naval Bose. Next morning on the 31st Dec. the National Flag of India was again unfurled at the official residence of the Chief Commissioner by Netaji. And we took off for Rangoon.

The programme was to reach Rangoon and declare the establishment of Advance Headquarters of Azad Hind Government there. However, when we were nearly half way between Andaman and Rangoon, a message came by wireless that the enemy planes were invading Rumree Island near Akyab on the western coast of Burma and it was considered undesirable to proceed to Rangoon at that moment. I have a feeling that it was a preplanned thing to keep the people in Andamans under the impression that we were proceeding to Burma, while actually Netaji was to proceed to

Bangkok as the guest of the Thai Government and then to move to Rangoon after a week or so. However, Netaji ordered the plane to proceed to Bangkok where arrangements were made for us to stay at Ratua Konshin Hotel, very near the Royal Palace.

All the arrangement being ready for starting our Advance Headquarters in Burma, we flew to Rangoon and Netaji occupied as his residence an impressive building previously belonging to a Parsee High officer of British days. He was given a warm welcome both by the Burmese and the Indians on his arrival at Rangoon. Soon after his arrival Netaji started preparations for sending the I.N.A. contingents to Indo-Burma border to start the war of liberation. Major Gen. M.Z. Kiani as Commander-in-Chief of one full division, with Lt. Col. Inayat Kiani commanding a Regiment under him. Maj. General Shaw Nawaz Khan, Col. Gulzara Singh and Col. Pritam Singh, as commanders of various regiments were sent to various fronts. We had some difficulty with command of forces on battle front.

Naturally the Japanese had more senior officers than we had and according to code no senior officer could work under the command of a junior officer. Yet, it was not possible to allow I.N.A., i.e. our forces of liberation of India to serve under any foreign and, it was not possible to allow the Japanese to act independently command. That was totally unacceptable to Netaji. However, after long negotiations, it was mutually agreed that while in Burma, the fighting forces may remain under all Japanese senior officers command, after entering Indian command and the Japanese contingents under the Japanese and they would work and fight in complete co-operation, and with complete understanding. A Committee of Indian and Japanese officers was formed. The Japanese wanted that the Chairman of the Committee be a Senior Japanese Officer. But, Netaji did not agree. And this was left undecided to be settled at very meeting according to the situation.

There were some Indians in Burma who were detained in Prison because they did not abide by the decisions of the Japanese to surrender their assets to the Japanese, after the British left Burma and the Japanese occupied the territory. After Netaji's arrival, a massage reached him about these Indians. I was sent to meet them in prison. I was surprised to find my old friend, Mr. S.M. Bashir, who was my close comrade in Japan in my national congress work there. He was a staunch nationalist and I could not believe the Japanese version that he was anti-I.N.A. He had a large rubber factory in Rangoon and he had refused to hand over that to the

Japanese. There were other similar cases. In the presence of the Japanese officer who went with me, I explained the purpose and the programme of the I.N.A. and for the satisfaction of the Japanese, I rebuked them for not co-operating. Bashir got up and refuted the charge and said they were all prepared to give not only the properties but also their life for Indian's freedom. "But that must be India's freedom". I assured them that justice will be done and returned to report the whole story to Netaji".

After some discussion with Netaji, we decided that we should tell the Japanese frankly that Indians in Burma were not enemies but allies of ours. Therefore, it was wrong even according to international practice of allies. I told them that all the Indians, throughout East Asia, from Japan to Burma, were the subjects and the citizens of free India; and it was for our Government to decide things about them. They argued that to fight the war, in mutual interest, we needed material those Indians had. I agreed and told them that we would find our ways and means to achieve that end. I suggested to Netaji that in response to his appeal for total mobilisation of the resources of Indians in East Asia to fight our war of liberations. We should persuade the Indian industrialists and prosperous traders to formally surrender their concerns to the Azad Hind Government and declare so. On our part, as we had no time to take care of those establishments our agents to manage their respective concerns and supply such goods as they manufactured and as we needed for our common war efforts. Netaji promptly agreed and asked me to tackle the Indians.

I had already such an assurance from those whom I met in Jail. I told the Japanese that whatever we needed from the Indians for our war efforts, that would come through us. As raw materials were needed for manufacturing things, we asked them to help us either by importing from other territories under them or securing from the Burmese. They in response to Netaji's call all Indian factories were surrendered to Azad Hind Government and without disturbing the working capacity, as mentioned above, they were allowed to manufacture goods required by the fighting forces. We i.e. the Japanese, supplied materials as and when required and paid minimum wages to the workers through us. The largest estate of Ziawadi, of Hariji of Dumraon, that produced sugarcane and had large sugar factory, was under the management of Shri Parmanandji, who joined our struggle and took leading part in various capacities. He placed the estate at the disposal of Azad Hind Government and the management continued as it was.

A Committee to collect donations for Netaji Fund was appointed by Netaji, of which Mr. Hamid, a multimillionaire of Burma, was made the Chairman and Shri S.M. Bashir, the Vice-Chairman. Collection of funds started with a big bang. Shri Hamid had already enrolled as total mobiliser by giving away his entire huge assets to Azad Hind Govt. and enrolling himself as volunteer of the Fauj. Netaji in his speeches always asked the Indians to take : "HAMID MIXTURE" to get intoxicated with the spirit of freedom. He once said, "Some say, Hamid has gone mad. I agree. I want every one of you Indians to get mad to achieve Victory and freedom of our motherland. We need such mad men and women." He declared more than once that he was not going to ask the Japanese allies for financial help before the Indians have given for the fight all they have. He said "We are fighting for Indians. We can ask others to help only when our own resources have exhausted. There can be no justification to beg from others before that." And the Indians wholeheartedly responded, irrespective of social, religious or another distinctions. Volunteers poured in for recruitment. Camp were started and the training started. Women vied with men and joined Rani Jhansi Camp as cadets and volunteers. Materials like textiles, medicines and grains were donated so liberally that, Gen, Takhin Aung San, the Prime Minister of Burma , once told me at a dinner in Delta area, that I gave in his honour while visiting the area at the same time, that he wondered whether Burma was the island of Burmese or of Indians. He said, "While we are unable to meet the expenses of even administration from taxes and Burmese contributions you just make and appeal and millions of rupees, hundreds of tons of rice, gold medicines etc. in large quantities pour in." They were openly jealous of our position and popularity of Netaji. Another friend of mine in Burma's Government, Takhin Tan Tun, a communist and Minister of Agriculture, came to me and asked me to help him in collecting funds for his government. Takhin U Nu, Prime Minister of Burma after the War, was very friendly with us and was always prepared to co-operate whenever I approached.

By the end of 1944 our Azad Hind Fauj Jawans were already fighting on different front, inside India, and had liberated some parts of our motherland. Netaji wanted our Headquarters to move forward. Azad Hind Dal was organised to prepare the administrative wing of our government to take over the responsibility of civil administration in liberated areas. Netaji appointed. Lt Col. Ehsan Qadir as the leader and myself as the Deputy leader of Azad Hind Dal and asked us to proceed to Maymyo. We had to travel in coal loaded wagons. Netaji himself was present at the railway platform of Rangoon to send us off. At night our train was attacked by enemy planes, but we escaped any casualty. The bomb fell just outside the railway station by the side of the line and made more than 10 feel deep ditch. In the morning we were received at the Ziawadi railway station by Shri Parmanandji and we were escorted to his residence where we had a rest and lunch.

Immediately after the establishment of our Headquarters in Rangoon was announced, Netaji addressed himself to get our forces ready to march towards Indo-Burma border. Vigorous training of our Jawans in various types of Guerilla warfare and jungle operations were undertaken in various camps. Units of Rani Jhansi Regiment also started vigorous practice. As October approached we also decided to celebrate the first anniversary of the formation of the Azad Hind Government on an impressive scale. Apart from other programme one particular event must remain memorable for all those who participated in it. On 18th Oct. 1944, at about 10 a.m. a grand parade of a full regiment was arranged at the parade ground outside Rangoon, when all the minister present in Rangoon, all the officer of the I.N.A and a large number of High officers of the Japanese Army in Rangoon were invited and were present. Netaji was to address the contingent.

The programme started exactly in time. After preliminaries. Netaji went to the rostrum to receive the salute and march past started. Just then an AcAc shell burst hitting a Jawan and blowing off his head. We could not understand where did the shell come from. But General Shah Nawaz Khan, immediately went to Netaji and asked him to come down. Netaji unmindful of his request, remained standing. This made Gen. Shah Nawaz unhappy and he told Netaji that the danger is approaching and he would not allow him to play with the life of a full Regiment beside Netaji's himself. Other senior officer also jumped to the rostrum and strongly pleaded for that he comes down without delay. Netaji, most reluctantly came down the rostrum and the Jawans were ordered to quick march to safety in bush or barracks. We, along with Netaji hurried to a nearby bamboo bush and took shelter there. Within seconds after that more than twenty enemy fighter planes swooped over the ground and riddled the whole area, shelling the ground and vicinity indiscriminately for nearly twenty minutes. Very fortunately, there was not a single casualty thanks due to the thick bamboo bush and timely warning of our AcAc shell. Had we not left the place so quickly, this might have proved the greatest tragedy and might have put our whole plan of future fight to a halt. The existence of the whole Regiment of I.N.A. was at stake, besides the large number of our senior officers and

Netaji himself. His car went to another station, about fifteen miles ahead, where our train was resting for the day. We travelled only at night, to avoid enemy vigilance. Next morning, having reached Mandalay, we travelled to Maymyo the Hill station of Burma, by road and were accommodated in spacious Government English High School. Our contingent consisted of administrators, office assistant, stenographers, engineers, electricians, mechanics, some military guards and volunteers, including an unit of Rani Jhansi Regiment. Advance units of Azad Hind Dal volunteers had already gone ahead of us and were awaiting our arrival in various places on way to the Indian border.

After a few weeks Netaji also arrival from Rangoon. Advance Headquarters of Azad Hind Fauj and Government were announced to have been established there. Pending Netaji's arrival we had organised the inhabitants of Maymyo to start working for the movement. An office of the Independence League was started. Women section of the League was also organised and young Indian women enrolled to be the members of the Rani Jhansi Regiment. We were anxious to march forward. Gen Chatterjee was appointed the Governor of liberated area. We were anxiously waiting news of progress from the Front lines. But, the Japanese informed us that they were receiving no message from the fighting front. From Indian source we learnt that our forces were suffering due to shortage of food and medicines. Netaji immediately decided to send a Mission to the front to assess the situation and to carry some medicine. ration and cash for the Fauj.

In the meantime, one night, our camp was subjected to heavy bombardment by the enemies. Just after dinner, at about 9 p.m. waves of bombers carried on continuous bombing for nearly culvert and keeping them there under the bridge. About fifteen of them were in another shelter the entrance of which were completely blocked by a bomb that fell nearby throwing large chunks of earth to the entrance. After the raid, when I was going around to check the casualty, I heard some noise from one of the shelters. Volunteers were immediately called, the blocked entrance was cleared and all the Ranis were safely brought out. Very fortunately, there was no casualty in our camp in that night's raid, though most of our vehicles were damaged and the building was badly damaged. Next morning Netaji visited the camp and we were ordered to shift to other places and Gen. Chatterjee, Capt Rawat, A.D.C. to Netaji, and myself escorted the Rani to a well protected area in a thick wood by the side of I.N.A. hospital. On our way we encountered a reconnaissance enemy plane flying very low and I had to stop the truck, order the running from one tree to another to avoid the enemy's eyes. Later, he himself told me that never in his life he had run for safety like that. We ourselves moved to a Reserve forest where thatched barracks were immediately constructed for us. I got some materials collected from the fallen school building and our mechanics and carpenters built a nice little hutment with a dining-cum-sitting room and a bedroom, bath attached, within three days for me.

After a few days, according to plan, we started on our trek to the battle fronts. Gen. Alagappan, the Supply and Health Minister, Gen. Chatterjee, Minister of Finance and Governor designate for liberated area, and myself along with some of our aides and officials of India Independence League of Indo-Burmese border area, started from Mandalay in a car and a truck with loads of sweet packed in gunny bags. We had to leave the vehicles on the eastern bank of Irrawady river because the available boats could not carry them across. We unload the ration and other belongings and carried to the western coasts and therefrom we managed to secure two trucks to take us forward. It took us several days to reach More and Tamu travelling at nights and hiding in some safe bush during the days, to avoid enemy reconnaissance. The party had to face unusual hazards including some accidents and breakdown of our transport. Trucks had to pass on narrow strip of roads with high hills on one side and deep river on the other and all this in dark nights because we could not use head lights for fear of being detected by the constant enemy planes flying over head. We also met our comrades in some places, including wounded and ailing Jawan brought back from the front, parties of Azad Hind Dal etc. We distributed ration and money to our contingents according to need.

At More we found our camp on the bank of a river waiting for us to arrive and give them line clear to proceed to the liberated areas to take over the Civil Administration. Shri D.M. Khan was in command.

As it was necessary to assess situation and get first hand information before asking our administrative machinery to proceed further, we decided to visit the fighting front and see the thing for ourselves. We crossed the official border between India and Burma that was shown by a sign Board of British days. Some Japanese news men had also accompanied us and they promptly took our snaps. We met enemy planes on the way. But they could no do any harm because the mountain roads were so zigzag that by the time they located us we took another turn and went out of their sight. At last at about midnight we reached Chamol, a place where he had to leave the truck and walk down the hill to reach the underground headquarters of Gen. Kiani's Division. There I was so delighted to meet Major Hassan, Col. Pritam Singh and Col. Enayat Kiani, the latter being the commander of the contingent presently fighting very near Imphal a few miles ahead of us. They were in high spirit.

Next day we paid a visit to Gen. Yamamoto. the Div. Commander of the Japanese Army, about a mile away on the other side of hill. Gen Alagappan and myself visited him because Gen Ghatterjee met an accident just a few hours before when an enemy shell burst from the opposite hill and a splinter slightly burnt his abdomen and he was lying in the shelter. The Japanese Commander gave us the information regarding the existing position of fighting front. Although, he did not say so, I realized that they were not in a position to do much to help the fight. They were not able to supply ration to our Jawan, their transport and communication had almost broken down. Our injured and sick Jawans had neither medicine nor other aid. On the other hand the Monsoon was fast approaching and that would flood all the rivers making supply position almost impossible. And then in that condition, even withdrawal would become impracticable. I, therefore, felt that our troops had to withdraw to Rangoon and be reorganised. I was confident, after the rainy season, it would have been possible for us to return to Manipur and give a good fight. In the mean time, I felt we could collect money, materials and ration from the Indians and equip our forces sufficiently to continue the fight and liberated Eastern part of Assam, including Manipur. Although Gen. Chatterjee did not agree with me, I decided to report to Netaji on those lines after returning to our Headquarters. Having finished our work, I became anxious to return. We returned to our camp at More on the following day and an immediately started for Mandalay & Maymyo. At Yeu, our Transport Depot, we changed our means of transport and travelled by our own cars and jeeps. After a hectic journey, we reached Mandalay on 7th June, 1944, only on learn that Netaji had already left Maymyo for Rangoon and had asked us to proceed to Rangoon.

The journey to Rangoon was equally trying and we had to face the fury of unusually heavy rain during the journey. Having returned to Rangoon we met Netaji, who informed us that he had already received report about the deteriorating condition on front and had ordered for the withdrawal of troops from Imphal (Manipur) sector before the rain set in and the rivers are flooded. Work had already started in Rangoon to reorganise the Azad Hind Fauj and to improve supply and Transport condition. We needed rice, medicine and money to replenish our stocks. Netaji asked me to form a team and to tour for the purpose. The Delta area, south of Rangoon was considered the rice bowl of Burma. The area was not yet tackled. We also expected donations to our War fund from the Indians of Delta.

I organised a team consisting of my friend and industrialist, Mr. S.M. Bashir, Mr. Nachiappan, and a number of other members of the Indian Independence League who were well acquainted with that area. We requisitioned a motor boat and started on our tour, probably in the third week of June. There were a large number of Chattiar owning rice mills. There were flourishing Muslim merchants and also a large number of stockists of medicine. They all came forward and liberally contributed to our fund. Some of Indian ladies donated also their gold ornaments. We received several hundred tons of rice for our Fauj, stock of medicine and nearly two crores of rupees in cash. We had also places. Mr. Bashir was very helpful in our efforts because he knew the people of the area and was well known to them. When we returned to Rangoon and reported the result to Netaji, he was very satisfied.

In Sep 1944, Netaji asked me to proceed to the Philippines and China to collect funds and to inspect the work of the League and Azad Hind Volunteers Corps. after Saigon I had to take a seat in a bomber that took me to Shanghai after a night's halt in Hainan. Immediately on arrival at Shanghai, I started visiting various camps of the I.N.A. volunteers where the training had started by Captain B. Narain, an Ex-Army officer. I called a meeting of the Indians of Shanghai in the local Gurudwara and appealed for men and money. I also sent a representative to Tientsin and Dairen with our appeal for funds. The response was very encouraging. Volunteers also started pouring in for recruitment. Quite a number of young Sikh women enrolled themselves for training and wanted to be sent to the front as early as possible. I had also made some changes in the structure of the Indian Independence League of Shanghai. Mr. Jalal Rahman, a tried national worker of Japan and Shanghai India National Association, was made the chairman of the China Territorial Committee, Shri Nanik Ram an old merchant was nominated as the Chairman of the Shanghai branch and concurrently Treasurer of the Territorial Committee along with one Harnam Singh. In the meantime, by the end of Nov. 1944, I was informed by the Japanese Liaison Officer, that Netaji was arriving at Shanghai with his party for a short visit on his way back from Tokyo. I received them at the Air Port. The journey had to be kept a secret. The party was escorted to Cathey Hotel where a suite and about 10 other bed rooms were reserved for them. We held a number of meetings of the local Indians where Netaji spoke at length about the achievements of our Azad Hind Fauj on various fronts. He also visited the Training Camps for volunteers an also the Gurudwara where the women volunteers of Rani of Jhansi Camp presented a guard of honour. Netaji also visited Nanking where some Indians were residing. His party consisted of Gen. M.Z. Kiani, Gen. A.C. Chatterjee, Col. Habibur Rahman and his personal staff. As the birth day of Netaji was approaching, I decided to stay for the celebration in Shanghai to encourage the League and Fauj officials and Volunteers. Before leaving Shanghai, Netaji had asked me to visit Tokyo returning to Burma to attend to some pending work regarding the printing of currency notes. Actually, I felt, he wanted me to meet my family in Tokyo before returning to the front.

The celebration of Netaji's birth day was a grand function. I inspected the volunteers, hoisted national flag. I received Guard of Honour by them and Rani of Jhansi volunteers. I spoke on various functions. I distributed sweet meats among the children at Gurudwara. At the main function where I inspected the parade and guard of honour was presented to me a large number of Japanese, German and Italian high official and Army officers, besides the representatives of the Chinese Government attended the function, in spite of the biting cold. Assured of continued efforts by Rahman, Nanik Chand and Harman Singh and other members of the League office in Shanghai, I left China for Tokyo by a plane on 10th February, 1945 reaching Nagasaki after a few hours. From Nagasaki I had to travel by train, reaching Nagasaki after a few hours. From Nagasaki I had to travel by train, reaching Tokyo on 13th Feb. There my two elder daughters, Asha (Bharati) and Tulu (Razya) were on the platform to receive me besides the Japanese official, and Rama Murti, the Chairman of the Japan League.

Although I did not like it, I was detained in Japan for more than a month for want of transport facilities. The enemy reconnaissance had also increased. My wife and children wanted to go to the front and work there for the country. Taking everything in to consideration, that was not possible. My third daughter and my son, the youngest one were already in a far off forest village, sent for safety by the authorities. I found that my wife was ailing and was almost invalid due to Arthritis. I, therefore, wanted to take the two elder daughters with me. However, Japanese knew that the War was coming to an end and told me that unless I wanted my wife to be left to die unattended, I should not take away both of my grown up daughters from her. Helplessly, I had to leave the younger one (Tulu) to look after the mother. But, Asha, the eldest was determined to accompany me. She said Netaji had promised her that. I agreed and got her ready to the journey.

Our journey back was full of hazards and very exciting. We travelled by train from Tokyo to Nagasaki. From there after a few days we were flown to Taihoko (south Taiwan) in a civilian plane. On the way we encountered enemy reconnaissance plane and were asked to tighten our belt for any emergency. However, we landed at Taihoku air port safely and stayed in Railway Hotel for nearly a month, again for want of transport facilities. Every night enemy bombers dropped bombs near about the places. Then we were asked to proceed to central Taiwan (Taichu) by train. On the way at about midnight, train stopped because enemy planes had bombarded the track and train could not proceed further. Early next morning when the train started, on the way it had to pass through a tunnel up the hill. The engine failed to draw the train. We had to get down and all the passengers had actually to push the train through the tunnel. The Governor of Taichu received us at the Railway station on arrival at Taichu and escorted us to a Japanese hotel, the best of the town. We were given a suite of rooms. But, here too, every forenoon we had undesirable visitors, the enemy planes. As soon as the danger siren sounded we had to rush to a shelter by the side of a nearby canal. The fighter planers shelled the area mercilessly. One day while we were in the shelter a bullet aimed at the hotel hit its window, pierced through the paper sliding door in to my sitting room, hit the telephone and lodged on the mat there. When we returned we found it lying there.

There after authorities decided that every morning we should be escorted to a far off village temple or in some bush for safety. Thereafter our daily routine was to take our breakfast in the hotel and then rush in a car or a jeep to some far off Buddhist Temple and spend the day. Some days we spent our days in the hutment of a Formosan (Taiwanese) farmer, who would prepare rice and some vegetables for us, for our lunch. One day I asked them to get some spice like chili, garlic, onion, etc. and their cooking oil and prepared Indian curry. And we enjoyed it with rice that they used to eat. They were so happy that they wanted me to come every day. I found that they liked spiced vegetables or meat as we do.

Our departure from Taichu was again unusually delayed due to lack of transport. At last in the third week of April, our Japanese friends informed me that an Army plane was flying to Saigon that night and we may be able to take advantage of this facility. I immediately agreed. We went to the air strip at about midnight. The driver had to search in the dark for the starting point for about half an hour to locate the place. At last the Commandant of the Base addressed the crew as follows: "You are going to the south. As you know the plane is very new and you have the responsibility of carrying valuable guests of another country, you must do your duty fully conscious of your country's honour." He perhaps did not know that we could understand his language. Asha asked me if I understood what he meant. I noded, and said we have to face the situation. So we left at about 1 a.m., stopped at about 9 a.m. in a small place, pushing the plane to a hiding place under a tree and then walking about two miles to rest for the day. In the evening we again took off on our final hope arriving next morning at Saigon and thence to Bangkok airport in the afternoon. I was greatly concerned about my daughter because she was so young and this was her first experience. But, she proved courageous beyond expectation and calmly faced all that came, At Bangkok we learnt that our troops had withdrawn from Rangoon and they were coming to Bangkok with Netaji, we waited there for his arrival. He arrived after a few days with the contingent of Rani Jhansi and some officers of Azad Hind Fauj. He declared that "our fight had not ended. We lost only the first battle and our men had done marvellously well. We will reorganise our Force and march again." A camp for the training of Rani of Jhansi cadets was started and training started. My daughter Asha was admitted as a cadet. Training in other camps were started. Consultations were held for future steps. Collection of funds and materials were started. But, Netaji knew that the Japanese were not in a position to continue the fight and we had to find some other means to continue our fight on some other front if India could not achieve freedom after that war. When in Tokyo, Netaji had approached the Japanese to help him in contacting the Soviet embassy. But the Japanese did not agree. When Netaji told me about it after returning from Rangoon, I told him that there were some other ways to approach the Soviet.

Early in 1945, when it became evident that Japan may not be able to continue war for long, and when they refused to allow Netaji to contact the Soviet Embassy in Tokyo, we decided to make direct effort, secretly, to contact Communists in China. Netaji was determined to continue our fight for freedom from some other theatre. He calculated that the Anglo-Soviet friendship was a marriage of convenience and might not survive long after the war. Thus was decided to seek collaboration with U.S.S.R. in case India was not free after the war.

I informed Netaji that when I visited Yanching University in 1938, I had met a number of Chinese professors who were prominent members of the Chinese Communist Party and were friendly of India. They could be contacted through Hanoi. This had to be kept guarded secret from the

Japanese. Accordingly, Netaji sent Gen. Chatterjee and myself for collection of funds. Later I proceeded to Hanoi. ostensibly, for the same purpose. There I contacted the revolutionary Vietnamese and two trusted young men were despatched to Chungking, the Headquarters of Generallissimo Chiang Kai Sheck Government of what was called Nationalist China, to contact and negotiate with the Chinese Communist leaders to help us in surrendering to Soviet Forces in Manchuria when the Japanese surrendered to them.

I was confident that when Japan's defeat became imminent, U.S.S.R. would not leave the strategic Manchuria to be occupied by the Anglo-Americans. Unfortunately, Japan's collapse came earlier than expected, due to American atom bombing. And, our plan did not materialise. On August 17th, 1945 Gen. Chatterjee, Major Abid Hasan, John Thivy, Col. Gulzara Singh, Col. Pritam Singh and Debnath Das arrived at Hanoi, quite unexpectedly, and informed me that Netaji had left for Japan. They joined me and were accommodated in the same house where I was staying with some Japanese civilian officials. On the evening of 18th August, Tokyo Radio announced Netaji's plane crash in Taihoku, the capital of Taiwan, and his demise. We did not believe it. I thought it was a planned as camouflage to mislead the enemy.

The North Vietnam was to be occupied by the Chinese Forces and the British Forces were to occupy south of the 17th parallel latitude. This news came to us to our great relief. After a while, where the Chinese Forces arrived and occupied North Vietnam with their Headquarters at Hanoi, under the command of Gen. Lo Han, Gen. Chatterjee and myself called on him by appointment and offered to be arrested. But, he refused and asked us as to why should he arrest us. The conversation was interesting; and, if I remember correctly, it was as follows:

General Lohan	:	What have you done to be arrested?
Sahay	:	We fought against the British.
Gen.	:	Did you fight against the Chinese?
Sahay	:	Netaji asked us not to do so.
Gen.	:	But, you collaborated with our enemies no?
Sahay	:	Yes, that was the tragedy. We collaborated with your enemies and you collaborated with ours. But, neither of us fought for them, did we?

The General was silent for a moment and then he laughed and said, "You may go and live as free man or go away wherever you want. No Britisher can touch you within my territory, unless my Government ask me to hand you over to them ."

Thus, till 22nd December, 1945, we remained free men and went about as such. On 20th December, a Sindhi merchant of Hanoi, Mr. Kewal Ram, came and informed me that a British Colonel Wilson, had arrived and wanted me to go and meet him. I had already learnt that a British Military Mission under Col. Wilson had come to Hanoi and was making enquiries about us. Two days earlier, my car was removed from my gardage at midnight by some armed men, supposed to be the agents of Col. Wilson. I told Kewal Ram that I knew why I was called but I was no prepared to go. I said, "As I am a Minister of Azad Hind Government and Col. Wilson is just an Army officer, my rank was higher than that of a Colonel. If he wants to meet me, please ask him to come and see me at my residence." Kewal Ram was upset and pleaded with me saying that he can arrest me by force. I told him, "You are just a messenger and should take a message to him." Very reluctantly he went back only to return with in a short time to report that the Colonel had agreed to visit me an wanted time to be fixed.

The next day 21st of December, the monthly Azad Hind Day and I invited Col. Wilson to come and have tea with me. I had the national flag of India and that of Ho Chi Minh's Vietnam beautifully displayed on the wall of my drawing room along with the photos of Netaji and Ho Chi Minh. The Colonel stared at them rather with interest. He told us frankly that he was sent to "Collect" us. I told him equally frankly that we were prepared provided we are taken to Delhi. He said he would consult his Headquarters at Singapore and would meet again the next day.

The next day, i.e. 22nd Dec. 1945, at about 5 P.M. two cars pulled up in front of my residence to escort us, as arranged. On our way, Colonel was waiting at the pavement and entered my car and told me that, instead of meeting at the appointed place, we would proceed to his office. He told us that he had received instructions that air transport was coming to fly us on the following morning via Saigon. When we reached his office a Chinese unit formally handed us over to the British and withdrew. On our request Col. Wilson readily agreed to escort us to our residence to collect our belongings. I distributed the heavy items among my neighbours and servants and packed my bedding and suitcases to be taken with us. I had already arranged with my Vietnamese comrades to broadcast our arrests from their station the same day and they, kindly, did it.

We spent the night at the office of Col. Wilson and were next morning flown to Saigon, Where we spent the night in some barrack. On arrival at Saigon airport when our luggages were unloaded I found that one of the suitcases, containing important document, cash and clothing, was missing. Evidently, it was deliberately removed by Colonel's men. I wrote to the Colonel complaining. But, there was no reply. The next morning, on 24th. Dec. 73, we were flown to Singapore where were lodged in two different Jails-Myself, Gen. Chatterjee, John Thivy and Abid Hasan in Pearl Hill Prison and Col. Gulzara Singh and Col. Pritam Singh in notorious Changhi Prison. (Deb Nath Das had already slipped out to Thailand before our arrest). In jail we were lodged in single cells with just one wooden Chowki, two blankets and a bucket for easing. Every morning we had to carry our buckets to a ditch, empty them, clean them and bring them to our cells. After entering the prison. I took things easy and made myself at home.

I wrote to my wife in Japan to inform her about my arrest. I told her that I was prepared to face the worst gladly, and that I was proud of what I had done to serve the cause of my country's freedom. I asked her to return home and take proper care of the children. During my last visit to Tokyo, before the end of the war, I had brought my eldest daughter Asha (Bharati) with me to Bangkok and she had joined the Rani Jhansi Regiment as a Cadet and with in very short time of training she had become an officer in the rank of 2nd Lieutenant. I did not know her fate. After being detained in solitary cells for some time, we were later taken to better solitary cells, meant for European prisoners, with sanitary toilet attached. Australian soldiers, working as wardens, became friendly with me and used to bring informations regarding happenings in India. We were also allowed to spend the day time with other I.N.A. prisoners in an enclosure with in the jail. My younger brother, Satya Dev Sahay, who was incharge of Intelligence of Azad Hind Government, was in hiding in Singapore and Malaya. He contacted me with the help of Indian wardens of the Jail and used to supply Indian food every day and other needed articles through them. Later we secured permission to get our daily meals openly from Indian friends in Singapore. I became friendly with the English Jailor by helping him in translation work. Gradually, I received all amenities of life like laundry, hot water for shaving etc. with the permission of the Jailor. I was also made-in-charge of jail bakery and pantry where best of cakes and pastries of Singapore were made for white officers in the city. I enjoyed cakes and coffee every afternoon. Indian wardens of the Jail greatly respected us as patriots and were very helpful. I took to walking and running around the compound every afternoon before taking a good shower bath.

In Feb. 1946, one Rai Bahadur Bakshi Badrinath of the Intelligence Dept. of the Govt. of India, came to Singapore to Interrogate us. Gen Chatterjee and Major Abid Hasan were greatly harassed by him during the interrogation. When they told me about their experience I decided to be tough with him when my turn came. I told him at the outset that I would tell him frankly and fearlessly what I knew and what I did, if he dealt with me like a gentleman, I reply to his queries I gave a detailed factual reply at every point. I think he was convinced that I was not trying to conceal anything. I gave him more than he wanted, so much so that he once remarked that I was myself trying to put the noose round my neck. I retorted, "Rai Bahadur I know, Your British bosses know what I have during the last twenty-five years. They would not spare me if I even kept mum. I am prepared to go to gallows proudly. If I am saved. I would be certainly not due to any mercy from your bosses but only due to the strength of my countrymen"

I did not know much about the negotiations that were then going on in Delhi nor about the Great Trial of my brave comrades of the I.N.A. in Red Fort. until the Australian warden came to my cell at 10.30 P.M. and informed me that Shah Nawaz, Prem Saigal and Gurubaksh Dillon were Court Martialled, acquitted and cashiered at Red Fort and were defended by Jawaharlal Nehru and Bulabhai Desai. Later H.N. Kunzru, P.N. Sapru and Kodanda Rao visited us in Jail and told us that efforts were being made to release us. I told them that our release was not as important as the freedom of India. On 19th March 1946, Jawahar Lal Nehru visited us. I knew about his visit to Singapore a couple of days back from the Indian Warden and I had written a welcome address for him in Hindi verses. I had it written in beautiful letters. And made two copies outside the jail with the help of my brother Satya Dev Sahay. Before Jawaharlal visited us in Jail, Satya Dev, had already presented a copy to him. So when he visited us and when I presented it to him, he remarked, "I have already received it."

The Jailor informed me on 26th March, 46, that we were to be unconditionally released on 30th March, 46, because the Civil Authorities were to take over the administration of Singapore I came back to my barrack and told my comrades in a depressed tone that I had a bad news for us. Many were scared and pressed me to divulge it. Then I told them that we were to be released unconditionally; and they cursed me for frightening them. I said, my problem was that, while I was enjoying all the amenities of life in Jail, once out I did not know where were I to go and how to manage without funds. Earlier, a batch of Indian Civilian prisoners of the I.N.A.

were also brought from Bangkok, including Parmanandji, Sardar Isar Singh, Pandit Raghunath Sharma and others. They informed me that my daughter, Lt. Bharati (Asha) was safe and with the family of Pt. Raghunath Sharma. I was greatly relieved.

Eleven days after Jawaharlal Nehru came to see us, we were released on 30th March 1946, in the morning at 9 a.m. I dressed up in full I.N.A. uniform with shining top boots all complete and went to the superintendent to take leave. He looked at me, smiled and said, "It seems you are going to fight again." I replied, "Our fight is not yet over. India must win her freedom before our fight ends." And we parted. Many patriotic Indians greeted us at the gate, even garlanded us and escorted us to their respective homes. I was taken to one Major Misra's House where I stayed for nearly four months before I was permitted to return home. My daughter Lt. Bharati came and joined me there from Bangkok. Thus ended my life as a soldier of NETAJI and his Arazi Hukumate Azad Hind.

Jai Hind.

Appendix-II

Interrogative Report of Anand Mohan Sahay[1] (Extract)

Great Asia Conference

12. In about Sep 26 (1926), the Japanese organised a gathering called the "Great Asia Conference" at Nagasaki. Delegates were invited by the Reception Committeee from all over ASIA but as none could come from INDIA the following were accepted as Indian delegates :–

(a) Rash Behari Bose

(b) Keshio Ram Sabarawal (Punjabi) – Deported by the Japanese in 1937 on suspicion of having Russian contacts. Last seen by H/1459 at Dairen in 1937.

(c) Vidhya Dhar Bakshi – Left JAPAN about 1926.

The conference was also attended by representatives from China, Philippines, Java and SIAM. Resolution on Asiatic unity to accomplish the "Resurgence of ASIA" were passed. Raja Mahendra Pratap – then in Manchuria, was also to come to Japan for the Conference, but he was refused entry because he had no passport, and was returned by the same steamer to Tientsin or Dairen.

Business Trip in the Far East and Visit to India

13. In Nov 26 H/1459 went on a tour to Hong Kong, Bangkok , Malaya, Ceylon and India, for business purposes. In India he visited Dr. Rajendra Prasad, M. Gandhi, S. C. Bose and other political leaders of his acquaintance. He informed them of the ignorance of the Japanese

---

1. C.S.D.I.C. Report I.N.A. Papers. H/1459 number was allotted to Anand Mohan Sahey. Other prominal leaders of the I.N.A. Who were interogeated by the C.S.D.I.C. were allotted similar numbers. These reports of the C.S.D.I.C. which are frequently mentioned in these document are available in the National Archives of India amongest I.N.A. papers which were previously in the custody of the Historical Section of the Ministry of Defence, New Delhi. Some of these reports are available amongst the War Office Papers at the Public Record Office, London. Sahey's account is very important for understanding the Japanese Policy towards I.N.A.

about conditions, political, cultural and spiritual, in India. During this visit H/1459 married the daughter of Urmila Devi, a national worker of Calcutta and sister of the late C. R. Das. By this marriage he has 3 daughters and one son. As he had always intended to return to India he had his children registered with the British Consulate at Kobe, to ensure their Indian nationality. His eldest daughter is now in Bangkok with the family of Pt. Raghunath Sharma. The rest of his family is in Tokyo.

The Return to Japan

14. H/1459 and his wife left Calcutta in Sep 27. They broke their journey at Singapore for business reasons, and reach Kobe in October. Soon after their arrival in Japan H/1459 delivered a speech under the auspices of the India Club on the situation in India.

Raja Mahendra Pratap in Japan

15. About the end of 1927 or early 1928 Raja Mahendra Pratap visited Kobe and H/1459 arranged a public meeting of the Indian to unable Raja Mahendra Pratap to express his views. At this meeting Raja Mahendra Pratap described his own activities in Germany during the war of 1914/1918 and his subsequent work in Afghanistan, Moscow, America and China. He claimed that he had collaborated with the Germans to secure armed assistance for the liberation of India and described how later on he was received by Amir Amar Ullah in Kabul and by the Soviet leaders in Moscow. Raja Mahendra Pratap possessed a number of photographs of his visits to foreign countries which he showed to his audience.

16. The Indian National Congress Committee in Japan had the following objects:–

(a) Political and cultural propaganda in order to create better understanding and friendhsip between India and Japan.

(b) To make efforts to raise the prestige of the Indian Merchants in Japan in the eyes of the Japanese and thus to secure better facilities for trade.

(c) Helping Indian students in their higher studies.

In order to achieve this H/1459 started a monthly journal called "Voice of India" and established a boarding house called "India Lodge" in KOBE. He also made efforts to foster unity between the various Indian communities, and to develop national feelings.

National anniversaries were observed on 4 occasions in the year:–

(a) Indian Independence Day (26 January)

(b) Id

(c) Diwali

(d) Parsi New Year

Outbreak of War in Europe

17. Soon after the outbreak of War in 1939 H/1459 called a meeting of the Indians under the auspices of the Indian National Association at Kobe and after a review of the situation in India a resolution was passsed similar to that of the AICC which had protested against the Govt of India's declaration of war. More meetings were held, one of which was addressed by Raja Mahendra Pratap who said that the fullest advantage should be taken of the war to obtain freedom of India. H/1459 and Raja Mahendra Pratap teared Japan addressing meetings on the lines of Congress attitude towrads the war. H/1459 also wrote newspaper articles on the subjects, and issue pamphlets for the Indian National Association reproducing speehes and statements of Congress leaders as well as the correspondence between the Congress and the Govt of India on the India subject of the war and Congress demands. He frequently visited Shanghai in connection with this propaganda.

18. During one of these visits to Shanghai, a German journalist called on H/1459 for an interview during which H/1459 stated that India had no liking for Fascism or Nazism, and that Indians were equally against Imperialism. They would not support the British war effort because they were not convinced that the war was being fought in the cause of freedom or democracy as declared by the Allies. The German asked H/1459 to speak afterwards the German journalist asked H/1459 to introduce to him Indian announcers suitable for an Indian Session which was being introduced into the broadcast programme. H/1459 agreed on condition that nothing would be said against the Indian National Congress or its leaders in these broadcasts. H/1459 introduced to the German an educated Sikh watchman (name not remembered), who, he thinks, was evacuated by the British on the outbreak of war in the East. The description of the Sikh is:–

Height :– 5' 9"; Age :– 25 yrs;
Fair complexion; a shaven Sikh.

H/1459 as Author

19. The German Publicity Dept in Shanghai also produced WILL DURANT's book "Case for India" and asked H/1459 to write an introduction. He did so, recommending the book to those who wanted to know the facts about the British Rule in India. H/1459 had by now himself written a book in English on India. This had been translated by a publishing company under the joint names of H/1459 and T. Muto. The book was called simply "India". In 1935 H/1459 had written a small play called "In India" depicting scenes of the non-cooperation movement of 1920. He later learnt that this play had been banned by the Government of India. He wrote another booklet in English called "Coloured Ethiopia" which denounced Italian aggression against Abyssinia. He followed this is 1940 by a book in Japanese entitled "Doomsday of the British Empire", which was a denunciation of British Imperialist policy in India. H/1459 bore the expenses of all these publication from his own assets except for "Coloured Ethiopia" which he wrote for the Greater Asia Society at the request of Professor Nakatani.

Indian Political Parties Working in Japan at the Time of the Outbreak of War in Europe

20. There were three Indian Political groups in Japan which were carrying on propaganda for Indian freedom. They were:–

(a) Indian National Association–controlled by H/1459. Its represented the Indian community on various non-commercial matters and also served Indian merchats in their business affairs there being no Indian Chamber of Commerce or other similar institution. When, owing to tariff barriers imposed against Japanese goods and the retaliation of the Japanese by Tariffs on Indian raw materials, Indian merchats became commercially embarrassed, H/1459 put up to the Japanese the argument that the merchants could not held responsible for the policy of the govt of India. The Indian National Association also helped the merchants when their assets were frozen by the Japanese Govt.

(b) Raja Mahendra Pratap was the founder of the "World Federation" Movement and editor of a periodical of the same name. He did not enjoy much political following but was held in great esteem on account of his sacrifice and sufferings in the cause of India. His political ideology was unintelligible to most of the Indians and won little backing. With the help of contributions by Indians in Japan he purchased a piece of land at Kokubunji near Tokyo and built some huts where he lived and worked. His only ardent followers was a Sikh named Sohan Singh who had been living in Japan for a long time and was married to a Japanese girl.

(c) Indian Independence League–This was run by R. B. Bose who had some staugh supporters among the young Indians in Tokyo. Some of the Indian merchants in Kobe and Yokohama were his personal friends and he had a large number of intimate Japanese friends in both official and non-official circles. The following in particular were his satellities:–

(i) Desh Pande—Later went of Bangkok (believed drowned on torpedoed Japanese ship)

(ii) Miglani (Punjabi)– Was employed as an announcer at the Tokyo Broadcasting Station during the war. Still in Tokyo.

(iii) Raja Sharma –A South Indian who accompanied R. B. Bose to Bangkok; present wherabouts not known.

(iv) Gupta–Was a student in Tokyo and came to Malaya with R. B. Bose. In 1943 H/1459 saw him in Singapore, and later heard that he was working with the Japanese.

21. R. B. Bose and his associates were not very friendly with H/1459 because he was the official representative of Congress which, because of the well-known leanings of its leader Nehru, they suspected of socialism, H/1459 was on the other hand very popular among the Indians and was also respected by the Japanese intelligentsia.

Ever since the outbreak of the European War the antagonism of the IIL group towards H/1459 had been growing more acute and he found that the Japanese MP and a section of the Japanese Press were paying him some attention. An article was published in the "Nippon" of Tokyo, dannouncing H/1459 as a follower of Nehru, and at the same time R. B. Bose's grouup passed a resolution condemning the policy of the Indian National Congress. H/1459 replied with an article in the "Osaka Mainichi" repuiating the resolution and saying that it was foolish to think that a few Indians in Tokyo were wiser than the great brains of the Congress.

Differences in the Trinity

22. The unity of the 3 Indian political groups was superficial and in spite of all efforts could not last. Raja Mahendra Pratap was keen on joining hands with the Germans and Italians to which H/1459 and Bose did not agree. On one occasion BOSE suggested to H/1459 that they should obtain arms from the Japanese and send them to India. H/1459 did not agree because he did not think that arms would serve any unseful purpose under the conditions which existed in India and in the absence of any organised nation-wide revolutionary party. He argued that Congress was the only organised national body in India and that it could never welcome such a move. He told R.B. Bose that if Japan was prepared to help India with arms there must be some ulterior motive, but agree that provided Japan had no territorial or selfish design on India, and that India was in a position to sustain a nation-wide armed revolution, the proposal would bear consideration. Bose suggested that he had friends in India with whom he could communicate and whom he could interest in project. He claimed that the Japanese anthorities might also agree to give an undertaking that they had no ulterior motives in helping India. Bose refused to divluge the names of his friends in India and Japan through whom he hoped to secure all this. These discussions resulted in serious and immediate differences among the parties.

Outbreak of War in the East

23. On 8 Dec 41 H/1459 learnt that JAPAN was at war and later the same morning R. B. BOSE telephoned him calling him to a meeting in the Rainbow Restaurant to discuss the situation as it affected INDIA. H/1459 arrived at the rendezvous and found BOSE and some other Indians gathered there. He remembers the following :—

(a) R. B. Bose

(b) Desh Pande

(c) Lingam–A South Indian follower of R. B. Bose

(d) Raja Sharma

(e) Narain–A South Indian employed in some paper press.

(f) Ramamurti

(g) S. N. Sen–Bengali

(g) Rastrapal

The discussion which took place was quite informal. It was decided to call a meeting in Tokyo of Indians from all over Japan. Various suggestions for cooperation with the Japanese in order to achieve the freedom for India were also discussed. H/1459 suggested that before they obtain any help from the Japanese Govt they must have a categorical declaration that Japan had no territorial or other designs on India. H/1459 was authorised to call the meeting mentioned above.

24. H/1459 unofficially sounded his Indian friends in Kobe, Yokohama and Tokyo. He felt inwardly confused. On one hand were his staunch Congress feelings, which did not fit in with the aggressive creed of the Japanese: on the other there was the apparently excellent opportunity to liberate India which, he felt, should not be missed. He felt, however, most strongly that whatever was done, Indians should not merely exchange one master for another or become Japanese tools. He was strongly opposed to the idea of a Japanese Army invading India and after long deleberations and heart searching came to the conclusion that while the opportunity should not be missed, he personally should not accept the leadership of any movement which would be organised in Japan. He thus went against the wishes of his friends.

Indian Independence League Conference

25. The Indian conference was held in the Railway Hotel Tokyo on 26 Dec 41. R. B. Bose was elected President at the suggestion of H/1459. The following were the most prominent of the 30 Indians who attended:—

(a) S. C. Das	–	From Kobe
(b) S. Mangan Mal	– "	"
(c) Ramchand	–	From Yokohama
(d) Mahtani –	"	"
(e) D. W. Sadhani	–	" "
(f) H. N. Khoob	–	" "

(g) Hans Raj	–	from Kobe
(h) Rawal	–	" "
(i) Ramamurti	–	From Tokyo
(j) Deshpande	–	" "
(k) Lingam	–	" "
(l) Kishore	–	" "

Resolutions were passed:–

(a) To open branches of the IIL in Kobe and Yokohama.

(b) To call upon India to rise against the British and fight for freedom.

(c) To cooperate fully with the Japanese.

(d) To request the Japanese Govt to help India in achieving complete independence.

26. R. B. Bose took upon himself the task of negotiating with the Japanese Govt while H/1459 was entrusted with the organisational work of the IIL Branches in Japan. H/1459 consented to close down the Indian National Association in the interest of Indian unity.

Opening of IIL Branches

27. After having closed down the Indian National Association H/1459 handed over its funds (about Yen 6,000), to R. B. Bose. He then visited Kobe and Yokohama where he called public meetings of Indians and explained the significance of the war in India's fight for freedom. He explained the closing of the Indian Association and the handing of the leadership of a united movement to R. B. Bose, and advised his hearers to cooperate with the IIL. R. B. Bose had accompanied H/1459 to Kobe. At the termination of the meeting at KOBE a branch of the League was set up with the Mehta, a Punjabi businessman (Description:— about 50 yrs old, short stature, medium built, wheat complexion, wears glasses and is married to a Japanese woman) as Chairman. Mehta was told to select other office bearers himself.

28. H/1459 next opened a League branch at Yokohama. Mahtani, a Sindhi merchant (Description :— Age 50, medium height, well built, fair complexion), who was President of the Local Merchants Association, was requested to take up the work of Chairman.

29. Early in Jan 42 H/1459 accompanied by Deshpande went to Shanghai. They stopped in the Astor House Hotel and interviewed workers of

the Indian National Association. The Shanghai Indians did not agree to close down this Association immediately although they raised no objection to the opening of a branch of the IIL there. Nair, a South Indian living in Manchuria, was also on a visit to Shanghai at the instance of the Japanese. H/1459 learnt that he had already organised a local IIL with the help of Indians who were not members of the Indian National Association.

H/1459 held discussions with Nair on the subject of the IIL. (H/1459 had by this time made up his mind to agree to the continuation of the Indian National Association in Shanghai. Amongst other things he saw that the League would be considered a Japanese sponsored body and would therefore not be able to obtain relief for Indian destitues from the Swiss Consulate as the Indian Association was doint. H/1459 told Nair this, assuring him that the League and the Association would cooperate, and Nair agreed. Nair was accompanied by a Japanese officer (name not remembered) who told H/1459 to see that the Indian Independence Movement did not suffer. H/1459 assured the Japanese that to an Indian like himself the independence of India was very dear and that he would do all he could to maintain harmony and goodwill among the Indians.) (Note:— These two factions — for such they became – continued until after S. C. Bose's arrival. Loganadan (B 953) tried to solve differences in Sep 43 and the Association was finally closed by Hassan (H/1457) in Nov-Dec 43.)

30. H/1459 discovered that there were 2 other Indian groups functioning in Shanghai. One was led by Osman, a Punjabi watchmen in the service of the Japanese Navy, and the other, which had started at the outbreak of war inthe East and was called "Welfare Society" was led by Kapahi and Seth, both Pubjabi businessmen. Both these groups had Japanese backing. Osman's party was supported by the Japanese Navy. It consisted of Sikh and Pathan watchmen and had been formed sometime before the war in the East. Osman had come to Shanghai from Java with the help of the Japanese Navy after the outbreak of war in Europe. H/1459 had met him before on a couple of occasions and had found that he had not only fantastic ideas about the independence movement but that he was illiterate and completely ignorant of politics. The welfare Society under Kapahi and Seth was helped by Lt. Col. Akiyama of the Publicity Bureau of the

Japanese Army. Kapahi and Seth had lived in Japan for a number of years and knew many Japanese officers. (Note : Osman Khan, Hari Singh was still in Java in Nov 45 living near Bandoeng).

31. H/1459 met Osman, Kapahi and Seth separately. He appealed to them to unite in the interests of Indian independence and to merge their parties in the League.

All said they were ready to cooperate but insisted that as there was no capable leader for the IIL in Shanghai under whom they would come to serve, they should carry on their respective parties. Osman promised to attend any functions organised by H/1459 to show his cooperation H/1459 learnt that Kapahi, as leader of his party, was obtaining wheat flour from the Japanese and selling it at a high price to the Indians. This was the reason for his unwillingness to forego his leadership.

32. H/1459 addressed Indian gatherings at various places in Shanghai appeaiing for unity. The response was very encouraging. He then held 2 meetings on 26 Jul 42 (Indian Independence Day); there was a flag hoisting ceremony under the auspices of the IIL in the morning, and a public meeting under the auspices of the Indian National Association of China in the evening. To the flag hoisting ceremony Japanese officials and Chinese had also been invited and H/1459 hoisted the flag. He delivered a short speech on the importance of the Movement and called upon Indians to merge their differences and to rally round their flag. The public meeting in the evening was a purely Indian function and was presided over by J. Rahman. It was well attended and was addressed by H/1459. Desh Pande, Mahtani and a few others.

33. During his stay in Shanghai H/1459 also met Lt. Col Akiyama and told him that his support of Kapahi and Seth was deterimental to the Movement and should be withdrawan. Akiyama agreed. H/1459 insisted that the political work of the Indian National Association be handed over to the League. H/1459 was visited by a representative of the German Broadcasting Station, Indian Section, who complained that the Sikh announcer H/1459 had introduced previously was not efficient at his work (ref para 30). At his request H/1459 introduced 2 Punjabis, one named Kochhar and the other possibly Ram Sarup. Both had been in Japan as annoucers. These 2 worked for a time and were eventually repatriated to India during the course of the war

while H/1459 was in Bangkok. H/1459 is not aware whether they were given any instructions for secret work in India.

Mohan Singh's Goodwill Mission to Tokyo

34. About the middle of Mar 42 H/1459 visited the League Office and saw some new faces there. He had not been informed about any fresh arrivals. He was introduced to Mohan Singh (H/1050), Raghavan (H/1193), Goho (H/1357), Gill (B1190) and Menon, who informed him that they had come from Singapore buy did not disclose the object of the visit. Mohan Singh secretly gave H/1459 a letter from Swami Satianand Puri. The letter complained bitterly against Japanese behaviour and treatment. Puri expressed his desire to stay with H/1459 in Tokyo and talk over the whole matter in confidence. In talks with Mohan Singh and others H/1459 learnt the object and arrangements of the "Goodwill Mission". He decided, however, not to participate as he had not been informed of the arrival of the edelegates or of any proposed conference, and he informed Bose accordingly. Some of the delegates, however, lunched with him privately. Lingham and Nair came too, possibly to spy on the gathering. (Note: The Tokyo Conference is fully described "S" Sec Reports 1007, 1144 and 1310. Swami S. N. Puri of course was killed on the way to the Conference and thus did not stay with H/1459.)

H/1459 Rejoins R. B. Bose

35. After the delegates to the above conference dispersed in mid Apr 42, R. B. Bose summoned H/1459 to his office. Bose gave H/1459 detailed information about the conference and asked him to come to Bangkok where Bose intended to set up IIL HQ. At first H/1459 refused to accede to this request but when Bose insisted, he asked for time to think matter over. About a week later Bose invited him to a dinner arranged by some Japanese staff offers. Among these present were :—

(a) R. B. Bose

(b) Deshpande

(c) Nair

(d) Maj Ozeki

(e) Takeda

and about 5 other Japanese. H/1459 wasd formally requested by the Japanese officers to join the movement wholeheartedly. He found it difficult to refuse thus suddenly brought to bay. He wanted as far as possible to restrict Bose's power and he did not wish unnecessarily to antagonise the Japanese.

Furthermore he had recently spoken the telephone to Deb Nath Das in Bangkok. Deb Nath Das had pressed him urgently to join, for reasons which he would disclosed when they met. H/1459 accordingly agreed to join R. B. Bose.

To Bangkok

36. 11 May 42 was fixed as the day of departure from Tokyo and the following were selected to accompany Bose and H/1459 to Bangkok:—

(a) Desh Pande – Continued in the movement but was drowned when the steamer Awa Maru was torpedoed in Apr 45.

(b) Nair– Now in Japan

(c) Lingam–Now in Japan

(d) Gupta– was last seen in Singapore in 1943.

(e) Raja Sharma–Drowned in the Awa Maru.

(f) Parekh–Probably still in Malaya

(g) Ram Singh Rawal–A Punjabi merchant. Was in Bangkok at the time of surrender.

(h) Vinayaka Supanekar– A Maharathi student, joined INA.

(i) S. N. Sen– Now in Tokyo

About 7 May 42 a farewell party was given to the above by Japanese staff offrs in a restaurant near the Sanne Hotel. Almost all the Japanese officers who had attended the previous dinner were present. The Indians of Yokohama also gave a farewell party at the India Club. At this party H/1459 delivered a speech saying that if the Japanese Army wanted to go to India against the will of the Indians it would only do so by marching over his dead body.

37. On the night of 11 May 42 the party left Tokyo by rail for the Ise Shrine where it paid homage to the Japanese Gods. It was accompanied by a Japanese lieutenant (name not remembered) who remained with it throught the journey. The party sailed from Moji on

15 May 42 in a Japanese convey and disembarked at Saigon on 28 May 42. From Saigon to Bangkok it travelled on the following day by air.

In Bangkok

38. They arrived at Bangkok on 29 May 42 and were received at the aerodrome by some Japanese who took them to Renaissance Hotel, Suriwongse Road. A few days later a temporary IIL office was established and preparations were begun for the Independence Conference fixed for 15 Jun 42.

39. Deb Nath Das told H/1459 that the Indian community was extremely anti-Japanese because of arrogant Japanese behaviour towards Indians and because it was thought that Swami S. N. Puri had been murdered by the Japanese for his independent views H/1459 told Deb Nath Das of the need for the greatest caution as they could neither allow the Japanese to have their own way nor afford to antagonise them. Both agreed that their chief difficulty was the weakness of R. B. Bose's character.

40. The party left Singapore by air on 29 Oct 43 arriving at Tokyo via Manila and Fukuoka on about 1 Nov 43. Bose was received at the Haneda Aerodrome by leading Indians and high Japanese military and civil officials, and taken straight to the residence of the viscound Sibuzawa, where Bose and his personal staff were to be lodged. In the evening Bhonsle (B1189), Mak Raju (B 956) and H/1459 were moved to the Imperial Hotel.

41. On the following day all were taken to the Imperial Palace where they signed the Visitors' Book. Later they called on th Dowager Empress, Prince Chichibu and Prince Takamatsu. On this or on the next day visits were exchanged by Gen Tojo and S. C. Bose. H/1459 was present at Bose's interview with Tojo at his official residence. Bose suggested to him the handing over of the Andaman and Nicobar Islands to the PGI, and the issue of Indian National Currency. Tojo promised to consider the matters and to reply later. Bsoe also attended a press conference and expressed his views on the international situation, expanding on the formation of the PGI and on its declaration of war. The main object of Bose's visit to Tokyo was to attnd the Greater East Asia Conference. Bhonsle and H/1459 attended the Conference with him. They attended as observers and not as delegates as Bose

considered that he could not commit India, without the consent of the Indians in India, to the Co-prosperity Sphere Group sponsored by Japan. (Note :—Confirms "S" Sec Report 1407 para 24.) Maj Raju (B 956) and Hassan (H/1457) attended the Conference as visitors. The proceedings were fully published in the press.

42. On the last day of the Conference TOJO announced the decision of the Japanese Govt. to hand over the Andaman and Nicobar Islands to the PGI. The detailed plans of this handing over were discussed at a Conference at the official residence of the Navy Minister which Bose and H/1459 attended. The Navy Minister explained that the Islands were very important for strategic reasons, and that it would be difficult to hand over their defences to the PGI during the war. He agreed that the civil administration might gradually be transferred and suggested that a Conference be held between the PGI and the local Naval Command of the Islands to discuss plans of transfer. Bose suggested that Indian National Currency be issued in the Islands as soon as it was printed. The minister raised various practical objections to this although he did not object in principle. He said, when asked, that he would be unable to transport INA to the Andamans. (Note:— The document published at Appx "C" to "S" Sec Report 1407 dates these conversations as 12 Nov 43 and gives written answers to the points Bose raised.)

43. Bose accompanied by H/1459 and possibly Bhonsle also called on M. Toyoma, founder of the Black Dragon Society. This was purely social call and R. B. Bose was also present. Bose was entertained to various official and non-official dinners by Indians, Japanese and others including the German Ambassador and Toyama. Bose also addressed public meetings.

With a puse, and a meeting of Indian women. The party left the Andamans by air on 31 Dec 43 reaching Bangkok the same evening. (Note:— The above should be read in conjunction with the relevant portions of CSDIC 2 Sec Reports 956 and 978, and "S" Sec Reports 1208/and/71123/11/2).

Conference with Mutaguchi

44. After formal visits, there was a conference with Gen. Mutaguchi at which the following decisions were taken. They should be read in conjunctions with paras 28–31 of "S" Sec Report.

(a) Indian forces would work under Indian comds.

(b) In joint operations, the senior officer, whether Indian or Japanese, would take command.

(c) The Japanese authorities would not have the power to arrest members of the INA unless they were accused of a crime against the Japanese Army, and vice versa.

(d) Compliments would be paid to officers of both armies according to seniority.

(e) Indian offices would fly INA flags on their cars according to their ranks, and would be entitled to the same privileges as Japanese officers.

(f) On entry into India Indian National Currency alone would be used both by Japanese Army and INA. So long as Indian National Currency was not available Japanese Military notes of Burma would be the local tender to be withdrawan on the introduction of Indian National Currency.

(g) In liberated areas there would be no military administration and the PGI would take over as the Indo-Japanese forces advanced.

(h) Administration of liberated areas would be completely in the hands of PGI except in matters where operations necessitated military control. Such military control would be joint.

These discussions were kept secret.

45. At another meeting a Japanese staff officer explained with the help of a map the entire strategy of the impending operations to Bose, and on the following day Bose with his party returned to Rangoon.

Azad Hind Fauj

46. On his return from Maymyo, Bose proceeded to select men for the AHD from among the volunteers in Rangoon. Applicants for all services – engineers, and communications experts were available. On 5 Mar 44 Bose called a cabinet meeting and selected Capt (Lt. Col) Ehsan Qadir (B 978) as leader and H/1459 as deputy leader of the AHD. (Note : para 26 of CSDIC Report 978 refers). They were given two days' notice to move forward. The selected staff was assembled in the AHD Camp on the next day and on 8 Mar 44 the party left, arriving at Maymyo 3 days later. In Maymyo and the

AHD was accommodated in the English High School Building. The Japanese Army Reconstruction Staff assembled in Maymyo at the same time and on 20 Mar 44 a joint conference of the two staffs was held. In his address Gen Mutaguchi emphasised the necessity for mutual goodwill and confidence, and for a spirit of cooperation. He told the Japanese to think of the Indians as their brothers.

In mid Apr 44 the first batch of the AHD left for the front in groups with the Japanese forces while fresh reinforcements continued to arrive from the rear. A detachment of the Rani of Jhansi Regt also arrived at the same time and was lodged in the English High School Buildings. Bose accompanied by Col Chatterji, Gen Isoda and members of hs staff also came ot Mayamo and addressed a joint conference of the AHD and the Japanese Army Reconstruction Dept, Bose also addressed a group of Japanese Army officers bound for the front and warned them against bad behaviour towards Indian women, a thing which would entirely alienate Indian sympathy from them and mar their prospects of success.

Visit to the Front

47. In early May 44, under orders from Bose, H/1459 accompanied by Lt Col Chatterji (H/1454) and Lt Col Alagappan (H/1450) left for the front. This visit has been described in "S" Sec Reports 1403 and 1407. H/1459 says that Chatterji and Alagappan were going to look after the comforts of the INA and make arrangements for Hospitals, while those individuals hav shown that their mission was more general. H/1459 refers to halts at Yeu, Kalewa, Moreh, the visit to HQ 1 Div at Chamol, the photographing of the party by press correspondents who had followed from Moreh, and the shell bursts which wounded Chatterji (H/1454). He supports existing accounts of conditions at the front. H/1459 visited Yamamoto explained to the visitiors the situation in glowing terms and expressed great admiration of the work and esprit be corps of the INA. Fujiwara called on the visitors during the same evening on behalf of Gen Yamamoto. H/1459 pointed out to Fujiwara the urgent need for supplies, medicines, and transport, as the men were suffering terribly for lack of these things.

48. On return to Maymayo H/1459, Lt Col Chatterji and Lt Col Alagappan prepared a report on their tour to the front in which they described the hardships suffered by the INA and AHD because of lack of supplies, medicines, and transport, and reported the careless and unhelpful attitude of Hikari Kikan officers. They recommended that

the Hikari Kikan be abolished as soon as possible. (Note :— Chatterji (H/1454) at para 40 of "S" Sec Report 1407 claims most of the credit for this report).

The Last Plans and Intentions of Bose

49. As H/1459 is the last of the "HAOI Party" to be interrogated by this Section, it is not inappropriate to include here a summary of our information about the last intentions of Bose. H/1459 is the only one who has talked at all freely on this subject. He says that when he was in Japan in 1944-45 he called, as a minister of the PGI, on Shigemitsu the Foreign Minister, Sawada his deputy, and on Kodaki who was in charge of the Indian section he had gathered that Bose had wished in his last visit to Tokyo to contact the Russian ambassador, but that he was unable to do so because of lack of Japanese support. ISODA confirmed this to H/1459 when they met in Saigon in Jun 45. In May or Jun 45 Bose himself told H/1459 that he had asked the Japanese Army authorities to arrange a passage for him to Russia via Manchuria. The Japanese had said that this showed that he had lost confidence in them, and he had accordingly dropped it. Chatterji however put up to Southern Army HQ at Saigon in Jun 45 that some of the cabinet should go to Manchuria. This was turned down.

50. The future plans of Bose as obtained by SACSEA Commission No. 1 in Saigon from Japanese offrs were stated in that HQ letter No. 63/2/34/GSI (b) dated 6 Nov 45. Paras 1 and 4 and 5 read as follows :—

"Again in Jul as the situation was fast deteriorating for the Japanese, Bose sought permission, this time to enter USSR via Manchuria with a few selected members of his movement. No formal reply was made to this put Bose was advised to proceed to Tokyo in view of his request. Col Yano chief of the Ind Sec Southern Army HQ has been interrogated at some length on this point. He is emphatic that the Japanese decision to "respect Bose's views" does not denote that the Japanese Govt sought or received willingness from the Russians to accept Bose to go underground in their country. On the contrary, he believes that the Japanese Govt was then approaching Russia to use for peace and could not at this stage allow any complication which must have arisen from Bose's admission."

In the absence of any specific answer from Tokyo Bose intended to give himself up to the Chinese or American forces if on his arrival in

Tokyo the Japanese Govt did not permit him to enter Soviet Russia. But the fact remains that from Saigon Bose travelled in a plane which was taking Lt Gen Shidei to Manchuria Via Japan where the latter had been posted after surrender. Another source contends that there was no need for the Japanese to ask the Russians for Bose's entry for Bose wanted to go to MANCHURIA from where he thought he would be able to get in touch with the Russian forces and obtain necessary admission independently."

Conclusion

51. H/1459 has been engaged in political agitation for the greater part of his life. He was a well-known Indian political leader in Japan when war broke out and had a following probably as strong as that of R. B. Bose. At first excluded from IIL affairs, he claims, by his own suspicions, he has been in the front rank of IIL leaders ever since the Bangkok Conference and is probably one of the most capable. Becoming even more prominent with the arrival of S. C. Bose he became secretary to the PGI cabinet accompanied Bose to Tokyo in Nov 43 and to Rangoon in Jan 44 when the PGI was first established there. He was at Bose's right hand during the important discussions which led to the formation of the AHD and Chatterji's Govt in Mar 44. In May 44 he toured forward and in Nov 44 he began an extensive tour of China, the Philippines and Japan as Bose's personal representative. Returning to Bangkok in May 45 he became the last Minister of Manpower and under Bose's scheme for the dispersion of PHI VIP's went to FIC at the end of June.

52. With H/1459 his political activities in the IIL/PGI have been the natural culmination of his whole career, and it would be idle to expect him to become politically inactive if released now. He would accordingly be most dangerous if released in India or in British territory. Although he is not a Japanese subject there and of the fact that his family is still there, he should be returned to Japan as soon as possible, that he should be sternly prevented from taking any further part in politics. A nominal category of Black is recommended.[2]

2. Sahay came back to India and served as Indian's Ambassador at many places.

Appendix-III

Statement by Deb Nath Das Regarding Doubts About the Death of Bose[1]

27 March, 1953

Mothers, Sisters and Brothers of India.
Jai Hind

I am placing before you my first report on Netaji Subhas Chandra Bose, as the Ex-General Secretary, the Indian Independence League Headquarters. East Asia, and as the Special Officer entrusted with a great mission as per the order of Netaji on 17.5.45 and 16.8.45. I owe my compatriots an apology for the delay in submitting my findings; but I feel sure that considering enormous responsibility inherent in the task and the magnitude thereof, the development of a reactionary force in India-creating hostilities against the cause, the insurmountable difficulties arising out of sheer disability on the part of workers to move and work in various places of different countries, and the last but not the least, the extreme beggarly condition of the workers, you will condons this delay. Moreover, the complete disintegration of the I.N.A. and its subsequent neutralisation shattered its very foundation. The most disgraceful feature exhibited in the game of some result of some of our colleagues created no less difficulties in the way of our mission, due to difference in common outlook and doubtful co-operation almost amounting to sabotage.

The reported death of Netaji created three reactions in India :

(a) Some felt relief thinking that the greatest Indian Revolutionary Leader is gone and thus with him the stiffest resistance in their way to fame and fortunes and power.

(b) Some took it philosophically and believed that it was a call of Destiny and that Netaji died after the fulfilment of a great mission, destined as he was, in the eternal way of Eternal India.

(c) But the greater number of people believed that the 'Plane Crash' was no crash and that it was merely an item in accordance with

1. History of Freedom Movement Papers.

the Master plan, envisaged by Netaji and that the beloved Leader would appear in the historic moment in the shaping of India's destiny.

The first reaction sought to completely Quarantine Netaji's ideals; the second—typical of India's philosophic way—neutralised the very great love for Netaji by inaction and completes surrender to Fate. The third- a logical conclusion of political thinkers and workers of revolutionary faith and ideals - was ineffective, because of their differences in contents and approach, neutralising one another and thus dragging the issue in their own way rather than leading the issue to a higher plane in the true perspective, away from compartmental political gains.

The main Issue was thus sidetracked in the midst of landslides of psychological currents and cross currents.

The people of India, bereft of all guidance, looked askance to one another with a fond hope, but remained in the dark, hoping against hope, in India's way of faith in God. Netaji's ideals remained in mere story-telling and not in preaching and practising them.

Thus sandwiched between two forces, one unsympathetic and hostile and the other sympathetic but not serious to the highest pitch with a soldier's mind, we few, appointed by Netaji in his order of the Day, had therefore to gear our mind and action into two channels; firstly, to conduct in the way as was instructed by Netaji and endeavouring at the same time to contact him, and to ensure confidences in him, to keep our stature, moral and political, strictly that everything was done according to the Plan. In that process, all calmness and precision was observed with the absolute pre requiste that was needed. Secondly, we had also to investigate whether everything was also followed according to Netaji's plan since the operative part of the plan was entirely in the hands of Japanese Military Officers who took charge of him and as such the success of our mission hinged on the precision in the manner of execution of the solemn pledge undertaken by the Japanese Military Officers, concerned. We proceeded from both angles. We had to be extremely cautious and reserved since even more lapse of some words would cause still more difficulties and might jeopardise the success of the very mission. In the terrific suspense we walked on. Ours was a colossal task. Not a single Zone remained unapproached with hope and confidence in the course of the last seven years. My worthy colleagues stood all attention in their respective positions till the last moment.

Now, on a final checkup of the findings in regard to the whereabouts of Netaji Subhas Chandra Bose, we have come to the conclusion based on circumstantial evidence and individual contact that nothing whatsover was done by the operative machinery of the then Japanese Military authorities as solemnly promised as per the wish of Netaji.

According to our study through patient work into the Japanese ranks entrusted with the operative part of the Plan (First Phase) this failure on the part of the Japanese was deliberate and was attributed to the complete frustration of the defeated Japan and her anxiety to avoid, in every possible way, any further hostility of Britain (which was at that time ruling over our country) and America over the shielding of Netaji from the British clutch. Japan could not think of handing over Netaji to the British authorities as such an act would invariably mobilize Indian opinion against her, since Japan was conscious of Netaji's immense popularity in India; nor could she keep him (Netaji) underground away from British clutch, as it would, on the other hand, make the occupation forces in the South-eastern Asian region more embittered to the occupied Japan.

The Japanese Military authorities knew the mind of Netaji and had a glimpse of the Post War Revolutionary programme and the Leader's determination to form new alliance for the liberation of India and to open a new phase in India's struggle for freedom and life. The Japanese calculated that his resurgent appearance in the future would only cast doubt in Britain's mind towards Post war Japan's bonafides in her (Japan's) policy towards Britain and her Allies with whom the Post war Japan must cast her lot for many more years. Japan tried to save herself from wrath of both India and the Occupation forces in South-East Asia. At the same time an impression was created that the accident was one according to the Alternate plan apparently to cover up her defeatist mentality and frustrated stature. All this is not my hypothetical assertion–truth will come out if public investigation is made.

Now I should touch upon the plan chalked out by Netaji before he emplaned from Bangkok immediately after the termination of the South - East Asia war. As I was constantly with him in those fateful days and as I was fortunately taken into his fullest confidence, with regard to the Plan (Original and alternate) and was appointed to head the mission, I claim to speak with a certain amount of authority. From May 1945, Netaji began to think of new move because of overwhelming enemy forces. It was Netaji's plan to go to India (First Priority) and continue the country's liberation fight from some underground centre. Japan agreed to take Netaji from

Bangkok to somewhere in Bengal and agreed to take responsibility so far as the necessary transport was concerned. All other parapheranalis were made by us, from the middle of June,1945. This is known to some of my colleagues in the Cabinet of Azad Hind Government and some members of Armed Forces.

On that understanding, Netaji emplanned for Saigon, as according to the Japanese, it could have been easier him and his officers to go to India through Saigon, as there was vigilance of the Allied Forces on that route. Mr. S. A. Ayer Singh Colonel Habib-ur Rehman., Colonel Pritam Singh, Colonel Abid Hassan and myself accompanied Netaji early in the from Bangkok (Netaji arrived from Singapore on 16.8.45) morning of 17.8.45. After reaching Saigon only, the Japanese Military authorities seperated Netaji from the rest of us on the ground that there was no accommodation in the plane. Not only that, we were informed for the first time that he was to be taken towards Tokyo; nor had Netaji any idea of the whole picture.

Here I must emphasise the talk that passed on between us on one side and General Isoda, Chief of the Hikari Kikan, that was set up by the Japanese High Command to serve as the Liaison Department for conducting military affairs with the Supreme Command, I. N. A., on the other. It was 8 o'clock in the morning when we arrived at Saigon from Bangkok and we went straight from the aerodrome, to two houses for a little rest. In one house, Netaji (in one room), Colonel Habib ur Rehman and myself were accommodated; in another house, just adjacent were Mr. Ayer, Colonel Gulzara Singh, Colonel Pritam Singh and Major Hassan. Seven days and nights we had no rest we longed for it. I was first to be awakened and Netaji was found beside me. The first few words of Netaji (he spoke in Bengali) were; "You see, they are changing the Plan- I don't know why - just come and have a talk with General Isoda", I was stunned and Netaji was requested by me not to give his consent. I immediately felt a little helpless for the new move, so surprisingly made and that too at Saigon where we were placed in the most disadvantageous position having been far away from our own Armed Forces yet strong in moves and courageous in mobility. I found Netaji's face full of signs of restlessness; for the first time I found in him a little uneasiness and helplessness of a child. "Any way" hurry up, come to that room". Netaji said, I hurried up and found General Isoda and another Japanese Officer. Immediately I gave vent to my feelings that there should be no change in the plan and that Netaji must be taken to India – the only logical step for him: "Even if we are captured", I said "the people will come to know and help us". Netaji was listening - he did not utter a single word but his eyes spoke and I could understand his mind. General Isoda enumerated some difficulties; but they were minor and he suggested that the Alternate Plan be taken up. (The principal feature of the Plan was to keep Netaji safe somewhere in East Asia) and gave me an idea of bases and routes, General Isoda said, that there would be no difficulties and so long he lived, he would keep Netaji safe. I still refused to accept his suggestion. Netaji, then intervened and asked General Isoda; "Suppose I go towards Tokyo, all of them (he meant the whole party) are certainly coming with me. "Then, the other Military Officer said; "Your Excellency, there is no accommodation in the plane - we shall try to accommodate at least one officer to go with Your Excellency. "Netaji did not reply direct but turned towards General Isoda and said, "Do you think,General, they (The Party) will agree to leave me alone?" Then hurriedly he told me to call other Officers. Immediately I called Col. Habib-ur-Rehman and just told him the gist of the talk. Then I ran to the adacent house and called Sri S. A. Ayer, Col. Gulzara Singh, Col Pritam Singh and Major Hassan to hurry up and report to Netaji. They all came and all of us vehemently opposed General Isoda's idea and even questioned him about the change. All of us, including Col., Rehaman resented the idea of giving seat to one Officer only to accompany Netaji. Meanwhile, Mr. Hachiya, Japan's envoy to the Azad Hind Government joined us. Both General Isoda and Mr. Hachiya assured safety of Netaji and promised to provide conveyance to the rest of us at the earliest possible opportunity to follow Netaji. But still we argued. At this moment, another Japanese military officer came in and talked to General Isoda. The General told Netaji that just at 1 o'clock in the afternoon a plane was leaving towards Tokyo and that Netaji should hurry up–there was one seat more, he added. Yet, we all did not agree. Netaji at this moment said: "You all don't worry - General Isoda has promised to provide you all with transport within the shortest possible time", and then he turned towards General Isoda and just asked. "Could you not give one more seat? Let Das come with me - he knows the place and language and will be of some help to me." "Can't say now, Netaji", the General, said," any way, I shall try once more while we are at the aerodrome. " "Netaji, however, asked all of us to bring our kits, and said he (Netaji) would try once more in the aerodrome for giving us the facility." Well, let us try, you all come, if you don't get transport, come back, "Netaji said. And he gave some instruction with regard to steps to be followed. He looked determined, calm, and collected. It was 17th August, 1945."

We all went towards the aerodrome with our kits and three suitcases of gold ornaments and gold bars, donated by the people of East Asia towards the Netaji Fund Committee. It was only a 20 minutes' drive. When we had only a few minutes to talk, Netaji once more told General Isoda and Mr. Hachiya about the plane for us which they had promised. Meanwhile, we were anxious about the gold; when I talked to General Isoda that the treasure must go with Netaji, he told me that the plane was already overloaded and he did not know whether the pilot would agree. Netaji interrupted and told "it does not matter - these may come with you all." Immediately I submitted to Netaji : "The treasure must go with you, Sir , "And all other officers spoke in the same strain. I turned towards General Isoda and told him: "Why not ask one or two of your Japanese Officers to get down and make room for the treasure? Meanwhile, the propellor started so we did not wait for General Isoda's reply; Col. Pritam Singh, Major Hassan and myself took the three cases and just put them inside the Bomber and told Col, Habib-ur-Rehman to take care of them. Netaji embraced everyone of us and boarded the plane. We all shouted "Habib, take care of Netaji".

After three days, stay in Saigon, we were told that Netaji had gone towards Tokyo and that we were to follow him. But finally, only on 21-8-45 Mr. Ayer alone was flown to Tokyo and the rest of us were taken to Hanoi the same day, though at the time of explaining we were given no hint of our Hanoi destination. On 21-8-45 Major General A.C. Chatterji and Sri J.A. Thivy arrived at Hanoi from Singapore. They were misled too. Sri A.M. Sahay was already at Hanoi.

At Hanoi we heard of Netaji's reported demise over the Radio on 24th August 1945. On the 26th August just a week after Intellegence Department met me at Hanoi together with a Military Officer from Towloon the seat of Marshal Tarauchi's Headquarters and told me: "Netaji no Hikoki ochiru kotowa shinio shimasan. Das Sanwa Netaji no yu koto torini shitekudaisai mase," the exact translation of which as follows : "Don't believe the plane crash as a real crash, you adjust your movements and plans in accordance with the alternate plan of Netaji" (This alternate plan was to continue the freedom fight from a suitable place in East Asia, in case it was not possible for Netajhi to go inside India immediately), we consulted the plan and took note of new base. I took Col. Pritam Singh , Major Abid Hassan and Mr. J. A. Thivy into confidence and took all steps and precautions. Major General A. C. Chatterjee, Sri A, M. Sahay and Col. Gulzara Singh were all consulted. And I went ahead. My colleagues in different places in accordance with the Plan until I was arrested at Bangkok by the Occupation authorities of the Allied Powers in May, 1946 and brought to India on 30.8.46

These seven years we have worked with faith in man and God in co-operation with my trusted workers all over East Asia, in the midst of Himalayan odds and suspense. We very often had discussed the bonafides or otherwise of the Japanese Military officers who took charge of Netaji, we took the late Sri Sarat Chandra Bose into confidence. We did not, however, allow our mind to be prejudiced. The late Sri Sarat Chandra Bose gave me inspiration to proceed with my mission, since some allowances of time must be given in view of Japan's extremely delicate position, war-criminal's trial and other international complications and no less, the disguised hostility of the Power that be in Indian towards Netaji. We became very often restless though, we did not like to cast any doubt, lest that might be interpreted as a branch of faith. Moreover, so long there was the least chance of Netaji being contacted according to the alternate plan, any suspicion on our part towards the 'benefactor' would have been as if to destroy the very roof that gave him (Netaji) shelter. Hence we had to wait until Japan got rid of the occupation forces and enjoyed better channels for outside contact. Hence the delay in accordance with the strategic necessity. There was a historical necessity too, in case everything was done according to the plan, for Netaji's remaining underground for obvious reasons only to appear at the historical moment for shaping India's destiny.

We gave our last push as soon as Japan got rid of the bindings of the occupation period. Meanwhile, to our utter surprise Sri S. A. Ayer went to Japan and gave the report of his conducted tour. In his statement he did not care to go through the salient features and simply came to a conclusion of his own apparently to bury the great issue of such national importance. We were perplexed when we found to our utter surprise that he was inducing the Government of India to bring the so called ashes of Netaji. The Japanese authorities concerned, on the other hand, have been also trying to hush up the matter. The Government of India have not chosen to set up a Top-level Enquiry Commission as has been demanded by the people of India.

When all avenues to find out Netaji were exhausted and when we found after thorough investigation and minute scrutiny that nothing whatsoever was done by the Japanese military officers in matters of executing instruction to different bases, as they promised in accordance with the alternate plan, we tried our best to contact the Japanese officers concerned. Replies were available are only too vague. Most of them are dead silent.

Contact or no contact, we believe Netaji should naturally remain alive but, if Netaji is no more, we equally believe there is some foul play somewhere and that some heinous crime must have been perpetrated in our darkest moment of history. This is our charge. And the responsibility lies on those Japanese Military officers who took charge of Netaji. Those officers who are all living today can not shirk that responsibility. It is one thing if, due to changed circumstances, they failed to continue the task even though solemnly pledged but it is quite another when the life of Netaji is concerned. As one who knows Japan for the last twenty years and has worked with brave Japanese people in the making of that glorious history under the banner of Netaji my grateful heart goes to the Japanese people for all they did for us. I. N. A.'s contribution, service and sacrifice, which will remain written in golden letters, It is with that feeling I would appeal to the Japanese Government and its people to see that their fair name be not married with stigma in their relation with the I. N. A. and the Leader before the posterity. Hence I appeal to them in fairness to their love towards India to allow such enquiries vis-a-vis the reported plane crash in Taihoku on the 18.8.45 when the fate of India's most beloved son is involved.

We understand that the Government of India is making arrangements to bring Netaji's ashes to India. Why did not the Government of India form a Top Level Investigation Committee at the outset to investigate the reported death of Netaji a Committee representing all shades of Indian opinion and the public? Why did the Government choose to send just one man (Sri S. A. Ayer) to Japan for the said Investigation—a man who had been in Japan just for month or so and did not know the language and the country well and had to yield to a conducted tour? When he did know what transpired between the Japanese officers and us in the matter of the execution of the plan did not he find him in an independent position to question them for their (the Japanese officers) failures to keep up the pledge and the reason thereof. If not; why? If so, why should he choose to keep his fingings secret from us who are all piligrims to that 'journey's end'. The question of the person of Netaji is the concern of the people of the whole of India.

Now, again during all this seven-year period, the whereabouts of the gold, which rightfully belongs to the Indian Nation, has remained a mystery. I put up this matter many times in the Central I. N. A. Advisory Committee but Sri S. A. Ayer did not give any reply. It was after my interview with the United Press in Bangkok on the 23rd January this year, which we published in all major papers of Japan, Thailand and other parts of East Asia that the 'Oskan Mainichi', a leading daily of Japan came out with a three column banner that Netaji's have been found. It is also noteworthy that in that report the name of Mr. Rammurti Ex-President of the Indian Independence League, Tokyo Branch, who became multimillionaire overnight, was mentioned prominently. It is also known that Sri S. A. Ayer delivered the treasure to him. I understand Mr. Rammurti is now in India with his Japanese wife and as an old acquaintance of his, I would earnestly request him to explain to the people of India why he did not report this to the Government of India or to the I. N. A. Inquiry Committee or to the Central I. N. A. Advisory Committee al these seven years. He should also explain how he got the treasure and under what circumstances he got it. Is it a fact that he offered him service to the British Information Service in Tokyo as soon as the Occupation Troops landed in Japan?

Sri S. A. Ayer should also explain the reason of his silence over these particular points and, as one who was on the very spot at Tokyo and as one who chose only Mr. Rammurthi to deliver the sacred treasure he should explain the situation in the light of the information that might be at his disposal. It is also astonishing that inspite of repeated appeal of Indian community in Japan. India's envoys accredited in Japan did not take any action for the restoration of the national treasure from Mr. Rammurthi. Why have not the Government made any arrangements to interview and question those people whose names are prominently associated with the disappearance of the gold? The details of the treasure will be submitted to the Investigation Commision.

It is a glorious chapter of the Azad Hind Government how this national treasure voluntarily contributed by Indian mothers, sisters and brothers in East Asia to Netaji for the sacred cause was presented by loyal officers and men. Sri Yellappa, Colonel Misra, Lt. Nazir Hussain and Lieutenants Josephina and Stella (Rani Jhansi Regiment) become martyrs to protect the treasure. Our worthy colleagues Major General A. C. Chatterjee, Major General J. K. Bhonsle, Sri J.A. Thivy, Sri J. N. Bhaduri, Director Azad Hind Bank, Pandit Raghunath Sharma, Secretary, Finance Department, Indian Independence League, Thailand, Major Abid Hassan, Confidential Secretary to Netaji, SriE. Bhaskaran, confindential stenographer to Netaji, Sri U.C. Sharma and Sri C. Rai Narulla, Sri S. N. Dasgupta, Sri A.C. Das Sri P.N. Pillay - officers of the General Secretariat and Hav. Kundan Singh and Adya Prasad, personal orderlies to Netaji - to name only a few - who played a great part in protecting the treasure in toto will. I am sure, varify the details as correct.

It was the greatest moment of our life when the national treasure was delivered to Netaji's new Headquarters in full on evacuation from Rangoon. This sacred treasure belongs to the nation and anyone found guilty of appropriating so is a traitor to the country and must be punished accordingly. The findings will also throw light on the circumstances that led to the reported plane crash.

Will the people of India remain quiet and accept without any investigation the so called ashes of India's most beloved son?

It is beyond our comprehension to think why the Government of India have chosen not to set up an Investigation Commission for findings out the circumstances and evidence in connection with the reported 'Plane Crash'. A new situation has arisen by the Prime Minister's declaration for the first time in the Parliament recently that the Government of India are convinced about the death of Netaji. Why did not the Government of India take it to be a supreme moral duty to place before the people of India the reason of their conviction and the materials leading to their conviction. It is the question of life of one so dear to India and universally respected and cannot be disposed of light-heartedly. We do no know how a National Government could remain true to its character by choosing to withold publication of the materials concerning the life of India's greatest revolutionary, Could there be any relation in the policy making of the State, with the materials available at the disposal of the Government in connection with the reported 'Plane Crash' or any other incident? The people have the right to know the details and themselves to judges. We therefore appeal to the Government of India to form an Investigation Commission with the Chief Justice of India, judges of integrity and international repute like Dr. Radha Binode Pal and other distinguished citizen.

The question of bringing the 'ashes' of Netaji does not arise.

Mothers, Sisters and Brothers

We appeal to you to call upon the Government of India to take up the issue, lest the Posterity shuld blame us all of our indifference towards the fate of India's Man of Destiny.

I earnestly pray that Pandit Jawaharlal Nehru should exert his influence to order a through investigation into the issues I have raised in the report and thus satisfy the people's demand to know the real truth following the disapperance of Netaji. Let me pray the voice of millions will break the barrier of the vicious circle and reach and move the conscience of the Prime Minister of India.

I swear, in the name of God, in the name of those Martyrs who have died for our freedom and in the name of the people of India that my findings are not based on any hypothesis or imagination. If called upon by the Investigation Commission, I and my colleagues will prove what I have siad. I take the full responsibility of this Report, including the charges I have made, As a soldier, I have worked with utmost disciplines, as a solider, I submit to-day the findings to the people of India without mincing matters and as a soldiers, I will stand on duty to defend what I have said. I swear I have no political motive.

Let India take Netaji's issue- the great National Issue concerning the Life and Mission of India's greatest Revolutionary.

Let the sons and daughters of Eternal Hind remember that the deathlessness of Her Soul lies in what we do, not in what we are.

JAI HIND

N.B.
Submitted at a Press Conference
on the 27th March, 1953.[2]

(Deb Nath Das)

2. It was after this campaign that the Government of India appointed an Enquiry Commission to report on the death of S.C. Bose under Shah Nawaz Khan, in 1954.

Appendix-IV

Memoirs of Col. Yamamoto[1]

I think Mr. Subhas Chandra Bose was one of the greatest statesman who ever lived in modern India.

I, led by fate, had close relations with him from the time of his residence in Germany upto 10 months before his tragic death at Taipeh in Formosa.

There have been quite a few articles in newspapers and magazines after the termination of the War on Mr. Subhas Chandra Bose and the movement for Indian Independence. Most of them however contained many inaccuracies.

I am afraid the people of the coming generation might put undeserved blame on a number of Japanese and Indians who sacrificed themselves for Mr. Bose and Independence, and thereby might cause a breach in Indo-Japanese good relations.

I, as one of the men who worked with him for the independence of India, think it is my duty, to say what I know were the real facts.

Soon after the termination of the war, I was asked by the investigating officers of both the American and the British Armies to give whatever detailed information I had concerning the Indian Independence movement.

After interrogation of all my subordinate officers, the investigation in respect of me was the final one to close the case.

History of Freedom Movement Records N.A.I.

I revealed all the facts known to me and, at the same time, expressed my views.

"It was wrong to call our part in aiding India to attain her independence, as a conspiracy", I stated.

"There were no instructions nor any other papers from the General Headquarter indicating any conspiracy". "It was a cooperative action

1. History of Freedom Movement Papers. Col. Yamamato was in Berlin when he met Bose. At that time he was military attacke at Japanese Embassy.

taken by the provisional Indian government and the Japanese Army" I affirmed. What I wanted to say was that the Japanese Army never made use of India to win the war.

I can recall Mr. Bose making a speech with tears in his eyes, moved by the wholehearted support shown to him by the Japanese to win Indian Independence.

I thought it was Hikari-Kikan's duty (Espionage Counter Intelligence Corps) to materialise the wishes of the Japanese people then.

It was in the spring of 1940, I remember, that Mr. Bose fled from India to live in Germany.

In the early autumn, I met him for the first time. I was then serving at the Japanese Army Office at Berlin as a Colonel and received a telegram from Tokyo instructing me to report on Mr. Bose.

For sometime after Mr. Bose's arrival in Germany, the German Ministry of Foreign Affairs somewhat suspicious about his real intentions, but upon recognizing his worth, and bona fides, they treated him as a national guest.

Seeing that it was difficult to have an interview with him, I had him invited through Ambassador Oshima and Minister of Foreign Affairs, Ribbentroppe, to the official residence of the Japanese Embassy, where I met him for the first time.

Having gained the impression that he was a man of worth, I reported it to the G. H. Q., together with information about him gathered from German sources.

After that I had many chances to have talks with him when he visited Ambassador Oshima. There was about him no 'meanness ' such as one might come across in a political refugee, nor had he any sense of egoism, Simplicity marked his character. But he was a man of dignity. Any on who came in contact with him was impressed with his fierce fighting spirit for the cause of Indian Independence. Yet his speeches and actions were marked by the stamp of great gentlemanliness.

One evening when we had a conversation, he told me how he had got out of India and came to live in Germany.

It is as follows:

"I am confident that Indian Independence will be realised only at the cost of our blood."

And there is scarcely any hope of its realization through the creed of non-violence exhorted by Gandhi.

"Luckily I have had many supporters of my view among the younger group of the Congress."

When the European war, caused by the struggle between Germany and England, began I started to make public speeches to stir anti-British feelings and emphasisings the need to resort to force, being convinced that it was a great chance for the realisation of Indian Independence.

"I dared to do it though realizing that I would be put in prison for doing so. Sure enough, I was put in Prison not long after that."

"Now I was afraid that if I were to be kept in prison the best chance would be lost. Disguised as one who might belong to the scheduled castes, I travelled by the lowest class in the train and crossed the boundary , joining a caravan heading for Kabul. At the boundary pass, I slept among my co-travellers on the bare ground of the caravan inn."

"It was snowing heavily and was so cold that I had to take some liquor-up-to when I had never touched alcoholic drinks to keep myself warm and excape death from cold."

"At Kabul, receiving indications that the Afghan police authorities were after me, I hide myself amongst one caravan now and amongst another later."

"Finally, I came to think that it was useless to continue like that, Then, I visited firstly , the Japanese Legation, a fellow Asian legation, for help, where they politely refused to see me. The Minister was supposed to be absent then."

"Then I visited the German Legation in vain."

It was at the Italian Legation that the Minister condescended to see me and at once took steps to protect me. Both Italian and German ministers in cooperation made efforts to get a passport for me to go to Soviet Russia.

Knowing that the British police authorities had located me, I thought of entering Soviet Russia without a passport. Saying that they were able to get a passport for me at last.

"Thus I came to Germany through Soviet Russia".

After coming to Germany, Mr. Bose was broadcasting to India through German and Italian propaganda radio stations.

After the end of the year of his entering Germany, the Pacific war started.

And in the following year, 1942, it was reported that the Japanese army was going to start operations in Malaya.

Mr. Bose vigorously asked the Japanese GHQ, in Tokyo for his participation in the Malayan operations with the Japanese Army saying,

"Now that the whole situation has changed, I want to fight against the British army in Asia. I cannot expect to achieve any results through broadcasting from here (Europe)".

Thinking his desire as quite reasonable, I transmitted it to Tokyo Headquarters.

We waited and waited for an answer. And at last I got it, allowing him to come over to Japan if he could manage it. Meanwhile, he met with opposition from the German side against his going over to Japan.

The reason was because German officials of the Foreign Affairs Ministry made use of him as a "living encyclopaedia" on Indian Affairs.

Everytime they got questions concerning India, they went to him for his comments, clarifications and uptodate information. Inspite of their opposition he, according to Ambassador Oshima's advice, expressed to Fuhrer his desire to go over to Japan, "You can do as you wish to" said Fuhrer Hitler, accepting his proposal willingly.

"All that I want is the realization of India's Indpendence. So if you want to go over to Japan, I will do everything in my power to help you".

This reply from Hitler terminated all oppositions arising from officials of the Ministry of Foreign affairs.

It was about the end of 1942 that they reached an understanding about this.

Now, the only question left for him to solve was how to get to Japan. First of all, submarine was considered as the means of tranportation and he negotiated with the authorities concerned in Germany and Japan. As Germany and Japan too had no long-range submarines to spare for him, he came to think of the trip by air which then was generally considered as a dangerous one.

I was ordered to accompany him on his trip.

In 1942, an air trip to Asia was planned many times in Germany and Italy; each time failing to materialise. So great was his joy everytime he was notified of such a plan that he could not contain himself. And great was his disappointment when he was notified of its failure.

At the end of the year, I was ordered to return to Japan via Russia. On my leaving Germany I promised Mr. Bose that I would make efforts for him in Tokyo.

To my great joy, I was told by the Chief of Staff of GHQ that, Mr. Bose has decided to come over to Japan by submarine".

It was on the Java Island to the North of Sumatra that Mr. Bose, accompanied by his secretary *Hasan* put his first steps on Asia in the early part of May 1943.

Great efforts on the part of both Germany and Japan, and luck, made it possible.

Submarines of both the countries were scheduled to rendezvous at a certain point off the Southern Coast and they planned to use wireless signals just once to locate each other. Their plan proved to be a success and they could meet at sea. The sea was so rough then that Mr. Bose could not be trans-shipped. Drifting along for three days, they received a light signal from the German submarine saying that owing to fuel situation they were, to their great regret, compelled to tour back the next day.

Meanwhile, the sea had become a little calm. Taking this opportunity they joined the two ships with a rope and with the aid of this rope, Mr. Bose was transhipped successfully.

Returning home, I was relieved from the job in which I had participated till then and was transferred to the Hamamatsu Air Training School.

During the later part of March, I was ordered to take over the Iwakuro Kikan (Intelligence Organization). Soon afterwards, Mr. Bose arrived at the Savan Island. With him I flew to Tokyo and was lodged at the Imperial Hotel.

He expressed his view on Indian Independence so ardently that any person who interviewed him was impressed.

With all the interviews with press reporters, and all the busy life otherwise, he had to sit up late into the night.

He made it a point to make inspection tours of industrial plants, military barracks and schools when he had no interview to give.

It seemed to me that he was trying to improve himself every minute and fit himself for the independence and the reconstruction of India.

Of the Japanese food, he liked Tempura best.

The plan for the establishment of provisional Indian Government was proposed by him on the day previous to his scheduled departure for Tokyo.

To gauge the opinion on the part of Japan to his plan, he postponed his departurte for several days.

In the plan he had proposed to fight for Indian Independence with the help of Axis powers and army in accordance with international law.

This proposal met with no opposition from any of the authorities concerned, as they knew his worth well.

In July, he was fervently welcomed by Indians in Singapore. Upto then, Rash Behari Bose was the president of the Indian Independence League and with the speech of welcome for Mr. Subhas Chandra Bose the Presidentship was handed over to the latter.

The thing which most impressed me then was Mr. Rash Behari Bose's admirable attitude. All that occupied his mind always was Indian Independence and nothing else. He never thought of anything for his own interest. I wonder if it was due to his having accepted Japanese nationality that he was called, and regarded by some Indians as that cat's paw of Japan.

All his efforts and energy were directed towards bringing the members of the Indian Independence League together for the cause of *Indian Independence* and not for Japan. Regarding his talents and the hope pinned on him by the Indian people, they were not small in comparison with those attached to Mr. Chandra Bose; great were his efforts for the independence movement in spite of his old age and poor health. In appreciation of his services and merits, Mr. Chandra Bose recommended him as the Supreme Adviser to the League. Ever since his arrival in Singapore, Mr. Chandra Bose worked and worked like a fire ball.

He slept only 2 or 3 hours a day. With constant meetings with high ranking persons of the League and the Indian Army to keep himself up-to date as to how things were going on, and with the column of writing and broadcasting he performed and, the work of inspecting the Indian Army, making speeches for the members of the League in various places, etc he had scarcely any time for rest.

He was really a revolutionary statesman, but not much of an administrator nor a cold-blooded businessman.

On many occasions the members of the Hikari-Kikan were quite at a loss as how to meet his request, as it was often made all of a sudden, without giving any time for prior arrangements.

He believed in self-help and never asked unnecessarily for aid or advice. This was probably due to some extent to his having had no competent advisers but certainly due also to his own character.

His request to the Indians went always as follows:

"We Indians should be prepared to sacrifice as much as we can for the Independence of India. If Independence is gained without any effort on our part just like a X'mas present it has no worth. Youth should offer blood and one who is rich should offer his property". And he urged Japan saying, "I want Japan to accommodate us. We will repay her when independence is realized".

The amounts needed for the monthly expenditure of the provisonal Indian Government was supplied by me in cheque to him and I received I.O.U.S. with his signature in place of a receipt."

The expenditure of the Indian National Army was added as an other item to the amount specified as owing.

Mr. Bose once said "There is no way of paying Japanese who would be killed in action fighting with the Indian Army, but we will console their souls by enshrining and paying pension to their bereaved families".

I think he knew well that the Japanese Government had no intention of demanding payments for the aid given by them to the Indian Independence movement.

Still, I am sure, he would not be satisfied with receiving "charities". He had also his own reasons to be dissatisfied with Hikari-Kikan.

The first reason was because, I believe the Japanese Government did not exchange Ambassador with them when the Provisional Government was established despite the fact that the Japanese Government approved the Indian Government.

The reason on the part of the Japanese Government might have been that there was not much necessity for a diplomatic organization approach in the southern area under a military government scheme of things.

But they sent Ambassador Swada to the Burmese Government. So he might have felt it proper to expect an ambassador or a minister assigned to his government.

The Imphal operation was not staged as a means to invade India. Mr. Bose used to exhort ever since the day of his residence in Germany that when the Japanese staged any operation on India they should find their way into India first through Chittagong. Because in and around this district was the centre of the independence movement.

Only through the occupation of this district would the decline of the British influence be achieved.

But his plan was not adopted by the Japanese Army and Navy of as it was beyond their power to carry it out.

As far as I know, the Imphal operation was staged for the purpose of defending Burma.

The preparations were started during the autumn of 1944.

Then, he proposed:

(a) I want to have as many units of the Indian Army as possible sent to the front and have some front lines assigned to them.

(b) When Imphal is occupied, I want to have the occupation administration of the area commissioned to the Indian Provisional government. These two proposals were accepted by the Japanese Army of the Burma Area but it was not easy to have them materialise.

The first step of the operation was started with the army moving from Singapore to Burma.

As all the rail facilities were utilised for the transportation of ammunition to capacity, the army moved on foot.

Thus the Provisional Government moved to Rangoon in the early part of January 1944.

The biggest difficulty about the Imphal operation lay in supply at the front. The Indian army was assigned to various divisions of the Japanese army at the front and engaged in fighting as bravely and as well as we had expected.

Especially it was the case with the division led by Col. Kiani. But the Imphal operation ended in total failure on our part. The casualities on the Indian Army side were small in comparison to those on the side of the Japanese Army.

I think some of the reasons was that the Indian army retreated several; days earlier than the Japanese Army—under the advice of the Japanese Army.

Their well maintained military discipline was another reason. From the very outset of the operations, Mr, Bose insisted on sending his provisional government as far to the front as possible. As we suffered from inadequate supply of food, fuel and insufficient transporatation facilities, we could not afford to receive a large number of guests at the front.

So Lt. Gen. Isoda, Mr. Bose and his military advisers went to the front and we had the rest of the government staff awaiting on the way.

Soon after the termination of the Imphal operations, I had a talk on the outcome of the war with him.

"The enemy front at Burma became as tough as an iron wall". I said, "I think teh old military saying that the gateway to the invasion of India was still at its western barrier" still proved a truth.

I sound his opinion.

"Judging from the information so far obtained from Russia and knowing that their interest in India was rising" I ventured to ask him and "what do you think about seeking Soviet Russia's assistance". After a while he said, "As I have always told you I never refuse to get assistance from any countries as far as they are against Britain".

"And I am sure that India will not turn 'red' if they have friendly relations with Russia", he declared.

Appendix-V

Note by Office of Strategic Service on the Rise and Fall of the Indian National Army

The virtual disintegration of Subhas Chandra Bose's Indian National Army (I.N.A.) in the general Japanese retreat from Burma marks the latest failure in Japan's attempt to exploit Indian Nationalism in her war against the Allies in Southeast Asia. In the last few months large scale surrenders, revealing a radical decline in morale have rapidly reduced I.N.A. ranks. Remaining troops have presumably retreated with the Japanese into the Shan moutains towards Thailand. Bose the I.N.A. Commander in Chief, reportedly has fled to Bangkok, from where is allegedly reorienting his propaganda to longer range objectives.

The I.N.A. was established as the military arm of the Indian Independence League which the invading Japanese had organised throughout Southeast Asia in 1942. Bose's troops, operating in conjuction with a Japanese drive into India, were intended to engage in military infiltration, espionage, and anti-British propaganda urging the Indians to work for a Japanese victory in the interests of their own future independence. Japanese anti-British propagands,with its slogan of "Asia for the Asiatics", and the policy of singling out the Indian communities for especially favourable treatment undoubtedly carried a certain appeal to Indians in Southeast Asia. Furthermore, ever since the Russo-Japanese War of 1904, Japan has enjoyed increasing prestige as the one Asiatic nation able to establish herself as an independent equal of the Western powers. In the early years of the Pacific War, Japan's position in Asia was stronger than ever, and Great Britain's defeat in India may have seemed a matter of months. Expediency appeared to many Indians to require cooperation with the Japanese.

In Burma the Indian Independence League had been concerned largely with protecting the Indian minority from Burmese hostility until

1. O.S.S. Papers. No. 31428. U.S. National Armies Marlaglaw, U.S.A.

Bose arrived in 1943 to assume its leadership and to organise the "Indian National Army". In early 1944 Burma became the headquarters of the whole movement when the I.N.A. First Division was moved up from Malaya to aid the Japanese in the Manipur campaign. Bose an energetic and persuasive speaker, was probably most popular with those Indians who had some previous contact with political agitation or who came from his own province of Bengal. There Bose had won his largest following as one of the most turbulent and conspicuous of the nationalist leaders in India. In 1938 he served as President of the All-India Congress but, when re-elected in 1939, was virtually forced to resign after a clash with Gandhi and Nehru,who both distrusted his extremism. Subsequently, Bose organised his followers into the left-wing "Forward Bloc", which functioned as an opposition party to the Congress. Already at that time Nehru recorded his fear that Bose was turning fascist. In 1941 after another arrest, Bose escaped from India and was next heard from broadcasting for the Axis from Berlin.

In Bose the Japanese found an excellent potential puppet. He had frequently been imprisoned by the British in India, and his hatred for Great Britian was violent. He had long arged that there was no hope in the policy of compromise with the British which Gandhi was following,and that Indian Independence could be achieved only be force. Until June 1943 the Japanese used another man named Bose, Rash Behari Bose, to spread the idea of winning Indian freedom with Japanese aid. Rash Behari Bose had fled to Japan after having directed terrorist activities in the Punjab during the last war. In 1931 he organised the first Indian Independence League in Japan, which announced as its objective "the attainment of independence of India by all possible means." Until Subhas Chandra Bose arrived in Japan from Germany, the elder Bose was reorganised leader of the network of Indian Independence Leagues throughout Southeast Asia. When in June 1943 the younger Bose took over completely, Rash Behari apparently retired to Japan, and has since died.

Burma succeeded Malaya as the suitable headquarters for the Japanese sponsored Indian Independence movement not only because it was to be the staging area for the military attack on India but also because after Malaya it provided the largest Indian population outside of Indian upon which to draw for membership. At the time of the Japanese invasion over a half-million Indians remained in Burma. By far the greater part of them belonged to the laboring class, but a large number of Indian merchants also had heavy financial stakes in the country, accumulated through moneylending the rice-selling. Although many of these merchants fled to India in 1942, some left representatives to protect their interests and provided Bose's movement with a source of funds. The Japanese, contrary to Burmese desires, allowed the Indian community to retain control over all Indian-held property in Burma.

Indians in Burma have long been conscious of being a minority and are jealous of their status as a separate political group. The Burmese are openly hostile toward the Indians, considering them a meance to Burma's national and economic life. As early as 1922, Indians had formed a separate electrorate which, under British auspices, was incorporated into the present constitution in the face of Burma, opposition. Most of the educated Indians in Burma sympathized with the aims of the Indian National Congress, and although the imported laborers who formed the bulk of the Indian population were politically inactive before the war, Indian National Congress propaganda may have influenced them to a certain extent before they left India.

During early 1942 the Japanese conducted a campaign to persuade Indian prisoners of war in Hong Kong, Shanghai, and Singapore that they should fight along with the Japanese for the "liberation" of India. In June the Japanese sponsored a conference in Bangkok at which the I.N.A. war formally launched, and by November the Japanese claimed that the strength of the force was 16,000 troops. Disagreement between its first leader and Rash Behari Bose ended in the temporary disbandment of the I.N.A. In June 1943 Subhas Chandra Bose arrived from Germany and, besides taking over the Indian Independence League and the new I.N.A. as commander in Chief, became President, Premier, Foreign Secretary, and Defence Minister of the "Provisional Government of Free India". His extensive propaganda and recruiting campaign for the I.N.A. was at first conducted among Indian prisoners of War, of which about 70,000 were in Japanese hands, and among Indian rubber plantation labour in Malaya In February 1944 Bose moved I.N.A. headquarters to Rangoon and continued his recruiting from there.

Several factors aided Bose in his work. At that time British prestige was at lowest ebb. Enlistment afforded escape from POW camps, where conditions were bad, and a possible opportunity for Indians to return to their homes and families. Bose's propaganda spoke of the "the sacred soil of the mother land" and of raising the flag of free India in ever city,. town and village in India. Many Indians doubtless incerely believed that by joining the I.N.A. they would participate in achieving real Indian Independence. Furthermore, they were told that they would be welcomed by the British Indian Army, which would refuse to fight them, and that all India would rise to welcome them. Thus the general morals of the I.N.A. troops before their first engagement in Arakan was fairly high, and Japanese propaganda was able to aim at the British-Indian Army, urging desertion and telling of comrades-in-arms training outside of India to liberate their native country.

In the military engagements that followed, I.N.A. regiments were intended primarily to confuse British-Indian troops in the combat areas by shouting orders in Urdu or English, to encourage deserters, and to take full charge of fall British-Indian prisoners in order to persuade them to chage loyalties and join the I.N.A. cause. They were also used in forward reconnaissance and as screens for Japanese troops, often regarded with suspicion by the Japanese, I.N.A. forces were almost never employed as regular fighting units, and were assigned inferior equipment.

The first encounter between British-Indian and I.N.A. troops, a surprise engagement, took place a few miles north of Buthiadaung in Arakan. INA units were successful through trickery and civilian disguise in overpowering British Indian sentires and enabling the Japanese to capture a divisional headquarters. In the next encounter, however, an I.N.A. sikh, who had been encouraged to leave cover shouting slogans and invitations to desert, was riddled with British-Indian bullets.

Optimism aroused among the puppet Indians by initial military successes quickly disappeared. The ineffectiveness of the I.N.A. was clearly demonstrated at the time of the fathest Japanese advance into India in the spring of 1944. Japanese expectations had obviously been high and the British themselves had been uncertain how much confusion Bose's Indians could cause. Buit actual encounters proved that British-Indian troops would fight the enemy whether he was Indian or Japanese.

Three I.N.A. regiments, their morale evidently high, crossed the Chindwin in March 1944 for the Manipur Campaign and the much-heralded "March of Delhi". Indians trained as occupation officers for the "Indian Provisional Government" actually arrived in Tamu (on the frontier below Imphal) but were soon forced to retreat. Although the Japanese penetrated into India almost as far as Imphal, by June they were pushed back into Burma. I.N.A. troops withdrew in very poor condition. Disease swept their ranks, they were inadequately supplied and their morale fell sharply. Japanese officers in charge of I.N.A. intelligence operations in Manipur complained that while Japanese were being killed, I.N.A. men were no longer willing to die "for the cause of India's freedom".

Japanese failure in the Manipur campaign seriously impaired the strength of Bose's "Provisional Government"and dashed the Japanese hope for widespread local revolts against the British resulting from an invasion of Indian soil. Despite military reverses, however, Bose continued his propaganda. When the Gandhi-Jinnah meeting in the summer of 1944 was first scheduled , Bose urged Indians not to believe that a settlement between the Congress and the Muslim League could lead to independence. The failure of Gandhi and Jinnah to break the Indian political deadlock by a reconciliation between nationalist elements and compromise with the British restored some hopefulness to the Japanese-sponsored "Free India" movement, and in the fall of 1944 Bose talked of engaging the I.N.A. with Japanese aid in a new campaign to win Indian Independence by force.

In November 1944, in line with renewed Japanese emphasis on the Greater East Asia program, Bose visited Tokyo to establish closer relations between his "Provisional Government of India" and Japan. An exchange of diplomatic representatives was arranged in the hope of increasing collaboration and improving occasionally strained relations. In the past, members of the I.N.A. and even Bose himself had difficulties with Japanese military men in the field. Another troublesome problem had been the Burman puppet government's desire to liquidate all Indian claims to property in Burma. Also there had been conflict between Bose and the Japanese concerning propaganda directives beamed to India. With his own dilomatic representative in Tokyo, Bose may have hoped to have his India policies more effectively presented. At the same time, Tokyo's warm and impressive welcome of Bose indicated that the Japanese still considered his role important to their war effort.

Although in the 1944-45 winter operations in Burma, isolated I.N.A. units belonging to the fresh and untried second division are said to have fought with determination, the I.N.A. as a whole continued to be an ineffective device for Japanese exploitation of anti-British sentiment in India. I.N.A. strength in March 1945 was estimated to have declined to about 35,000. Since February, when at Bose's request the I.N.A. was given a defensive position on the Irrawaddy, its troops, in units varying in strength from 200 to 3000, have surrendred on a large scale.

Index

H

I

R

T

U

V

W